Grammar Dimensions
Book Four

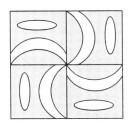

Grammar Dimensions

Book Four

Form, Meaning, and Use

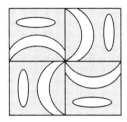

Jan Frodesen

*University of California
Los Angeles*

Janet Eyring

*California State University
Fullerton*

**Heinle & Heinle Publishers
A Division of Wadsworth, Inc.
Boston, Massachusetts 02116 U.S.A**

This book is dedicated to our parents,

Jeanne and George Frodesen

and

Lavon and Joseph Eyring

Photo Credits:

Photo on page 21 by Torin Halsey appears courtesy of Wichita Falls Times and News Record.

Photos on pages 39, 124, 164, 247 (middle), 307, 362 courtesy of Pat Martin.

Photo on page 81 by Ken Regan appears courtesy of Special Olympics International.

Photo on page 86 by Don Clegg appears courtesy of Carle Foundation Hospital.

Photos on page 124: Akita courtesy of Chiheisen Akitas; Airedale by Pat Martin; Boston Terrier by Pat Martin, courtesy of Susan Laesch; Bulldog courtesy of Patti Austin; Dachshund courtesy of Betty Snyder.

Photos on page 125: Doberman, German Shepherd, and Shih Tzu by Pat Martin; Dalmation by Pat Martin, courtesy of Dennis Phillips; Pekingese courtesy of Hetty Orringer; Poodle courtesy of Eileen Fox.

Photo on page 151 courtesy of Zabrina Atkins.

Photo on page 182 by Pat Martin appears courtesy of James Strong.

Photos on page 247 (left and right) appear courtesy of Carole Williamson.

Photo on page 258 appears courtesy of U. S. Department of Interior—photo # 089075b.

Photo on page 268 appears courtesy of United Nations—photo # 44070.

Photo on page 285 appears courtesy of NASA.

Photo on page 289 appears courtesy of Culver Pictures.

Photos on page 335 and 375 appear courtesy of Jan Fisher.

Photo on page 388 (left) appears courtesy of the Australian Overseas Information Service.

Photo on page 388 (right) by J. K. Isaac appears courtesy of United Nations—photo # 141452.

Photo on page 389 appears courtesy of AP/Wide World Photos.

The publication of the Grammar Dimensions series
was directed by the members of the Heinle & Heinle
ESL Publishing Team:

David C. Lee, Editorial Director
Susan Mraz, Marketing Manager
Lisa McLaughlin, Production Editor
Nancy Mann, Developmental Editor

Also participating in the publication of this program were:

Publisher: Stanley J. Galek
Editorial Production Manager: Elizabeth Holthaus
Assistant Editor: Kenneth Mattsson
Manufacturing Coordinator: Mary Beth Lynch
Full Service Production/Design: Publication Services, Inc.
Cover Designer: Martucci Studio
Cover Artist: Susan Johnson

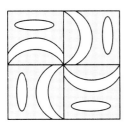

Table of Contents

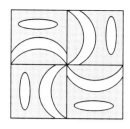

Preface to *Grammar Dimensions: Form, Meaning, and Use*

To the Teacher

ABOUT THE SERIES

With the recent emphasis on communication, the teaching of grammar has often been downplayed, or even overlooked entirely. Although one would not want to argue the goal of having students be able to communicate successfully, it is important to recognize that a major means to this end is to teach students to use grammatical structures. Some grammatical structures may be acquired naturally without instruction, but it is assumed by the creators of this series that explicit focus on the troublesome aspects of English will facilitate and accelerate their acquisition. The teaching needs to be done, however, in such a way that the interdependence of grammar and communication is appreciated.

In this regard, it is crucial to recognize that the use of grammatical structures involves more than having students achieve formal accuracy. Students must be able to use the structures meaningfully and appropriately as well. This series, therefore, takes into account all three dimensions of language: syntax/morphology (form), semantics (meaning), and pragmatics (use). The relevant facts about the **form, meaning,** and **use** of English grammatical structures were compiled into a comprehensive scope and sequence and distributed across a four-book series. Where the grammatical system is complex (e.g., the verb-tense system) or the structure complicated (e.g., the passive voice), it is revisited in each book in the series. Nevertheless, each book is free-standing and may be used independently of the others in the series if the student or program needs warrant.

Another way in which the interdependence of grammar and communication is stressed is that students first encounter every structure in a meaningful context where their attention is not immediately drawn to its formal properties. Each treatment of a grammatical structure concludes with students being given the opportunity to use the structure in communicative activities. The point of the series is not to teach grammar as static knowledge, but to have students use it in the dynamic process of communication. In this way grammar might better be thought of as a skill, rather than as an area of knowledge.

It is my hope that this book will provide teachers with the means to create, along with their students, learning opportunities that are tailored to learners' needs, are enjoyable, and will maximize everyone's learning.

ABOUT THE BOOK

This book deals with grammatical forms that are needed for cognition and technical/academic reading and writing. It reveals to students the subtleties of certain grammatical structures and their workings in discourse.

Units that share certain features have been clustered together. No more than three or four units are clustered at one time, however, in order to provide for some variety of focus. As the units have been designed to stand independently, it is possible for a syllabus to be constructed that follows a different order of structures than the one presented in the book. It is also not expected that there will be sufficient time to deal with all the material that has been introduced here within a single course. Teachers are encouraged to see the book as a resource from which they can select units or parts of units which best meet student needs.

Unit Organization

TASKS

One way in which to identify student needs is to use the **Tasks**, which open each unit as a pre-test. Learner engagement in the Tasks may show that students have already learned what they need to know about a certain structure, in which case the unit can be skipped entirely. Or it may be possible, from examining students' performance, to pinpoint precisely where the students need to work. For any given structure, the learning challenge presented by the three dimensions of language is not equal. Some structures present more of a form-based challenge to learners; for others, the long-term challenge is to learn what the structures mean or when to use them. The type and degree of challenge varies according to the inherent complexity of the structure itself and the particular language background and level of English proficiency of the students.

FOCUS BOXES

Relevant facts about the form, meaning, and use of the structure are presented in **Focus Boxes** following the Task. Teachers can work their way systematically through a given unit or can pick and choose from among the Focus Boxes those points on which they feel students specifically need to concentrate.

EXERCISES

From a pedagogical perspective, it is helpful to think of grammar as a skill to be developed. Thus, in this book, **Exercises** have been provided to accompany each Focus Box. Certain of the Exercises may be done individually, others with students working in pairs or in small groups. Some of the Exercises can be done in class, others assigned as homework. Students' learning styles and the learning challenge they are working on will help teachers determine the most effective way to have students use the Exercises. (The Instructor's Manual should be consulted also for helpful hints in this regard.)

ACTIVITIES

At the end of each unit are a series of **Activities** that help students realize the communicative value of the grammar they are learning and that offer them further practice in using the grammar to convey meaning. Teachers or students may select the Activities from which they believe they would derive the most benefit and enjoyment. Student performance on these Activities can be used as a post-test as well. Teachers should not expect perfect performance at this point, however. Often there is a delayed effect in learning anything, and even some temporary backsliding in student performance as new material is introduced.

OTHER COMPONENTS

An **Instructor's Manual** is available for this book. The Manual contains answers to the Exercise questions and grammatical notes where pertinent. The Manual also further discusses the theory underlying the series and "walks a teacher through" a typical unit, suggesting ways in which the various components of the unit might be used and supplemented in the classroom.

A student **Workbook** also accompanies this book. It provides additional exercises to support the material presented in this text. Many of the workbook exercises are specially designed to help students prepare for the TOEFL (Test of English as a Foreign Language).

To the Student

All grammar structures have a form, a meaning, and a use. We can show this with a pie chart:

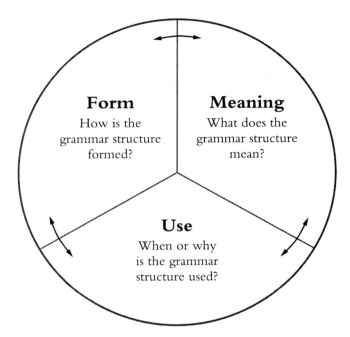

Often you will find that you know the answer to one or more of these questions, but not to all of them, for a particular grammar structure. This book has been written to help you learn answers to these questions for the major grammar structures of English. More importantly, it gives you practice with the answers so that you can develop your ability to use English grammar structures accurately, meaningfully, and appropriately.

At the beginning of each unit, you will be asked to work on a **Task**. The Task will introduce you to the grammar structures to be studied in the unit. However, it is not important at this point that you think about grammar. You should just do the Task as well as you can.

In the next section of the unit are **Focus Boxes** and Exercises. You will see that the boxes are labeled with **FORM, MEANING, USE,** or a combination of these, corresponding to the three parts of the pie chart. In each Focus Box is information that answers one or more of the questions in the pie. Along with the Focus Box are Exercises that should help you put into practice what you have studied.

The last section of each unit contains communicative **Activities.** Hopefully, you will enjoy doing these and at the same time receive further practice using the grammar structures in meaningful ways.

By working on the Task, studying the Focus Boxes, doing the Exercises, and engaging in the Activities, you will develop greater knowledge of English grammar and skill in using it. I also believe you will enjoy the learning experience along the way.

Diane Larsen-Freeman

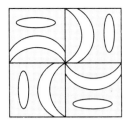

Acknowledgments

Series Director Acknowledgments

As with any project this ambitious, a number of people have made important contributions. I need to thank my students in the MAT Program at the School for International Training and audiences worldwide for listening to me talk about my ideas for reconciling the teaching of grammar with communicative language teaching. Their feedback and questions have been invaluable in the evolution of my thinking. One student, Anna Mussman, should be singled out for her helpful comments on the manuscript that she was able to provide based on her years of English teaching. A number of other anonymous teacher reviewers have also had a formative role in the development of the series. I hope they derive some satisfaction in seeing that their concerns were addressed wherever possible. In addition, Marianne Celce-Murcia not only helped with the original scope and sequence of the series, but also provided valuable guidance throughout its evolution.

I feel extremely grateful, as well, for the professionalism of the authors, who had to put into practice the ideas behind this series. Their commitment to the project, patience with its organic nature, and willingness to keep at it are all much appreciated. I insisted that the authors be practicing ESL teachers. I believe the series has benefited from this decision, but I am also cognizant of the demands it has put on the authors' lives these past few years.

Finally, I must acknowledge the support of the Heinle and Heinle "team." This project was "inherited" by Heinle and Heinle during its formative stage. To Dave Lee, Susan Mraz, Lisa McLaughlin, and especially Susan Maguire, who never stopped believing in this project, I am indeed thankful. And to Nancy Mann, who helped the belief become a reality, I am very grateful.

Author Acknowledgments

A number of people have contributed to this book's form and meaning (to borrow from our series' subtitle), and we would like to extend our heartfelt thanks to them.

We are most grateful to Diane Larsen-Freeman, our series director, for her constant guidance, her insights about grammar and the teaching of grammar, and her many valuable suggestions on drafts throughout this project. No doubt the long distance telephone companies have profited greatly from our numerous cross-country conversations on grammar and pedagogy, but so have we. We would also like to thank Marianne Celce-Murcia, whose careful reading and extensive feedback on our drafts helped us immensely in shaping these materials. We greatly appreciate her generosity in sharing her expertise.

We would like to thank the following manuscript reviewers for their valuable advice and suggestions: Dennis Godfrey (West Chester University), Gilbert Couts (American

University), Katherine Leffell (University of Alabama), John Miller (University of Southern Mississippi), Duane Ratzlaff (Christ College Irvine), and Sarah Gray (UC Santa Barbara).

All of the staff we worked with at Heinle and Heinle were very supportive during the development of this book; we are grateful to them for their support. We wish to thank especially our project editor, Nancy Mann, for her enthusiasm, patience, and assistance in coordinating the various facets of the project. We owe many thanks to Dave Chang, Production Coordinator at Publication Services, for his careful supervision of this book's production and constant attention to our concerns; Dave truly meant it when he said he would assist us in any way he could. Finally, we wish to thank our families and friends for their support and encouragement from start to finish. Now we know why so many acknowledgments end with: "We couldn't have done it without them."

1

Verb Tenses in Discourse

Task

You can define yourself in many ways: by your values and personality traits, through your accomplishments, and by your appearance, among other things. Another way to define yourself is by the groups to which you belong.

Gordon Allport, a Harvard psychologist, used the term *in-groups* to describe the groups that individuals are a part of at one time or another. By in-groups, he didn't mean popular social groups, but rather all the groups that an individual identifies with. Some groups, called *ascribed groups*, you are born into, such as your family, your ethnic group, your hometown and your nationality. Others, called *achieved groups*, you become a part of through your activities and involvements, such as going to school, creating groups of friends, entering a profession or getting married. Some in-groups are permanent—you can't change the circumstances of your birth—but others change as your activities, beliefs, and loyalties change.

As an example of in-groups, here are some of the in-group memberships, both past and present, of Kay, a Thai-American woman in her mid-thirties.

the family she grew up in
her own family (husband Phil and child Andrea)
Thai (ethnic group)
native speakers of Thai
Bangkok (the city she was born in)
Chicago (where she lived from ages 8 to 18)
Palo Alto, California (the city she lives in now)
her girlhood circle of friends
the Girl Scouts
her elementary and secondary school
Princeton University
Stanford Medical School
physicians (her profession)
the Buddhist religion
the National Organization for Women

her neighborhood volleyball team
the Sierra Club
the Democratic party
the United States

Make a list of some in-groups to which you belonged as a child (pick an age between five and 12 years old.) Some of these groups might be the same as present ones. In a paragraph, describe one of your childhood in-groups that was especially important to you at that time and explain why it was important. Next, make a list of in-groups that you belong to now. Choose one that is significant in your present life, and write a paragraph describing your involvement in it.

In a third paragraph, state which of your present in-groups you believe will remain significant groups for you 10 years from now. Also speculate on what you think will be some new in-groups for you in the future—e.g., a new school, a profession, your own family (as contrasted to your family of origin)—and when you think that might happen.

Compare your lists for the first two paragraphs with those of two or three other class members. Discuss which groups on your childhood lists have changed and which have remained important groups to you at the present time. Save your paragraphs; you may use them later in the unit.

Focus 1

FORM ● MEANING

The English Verb System: Overview

FORM
MEANING

- Verbs in English express how events take place in time. The verb tenses give you two main kinds of information about an event (an action or state):
  - The **time frame** in which the event takes place: now, at some time in the past, or at some time in the future.
  - The **relationship of the event to the time frame:** whether, for example, the event occurs at a point (or points) in time or extends for a period of time. This relationship is called **aspect.**
- The English verb system combines information about *time frame* and *aspect* in 12 different ways:

Aspect	Time Frame		
	Present	**Past**	**Future**
Simple Tense Ø aspect (at that time)	work/ works speak/ speaks (simple present)	worked spoke (simple past)	will work will speak (simple future)
Progressive Aspect (in progress at that time)	am/ is/ are working am/ is/ are speaking (present progressive)	was/ were working was/ were speaking (past progressive)	will be working will be speaking (future progressive)
Perfect Aspect (before that time)	has/ have worked has/ have spoken (present perfect)	had worked had spoken (past perfect)	will have worked will have spoken (future perfect)
Perfect Progressive Aspect (in progress during and before that time)	has/ have been working has/ have been speaking (present perfect progressive)	had been working had been speaking (past perfect progressive)	will have been working will have been speaking (future perfect progressive)

Please note that there are many ways to express the future time frame in English. The chart above gives examples of the future using *will* only.

Exercise 1

In his autobiography, *The Hunger of Memory,* Richard Rodriguez describes his struggles growing up in two different worlds: Mexican culture and the American educational system. The following passages are from his book. Underline the verbs of main clauses in each sentence. Then state the time frame for each passage: present, past, or future. Circle words such as time adverbs that help to signal the time frame.

1. (a)From an early age I knew that my mother and father could read and write both Spanish and English. (b)I had observed my father making his way through what, I now suppose, must have been income tax forms. (c)On other occasions I waited apprehensively while my mother read onion-paper letters air-mailed from Mexico with news of a relative's illness or death. (d)For both my parents, however, reading was something done out of necessity and as quickly as possible.

2. (a)Lately, I have begun to wonder how the family will gather even three times a year when [my mother] is not there with her phone to unite us. (b)For the time being, however, she presides at the table. (c)She—not my father, who sits opposite her—says the Grace before Meals. (d)She busies herself throughout the meal.

3. (a)Someday . . . you will all grow up and all be very rich. (b)You'll have lots of money to buy me presents. (c)But I'll be a little old lady. (d)I won't have any teeth or hair. (e)So you'll have to buy me soft food and put a blue wig on my head. (f)And you'll buy me a big fur coat. (g)But you'll only be able to see my eyes.

4. (a)The third of four children, I had been preceded to a neighborhood Roman Catholic school by an older brother and sister. (b)But neither of them had revealed very much about their classroom experiences. (c)Each afternoon they returned, as they left in the morning, always together, speaking in Spanish, as they climbed the five steps of the porch.

5. (a)Visiting the East Coast or the gray capitals of Europe during the long months of winter, I often meet people at deluxe hotels who comment on my complexion. (b)(In such hotels it appears nowadays a mark of leisure and wealth to have a complexion like mine.)(c)Have I been skiing? In the Swiss Alps? (d)Have I just returned from a Caribbean vacation? (e)No. I say no softly but in a firm voice that intends to explain: My complexion is dark.

6. (a)[My nephew] smiles. (b)I wonder: Am I watching myself in this boy? (c)In this face where I can scarcely trace a family resemblance? (d)Have I foreseen his past? (e)He lives in a world of Little League and Pop Warner. (f)He has spoken English all his life. (g)His father is of German descent, a fourth-generation American.

7. (a)I had known a writer's loneliness before, working on my dissertation in the British Museum. (b)But that experience did not prepare me for the task of writing these pages where my own life is the subject. (c)Many days I feared I had stopped living by committing myself to remember the past. (d)I feared that my absorption with events in my past amounted to an immature refusal to live in the present.

From Richard Rodriguez, *The Hunger of Memory*. Copyright © 1982 by Richard Rodriguez. Reprinted with permission of David R. Godine, publisher.

Exercise 2

Exchange the three paragraphs you wrote for the Task with a classmate. After reading your classmate's paragraphs, decide whether there is a consistent time frame used for each paragraph. If so, identify the time frames. Report your results to your classmate to see if she or he agrees. Discuss any changes you think should be made in verb tenses.

Focus 2

FORM ● MEANING ● USE

Moment of Focus

- Each time frame (present, past, and future) has a moment of focus.
- The moment of focus can be a point of time or a period of time.

	Present	**Past**	**Future**
Moment of Focus	now	specified time in the past	specified time in the future
Point of Time Focus	**(a)** Her son is 4 years old **today.**	**(b)** The tornado touched down **just before dawn.**	**(c) On Saturday, morning,** they will leave for their honeymoon.
Period of Time Focus	**(d)** Her son listens to music for hours at a time.	**(e) During the early nineteenth century,** millions of Italians migrated to the United States.	**(f) In the decades to come,** computer technology will change our lives even more.

- It may be stated explicitly by a time signal such as a time adverb, or it may be implied in the context.

Explicitly Stated Time Focus	**(g)** I can't talk **now;** I'm trying to study.	**(h)** Until the end of **the Cretaceous Period,** dinosaurs had roamed the earth.	**(i) After you finish that chapter,** I'll give you a ride to school.
Implied Time Focus	**(j)** Her son goes to a private school.	**(k)** Dinosaurs evolved into towo distinct groups.	**(l)** The weather will continue to be warm and sunny.

- In discourse, the moment of focus may be the same for a number of sentences, or it may change from sentence to sentence:

Same Point of Focus	**Changing Point/Period of Focus**
(m) When Kay first moved to Chicago from Bangkok, she had a hard time adjusting to her new life. She idn't like the food at school. Other children eldom talked to her, and she had no one to play with.	**(n)** Kay met Phil **the summer after she graduated from college.** They dated **for two years. When they got married,** it was on the same date, July 15, that they had first met. **This year they celebrated** their 15th anniversary.

Exercise 3

The following oral interview passages are from Studs Terkel's book *The Great Divide,* in which Americans talk about their lives and their thoughts on changes in America. Divide up into groups and take turns identifying the moment or moments of focus for each passage. Discuss and determine whether each moment of focus is (1) a point of time or (2) a period of time and whether it is explicitly stated or implied.

1. (a)Right now, he's working the night shift at a twenty-four hour service station, with ten or twelve pumps. (b)He pumps the cash register. (c)His goals are very short-term, to get through the day.

2. (a)When I was a kid, I wanted to be a beatnik. (b)It meant reading poetry, getting my life experience, and finding obscure little crevices in the culture. (c)Students today, the beatniks of now, don't watch prime-time television. (d)They watch weird old re-runs . . .

3. (a)Back in the early eighties when the draft-resistance movement began, many of us who were resisters first appeared in public. (b)We debated representatives of Selective Service. (c)Frankly, we'd usually make them look pretty silly.

4. (a)In the last five years, there's been much more discussion of ethics on the campuses. (b)Remember, many of the young people of the sixties are the professors of today and they haven't changed their basic beliefs.

5. (a)A friend of mine, who is forty, had been a stock analyst on Wall Street fifteen years ago. (b)She married, had babies, raised her children, and now wanted to go back. (c)They said, It doesn't matter what you did before.

6. (a)I would like to be chief of police. (b)I'll probably apply for jobs. (c)If nothing happens, I'll go to Cape Cod, build a house, and look at the waves.

7. (a)[My students] have learned how to take college tests. (b)They score high, especially in math. (c)They are quite verbal. (d)They give the impression of being bright. (e)Encouraged by their families, they come with the conviction that education is something they want, something they need. (f)But their definition of education is something else.

From Studs Terkel, *The Great Divide.* Copyright © 1988 by Studs Terkel. Reprinted with permission of Pantheon Books, a division of Random House, Inc.

Focus 3

USE

Tense Shifts in Discourse

USE

- Changes in verb tense from one sentence to the next are common in discourse. The tense may change within the same time frame, such as from present perfect to simple present:
  (a) Self-help groups **have become** very common all over America. These groups **assist** people with everything from weight problems to developing self-esteem.

- Being consistent in tense usage means to keep verbs in the same time frame (past, present, future) unless you have changed the moment of focus. Time frame shifts are often signaled by explicit time markers (e.g. *last week, currently, next year*).

          Past time   **Present time**

(b) Vera **graduated** from college **last June.** She **now works** for a law firm.

          Present time

She **has worked** there **for a month.**

The second sentence above shifts to present time, using *now* to signal the shift. The third sentence shifts tense but remains in the present time frame. If the third sentence used a past time reference, it would be ungrammatical:

(c) Vera **graduated** from college last June. She now **works** for a law firm.

       NOT: She **had worked** there for a month.

Exercise 4

Each of the following passages has one sentence with an inappropriate verb tense for the context. Identify the sentence that has the error and correct it. Correction may involve changing the verb tense or using an explicit time marker to signal the shift in frame of reference. More than one verb tense could correct some errors.

> **EXAMPLE:** (a)I am taking this coat back to the store. (b)Someone had burned a hole in in it. (c)One button is missing too.
>
> **Frame of reference**: *Present*
>
> **Error**: (b)
>
> **Correction**: Someone *has burned* a hole in it or Someone *had burned* a hole in it *before I bought it.*

1. (a)My music class is really interesting. (b)We have been studying the history of American jazz and blues. (c)I will have been taking this course for six weeks.

2. (a)Sula's in-groups include her softball team. (b)She had belonged to this team for three years. (c)Last year she played second base, but this year she is playing first base.

3. (a)Japanese researchers had demonstrated that a human virus can cause rheumatoid arthritis in mice. (b)The virus, HTLV-1, is capable of inserting its own genetic information into the genes of its host. (c)It causes leukemia and two rare nerve disorders.

4. (a)Although Elvis Presley has been dead for decades, his legacy lives on. (b)For example, there was a computer game "In Search of the King." (c)And the Jockey Club registry lists the following thoroughbred horses: Elvis Pelvis, Triple Elvis, Elvis' Double, Jailhouse Rock, Blue Suede Shoes, and Love Me Tender.

Focus 4

Rhetorical Functions of Time Frame Shifts in Discourse

USE

- Verb tense shifts to a different time frame often occur when you move from statements that introduce a topic to ones that provide further information about the topic.
- Some reasons that you shift verb tenses in speaking and writing are
  - to explain or support a general statement with past description or elaboration on a topic:
    - **(a)** My family has many happy memories in this church. **All of my brothers and sisters were married here.**
  - to support a claim about the present with examples from the past:
    - **(b)** Our school is helping to conserve natural resources. **We recycled tons of aluminum last year. We started using paper cups instead of Styrofoam™ ones.** This year we hope to double the amount of recycled materials.
  - to provide background information about a topic:
    - **(c)** Wichita Falls has an interesting history. **It became a town over 100 years ago, when the railroad started a route through that area. The land that was to become Wichita Falls was a prize in a poker game.**
  - to express a comment or an opinion about a topic:
    - **(d)** Last year our city witnessed an increase in the number of people who volunteered their time for organizations that help those in need. Donations to these organizations also increased. **We need to continue this assistance to others less fortunate than we are.**
  - to support a general statement about change by comparing past and present situations:
    - **(e)** The social connections of Americans have changed during the last century. **In the past, individuals depended on their extended families and neighborhoods for social activities. Today many Americans live far from their extended families and do not know many of their neighbors.**
- Note that the simple present and present perfect tenses often "frame" topics: We frequently use them to introduce topics, to make topic shifts, and to end discussion of a topic. These tenses often express general statements that the speaker believes hold true at the present.

Exercise 5

Here are more passages from Studs Terkel's interviews in *The Great Divide*. Discuss the reasons for the verb tense shifts in each passage in class. Which passages change tenses within a past or present time frame? Which passages change time frames? Which verb tenses did the speaker use to introduce topics in these passages?

1. (a)This kitchen is part of the old house. (b)My great-grandparents bought the place around 1895 or somewhere in there. (c)I'm fourth generation.

2. (a)I think the American dream for most people today is just survival. (b)When people came here from the old country, it was for a better life, not just survival. (c)I see that people that come over today seem to prosper faster than the ones who were born here. (d)Maybe it's because they know what it is to do without.

3. (a)The marketplace has changed in another way. (b)We have major class shifts in America. (c)The middle class, as traditionally known, is disappearing—being split. (d)You have a growing upper class.

4. (a)The role of the radio personality has changed greatly in the last decade. (b)Back then, we were given a pile of records and a few flip cards to read. (c)Keep the conversation to a minimum. (d)I once worked for a guy who had a stopwatch. (e)If you talked over eight seconds, you'd get in trouble. (f)Today, people want to hear what the individual has to say. (g)In the old days, we could squeeze in eight, ten records an hour. (h)Now I'm lucky if I get in two.

5. (a)I keep my mouth shut with a patient when it comes to politics. (b)I once said something about a senator. (c)I thought it was normal conversation. (d)The patient was for the most part in love with this particular senator. (e)I never saw that patient again.

6. (a)Some of the old AMA★ homilies were true. (b)The doctor was a single person working in a community. (c)He went to the same church, had to meet the same people every day. (d)If someone was down on his luck, he'd put the bill on the tab. (e)He was certainly one of the most prestigious people in the community. (f)Today, under the high-tech alienation quality of the health-care system, doctors are way down on the list.

7. (a)I've been arrested five times. (b)I'm considered somewhat of a freak because I'm the police chief's wife. (c)I would march with my placard, hoping that the police wouldn't see me. (d)If I saw a policeman, I would hide behind my sign. (e)But they always saw me and they said, Aha there she goes, the crazy wife of the police chief. (f)The police all hate my husband, so they think I'm exactly what he deserves.

★ American Medical Association

From Studs Terkel, *The Great Divide*. Copyright © 1988 by Studs Terkel. Reprinted with permission of Pantheon Books, a division of Random House, Inc.

Exercise 6

The following passage describes the life of Tabora, a recent Mexican immigrant to the United States who currently makes his living as a day laborer. *El mosco* is the gathering place where men wait for employers to pick them up for a day's work.

Underline the main clause verbs in each sentence. Identify the time frame for each paragraph: past, present, or future. Put brackets [ ] around time frame shifts (e.g., present to past time reference) within a paragraph. Circle any explicit time markers that signal time frame shifts. Discuss why you think the writer shifted time frames within a paragraph in class. Is he giving an example? Is he elaborating by providing background information about Tabora's past? Do new paragraphs signal tense changes? Where does *but* help to signal a time reference change?

(1)Tabora is small, jumpy, talkative. (2)He tells tales of stealing onto trains at midnight, full of the desperation of solo migration. (3)He knew no one when he got to L.A. eight months ago, but he quickly heard of La Placita, a church near Olvera Street on the edge of downtown, long a magnet and refuge for Latino immigrants. (4)It's one of several churches that temporarily house migrants. (5)From there he makes his daily assault on the Los Angeles job market.

(6)What he has in mind is anything but *el mosco*. (7)In Houston, where he first heard of such sites, he rarely got work by waiting at the corners. (8)And when he arrived in L.A., he avoided the *moscos,* instead walking down the streets, striking up conversations, following rumors of work. (9)In December, for instance, he rushed downtown after hearing that toy factories were hiring box loaders. (10)That time, there were no jobs.

(11)But other times he's been luckier. (12)Tabora has manned a snow-cone cart for three months, varnished furniture in a factory at $2.50 an hour for a month, helped a welder for a month. (13)Both the factory owner and welder were Latinos he met by chance; both, in the end, were unable to pay him what he was due. (14)Between jobs he has fallen back on *el mosco.* (15)There he has landed four-day jobs with Armenian immigrants as a painter and ditch digger, and he has gone for three weeks without being hired. (16)All told, Tabora has worked only five of the months he's been here and has sent home money once. (17)He still sleeps in a free shelter.

(18)He'll use the *moscos* until the next steady job comes along, he says, and again if the next job disappears. (19)If you believe Tabora, the only way to remove him and the others from *el mosco* is to give them work.

(Excerpted from "El Mosco," Bruce Kelley, *Los Angeles Times Magazine,* March 18, 1990.)

Focus 5

Simple Present Tense
in Past Narratives

USE

- The simple present tense is sometimes used in conversation and informal story telling to express past events. This use of present tense helps to make stories more vivid and immediate to the listener or reader. Often the first part of the story starts in the past and then shifts to the present tense.

  (a) Joe **had** never **been skiing** until last winter. So one frosty day he **decides** he's going to try it, and he **heads** out for the slopes. Well, he **gets** to the top of a mountain, **pushes** off on his poles, and then he **realizes** that he doesn't have the slightest idea about how to stop. The next thing he **knows**, his face **is** in the snow, and his skis are in the air. A woman from the ski patrol finally comes to help him up, and she **suggests** that he might want to take a few lessons. But of course, Joe, he **thinks** he can learn everything by himself.

- The present progressive form (*be* + verb + *ing*) can be used in informal narrative to make the events seem even more immediate, as if they were happening at the moment:

  (b) So I**'m walking** through the woods and it**'s getting** dark – I mean <u>really</u> dark. And I**'m thinking**, I could be lost all night in the middle of nowhere. I**'m listening** to see if I can hear my friends, but all I**'m hearing** are owl hoots and faint rustlings in the bushes near the path. I**'m getting** more and more nervous by the minute.

Exercise 7

Rewrite these descriptions of past events in the present tense to make them seem more immediate. Your teacher will call on some of you to read what you've written.

1. (a) Well, the earthquake hit about 4:00 A.M., and of course, I was in bed, sound asleep. (b) But that jolt woke me right up, and I jumped out of bed. (c) So the first thing I did was to try to get to a doorway, but I couldn't even make it to the door because everything was shaking so much in the room, and I was afraid that the bookcase in my bedroom was going to fall on me. (d) Anyway, I was just about to make a dive under my desk when it stopped.

2. (a) Yesterday, my sister had a birthday party with three of her friends, and they all brought presents for her. (b) First they sat around listening to music and talking, and then they went out to the pizza place for dinner. (c) After dinner, they came back to the house, and my sister started opening her presents. (d) The first one she opened was a watch. (e) She thought it was really nice and put it on. (f) Then she opened the next one, and that was a watch too! (g) She didn't quite know what to do, but she decided to put it on her other wrist. (h) Then, she got to the last present. (i) Fortunately, it didn't look like it was going to be a watch because the box was square. (j) She opened the box and inside was a travel alarm clock. (k) By that time, everyone was laughing, and my sister was wondering if her friends were trying to tell her something.

Exercise 8

Think of a folktale, fairy tale, ghost story, or other story you know well. Tell the story in simple present tense, either orally or in writing (your teacher will tell you which form to use), to involve your listeners or readers more directly in the events.

Activities

Activity 1

As this unit discusses, being consistent with tense does not mean that you should keep the same tense in every sentence of a paragraph or text, but that you should have a consistent time frame (past, present, or future) unless you intend to change the moment of focus. Scan some comic strips in the newspaper to find strips that have a variety of verb tenses within them. In groups, discuss what the frames of reference are for each, and why tense changes occur. As a variation of this activity, cover up or blacken the verbs in comic strips. Then give another classmate the base forms of the verbs and see if she or he fills in the same tenses as the original. Discuss any differences in choices.

Activity 2

Select several paragraphs of something you find interesting from a textbook or other book. Analyze the verb tense use in the paragraphs. What types of verb tense shifts or time frame shifts occur? Analyze the reasons for tense or time frame shifts.

Activity 3

Take a look at a piece of writing you or a classmate has done recently: an essay or other type of paper, for example. Analyze the types of verb tense shifts you see. Do you think verb tenses are used appropriately?

Activity 4

Compare one of the in-groups you used to belong to with one that you belong to now. For example, you could compare two organizations, two schools, two neighborhoods, two groups of friends, etc.

Activity 5

Have a contest to see who can tell the best stories. Consider categories such as most humorous, most embarrassing, or most frightening. Tell your stories using present tense verbs to make them more vivid for your listeners.

2

Verbs
Aspects and Time Frames

Task

In Unit 1, the Task asked you to consider your in-groups, based on Gordon Allport's definition of that term. As you know, in-groups change over time; individuals may join new in-groups throughout their lives. At times, the process of joining a new group can be uncomfortable. Most people have had the experience of being a new member of a group and, for whatever reasons, feeling as if they didn't belong.

In *Lives on the Boundary,* Mike Rose describes well the sense of being an outsider that many students experience upon entering college, especially those who are among the first in their families to attend college:

> People are taking notes and you are taking notes. You are taking notes on a lecture you don't understand. You get a phrase, a sentence, then the next loses you. It's as though you're hearing a conversation in a crowd or from another room — out of phase, muted. The man on the stage concludes his lecture and everyone rustles and you close your notebook and prepare to leave. You feel a little strange. Maybe tomorrow this stuff will clear up. Maybe by tomorrow this will be easier. But by the time you're in the hallway, you don't think it will be easier at all.

(From Mike Rose, *Lives on the Boundary,* New York: Penguin Books, 1990.)

The experience of Lindo Jong in Amy Tan's novel *The Joy Luck Club* offers an example of someone feeling like an outsider when joining another family as the result of marriage. Upon her marriage to Tuan-yu, Lindo Jong has gone to live with his family in accordance with Chinese custom. She has already sensed that she will not get a warm welcome from her mother-in-law, Huang Taitai:

> No big celebration was held when I arrived. Huang Taitai didn't have red banners greeting me in the fancy room on the first floor. Tuan-yu was not there to greet me. Instead, Huang Taitai hurried me upstairs to the second floor and into the kitchen, which was a place where family children didn't usually go. This was a place for cooks and servants. So I knew my standing.
>
> That first day, I stood in my best padded dress at the low wooden table and began to chop vegetables. I could not keep my hands steady. I missed my family and my stomach felt bad, knowing I had finally arrived where my life said I belonged.

(From Amy Tan, *The Joy Luck Club,* New York: Ivy Books, 1989.)

Think of a situation in which either you, someone you know, or a character in a novel or film felt like an outsider upon joining a new in-group. In a paragraph, describe the situation and explain how you, another person, or the fictional character responded to the situation.

Focus 1

Review of Simple Tenses

USE

- Simple tenses do not have aspect. The simple tenses include simple present, simple past, and simple future. We use simple tenses to express:
  - general ideas, relationships, and truths:
    - **(a)** Our in-groups **help** to define our values.
    - **(b)** Immigrants to America in the mid-nineteenth century **included** large numbers of Chinese.
    - **(c)** Families **will** always **be** important to most of us.
  - habitual or repeated actions:
    - **(d)** Our family **visits** my grandparents after church every Sunday.
    - **(e)** Almost every year we **celebrated** my great aunt's birthday with a family picnic.
    - **(f)** The club **will collect** dues once a month.
  - mental perceptions or emotions:
    - **(g)** Kay **thinks** she has chosen the right profession.
    - **(h)** People once **believed** the earth was flat.
    - **(i)** You **will love** the new puppy.
  - possession or personal relationships:
    - **(j)** Phil **has** three brothers.
    - **(k)** We **owned** a station wagon, but we traded it in for a compact car.
    - **(l)** By next month, Andrea **will have** a complete set of encyclopedias.
  - time frame and moment of focus:
    - **(m)** The media **reports** that new evidence has been presented in the trial.
    - **(n)** When the United States **passed** the Chinese Exclusion Act in 1882, 100,000 Chinese were living in the United States.
    - **(o)** Phyllis **will call** you Thursday morning; I hope you will not have left for Omaha by then.

Exercise 1

Go back to the passages in Exercises 1 and 3 in Unit 1. Find an example of a verb with each of the following meanings. Write down your choices and prepare to discuss them in class.

1. past repeated action
2. present habitual action
3. past perception
4. future possession
5. past moment of focus

Focus 2

Review of Progressive Aspect

USE

- Progressive tenses, as shown in Focus 1 of Unit 1, include a form of *be* + a present participle (verb + *-ing*).
- The progressive aspect in English shows the relationship of events to the basic time frame and the moment of focus. We use progressive tenses to express:
  - actions already in progress at the moment of focus: When Phil **gets** home from work, Andrea **is** often **studying.**
    - **(a)** I **was driving** to the restaurant when I **saw** the meteor shower.
    - **(b)** She **will be working** the night shift when my plane **arrives.**
  - actions at the moment of focus in contrast to habitual actions:
    - **(c)** Eric usually goes out to eat four or five times a week. This evening, however, he **is cooking** dinner at home.
    - **(d)** During my childhood, the robins usually took up residence in the old apple trees every spring. One summer, though, they **were building** nests in every corner of the garage.
  - repeated actions:
    - **(e)** She **is** constantly **reminding** me to water the plants.
    - **(f)** When he was young, my older brother **was** always **getting** into trouble.
  - temporary situations in contrast to permanent states:
    - **(g)** Kendra **works** in the principal's office, but she **is helping** the new school nurse organize files this week.
    - **(h)** We will move into our new home in the country next spring, but until then we **will be renting** an apartment in the city.
  - periods of time in contrast to points of time:
    - **(i)** Yesterday the students **discussed** the projects they **were working** on this semester.
  - uncompleted actions:
    - **(j)** Sara **is doing** volunteer work for the homeless this summer.
    - **(k)** When I last saw Christian, he **was** still **planting** his vegetable garden.

15

Exercise 2

Underline the progressive verbs in the passages below. On a separate sheet of paper, write down what additional information the progressive aspect expresses for each verb. (Refer to the uses presented in Focus 6.)

1. (a)I am sitting under a sycamore by Tinker Creek. (b)I am really here, alive on the intricate earth under trees … (c)What else is going on right this minute while ground water creeps under my feet? (d)The galaxy is careening in a slow, muffled widening. (e)If a million solar systems are born every hour, then surely hundreds burst into being as I shift my weight to the other elbow. (f)The sun's surface is now exploding; other stars implode and vanish, heavy and black, out of sight. (g)Meteorites are arcing to earth invisibly all day long. (h)On the planet the winds are blowing: the polar easterlies, the westerlies, the northeast and southeast trades. (From Annie Dillard, *Pilgrim at Tinker Creek,* New York: Bantam, 1974.)

2. (a)For the twentieth time, Mr. Death Bredon was studying the report of the coroner's inquest on Victor Dean. (b)There was the evidence of Mr. Prout. (c)"It would be about tea-time. (d)Tea is served at 3:30, more or less. (e)I was coming out of my room on the top floor, carrying my camera and tripod. (f)Mr. Dean passed me. (g)He was coming quickly along the passage in the direction of the iron staircase. (h)He was not running—he was walking at a good pace. (i)He was carrying a large, heavy book under one arm. (j)I know now that it was *The Times Atlas.* (k)I turned to walk in the same direction that he was going. (l)I saw him start down the iron staircase; it is rather a steep spiral. (m)He had taken about half a dozen steps when he seemed to crumple together and disappear." (From Dorothy Sayers, *Murder Must Advertise,* New York: Harper and Row, 1961.)

Exercise 3

Decide whether a simple tense or progressive tense is appropriate for each blank and fill in the blank with the correct form of the verb in parentheses.

1. Andre (a) _____(come) from Brazil and (b) _____(be) a native speaker of Portuguese. Currently he (c) _____(study) English at the University of Colorado. He (d) _____(take) two courses: composition and American culture.

2. When Kay (a) _____(live) in Chicago as a child, she (b) _____ (take) the bus to school every day. Often when she (c) _____(get) off the bus after school, her mother (d) _____(wait) for her to walk her home.

At that time, her father (e) _____(have) an office in downtown Chicago, and usually he (f) _____(work) when Kay (g) _____(finish) her day at school.

3. One of my most important in-groups (a) _____(be) my church group. Right now we (b) _____(provide) lunches for homeless people in the city park. Also, some of us (c) _____(tutor) junior high students in math and English for the summer. Others in my group (d) _____(spend) part of the summer doing volunteer work at senior citizen centers. We all (e) _____(feel) that we (f) _____(gain) a great deal ourselves by participating in these activities.

4. Next summer our family (a) _____(have) a reunion during the July 4th holiday weekend. My uncle from Finland (b) _____(try) to come, but he (c) _____(start) a new business this year, so it (d) _____(be) difficult for him to get away. Another uncle (e) _____(spend) the whole summer with us. He (f) _____(work) at my mother's travel agency from June through August.

5. Ramon (a) _____(belong) to the Photography Club at school. This week he (b) _____(learn) how to take good close-up shots of people. At the moment, he (c) _____(drive) us all crazy by constantly taking our pictures!

6. For many immigrants to the United States, their home countries (a) _____(remain) an important in-group long after they have left. Even while they (b) _____(learn) a new language, many (c) _____(look to) speakers of their native language as an in-group who (d) _____(understand) their struggles to adapt to a new way of life.

17

Exercise 4

Ask another classmate to tell you five things he or she does now as a result of in-group associations. Write a sentence for each, using present time reference verbs. Report one or two of the sentences you find most interesting to the rest of the class.

EXAMPLE: Martin plays the saxophone with a jazz band.

As a student at Northwestern, he is majoring in environmental sciences.

Focus 3

USE

Review of Perfective Aspect

USE

- Perfect tenses, as was shown in Focus 1 of Unit 1, are formed by *have (has, have, had, will have)* + a past participle (verb + *-ed* or irregular form).
- Perfect tenses express events (including actions or states) that happen before another event. The perfective aspect indicates a relationship between an event and the moment of focus: past, present, or future.
- We use perfect tenses to express:
  - events that happen before the moment of focus:
    - **(a)** To date, Mark **has taken** off five days from work for vacation time.
    - **(b)** When I last spoke to my mother, she **had written** me a letter and **had mailed** it, so she didn't want to repeat her news over the telephone.
    - **(c)** By this time tomorrow, even more acres of the rain forest **will have been destroyed.**
  - events that began in the past and continue to be true at present in contrast to completed events:
    - **(d)** My parents **have lived** in their house for 40 years; this year they are remodeling the kitchen.
    - **(e)** My grandparents **lived** in a house on Tower Avenue until they died.
  - events that the speaker believes are relevant to the moment of focus in contrast to unrelated events:
    - **(f)** I **have** just **finished** that chapter, so I can help you answer the questions at the end of it. (My finishing the chapter is relevant to my ability to help.)
    - **(g)** I **finished** the assignment for history. Then I played video games. (The two events are related only sequentially.)

Exercise 5

Underline the present perfect and past perfect verbs in the following passages. Explain what information is expressed by the perfective aspect of these verbs. Which kinds of information listed in Focus 3 are expressed? (A perfect verb can convey more than one kind of information.)

EXAMPLE: 1. (d) had seen—past perfect

Information: events before the moment of focus; relevant to the moment of focus

1. (a)By 1851, in a matter of three years, there were 25,000 Chinese in California. (b)Fatt Hing was one of these 25,000. (c)His story is typical of the pioneer Chinese, many who came with him and many who came after him. (d)As a lad of nineteen, Fatt Hing <u>had</u> already <u>seen</u> and <u>heard</u> and <u>learned</u> more about the world than most of the men in his village, who had seldom set foot beyond the nearest town square. (e)For Fatt Hing was a fish peddler who went frequently from Toishan to Kwanghai on the coast to buy his fish to see at the market. (f)Down by the wharves, where the fishing boats came in, Fatt Hing had often seen foreign ships with their sails fluttering in the wind. (g) He had seen hairy white men on the decks, and he had often wondered and dreamed about the land they came from. (From Betty Lee Sung, *The Story of the Chinese in America,* New York: Collier Books, 1971.)

2. (a)The dog has got more fun out of Man than Man has got out of the dog, for the clearly demonstrable reason that Man is the more laughable of the two animals. (b)The dog has long been bemused by the singular activities and the curious practices of men, cocking his head inquiringly to one side, intently watching and listening to the strangest goings-on in the world. (c)He has seen men sing together and fight one another in the same evening. (d)He has watched them go to bed when it is time to get up, and get up when it is time to go to bed. (e)He has observed them destroying the soil in vast areas, and nurturing it in small patches. (f)He has stood by while men built strong and solid houses for rest and quiet, and then filled them with lights and bells and machinery. (From James Thurber, *Thurber's Dogs, A Collection of the Master's Dogs, Written and Drawn, Real and Imaginary, Living and Long Ago,* New York: Simon & Schuster, 1955.)

3. (a)On the morning of December 19, the snow had finally stopped, and a bright sun had come out and melted enough of it so that the cottages could be seen to be prettily, even lavishly, painted. (b)The High Street, down to the bridge, was fascinating, or beguiling, or weird, depending on one's tastes. (c)It looked like it had been done by a convention of crazy housepainters. (d)Perhaps bored with the usual limestone, in this limestone belt of Northamptonshire, they had gone rioting with ice-cream parlor colors: a hint of strawberry here, of lemon there, and farther on, a glimmer of pistachio, and then a sudden splash of emerald. (From Martha Grimes, *The Man with a Load of Mischief,* New York: Dell Publishing Co., Inc., 1981.)

4. (a)Today, amnesia is much easier to come by. (b)As technology has become more hyperactive, we, the people, have become more laid-back; as the deposits in its memory bank have become more fat, the deposits in man's memory bank have become more lean. (From Studs Terkel, *The Great Divide: Second Thoughts on the American Dream,* New York: Pantheon, 1988.)

Exercise 6

Choose either the simple present or the present perfect form to fill in each blank.

(1)Some trend forecasters _____(believe) that Americans _____

(begin) to reject the self-centered values of previous decades. (2)According to the forecast-

ers, Americans now _____(tend) to be more family-centered rather than fo-

cused on their individual desires. (3)It _____(seem) that Americans_____

(change) their attitudes about their work too; they _____(feel) that good per-

sonal relationships _____(count) as much as success in one's work. (4)Based

on recent evidence, some people _____(stop) working overtime and on

weekends and _____(started) to devote more time to family and friends.

(5)In short, many people, especially in urban cultures, _____(shift) their

energies from developing capital to developing relationships. (6)However, the evidence

also _____(suggest) that some _____(have) trouble adjusting

to the lowered standard of living resulting from this change. (7)Making less money

_____(mean) consuming less, and this _____(not, is) easy. (8)As

the saying _____(go), you can't _____(have) your cake and

_____(eat) it too!

Exercise 7

Decide whether you should use a simple tense (present, past) or present perfect of each
verb in parentheses to fill in the blanks.

The Hotter'N Hell Hundred

1. Near the Texas-Oklahoma border, where the wind never _____(seem) to

   stop, where the sun _____(broil) the blacktop and _____(sap)

   the strength, the cyclists _____(come) each year.

2. They _____(come) to Wichita Falls, Texas, by the thousands to ride in

   what _____(become) the largest 100-mile bicycle race in the world—the

   Hotter 'N Hell Hundred.

3. The race _____(take) place on Labor Day weekend at the beginning of September, when temperatures _____(regularly, soar) past 100 degrees.

4. The oddity of this race is that, with each passing year, it _____(become) more and more a symbol of Wichita Falls, a city that, until recently, _____ (be, hardly) a cycling bastion.

5. In days past, the sight of a bicyclist _____(cause) heads to turn in the pickup truck.

6. Tornadoes _____(be) once more numerous than bicyclists in Wichita Falls.

7. Actually, in the past, this town _____(be) much better known for its drinking establishments.

8. At one time it _____(have) so many bars that some people _____ (call) it Whiskeytaw Falls.

9. The Hotter'N Hell Hundred _____(start) in 1982 when a postal worker _____(suggest) a 100-mile bike ride in 100-degree heat to celebrate Wichita Falls' 100th birthday.

10. Today, the race _____(command) the attention of almost the whole city as race weekend _____(approach).

(Adapted with permission from "It's the hottest little ol' race in Texas," J. Michael Kennedy, *Los Angeles Times,* September 2, 1991.)

Exercise 8

Decide whether you should use a simple future or future perfect tense of each verb in parentheses to fill in the blank.

(1)Our class has been discussing which in-groups we think _____ (be) or _____ (be, not) important to us ten years from now. (2)Hua says she knows her family _____ (remain) an important in-group forever. (3)However, she thinks her associations with some campus groups, such as the French Club, _____ (end) by the time she graduates. (4)Kazuhiko thinks that he _____ (be) married for several years by that time. (5)He hopes he _____ (have) a few children of his own. (6)He believes his future family _____ (represent) his most important in-group in ten years. (7)Jose predicts that he _____ (become) a famous physicist by that time and that one of his important in-groups _____ (be) other Nobel Prize winners.

Focus 4

Review of Perfect Progressive Aspect

USE

- Perfect progressive tenses include present perfect progressive, past perfect progressive, and future perfect progressive. They are formed by *have (has, have, had, will have)* + *been* + a past participle (verb + *-ing*).
- Together, perfect and progressive aspects express:
  - uncompleted actions in contrast to completed actions at the moment of focus:
    - **(a)** The jury **has been discussing** the evidence. They still haven't reported their verdict.
    - **(b)** The jury **has discussed** the evidence for a week. They will soon report their verdict for the defendant.
  - continuous processes versus repeated actions:
    - **(c)** The construction workers **had been pounding** nails for hours when we finally asked them to give us some peace and quiet.
    - **(d)** Pat **had pounded** that nail in twice, but it kept falling out of the wall because the hole was too big.

Exercise 9

State whether the perfect progressive verbs in the following sentences indicate (a) uncompleted rather than completed action or (b) continuous rather than repeated action.

1. The class has been trying to guess the answer to the riddle all day, but they haven't figured it out yet.
2. Marlo will have been working at the zoo for two years at the end of August.
3. The sad-looking stranger had been showing everyone a photo of a smiling young woman and had been asking if anyone had seen her, but no one could help him in his search for his missing daughter.
4. Scientists have been speculating as to why dinosaurs became extinct. Although they have several theories, they're still not sure what happened.
5. My next door neighbor is practicing her voice lesson. She has been singing the same scale over and over for 20 minutes. It's driving me crazy!

Exercise 10

Decide whether the verbs in parentheses should express an action, event, or situation completed at a specific time in the past (simple past) or one that started in the past and continues to the present (present perfect or present perfect progressive). Write the appropriate form for each verb in the blank.

1. (1)Alfredo _____ (join) the Friends of the Theater in his community five

years ago and _____ (be) an active participant in this group ever since.

(2)It _____ (remain) one of his favorite leisure activities even though he

_____ (stop) trying out for roles in the plays last year because he _____

(be) too busy. (3)As a member, he _____ (help) promote the plays. (4)At

times, he _____ (look for) costumes for the actors. (5)For last month's play,

he _____ (work) with the props crew to get furniture and other props for the

stage sets. (6) He _____ (find) an antique desk to use for one of the sets, and he also

_____(make) a fireplace facade. (7)Most recently, he _____(try)

to get more businesses to advertise in the playbills.

2. (1)Last week, Vera _____(start) working for a law firm. (2)She _____(work) since she was 16, but the last time she _____ (have) an office job _____(be) when she _____(be) 20. (3)So far at the law firm, she _____(do) a lot of work on the computer. (4)She also _____(research) information for one case. (5)She _____(tell) me the other day that she _____ (enjoy) the research more than the computer work.

Exercise 11

From Ms. H's choice of verb tense below, would you say that her "vowel affairs" have ended or not?

"All right! All right! If you want the truth, off and on I've been seeing *all* the vowels — a, e, i, o, u. . . . Oh, yes! And *sometimes* y!"

The Far Side. Copyright 1991, FarWorks, Inc. Dist. by Universal Press Syndicate. Reprinted with permission. All rights reserved.

Focus 5

Summary: Present Time Frame

FORM
MEANING
USE

Form	Meaning	Use	Example
SIMPLE PRESENT base form of verb or base form of verb + −*s*	now	timeless truths	**(a)** children **need** social interaction to develop language.
		habitual actions	**(b)** Kay **plays** on a volleyball team once a week.
		mental perceptions and emotions	**(c)** Kay **considers** her Thai heritage an important in-group.
		possession	**(d)** Andrea **has** a red bicycle.
PRESENT PROGRESSIVE *am/is/are* + present participle (verb + −*ing*)	in progress now	actions in progress	**(e)** I **am** now **completing** my Bachelor's degree in Spanish.
		repetition or duration	**(f)** Kay **is throwing** the ball to Andrea.
		temporary activities	**(g)** Kay's brother **is staying** with her this summer.
		uncompleted actions	**(h)** Phil **is making** dinner.
PRESENT PERFECT *have/has*+ past participle (verb + −*ed* or irregular form)	in the past but related to now in some way	situations that began in the past, continue to the present	**(i)** Kay **has belonged** to the Sierra Club for four years.
		actions completed in the past but related to the present	**(j)** Kay **has applied** to several hospitals for positions; she is waiting to hear from them.
		actions recently completed	**(k)** Andrea **has** just **finished** junior high school.

Form	Meaning	Use	Example
PRESENT PERFECT PROGRESSIVE *have/has* + *been* + present participle (verb + *-ing*)	up until and including now	repeated or continuous actions	**(l)** Both Kay and Phil **have been playing** volleyball since they were teenagers. **(m)** This weekend Phil **has been competing** in a tournament, which ends tomorrow.

Exercise 12

Choose simple present, present progressive, present perfect, or present perfect progressive for each blank. More than one answer could be correct; be prepared to explain your choices.

(1)Inés _____(consider) her neighborhood in East Los Angeles to be one of her most important in-groups. (2)She _____(live) in this neighborhood since birth, and she _____(know) almost everyone in it. (3)Most of the people in the neighborhood _____(be) from Mexico, but some _____(be) from Central American countries. (4)Mr. Hernandez, who _____(live) next door to Inés, always _____ (insist) that he _____(live) the longest time in the neighborhood. (5)However, Mrs. Chavez, whom everyone _____(call) "Tía," usually _____(tell) him to stop spreading tales. (6)Mrs. Chavez _____(claim) that she _____(be) around longer than anyone. (7)Inés _____(watch) many of the children younger than herself grow up, and she often _____(think) of them as her little brothers and sisters—the ones she _____(like), that is. (8)Just as her older neighbors _____(do) for her, she now _____(help) her younger neighbors keep out of trouble and _____(give) them advice.

Focus 6

Summary: Past Time Frame

FORM
MEANING
USE

Form	Meaning	Use	Example
SIMPLE PRESENT	at a certain time	past events in informal narrative	**(a)** So on Friday, Terry **calls** Lila and **tells** her to be ready for a surprise.
SIMPLE PAST verb + -*ed* or irregular past form	at a certain time in the past	events that took place at a definite time in the past	**(b)** Kay **joined** the Girl Scouts when she was 8.
		events that lasted for a time in the past	**(c)** Phil **attended** Columbia University for two years as an undergraduate.
		habitual or repeated events in the past	**(d)** Kay **went** to Girl Scout camp every summer until she entered high school.
		past mental perceptions and emotions	**(e)** Kay always **knew** that she **wanted** to be a doctor.
		past possession	**(f)** Although she **didn't have** a car in college, Kay **owned** a bicycle.
PAST PROGESSIVE *was/were* + present participle (verb + -*ing*)	in progress at a time in the past	events in progress at a specific time in the past	**(g)** At midnight last night, Kay **was** still **making** her rounds.
		interrupted actions	**(h)** Kay **was talking** to one of the nurses when Phil called.
		repeated actions and actions over time	**(i)** Andrea **was acting** in a community theatre play for a month last year.

Form	Meaning	Use	Example
PAST PERFECT *had* + past participle (verb + *-ed* or irregular form)	before a certain time in the past	actions or states that took place before another time in the past	**(j)** Before starting medical school, Kay **had taken** a long vacation.
PAST PERFECT PROGRESSIVE *had* + *been* + present participle (verb + *-ing*)	up until a certain time in the past	continuous events taking place before other past events	**(k)** By 9:00 P.M., Andrea **had been studying** for two hours.
		events interrupted by other past events	**(l)** Phil **had been working** on his computer when the power went out.

Exercise 13

The comic strip below uses the following tenses: simple present, present progressive, simple past, past progressive, and past perfect. Find an example of each of these tenses in the comic strip, then identify one verb phrase from the strip that expresses each of the following meanings:

1. event in progress
2. present situation
3. event completed in the past before another event
4. action completed at a definite point in the past
5. event in progress at a specific time in the past

Reprinted by permission of U. F. S. Inc.

Exercise 14

In *The Man Who Mistook His Wife for a Hat,* Dr. Oliver Sacks writes about his experiences treating bizarre neurological disorders. The passage below summarizes part of Dr. Sacks' true story of Dr. P, the man of the book's title. Read the passage first. Then, for each blank, choose a simple past, past progressive, past perfect, or past perfect progessive form of the verb in parentheses. More than one tense might be possible for some blanks. Prepare to explain your choices.

(1) Dr. P <u>was</u>(be) a distinguished musician. (2) For many years, he _____(be) a singer; later he _____(become) a teacher at the local School of Music. (3) It _____(be) at this school that others _____(begin) to observe Dr. P's strange problem. (4) Sometimes Dr. P _____(not recognize) faces of people he _____(know). (5) Sometimes he _____(see) faces where there _____(be) none: on a water hydrant, for example, or on the carved knobs of furniture. (6) When Dr. P finally _____(go) to Dr. Sacks' clinic, these events _____(go on) for years.

(7) At the clinic, it _____(be) while Dr. Sacks _____(examine) Dr. P's reflexes that the first bizarre experience _____(occur). (8) Dr. Sacks _____(take) off Dr. P's left shoe to test his reflexes. (9) He later _____(leave) Dr. P for a few minutes, assuming Dr. P would put the shoe back on. (10) When Dr. Sacks _____(return) to his examining room, Dr. P _____(not put) the shoe on. (11) Dr. Sacks _____(ask) Dr. P if he could help, and Dr. P _____(say) that he _____(forget) to put the shoe on. (12) Finally, Dr. P _____(look) down at his foot and _____(ask) if his foot _____(be) his shoe. (13) When Dr. Sacks _____(point) to Dr. P's shoe nearby, Dr. P _____(tell) him that he _____(think) the shoe _____(be) his foot!

29

(14)Later, as Dr. P _____(get) ready to leave, he _____(start) to

look for his hat. (15)He _____(reach) for his wife's head and _____

(try) to put it on. (16)Poor Dr. P _____(mistake) his wife for a hat!

(Adapted with permission of Oliver Sacks from *The Man Who Mistook His Wife for a Hat and Other Clinical Tales,* Oliver Sacks, New York: Harper and Row, 1987.)

Exercise 15

It is doubtful that any of your in-groups include trees; in the ancient Greek myths, however, more than a few family members ended up as flora of one sort or another. The following passage tells the story of the mythological character Dryope. For each blank, choose a simple past, past progressive, past perfect, or past perfect progressive form of the verb in parentheses. More than one choice could be possible. Prepare to explain your choices.

(1)One day Dryope, with her sister Iole, _____(go) to a pool in the forest. (2)She _____(carry) her baby son. (3)She _____(intend) to

make flower garlands near the pool for the nymphs, those female goddesses of the

woodlands and waters. (4)When Dryope _____(see) a lotus tree full of

beautiful blossoms near the water, she _____(pluck) some of them for her

baby. (5)To her horror, drops of blood _____(flow) from the stem; the tree

_____(be) actually the nymph Lotis. (6)Lotis _____(flee) from

a pursuer and _____(take) refuge in a tree. (7)When the terrified Dryope

_____(try) to run away, she _____(find) that her feet would not

move; they _____(root) in the ground. (8)Iole _____(watch) help-

lessly as tree bark _____(grow) upward and _____(cover)

Dryope's body. (9)By the time Dryope's husband _____(come) to

the spot with her father, the bark _____(reach) Dryope's face. (10)They

_____(rush) to the tree, _____(embrace) it, and _____

(water) it with their tears. (11)Dryope _____(have) time only to tell them that

she _____(do) no wrong intentionally. (12)She _____(beg) them to bring the child often to the tree to play in its shade. (13)She also _____(tell)

them to remind her child never to pluck flowers and to consider that every tree and bush

may be a goddess in disguise.

Exercise 16

Retell Dryope's story in Exercise 15 in an informal narrative style. Use present tense verbs instead of past tense verbs.

Focus 7

FORM ● MEANING ● USE

Summary: Future Time Frame

FORM
MEANING
USE

Form	Meaning	Use	Example
SIMPLE PRESENT	already planned or expected in the future	definite future plans or schedules	**(a)** Kay **completes** her residency next May.
		events with future time adverbials (*before, after, when*) in dependent clauses	**(b)** After Kay **finishes** her residency, she plans to take some time off from work.
PRESENT PROGRESSIVE		future intentions	**(c)** I **am leaving** at 7:00 A.M. tomorrow.
		scheduled events that last for a period of time	**(d)** The family **is spending** the Christmas holidays in Boston.
BE GOING TO FUTURE *am/is/are going to* + base verb	at a certain time in the future	probable and immediate future events	**(e)** The movie **is going to start** in a few minutes.
		strong intentions	**(f)** I **am going to finish** this no matter what!
		predictions about future situations	**(g)** When you get older, you**'re going to wish** that you had saved more money.

Form	Meaning	Use	Example
SIMPLE FUTURE *will* + base verb		probable future events	**(h)** Buddhism **will** most likely **remain** one of Kay's in-groups.
		willingness	**(i)** I **will help** you with your homework this evening.
FUTURE PROGRESSIVE *will* + *be* + present participle (verb + *-ing*)	in progress at a certain time in the future	events that will be in progress at a time in the near future	**(j)** Kay's parents **will be driving** from Chicago to Palo Alto next week.
		future events that will last for a period of time	**(k)** Kay's family **will be staying** in Palo Alto until she finishes her residency.
FUTURE PERFECT *will* + *have* + past participle (verb + *-ed* or irregular form)	before a certain time in the future	future events happening before other future events	**(l)** Kay's parents **will have left** Palo Alto before Andrea starts school.
FUTURE PERFECT PROGRESSIVE *will* + *have* + *been* + present participle (verb +*-ing*)	up until a certain time in the future	continuous and/or repeated actions continuing into the future	**(m)** By the end of this year, Kay **will have been living** in California for four years.

Exercise 17

Choose an appropriate future reference verb tense—present, present progressive, simple future, *be going to,* future progressive, or future perfect—to complete the dialogue below between Justin and his friend Patty. More than one verb tense might be appropriate for some blanks. Read the dialogue with a classmate. Discuss any differences in the choices you made.

Justin: My brother (1) _____(leave) tomorrow for his third trip to Europe

this year!

Patty: What time (2) _____(he, go) ?

Justin: His plane (3) _____(take off) really early—at 6:00 A.M., I think, so he (4) _____(need) to get out of here by 4:00 A.M. or so. I (5) _____ (drive) him to the airport.

Patty: Why (6) _____(he, go) to Europe again?

Justin: It's for his job. He (7) _____(meet) his company's executives in Germany, and then he (8) _____(spend) a few days in Denmark. You know something? When I (9) _____(finish) school and (10) _____(get) a job, I (11) _____(have) an exciting life-style too!

Patty: Oh, really? And what (12) _____(you, do), if you don't mind my asking?

Justin: Not at all. Next summer, of course, after I (13) _____(graduate), I (14) _____(look) for a job for a while. With a little effort, I'm sure I (15) _____(find) a very challenging and lucrative position in my field. Five years or so from now, I (16) _____(save) enough money to put a down payment on a penthouse condominium. By that time, I (17) _____(made) enough to buy a flashy little sports car. I (18) _____(put) away enough money by then to rent a beach vacation home every summer.

Patty: It sounds as if you (19) _____(live) the good life!

Justin: Well, I just said I (20) _____(have) enough money to live like that. That doesn't mean I (21) _____(do) it. Actually, now that I think about it, I (22) _____(not, get) any of those things. At the end of the five years, I (23) _____(take) all that money I saved and (24) _____(buy) the largest sailboat I can afford. I (25) _____(quit) my job and (26) _____ (sail) around the world! Care to join the crew?

Activities

Activity 1

Sometimes actual written or spoken language doesn't seem to follow the rules you see in grammar books. However, often the larger context can provide an explanation that is consistent with the rule. For example, here is a "grammar rule" sentence to illustrate the use of the past perfect:

After his wife had left him, Macon met Muriel.

Our rule: The past perfect is used to indicate a past action (*had left*) before another past action (*met*). But now consider the first sentence of the novel *The Accidental Tourist,* by Anne Tyler:

After his wife left him, Macon had thought the house would seem larger.

This seems to be the reverse of the grammar rule! We can explain the verb *left* by saying that native speakers often use simple past when past perfect could be used. But how can we account for the use of the past perfect in the second part? Here's the rest of the novel's first paragraph to help you explain it. (Hint: Could the past perfect verb be used in relation to a verb or verbs other than *left?*)

Instead he felt more crowded. The windows shrank. The ceilings lowered. There was something insistent about the furniture, as if it were pressing in on him.

(From Anne Tyler, *The Accidental Tourist,* New York: Berkley Books, 1986.)

Activity 2

Find a place that you think would be interesting to observe nature or people: a quiet place outdoors, a school cafeteria, an airport, or a busy restaurant, for example. Spend at least 20 minutes in this place with a notebook to record observations of interesting sights and sounds. You might want to reread Annie Dillard's observations in Exercise 2.

Activity 3

Think carefully about a person you know very well. Describe what you think that person will be doing and how she or he will change in the next ten years or so.

Activity 4

Reread the passage by James Thurber in Exercise 3. Think of another animal that might have some very different opinions about the human race than humans tend to have about themselves. The animal could be a house pet, such as a canary; another domestic animal, such as a pig; or a wild animal, such as a wolf. Write a description of how this animal has probably regarded the human race.

Activity 5

Gordon Allport used concepts of in-groups and out-groups to develop a theory about how prejudices are formed. The very nature of in-groups meant that other groups were "out-groups." For example, if someone is Catholic, then non-Catholics would be "out-groups." Not all "out-groups" are at odds with each other. However, Allport believed that sometimes people treat certain out-groups as "the enemy" or as inferior to their group. As a result, prejudices toward those of other religions, races, or nationalities may form. Do you see evidence, in your school, community, or a larger context, of "out-groups" who are victims of prejudice? Working in groups, list some of the out-groups you think are discriminated against. Then describe the situation affecting one of these out-groups in an essay. State whether the situation has improved or gotten worse over time and whether you think it will have improved by the end of the next decade or so.

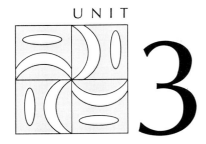

UNIT

3

Subject-Verb Agreement

Task

For over four decades, researchers for the Gallup Poll, which examines national trends, have been surveying Americans' reading habits and attitudes toward reading. They have asked people how often they read, what kinds of reading they do, and how reading compares with watching television as a leisure activity, among other things.

Take a poll of your class's reading habits by answering some questions used in the Gallup Poll. The categories for your responses are given in parentheses after each of the following questions below. As in the Gallup surveys, you may give "no opinion" if you do not want to answer a question for some reason. Try, however, to answer as many as possible.

Tally the results of your survey. Then write a brief summary of the results. Were any of them surprising? For the first question, the Gallup results for three polling periods are shown for you to compare your class's results. Some of the other results, taken from the 1990 poll, will be presented later in this unit.

Reading Survey Questions:

1. Do you happen to be reading any books or novels at the present time? (Yes / No)

2. When, as nearly as you can recall, did you last read any kind of book all the way through—either a hardcover book or a paperback book? (Within the last week / Within the last month / 1 to 6 months ago / 7 to 12 months ago / Over one year ago/Never)

3. During the past year, about how many books, either hardcover or paperback, did you read either all or part of the way through? (None / 1 to 5 / 6 to 10 / 11 to 50 / More than 50)

4. **(a)** Do you have a favorite author? (Yes / No)

   (b) If yes, who is it? (Any choice)

5. Which of these two activities—watching television or reading books—is

   (a) The most relaxing for you?

   (b) The best way to learn for you?

   (c) The most rewarding for you?

   (d) The most enjoyable way to spend an evening for you?

   Your choices for (a)–(d): Watching TV /Reading a book/ Both/ Neither

Gallup Results for Question 1	Yes	No
1990 Dec	37%	63%
1957 Mar	17%	83%
1949 Jan	21%	79%

From *Gallup Poll Monthly*, February 1991. Reprinted with permission from The Gallup Organization, Inc., Princeton, New Jersey.

Focus 1

FORM

Overview of Subject-Verb Agreement

FORM

- Subject–verb agreement often remains a persistent problem for advanced students of English. Even native speakers of English have trouble with some subject–verb agreement rules.
- Agreement refers to word forms or word endings that signal number (singular/plural) and person (1st, 2nd, 3rd). For example:

    3rd Person
    Singular
(a) She **watch<u>es</u>** television a lot.

    1st Person
    Plural
(b) We **watch** about two hours of television a day.

- The verb *be*, as you know, has several different present tense forms (*am, are, is*) and two past tense forms (*was/were*). For example:

    First Person
    Singular, Present:
(c) I **am** a senior now.

    Second Person
    Plural, Past:
(d) You **were** two of the people chosen for our poll.

- For all other simple verbs, agreement matters only with the **present** tense and with **the third person singular** (*he, she, it*) in contrast to other persons and numbers. For third person singular, an *-s* inflection is added to the base form of the verb:

3rd Person Singular	**Other Persons/Numbers**
(e) He **has** a library card.	I, You, We, They **have** a library card.
(f) She **reads** every day.	I, You, We, They **read** every day.

37

- If the verb is a complex one with *be* or *have* as the first part of the verb, *be* or *have* must agree in number with the subject:

  (g) The library **is closing** at 9:00 P.M.

  (h) One of the books that I **am reading** this month **has been listed** as a best-seller.

- Problems in choosing the correct verb form for the subject may arise for a number of reasons. Some of the most common are

  - Difficulty in identifying the head noun of a subject when the subject is long:

Subject	Predicate
Head Noun	**Verb**
(i) The main **reason** we decided to take a trip to the Rocky Mountains	**is** our interest in learning about the geological history there.

  - Nouns and pronouns that in some way have both singular and plural senses:

    (j) The pair of scissors you bought is really dull.

    (k) Every book in the library has been catalogued.

  - The fact that in English, the *-s* ending signals plural with nouns, but it signals third person singular with present tense verbs:

    Plural

    (l) Those comic book**s** make me laugh.

    Singular

    (m) That comic book make**s** me laugh.

This unit will cover many of the subject-verb agreement cases that are difficult for native and non-native speakers of English alike. It will present the traditional rules first, with a section on less formal usage at the end.

Exercise 1

To check for subject-verb agreement, first identify the subject of the sentence and then find the noun that is the head of the subject. In each of the following sentences, circle the *head noun* of the subject. Underline the verb.

> **EXAMPLE:** Many children's (parents) begin reading to them when the (children) are less than 3 years old.

1. Young people today are just as likely to read for pleasure as older Americans.
2. The reading survey finds some good news for those who appreciate reading as a pastime.
3. Today's Americans are more likely to read to their children than their parents were.
4. Reading to very young children stimulates them to learn to read sooner.
5. The impact of reading to children at an early age is dramatic.
6. There are signs of a coming surge in reading in America.
7. Despite television and its influence, reading seems to be coming back into favor.

Adapted from *The Gallup Poll Monthly*, February 1991, with permission of The Gallup Organization, Inc.

Focus 2

The Principle of Nonintervention

- The greater the distance between the subject head noun and the verb, the harder it may be to check for agreement. Particularly troublesome are cases in which phrases with plural nouns occur between the head noun and the verb:

**Head
Noun   Modifying Phrase with Plural Nouns**

(a) Another **poll**   of Americans' reading habits and attitudes **was taken** in 1990.

- The principle of nonintervention states: The speaker or writer should ignore all plural nouns in prepositional phrases or other structures that come between the subject head noun and verb.

- To determine agreement, disregard prepositional phrases and the following structures:
  - Compound prepositions

Compound Preposition

(b) The **library**, $\left\{\begin{array}{l} \text{together with} \\ \text{along with} \\ \text{as well as} \end{array}\right\}$ bookstores, **provides** reading materials.

- The noun phrase *not* + (other noun)

***Not* + Noun Phrase**

(c) The **child**, *not* her parents, **was** an avid reader.

- Relative clauses

Relative Clause

(d) **A child** who likes to read books and whose parents encourage reading often **does** better in school.

Exercise 2

The following sentences summarize information about the Gallup Poll's 1990 reading survey. Try this editing strategy to check subject-verb agreement. First put brackets [ ] around any modifying phrases following the head noun. Then underline the head noun. Finally, choose the appropriate forms in parentheses.

EXAMPLE: The library, [along with bookstores], ((provides), provide) reading materials.

1. The horror story writer Stephen King, together with romance novelist Danielle Steele, (was/were) the most popular of the authors named by the respondents.

2. One of the 1,019 respondents of the survey (claims, claim) that (he or she/they) started reading at the age of one!

3. Some respondents, in answer to the question of who their favorite living author is, (gives, give) the name of a writer who has died many years ago.

4. According to Judy Fellman, the President of the International Reading Association, one reason so many parents are reading to their children (is/are) the plethora of children's literature.

5. A father whose own parents read to him when he was young (is/are) more likely to read to (his/their) children.

6. James Michener, as well as V. C. Andrews, (ranks/rank) third in author popularity among those surveyed.

7. A person who belongs to one of the higher income groups (tends/tend) to read more.

8. According to the poll, the college-educated female, not the college-educated male, (is/are) the most prolific (reader/ readers), averaging 18 books a year.

Focus 3

FORM

Agreement with Correlative Conjunctions: *Both . . . and; Either . . . or; Neither . . . nor*

FORM

- When two subject noun phrases are connected by *both . . . and,* we use a plural verb:

    (a) Both **F. Scott Fitzgerald** and **Charles Dickens were** named as favorite authors in the 1990 reading poll.

- For *either . . . or* or *neither . . . nor,* the traditional rule is the **proximity principle**:
    - The verb should agree with the closest subject head noun.

        (b) Either the library or **bookstores have** current magazines.

        (c) Either bookstores or **the library has** current magazines.

        (d) Neither the book nor **the magazines discuss** this issue.

        (e) Neither the magazines nor **the book discusses** this issue.

- The proximity principle also governs agreement when one or more subjects is a pronoun:

    (f) Either you or **she is** going to be asked to give the answer.

    (g) Either Kay or **I am** going to the library this afternoon.

    (h) Neither the twins nor **he is** planning to go to the library.

    (i) Obviously, neither you nor **I am** interested in that topic.

Exercise 3

Select and circle the appropriate verb form and, in some cases, the correct noun phrase after the verb, for each sentence. In cases of *either . . . or* or *neither . . . nor*, use the proximity principle to select the verb.

EXAMPLE: Neither the books nor the bookshelf ((is)/are) mine.

1. Either books or a magazine subscription (makes a nice gift/make nice gifts) for someone.
2. For a less expensive gift, both bookplates and a bookmark (is a good choice/are good choices).
3. Neither the Russian novelist Leo Tolstoy nor the British writer James Joyce (was/were) known to more than 50% of the 1990 Gallup reading poll respondents.
4. She said that either the reserved book librarian or the librarians at the main checkout desk (has/have) the information you need.
5. Both reading and writing (is/are) what we consider literacy skills.
6. Either you or I (am/are) going to present the first report.
7. In my opinion, neither the front page of the newspaper nor the sports pages (is/are) as much fun to read as comics.
8. (Does/do) either the life-style section of the newspaper or the business section interest you?
9. I can see that neither you nor he (is/are) finished with your sections yet.
10. Both my brother and my parents (is/are) reading that new biography of Lyndon Johnson. Neither he nor they (has/have) read more than a few chapters, though.

Focus 4

FORM

Agreement with Non-count Nouns and Collective Nouns

FORM

- Non-count nouns in English include **mass nouns** such as *equipment* and **abstract nouns** such as *information*. These nouns are often troublesome because some of them may be count nouns in other languages.
  - Mass nouns and many abstract nouns take the third person singular form of the verb:
- **Non-count Nouns**
  - **(a)** The new gym **equipment has** just **been delivered**.
  - **(b)** That **information is** very helpful.

- Nouns that are *usually* non-count and take a singular verb in American English include:
  - **Mass Nouns**

homework	jewelry	grass	luggage
vocabulary	equipment	scenery	traffic
money	machinery	furniture	

  - **Abstract Nouns**

advice	behavior	research
information	health	transportation
knowledge	progress	violence
education		

- Collective nouns are nouns such as *class*, *team*, and *flock*, which define groups.
  - If the group is being considered as a whole, we use a singular verb:
    - **Collective Whole**
      - (c) The **class is going** on a field trip.
      - (d) The **team has been practicing** all week.
  - If the group is being considered as individual members, then you may use a plural form:
    - **Collective Individuals**
      - (e) The **class have disagreed** among themselves about where they should go on their field trip.
      - (f) The **team have** differing opinions about the best strategies to use in the game on Friday. Some think they should concentrate on defense, but others believe they should use a more aggressive strategy.

        In American English, plural verbs are not as commonly used with collective subjects as singular verbs are.
  - Frequently used collective nouns that usually take a singular verb but may, depending on meaning, take either a singular or plural verb include:
    - **Collective Nouns**

class	audience
committee	team
group	the public
family	

- Some collective nouns require plural verbs for agreement. They include:
  - *People* and *police*:
    - (g) The **people** of our state **are voting** for a new governor.
    - (h) The **police have asked** for more funds.
  - Nouns phrases derived from adjectives that describe people: *the young, the rich, the elite, the disenfranchised*, and so on:
    - (i) **The young want** to grow up fast, and **the old want** to be younger.
    - (j) Is it true that **the rich are** getting richer and **the poor are** getting poorer?

Exercise 4

Take turns giving oral responses to the following questions. Use the noun or nouns in bold print as the subject in your responses. The first one is done as an example.

1. What **transportation** do you prefer for getting to school?

   EXAMPLE: Well, the **transportation** I prefer **is** driving my own car, but since finding a parking space is difficult, I take the bus most of the time.

2. What is some good **advice** you've gotten during the past year from a friend, relative, or something you read?

3. What is some useful **information** you've learned in your English class?

4. What home office **equipment** do you think is the most helpful for your life as a student?

5. Do you think **violence** is ever justified? Explain.

6. In your community, do **people** regard the police as their friends or as adversaries?

7. Is your **knowledge** of sports good or poor?

8. Do you think **the homeless** are being neglected in our society?

Exercise 5

The following sentences describe activities of groups. Choose and circle an appropriate verb form for each.

EXAMPLE: The group ((has)/have) just left.

1. The audience for the political rally (was/were) huge.

2. The audience (seems/seem) to have mixed reactions to the President's speech; some people are cheering wildly, while others are booing.

3. My family (celebrates/celebrate) birthdays with a special dinner.

4. The city government (is/are) ordering a reduction in water usage.

5. I heard that the police (is/are) arriving any minute.

6. A swarm of bees (has/have) built a nest under the eaves of the roof. Look! The swarm (appears/appear) to be flying out in all directions from the roof.

7. The committee (has/have) expressed a number of different opinions on the topic of longer school hours.

8. The population of Phoenix (is/are) growing every year.

9. The population of that country (has/have) disagreed among themselves for years about immigration policies.

10. The disabled (is/are) are demanding more attention to their needs through legislation.

Focus 5

Subjects Requiring Singular Verbs

- Some singular nouns, noun phrases, or noun clauses may be potentially confusing for subject-verb agreement because they either look as though they are plural or may seem conceptually plural to you.
- The following take singular verbs:
  - Some common or proper nouns that end in -*s*:

    Courses (a) **Mathematics is** my favorite subject.

    Others: *physics, economics*

    Diseases (b) **Measles is** no fun to have!

    Others: *mumps, arthritis*

    Places (c) **Leeds is** where my aunt was born.

    News (d) **The news** from home **was** very encouraging.
  - Plural titles of books, plays, films, and so on:

    (e) *Tracks* **was written** by Louise Erdrich.

    (f) *Dances with Wolves* **has won** an Oscar for best film.
  - Plural unit words of distance, time, and money take singular verbs:

    Distance (g) **Six hundred miles is** too far to drive in one day.

    Time (h) **Two weeks goes** fast when you're on vacation.

    Money (i) **Fifty dollars is** a good price for that chair.
  - Arithmetical operations (addition, subtraction, multiplication, division):

    Addition (j) **Three plus seven equals** ten.

    Multiplication (k) **Four times five equals** 20.
  - Items that have two parts when you use the noun *pair*:

    (l) **My pair** of scissors **is** lost.

    (m) **A pair** of plaid shorts **was** on the washing machine.
  - Note, however, that you would use the plural if *pair* is absent:

    (n) **My scissors are** lost.

    (o) **Those plaid shorts were** on the washing machine.
  - Subjects that are clauses containing a subject and verb, even when the nouns referred to are plural:

    (p) **What we need is** more reference books.

    (q) **That languages have many differences is** obvious.
  - Gerund (verb + -*ing*) and infinitive (*to* + verb) clauses:

    (r) **Reading books and magazines is** one of my favorite ways to to spend free time.

    (s) **To pass all my exams is** my next goal.

Exercise 6

Imagine that you are competing on a quiz show. You are given several words, phrases, or numbers from which to choose answers to definitions. You must give your answers in complete sentences. Write statements providing the correct answers for each of the definitions. Begin each statement with the correct answer.

EXAMPLE: 366 is the number of days in a leap year.

1. the number of days in a leap year (364, 365, 366)
2. a disease that makes you look like a chipmunk (shingles, mumps, warts)
3. four (54 divided by 9, 100 divided by 20, 200 divided by 50)
4. a poem written by Chaucer ("the Canterbury Tales," "Great Expectations," "Guys and Dolls")
5. a common plumber's tool (a pair of scissors, a pair of pliers, a pair of flamingoes)
6. a city in Venezuela (Buenos Aires, Caracas, Athens)
7. what you most often find on the front page of a newspaper. (sports news, political news, entertainment news)
8. the study of moral principles (ethics, physics, stylistics)
9. the number of years in a score (ten, 20, 30)
10. a course which would discuss supply and demand (mathematics, economics, physics)

Exercise 7

What are your opinions and attitudes about each of the following topics? State at least two things that could complete each of the sentences below. Share some of your answers with the class.

EXAMPLE: What this country needs *is health insurance for everyone and better education.*

1. What this country needs ⎯⎯⎯⎯⎯⎯⎯⎯⎯⎯⎯⎯⎯⎯⎯ .

2. What I would like to have in five years ⎯⎯⎯⎯⎯⎯⎯⎯⎯⎯⎯ .

3. What's wrong with kids today ⎯⎯⎯⎯⎯⎯⎯⎯⎯⎯⎯⎯⎯ .

4. That working women should have pay equal to that of men ⎯⎯⎯⎯⎯ .

5. What really irritates me ⎯⎯⎯⎯⎯⎯⎯⎯⎯⎯⎯⎯⎯⎯ .

6. To become a well-read person ⎯⎯⎯⎯⎯⎯⎯⎯⎯⎯⎯⎯ .

(Possible verbs: *be, require, mean*)

7. What I find most frustrating about learning English ⎯⎯⎯⎯⎯⎯ .

8. Learning the rules of subject-verb agreement in English ⎯⎯⎯⎯⎯ .

46

Focus 6

Agreement with Fractions, Percentages, and Quantifiers

FORM

- With fractions, percentages, and quantifiers *all (of)* and *a lot of*, verb agreement depends on the noun or clause after them, which is usually in an *of* phrase. Agreement follows the general rules for these nouns or clauses:
  - With singular nouns, clausal subjects, or non-count nouns, we use a singular verb:

Singular Noun	(a) **One fourth of this book is** about British drama. (b) **Fifty percent of the book is** about poetry. (c) **All of the book seems** useful in one way or another. (d) **A lot of that book was** hard for me to read.
Clausal Subject	(e) **Half of what he says is** not true. (f) **About 50 percent of what I have to do at my job is** secretarial work. (g) **All of what you've said to me** sounds like good advice. (h) **A lot of what she has lost is** irreplaceable.
Non-Count Noun	(i) **Over half of the furniture is** new. (j) **Fifty percent of the water is** gone. (k) **All (of) our information is** up-to-date. (l) **A lot of our factory equipment was made in** Germany.

- With plural nouns, use a plural verb:

Plural Noun	(m) **One fourth of the students have** computers. (n) **Thirty-three percent of our computers have** hard disks. (o) **All (of) the computers need** to be checked. (p) **A lot of the students live** near the campus.

- With collective nouns, use either the singular or the plural:

Collective Nouns	(q) **One-sixth of our Spanish club has/have** relatives in Mexico. (r) **Five percent of the population is/are** Armenian. (s) **All of our class is/are** here. (t) **A lot of my family lives** in Pennsylvania. (u) **A lot of my family don't** get along with each other.

- With the quantifiers *each* and *every(one)*, the verb is singular both when the modified noun is singular and when it is definite (*the, this, her*, etc.) plural:

Singular Noun	(v) Each Every Each and every } book has been cataloged.
Definite Plural Noun	(w) **Each of her papers has gotten** an *A*. (x) **Every one of the students is** on time.

- The quantifier *a number of* takes a plural verb. *The number of* takes the singular:

Plural Noun	(y) **A number of students are taking** the TOEFL exam today.
Singular Noun	(z) **The number of students** taking the test **is** 175.

- According to traditional grammar rules, *none* always takes a singular verb in formal written English:

Singular Noun	(aa) **None of this book looks** helpful for my report.
Non-Count Noun	(bb) **None of the advice was** very helpful.
Plural Noun	(cc) **None of the magazines** I wanted **is** here.

SUMMARY: TRADITIONAL AGREEMENT RULES

	Singular Noun	Non-Count Noun	Plural Noun	Collective Noun
percentages	singular	singular	plural	singular/plural
fractions	singular	singular	plural	singular/plural
all (of)	singular	singular	plural	singular/plural
a lot of	singular	singular	plural	singular/plural
each, every	singular		singular	singular
a number of			plural	
the number of			singular	
none of	singular	singular	singular	singular

Exercise 8

Choose and circle the correct form of the verb for each sentence.

1. The 1990 Gallup reading poll reports that although 86 percent of Americans (has/have) bookshelves in their homes, 29 percent of them (reports/report) not reading a book during the past year.

2. According to the poll, 97 percent of the respondents (has/have) heard of Mark Twain, but only 12 percent of them (says/say) they have ever heard of the French writer Gustave Flaubert.

3. Although over three fourths of those surveyed (states/state) that they have heard of William Faulkner, only one third of this population (has/have) ever read a book by him.

4. Only 9 percent of Americans (belongs, belong) to a book club.

5. Over one third of the group (claims/claim) to know someone who is illiterate.

6. Our class recently did a study of where some of our resources come from. Eighty percent of our city's drinking water (comes/come) from a reservoir. Thirty-seven percent of the petroleum we consume (is/are) imported from other countries.

Exercise 9

Use the information below from the Gallup poll to write five sentences about responses of the people surveyed. For subjects, you could use any of the following: respondents, people surveyed, Americans, those who responded.

> **EXAMPLE:** *Almost three fourths of the respondents believe they spend too little time reading books for pleasure.*

Question: Thinking about how you spend your non-working time each day, do you think that you spend too much time or too little time . . .

	Too Much	Too Little	About Right	No Opinion
Watching television	49%	18%	31%	2%
Reading newspapers	8	54	35	3
Reading magazines	6	65	24	5
Reading books for pleasure, recreation	7	73	16	4
Reading books for work, school, etc.	9	62	19	10

(Adapted from *Gallup Poll Monthly,* February 1991)

Exercise 10

Write six sentences describing the members of your class (or some other group you are familiar with), using the words in parentheses as the subjects.

EXAMPLE: The number of *female students in my class is 12.*

1. (The number of) _____ .

2. (Each) _____ .

3. (None) _____ .

4. (All) _____ .

5. (A lot of) _____ .

6. (A number of) _____ .

Exercise 11

The chart below presents statistics from another Gallup Survey; this one asked pet owners information about their pets. The numbers represent percentages. Complete each of the sentences below by summarizing one of the findings of the survey.

Question: By any chance, has your pet ever done any of the following:

	Dog Owners	Cat Owners
Gone to a veterinarian	94%	86%
Gone to a pet groomer	43	7
Gone to an obedience training class or school	15	•
Been included in somebody's will	2	1
Gone to a pet counselor or psychiatrist	•	•
• Less than 1 percent		

From *Gallup Poll Monthly*, September 1990. Reprinted with permission from The Gallup Organization, Inc., Princeton, New Jersey.

EXAMPLE: *Almost all of the cats have been to a veterinarian.*

1. Almost all _____ .

2. Almost none _____ .

3. Almost every _____ .

4. A lot of _____ .

5. Not a lot of _____ .

Exercise 12

Fill in each blank of the following radio news report with a verb form that would be appropriate for formal English use.

Here is the latest report on the aftermath of the earthquake. As most of you know, the earthquake has caused a great deal of damage and disruption to our area. A lot of the houses near the epicenter of the quake _____ badly damaged. A number of trees _____ uprooted in that area also, so be careful if you are driving. All the electricity _____ shut off for the time being. Water _____ turned off also. None of the freeways in the vicinity _____ currently open to traffic. Almost every side street _____ jammed with drivers trying to get back home. The number of deaths so far _____ two. All people _____ urged to stay at home if at all possible.

Focus 7

Agreement with *Majority* and *Minority*

FORM

- The nouns *majority* and *minority* can also be troublesome when it comes to subject–verb agreement because they have several meanings.
  - If *majority* has an abstract meaning of "superiority of number," it takes a singular verb. If it has a specific percentage meaning (e.g., over 50%), either a singular or plural verb may be used:

Majority: Superiority of Number	Majority: Specific Percentage
(a) The large majority is discontent with the government.	**(b)** We needed a 75% majority to approve the proposition. However, **the majority has/have** voted against it.

- Likewise, when *minority* has an abstract meaning of "inferiority of number" it takes a singular verb. When *minority* expresses a numerical percentage (less than 50%), it may take either a singular or a plural verb:

Minority: Inferiority of Number	Minority: Specific Percentage
(c) Only **a small minority appears** to support the government's current policies.	**(d) A minority has/have failed** to pass the bill into law. Only 40 percent supported it.

- When *majority* or *minority* refer to most of an **explicit set** of persons, such as Americans, students, or Republicans, we use a plural verb:

Majority: Specific Set	Minority: Specific Set
(e) A majority of the students favor less homework.	**(f) A minority of the students believe** that more homework is needed.

Summary of Agreement Rules	
Meaning	**Verb**
Abstract: Numerical superiority	Singular
Numerical inferiority	Singular
Specific percentage	Singular or plural
Explicit set of persons	Plural

Exercise 13

Decide which meaning of *majority* or *minority* is expressed in each of the following contexts and then circle the appropriate verb.

1. A majority of the people in the 1990 Gallup reading survey (does/do) not know who the author of *A Tale of Two Cities* is. In fact, only a small minority of the respondents — 17% — (knows/know) who wrote this nineteenth century British novel.
2. Of books that the survey respondents last read, the majority (was/were) novels.
3. I'm convinced that the great majority (is/are) optimists at heart and that a minority (has/have) a pessimistic outlook on life.
4. It has been rumored that during the spring congressional session, the majority (plans/plan) to vote in favor of increasing the minimum wage.
5. (Does/do) the majority of students in your class happen to be reading a book or novel at the present time?
6. The majority of immigrants (have/has) contributed greatly to our society.

Exercise 14

Following are the results of question 6 in the Task for the Gallup 1990 survey. Write five sentences summarizing some of the information. Use *majority* or *minority* as subjects of your sentences and one of the following verbs in present tense: *say, state, claim, report, believe,* or *think.*

> **EXAMPLE:** *A very small minority of those surveyed think that neither watching TV nor reading a book is the most enjoyable way to spend an evening.*

Question: Which of these two activities — watching television or reading books — is:

	Watching TV	Reading a Book	Both	Neither	No Opinion
The most relaxing for you	45%	48%	3%	3%	•
The best way to learn for you	31	60	6	2	1
The most rewarding for you	33	61	3	2	1
The most enjoyable way to spend an evening for you	52	34	5	8	1

• Less than 1 percent

From *Gallup Poll Monthly*, February 1991. Reprinted with permission from The Gallup Organization, Inc., Princeton, New Jersey.

Focus 8

Exceptions to Traditional Agreement Rules

USE

- Some of the agreement rules presented in this unit are observed mainly in formal English contexts, especially in formal written English.
- The following are cases in which native speakers of English frequently do not follow the traditional rules, especially in spoken and less formal written English:
  - When *either* or *neither* is the head noun of a subject followed by a prepositional phrase, the traditional nonintervention principle favors a singular verb. In contexts other than formal English ones, many native speakers of English use a plural verb:

(a)	**Formal:**	Either of the outfits **is**	⎫ appropriate.
(b)	**Less Formal:**	Either of the outfits **are**	⎭
(c)	**Formal:**	Neither of the choices **is**	⎫ objectionable.
(d)	**Less Formal:**	Neither of the choices **are**	⎭

- Plural verbs with *either* or *neither* head nouns are also becoming more acceptable in written English, especially with *neither*; for example, plural verbs are sometimes used with *neither* in newspapers.
  - When subjects are joined by *either . . . or* or *neither . . . nor*, the proximity principle says the verb should agree with the closest subject. Native speakers of English often use plural verbs with two singular subjects joined by these conjunctions, especially with *neither . . . nor*:

(e)	**Formal:**	Either my parents or John **has**	⎫ the car.
(f)	**Less Formal:**	Either my parents or John **have**	⎭
(g)	**Formal:**	Neither King nor Steele **is a favorite author of mine.**	
(h)	**Less Formal:**	Neither King nor Steele **are favorite authors of mine.**	
(i)	**Formal:**	Neither you nor I **am**	⎫ prepared for the exam.
(j)	**Less Formal:**	Neither you nor I **are**	⎭

- When *none* + a prepositional phrase is the subject, the traditional rule says to use a singular subject. Many native speakers of English use plural verbs when *none* is followed by a plural noun phrase:

(k)	**Formal:**	None of the magazines **is**	⎫ in the kitchen.
(l)	**Less Formal:**	None of the magazines **are**	⎭

- When *there* is used to introduce topics, the traditional rule says that the verb should agree with the noun phrase that is the logical subject. In informal usage, speakers often use a singular verb with plural nouns, especially the contraction *there's*:

(m)	**Formal:**	**There are**	⎫ three books here that you might like.
(n)	**Less Formal:**	**There's**	⎭

- Most of these less formal forms are becoming more common in all but the most formal written English contexts. *There are* is usually used with plural noun phrases in written English, however.

Summary: Formal versus Less Formal Usage				
Either of the	+	(plural noun)		
Neither of the	+	(plural noun)	*Formal:*	*Less formal:*
Either (noun)	+	(singular noun)	singular	singular or plural
Neither (noun)	+	(singular noun)	verb	verb
None of the	+	(plural noun)		

Exercise 15

Decide which of the following statements have verb forms that would be appropriate for formal written contexts. (In these contexts, you want to use the traditional verb agreement rules.) Your teacher will call on you to state which ones would be acceptable for other written or spoken contexts.

1. Neither of those political surveys are valid because the sample was not random.
2. I am sure that either Professor Tori or Professor Kline have already addressed the issues you mention.
3. As far as we know, none of the experiment's results has been duplicated to date.
4. There's some results that will surprise you.
5. Neither Dr. Gonzalez nor Dr. Mitchell are presenting the findings of their studies until the results are checked again.
6. In conclusion, either of the textbooks I have reviewed is an excellent choice for an introductory chemistry course.
7. We have reviewed the report. None of the figures seem correct; they should be checked again.
8. Either of the reports submitted are useful for further study of this environmental problem.
9. Neither the campus medical center nor the library is safe should a strong earthquake occur.
10. Either you or I are responsible for this month's financial report; please let me know if I should submit it.
11. Neither of the claims Senator Holmes presented is justified.
12. There's a number of errors in this report.

Activities

Activity 1

Following are some examples of spoken and written English that were found in the newspaper. Discuss the traditional rules of subject–verb agreement that have not been observed in class. How do they illustrate some of the troublesome cases of subject–verb agreement? (Why do you think the speaker/writer used a singular or plural verb in each situation?)

"I have decided that everyone in these type of stories are rich." (Quoted statement by an actress in reference to a TV movie she appeared in.)

"Her expertise in the water as a lifeguard and her understanding of ocean currents, coupled with the fact that she is a strong swimmer, makes her a strong competitor." (Quoted comment about a champion swimmer)

"I know there is going to be a major hassle with certain smokers, plus there is going to be a lot of attempts to bypass the regulation." (From a letter to the editor about no smoking regulations)

"... the chances of him coming back in the next eight years was very unlikely." (Quoted comment about a politician who ran for President)

"In the Jewelry Center, All That Glitter Sure Is Gold" (Headline for a feature article)

Activity 2

Ask another class (or a group of teachers) to answer the reading habits survey. Tally the results and write a survey report comparing them to your class's results.

Activity 3

Survey a group of people about the Gallup Poll question in Exercise 9. Write a paragraph comparing the results of the Gallup Poll survey with your results.

Activity 4

The caption of the cartoon below from the *New Yorker* conforms to the traditional grammar rule of using a singular verb form with *either* + prepositional phrase.

"By the way, does either of you chaps happen to know anything about Bonsai?"

Drawing by Weber; © 1990 The New Yorker Magazine, Inc.

Usage surveys have suggested that native speakers of English often use plural verbs with *either* + prepositional phrases with plural count nouns. The surveys used a statement, however, not a question. What do you think native speakers would choose for a question form, the cartoon version or: "By the way, *do* either of you chaps happen to know anything about Bonsai?" Give ten or more native speakers some sample questions (e.g., "Do/does either of you boys have a match?" "Is/Are either of you going to come with us to the movies?" "Has/have either of your parents worked in a bank?") and ask them to choose which form they would use. Report your results.

Activity 5

Write an essay expressing your views about society's treatment of one of the following groups of people: the poor, the disabled, or the elderly.

Activity 6

Review the subject-verb agreement rules for this chapter. Decide which ones are the most troublesome for you and/or the cases that you encounter most frequently when you write in English. Make a list of these and use it for an editing checklist. Keep a chart of your subject-verb agreement errors to note your progress in correcting them.

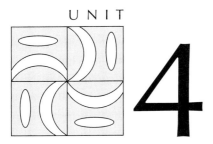

Perfective Modals

Task

MR. RETROSPECT'S HINDSIGHT AND ADVICE

Mr. Retrospect is an advice columnist for a daily newspaper. His specialty is telling people what they should have done after the fact. If you were writing Mr. Retrospect's column, how would you respond to each of the following letters? Write a brief reply for each.

Dear Mr. Retrospect:

A few weeks ago I asked a woman out to dinner. She seemed pleased with the invitation, but when my mother and I arrived at her house to pick her up, she looked shocked and said that she suddenly felt ill and couldn't go. She didn't look sick to me. What do you think must have made her change her mind? I must say, I'm a rather handsome guy, so I don't think it was my appearance.

Henry

Dear Mr. Retrospect:

On a recent trip, I visited a relative I don't know very well, one of my great aunts. She lives in a very rural area; the nearest large city is 300 miles away. I'm her only nephew, so she was really looking forward to my visit. Everything was fine until we sat down to eat. When I asked her what was in the stew she had just served, she announced, "Possum and squirrel." I was so shocked that I refused to eat anything and had to leave the table. I'm afraid that I hurt my great aunt's feelings even though later I said I was sorry. Now I am wondering what I could have said to be more polite.

Wild animal lover
(well, squirrels, anyway)

Dear Mr. Retrospect:

My hairdresser recently talked me into a new hairstyle that made me look like a porcupine. I hated it! Unfortunately, he thought it looked great. After he finished styling my hair, he proclaimed "It's you!" How do you think I should have responded?

Sally

Focus 1

Review of Perfective Modal Forms

- Like other modals in English, perfective modals have a number of meanings. The forms of perfective modals, however, are fairly simple.
  - Perfective modals in the **active voice** have the form modal + *have* + past participle:

	Modal +	***Have*** +	**Past Participle**	
(a) You	**should**	**have**	**seen**	that film.
(b) They	**must**	**have**	**come**	from miles away.

  - The **passive** form of perfective modals consists of modal + *have* + *been* + past participle:

	Modal +	***Have*** +	***Been*** +	**Past Participle**	
(c) That concerto	**should**	**have**	**been**	**played**	more slowly.
(d) His house	**must**	**have**	**been**	**built**	in the Victorian era.

  - You may use some perfective modals with a **present participle:**

	Modal +	***Have*** +	***Been*** +	***V-ing***	
(e) I	**must**	**have**	**been**	**dreaming!**	
(f) We	**could**	**have**	**been**	**playing**	tennis!

  - In **negative** forms, *not* follows the modal:

	Modal +	***Not*** +	***Have*** +	**Past Participle**	
(g) The game	**might**	**not**	**have**	**ended**	yet.
(h) You	**may**	**not**	**have**	**read**	that carefully enough.

Exercise 1

Underline the perfective modals in the following passage.

(1) My friends and I discussed the letters Mr. Retrospect received and the responses we would make to them. (2) Josef thought that Henry **must have been** born on another planet. (3) Inna agreed and added that his mother **couldn't have known** much about dating etiquette either. (4) Takiko thought Henry's date **might have called** him later and told him what the problem was. (5) For a response to his letter, we **would have informed** Henry that his date **may have been** a bit surprised to find out that Mom was chaperoning and that next time Mom should stay home. (6) As for the Wild animal lover's dining experience, we all agreed that we **couldn't have eaten** that dinner either, but we **wouldn't have wanted** to hurt the great aunt's feelings. (7) I suggested that he **might have said** he was allergic to squirrel or possum. (8) That **wouldn't have strayed** too far from the truth since he probably **would have gotten** sick from eating the dinner. (9) Finally, concerning the last letter, we disagreed about how Sally **should have responded** to her hairdresser. (10) Rosa thought Sally **could have asked** the hairdresser to restyle her hair. (11) Marty said she **might have told** him that her spiked hair could hurt someone. (12) We all concurred that Sally **should have found** out what her hairdresser planned to do before he styled her hair. (13) We also agreed that the hairdresser **must have been** thinking only of his own preferences and that Sally should look for a new stylist.

Focus 2

MEANING ● USE

Advisability/Expressing Judgments of Past Situations: *Should Have, Could Have, Might Have*

MEANING
USE

- As modals expressing advisability, *should have* (and its negative form *should not*), *could have*, and *might have* convey judgments about something that did not happen:
  - **(a)** You **should have gone to bed earlier.** (but you didn't)
  - **(b)** They **shouldn't have spent** so much money. (but they did)
  - **(c)** The teacher **could have warned** us that we would have to know all the math formulas for the test. (but she didn't)
  - **(d)** Rob **might have written** us that he was coming. (but he didn't)

- Modals of advisability can express criticism, regret, irritation, or anger. The speaker's attitude depends on the context and also on the person of the subject.

  - *Should have* and *should not have* with second or third person subjects often imply criticism. With a first person subject, they may express regret:

Criticism	Regret
(e) Brenda should have treated her sister better. She wasn't very nice to her.	**(f) I should have treated** my sister better. Now she won't even talk to me, and it's all my fault.
(g) You shouldn't have taken the day off from work. It created a burden for everyone else.	**(h) I shouldn't have taken** the day off from work. Now I'm even more behind.

  - *Should have, could have*, and *might have* can all express irritation, anger, or reproach about an event that did not occur:

    (i) You $\left.\begin{array}{l}\textbf{should}\\\textbf{could}\\\textbf{might}\end{array}\right\}$ **have called** us when you were in town. We didn't even know you were here.

  - *Could have* and *might have* often imply a stronger criticism than *should have*. They may suggest a lack of thoughtfulness or courtesy:

    (j) You **could have asked** me if I wanted some dessert.

    (k) She **might have waited** for us and **offered** us a ride so that we didn't have to walk two miles in the rain.

  - *Could have* more directly expresses capability than *should have* or *might have* does:

    (l) Ian **could have offered** to contribute to the cab fare. He certainly had the money to do so.

Exercise 2

Make a statement expressing a judgment about each of the following situations. Use *should have, could have,* or *might have* perfective modals in your response. Examples are given for the first one; make up one other for that one.

1. A friend failed a test yesterday.

   EXAMPLES: *She **could have spent** more time studying.*
   *She **might have asked** her teacher for help before the test.*

2. One of your classmates returns a paperback book to you with the cover torn. When you gave it to him, the cover was intact.

3. A manufacturing company is charged with pouring chemical waste into the river.

4. You were stopped by the police while driving your car. Your license plates had expired.

5. A neighbor locked herself out of her apartment and didn't know what to do.

6. A friend wanted to get a pet but her roommates didn't like cats or dogs.

61

Exercise 3

The following account chronicles the unfortunate experiences of the Hockney family—Ralph, Jane, and their son Andy—at a hotel where they recently spent a vacation. For each situation, state what you think the hotel staff or the Hockneys should have, could have, or might have done. For (1), two examples have been given; think of one other that might be appropriate for that situation.

1. When the Hockneys arrived at the hotel, the front desk clerk was talking on the phone to her boyfriend and ignored them.

   She could have at least acknowledged their presence.
   The Hockneys should have looked for another hotel!

2. When the clerk finally got off the phone, she told the Hockneys that, by mistake, their rooms had been given to someone else. However, several rooms would be available in four hours.

3. The Hockneys decided to have lunch in the hotel restaurant. Their waiter, who had a bad cold, kept coughing as he took their orders.

4. When the food arrived, Jane's soup was so salty she could feel her blood pressure rising by the second, Ralph's pork chop was about as edible as a leather glove, and Andy's spaghetti looked like last week's leftovers.

5. When the Hockneys were finally able to check into their rooms, the bellhop who brought up their bags forgot one of them in the lobby. Instead of getting it, he rushed off, explaining that he had to catch a train in ten minutes.

Exercise 4

Of the advisability modals, *should have* seems to have the greatest possible range of emotions: regret, desire, irritation, anger, even condemnation. Analyze the following statements in terms of the emotions you think each speaker is expressing and write down your conclusions.

1. Scotty, you knew you should have taken your shoes off when you came into the house, honey. Now I have to clean up all this mud.

2. You should have seen the lightning storm last night. It was really exciting!

3. Congressman Darren's behavior is reprehensible. He never should have accepted the illegal funds to finance his campaign.

4. Denise, I feel so bad that you moved all that stuff by yourself. You should have told me. I would have been glad to help you.

Focus 3

Advisability/Expressing Obligations and Expectations: *Be Supposed to Have, Be to Have*

MEANING
USE

- In addition to true modals, a few phrasal modals also express advisability in perfective forms:
- *Be supposed to have* refers to something planned or intended that did not occur when *be* is a past tense verb:

  (a) We **were supposed to have taken** our exam on Friday, but our teacher was sick.

- *Be supposed to have* expresses expected completion when *be* is a present tense verb:

  (b) We **are supposed to have made up** the exam by next week.

- *Be to have* expresses meanings similar to *be supposed to have*. It is more common in formal English:

Past Event That Did Not Occur	Future Expectation
(c) I **was to have graduated** in June, but I need to take two more courses for my degree.	**(d)** Governor Carroll **is to have handed in** his resignation by Friday.

Exercise 5

Complete the sentences to make statements about yourself and one of your classes.

1. I was supposed to have _____

   this year, but _____ .

2. In my _____ class, I am supposed to have _____

   _____ by (day or date) _____ .

3. I was to have _____ last

   (insert time phrase: weekend/month, etc.) _____ ,

   but _____ .

Exercise 6

Interview a classmate to find out three things that she or he was supposed to have done during the last month but didn't do. Report at least one of them to the class and explain why it didn't happen.

> **EXAMPLE:** *Fan was supposed to have gone to the mountains last weekend, but her car broke down before she even got out of town.*

Focus 4

MEANING ● USE

Inference/Making Deductions from Past Evidence:
Must Have, Can't Have, Should Have, Would Have

MEANING
USE

- Perfective modals express two kinds of inference: inferred certainty and inferred probability.
- *Must have* and *can't have* express **inferred certainty** that something happened or didn't happen.
  - *Must have* indicates that the speaker is quite sure something happened:
    (a) Our chemistry experiment failed. We **must have followed** the procedures incorrectly.
  - *Can't have* is the opposite of *must have*. It expresses negative certainty, the belief that something is impossible or unbelievable:
    (b) We **can't have performed** the procedures incorrectly! I read every step carefully both before and after we did the experiment to make sure.
- The two examples above represent strong inferences, not facts; both express their claims with certainty, but one must be wrong!
- *Should have* expresses **inferred probability**. It conveys an expectation about a past event.
  - The speaker may know that what was expected did not occur:
    (c) We **should have gotten** a chemical reaction when we heated the solution, but nothing happened. I wonder what went wrong.
  - In other cases, the speaker may not know whether or not the expectation has been fulfilled:
    (d) Let's check on our second experiment. The powder **should have dissolved** by now.
  - Unlike *must have*, *should have* does not express inferred certainty:
    (e) If the test tubes aren't here, Brian **must have taken** them.
    (f) NOT: If the test tubes aren't here, Brian **should have taken** them.

- *Would have* may also express inferred probability. We use it to speculate about what happened if we accept a certain theory or assume certain conditions.
    - The condition may be stated:
        (g) If our observations are correct, the burglary **would have occurred** shortly after midnight.
    - The condition may be implied:

Example	Implied Condition
(h) About one hundred seconds after the big bang, the temperature would have fallen to one thousand million degrees.	if the big bang model is accepted as part of the history of the universe

(From: Stephen Hawking, *A Brief History of Time: From the Big Bang to Black Holes*, Bantam, 1990.)

- We use the modal form *would have* instead of simple past tense (e.g., *fell*) in the example above because even though the big bang theory is generally accepted, it is still a hypothetical explanation.

Exercise 7

The following sentences represent some deductions about how native languages are learned. Fill in the blanks, using *must have, can't have,* or *should have* and the correct form of the verb in parentheses.

1. Since the number of possible sentences in any language is infinite, we _____ (learn) our native languages by simply storing all the sentences we heard in a "mental dictionary."

2. Children _____ (develop) their ability to speak their native languages by learning rules from adults because adults are not conscious of all syntactic, phonological, and semantic rules either.

3. A child _____ (acquired) his/her native language by the age of 5; if not, we suspect that something is physically or psychologically wrong.

4. When a native English-speaking child says words like *bringed, throwed,* and *doed*, this shows that she or he _____ (construct) a rule for the past tense.

5. Similarly, if a child says words like *tooths* and *childs*, we speculate that she or he _____ (overgeneralize) the rule for regular plurals.

Exercise 8

The following passage from Stephen Hawking's book *A Brief History of Time; From the Big Bang to Black Holes* describes what physicists believe probably happened after the big bang. Identify the perfective modals that express probability. Why does Hawking use these forms instead of simple past tense?

(1) Within only a few hours of the big bang, the production of helium and other elements would have stopped. (2) And after that, for the next million years or so, the universe would have just continued expanding, without anything much happening. (3) Eventually, once the temperature had dropped to a few thousand degrees, and electrons and nuclei no longer had enough energy to overcome the electromagnetic attraction between them, they would have started combining to form atoms. (4) The universe as a whole would have continued expanding and cooling, but in regions that were slightly denser than average, the expansion would have been slowed down by the extra gravitational attraction. (5) This would eventually stop expansion in some reasons and cause them to start to recollapse.

(From: Stephen Hawking, *A Brief History of Time; From the Big Bang to Black Holes*, Bantam, 1990.)

Exercise 9

To review modal uses so far, return to the letters at the beginning of this chapter. Which of the letters in the task has a modal expressing advisability? Which has an inference modal? Identify the perfective modals the letter writers used. Did you use these same modals in your answers? If you did, share some of your answers with the class. If not, write a one-sentence answer to each now, using these modals in perfective forms.

Focus 5

MEANING ● USE

Possibility/Expressing Guesses About Past Situations: *May Have, Might Have, Could Have, Can Have*

MEANING
USE

- Use possibility perfective modals to make statements about the past when you are not sure what in fact happened.
- *May have* and *might have* indicate that the speaker doesn't know if an event has occurred but has reason to believe that it has:
  (a) The movie **may have** already **started**. There are only a few people in the lobby.
  (b) I **might have gotten** an *A* on the test. I think I knew most of the answers.

- *Might have* sometimes expresses a weaker probability than *may have*. The speaker implies that the situation described is possible but not necessarily likely:

More Probable	Less Probable
(c) I **may have met** him a long time ago. Both his name and face are very familiar.	**(d)** I **might have met** him a long time ago, but I doubt it. He doesn't look at all familiar.

- *Could have* often expresses weaker possibility than *may have*. It can imply that other explanations may account for a situation or condition:

  (e) This car seems to be out of alignment. It **could have been** in an accident.

- We also use *might have, could have,* and *can have* in questions.
  - *Might have* and *could have* in questions express guesses about a past event:

    (f) Might Carol **have been** the one who told you that?

    (g) Could too much water **have killed** the plants?

  - We use *can have* only in questions and usually with **be**:

    (h) Can that **have been** Tom on the phone? I didn't expect him to call back so soon.

- We can paraphrase the first sentence in example (h): Is it possible that Tom was on the phone?

Exercise 10

Each numbered group of statements below expresses deductive certainty about the cause of a situation. For each, write an alternate explanation, using a perfective modal that expresses possibility. An example is given for the first one. Can you think of any others?

1. Look! The trunk of my car is open! Someone must have broken into it!

   Alternate explanation: *You may have forgotten to shut it hard and it just popped open.*

2. Carlos usually gets off of work at 5:00 and is home by 6:00. It's now 8:00 and he's still not home. He can't have left work at 5:00.

3. Our English teacher didn't give us back our papers today. She must have been watching TV last night instead of reading them.

4. We invited Nora and Jack to our party, but they didn't come. They must have found something better to do.

5. Christopher Columbus went looking for India and ended up in North America. He must have had a poor sense of direction.

MEANING ● USE

Conditioned Result/Expressing Results of Contrary to Fact Conditions: *Would Have, Could Have, Might Have*

MEANING
USE

- **Perfective modals** *would have, could have,* and *might have* are hypothetical results of conditions that are contrary to what actually happened:

Contrary to Fact Condition	**Hypothetical Result**
(a) If Jung had arrived before noon,	he **would have seen** us.

Actual Condition	**Actual Result**
(b) Jung arrived after noon,	so he missed seeing us.

- *Would have, could have,* and *might have* differ in the degree of probability expressed about a hypothetical result:

Modal	Speaker's Belief if Condition Were Real	Example
would have	certain result	**(c)** If I had been at that intersection ten minutes earlier, I **would have seen** the accident.
could have	possible result; capable of happening	**(d)** If the car had stopped for the light, the accident **could have been avoided.**
might have	possible result; a chance of happening	**(e)** If June had been wearing her seat belt, she **might have escaped** injury.

- We also use *would have, could have,* and *might have* in statements that imply a condition contrary to fact; that is, the conditions aren't actually stated. These statements may express a missed opportunity or a rejection of one option for another:

Example	Implied Contrary to Fact Condition	Implied Fact
(f) Tim would have been a great father.	if he had been a father	Tim is not a father
(g) I could have gone to medical school	if I had wanted to go to medical school	I did not go to medical school.
(h) Hannah might have made the debate team	if she had tried out for the debate team . . .	Hannah is not on the debate team.

Exercise 11

For each sentence, give two possible result modals that would fit the blanks, using the verb in parentheses as the main verb. For each, write an explanation of the difference in meaning and/or use between the two modals you choose.

> **EXAMPLE:** If the weather had been nicer, they _____ (stay) longer at the beach.
>
> (1) would have stayed
>
> (They definitely wouldn't have left so early; they had intended to be there longer.)
>
> (2) could have stayed
>
> (It would have been possible to stay longer; this form might be used if cold or rainy weather forced them to leave.)

1. If Sam had been better prepared for the interview, he _____ (get) the job.

2. They _____ (watch) the sunrise with us if they had gotten up earlier.

3. If you had let me know you needed transportation, I _____ (drive) you to your appointment.

4. If we had been more careful about our environment, we _____ (prevent) destruction of the ozone layer.

5. The chairperson _____ (call off) the meeting if she had known so many committee members would not be here today.

Exercise 12

Make up a hypothetical result that could be true for you to follow each condition. Use perfective modals *would have, could have,* or *might have:*

EXAMPLE: If I had lived in the nineteenth century,

I would have owned a horse instead of a car.

I could have known what it was like to live without electric lights.

I might have wanted to be a farmer instead of going into business.

1. If I had lived in the nineteenth century,
2. If I could have picked any city to grow up in,
3. If I had been the ruler of my country during the last decade,
4. If I could have been present at one historical event before I was born,
5. If I could have been the inventor of any invention in use today,
6. If I had been born in another country,
7. If I had had different parents,
8. If I had been able to solve one world problem of this past century,

Exercise 13

What might be an implied condition for each of the following hypothetical statements? Write down a few of your answers for each sentence.

EXAMPLE: I could have won the race.

Possible implied conditions:

If I had just run a little faster at the beginning . . .

If I had trained harder . . .

1. I could have been a fluent Spanish speaker.
2. Xavier might have been the class valedictorian.
3. Susan Sarandon would have been perfect for that movie role.
4. You could have come with us to the planetarium.
5. Kenneth Chen would have been the best candidate for that office.
6. My speech might have been more successful.

Focus 7

Summary of Perfective Modals Used in Contrary-to-Fact Statements

FORM
MEANING
USE

Meaning	Modal	Example	Implied Fact
Judgment of past situation	*should have* *could have* *might have*	**(a)** He should have written. **(b)** You could have told me. **(c)** They might have called first.	He didn't write. You didn't tell me. They didn't call.
Expectation, obligation	*be supposed to have* *be to have*	**(d)** We were supposed to have left before Tuesday. **(e)** I was to have heard from her by now.	We were still there on Tuesday. I haven't heard from her yet.
Result of Stated Contrary-to-Fact Condition	*would have* *could have* *might have*	**(f)** He would have written if he had known you wanted him to. **(g)** I could have told you what happened if you had asked me. **(h)** They might have called if they had had time.	He didn't write. I didn't tell you. They didn't call.
Result of Implied Contrary-to-Fact Condition	*would have* *could have* *might have*	**(i)** Pam would have been a good counselor. (Implied: If she had been a counselor) **(j)** You could have stayed with us. (Implied: If you had wanted to) **(k)** Kit might have been elected class president. (Implied: If he had run for office)	She is not a counselor. You didn't stay with us. He was not elected president.

Exercise 14

Some of the perfective modals in the sentences that follow express contrary-to-fact meanings and some do not. Identify the modals that are contrary to fact. Then write down what meaning each contrary-to-fact modal has: (a) judgment of past event (b) expectation or obligation (c) result of a stated condition or (d) result of an implied condition.

1. The essay you wrote is rather brief. You could have developed your ideas more.
2. Would you see if the mail is here? It should have come by now.
3. The mail isn't here yet. The mail carrier might have been delayed by that big accident on Seventh Avenue.
4. Anita should have gone to law school. She would have been a good lawyer.
5. Seth could have turned in your assignment for you yesterday if you had let him know you wouldn't be able to attend class.
6. The conference was supposed to have started on Friday, but it was postponed until next month.
7. Elaine might have asked me before she took my dictionary. I needed it to write my paper.
8. I could have told you that the swimming pool would be closed today. You should have asked me before you drove over there.
9. You have so much patience with small children! You might have been a good elementary school teacher.
10. Scientists believe that life on Earth could have begun more than 3.4 billion years ago.
11. If some forms of algae and bacteria are 3.4 billion years old, then their ancestors would have been even more ancient.
12. If that lecture had gone on any longer, I would have fallen asleep.
13. We could have gone out of town for our vacation, but we decided to stay home and remodel the kitchen instead.
14. If that graphics course had been offered last term, I might have taken it.
15. The post office could have handled my package more carefully. Two of the cups inside were broken.

Focus 8

Prediction/Expressing Fulfillment of a Future Event: *Will Have, Shall Have*

MEANING
USE

- *Will have* expresses the completion of future events before another future time:
  (a) By the time you get this postcard, I **will have left** Portugal.
  (You will get this postcard in a week or so; I am leaving Portugal tomorrow.)
- *Will* is often contracted in spoken English:
  (b) At the end of this week, **I'll have been** in Athens for four months.
- *Shall have* has the same meaning as *will have*. We rarely use it in everyday American English. It is used in some types of formal English such as legal documents or decrees:
  (c) By this date next year, Boyton Chemical Co. **shall have reduced** its air pollutants by 30 percent.

Exercise 15

Use the information in the first and second columns to express what will most likely have happened by the time period in the third column. You may want to add an if or unless clause to your sentence if you think it is needed.

EXAMPLE: 1. *By July, the Changs' store* **will** have **been opened** *for seven months.*
2. *By 1994, Larry* **will have graduated** *from college.*

Time Period 1	Event of Time Period 1	Time Period 2
December	The Changs will open their computer software store	July
1993	Larry will complete all the requirements for his college degree	1994
May, 1990	Patty Schwartz and Roger Peterson got married	May, 2040
July	Brian will visit Alaska, the only state that he's never been to before	August
September 1	Winnie has vowed to learn ten new words every day	October 1
1964	laser first used for eye surgery	2014

Activities

Activity 1

Write five brief scenarios that describe thoughtless, rude, or somehow inappropriate behavior. Exchange scenarios with a classmate and write at least one judgment about each of the situations your classmate has written, using advisability modals *could have, might have,* or *should have.* Use a variety of modals in responding. Afterward, if time permits, share a few of your situations and responses with the class.

> **EXAMPLE:** You were riding a subway train to school, standing up because it was very crowded, and suddenly the train stopped. A woman next to you spilled her diet Dr. Pepper™ all over your new trench coat.
> *Judgments: She shouldn't have been drinking a soda on the train.*
> *She could at least have offered to pay for dry cleaning the coat.*

Activity 2

Be an amateur detective! The next time you are in a supermarket, observe the items that the person checking out in front of you has in his or her cart or basket. (This is one time when you might want to get behind someone who has a lot of groceries!) Try to note as many items as you can, but don't let the person know that you are doing it. Afterward, briefly describe the person and then write deductions and guesses about him or her based on the items, using perfective modals expressing inference and possibility. Here are a few examples:

> *He must have owned a cat because he was buying ten cans of Kitty Gourmet Meals.*
> *He had a case of beer and lots of chips and dip in his cart; he might have been getting ready for a Super Bowl party.*

Activity 3

If your situation is not conducive to supermarket snooping, this is a variation of Activity 2 that you can do in the classroom or as a homework assignment. Make up a grocery (or some other store) shopping list of ten or so interesting items; exchange your list with a classmate along with a few descriptive phrases about the person (e.g., young, female, athletic-looking) who supposedly bought them. Write deductions and guesses about the person, using perfective modals.

Activity 4

Find an article in a book, newspaper, or magazine that describes an unsolved or unexplained situation: a crime, an unusual occurrence, strange weather patterns, etc. Have a class discussion in which students take turns summarizing the unexplained events to the rest of the class and others offer probable or possible explanations, using inference and possibility perfective modals: *must have, can't have, may have, might have, could have.*

Activity 5

Write five sentences stating things that you would (could, might) have done or not done, or situations that would (could, might) have happened in the past if circumstances had been different. Choose one of your sentences to explain further in a paragraph.

> **EXAMPLE:** *If my family had not moved to the United States, I might not have learned English.*
> *If my parents had not helped me so much, I couldn't have gone to college.*

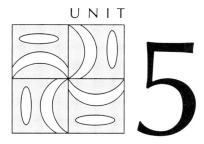

Stative Passives

Task

Does the diagram below look familiar? It illustrates the components of a mechanism that many of you have probably operated: the drivetrain of an automobile with manual transmission. Most people, however, don't know much about this machine they so frequently find themselves in, either as drivers or passengers. After reading the description below, identify the numbered parts of the drivetrain that have not yet been labeled, using terms in bold type.

A manual transmission is composed of a **gearshift**, a **clutch**, and the **transmission** itself. These are all parts of the drivetrain, which conducts the flow of power from the engine to the wheels. The front end of the drivetrain is known as the **crankshaft**; it is found inside the engine. The disc-shaped plate at the right end of the crankshaft, next to the **clutch disc**, is called the **flywheel**. These two components, the crankshaft and the flywheel, are powered by the engine. Located next to the clutch disc is the clutch **pressure plate**. It forces the clutch disc against the flywheel or releases it to change gears. Leading into the **transmission**, which is connected to the gearshift, is the **input shaft**. The input shaft is actually a continuation of the crankshaft and is linked to the **gears** inside the transmission. Emerging from the other side of the transmission is the **output shaft**; this part of the drivetrain is connected to the **driveshaft**. At either end of the driveshaft are found **u–joints**, which move in all directions and absorb movement. At the end of the rear u-joint is the **differential**, another set of gears, which is attached to the rear axle. Each side of the axle is rotated by the power transmitted from the differential.

(Adapted from *Auto Repair for Dummies,* by Deanna Sclar. Copyright ©1988 by Deanna Sclar. Reprinted by permission of Ten Speed Press, Berkeley, CA.)

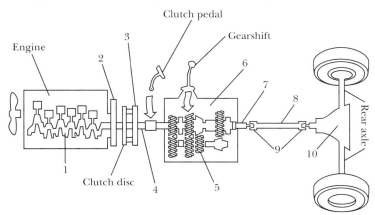

Focus 1

Review of Passive Verb Forms

FORM

You may have noticed that many of the verb forms in the description of the drivetrain were in the passive voice: **is composed, is found, is connected,** etc. But how many of them describe actions? Most of the passive verbs in the passage do not report activities; they describe the locations or connections of the various parts. Passive verbs that express action are called **dynamic passives**; passive verbs used for description are called **stative passives**.

- Use *be* + **past participle** to form passive verbs in English:

	Be	Past Participle	
(a) Disc brakes	**were**	**invented**	in 1902.
(b) Many advances	**have**	**been made**	in automotive technology.

- Modal verbs *(can, may, might,* etc.) may precede the *be* verb. The *be* verb will then be in the base form:

    (c) Antique cars **may** be seen at the Museum of Science and Technology.

- Stative passive verbs have the same forms as dynamic passives:

	Be	Past Participle	
(d) The input shaft	**is**	**connected**	to the gearshift.
(e) The American pioneers	**were**	**known**	for their courage.
(f) The classroom	**has been**	**designed**	for student interaction.
(g) Our house	**had been**	**located**	near a farm before we moved it into the town.
(h) Chaplin	**may be**	**regarded**	as one of our greatest film comedians.

- Sentences with dynamic passives may express the performer of the action **(the agent)** in a *by* phrase:

    (i) The electric motor car was invented **by William Morrison**.

- In contrast, sentences with stative passives do not have agents in *by* phrases, since they do not express action. If a stative passive occurs with a *by* phrase, *by* has another meaning, such as "near":

    (j) A variety of wildflowers **can be found** by the lakeshore.

Exercise 1

List all of the passive verbs in the Task paragraph describing the manual transmission drivetrain. Save your list for Exercise 2.

EXAMPLE: *is composed of*

Focus 2

Stative Passive in Contrast to Dynamic Passives

USE

- **Dynamic passives** express actions:

(a) The missing library book **was found** in the parking lot.	*Found, connected, called* all describe activities.
(b) Our telephone **was connected** yesterday.	
(c) Stella **was called** for a job interview on Tuesday.	

- **Stative passives** express states or conditions:

(d) The crankshaft **is found** inside the engine	*Found* describes location.
(e) The transmission **is connected** to the gearshift.	*Connected* describes a static condition.
(f) The box of gears above the rear axle **is called** the differential.	*Called* expresses a defining relationship.

Exercise 2

Which of the passive verbs from the Task paragraph, which you listed in Exercise 1, are stative passives? Which are dynamic passives?

EXAMPLE: *is composed of—stative*

Exercise 3

Answer the following questions with reference to the chart in Focus 2, which contrasts stative and dynamic passives.

1. None of the sentences in the chart has an expressed agent, that is, a performer of an action. Try to add a *by* phrase that expresses an agent to each sentence. Which sentences cannot take an agent without a change in meaning? Does this support the rule about agents stated in Focus 1?

   EXAMPLE: The missing library book was found in the parking lot *by a janitor.*
   (This sentence can take an agent.)

2. All of the stative passives in the chart are in the present tense. Change each stative passive to the past tense. What meaning differences result from these changes? Can you form a generalization about the verb tense for stative passives from these results? Are some meanings, such as static condition, more likely to be expressed in present tense?

   EXAMPLE: The crankshaft *was found* inside the engine.
   (This no longer sounds like a description but suggests that someone found the automotive part in the engine.)

Focus 3

FORM ● MEANING

Adjective Participles in Contrast to Stative Passives

FORM
MEANING

- Past participles used as adjectives after the verb **be** have the same form as stative passives:
  (a) I am **delighted** with the news.
- Adjective participles differ from stative passives in their meanings. Adjective participles express
  - temporary emotional states, attitudes, and feelings:
    (b) The doctors are **satisfied** with the results.
    (c) We had been **annoyed** by the long delay to board the plane, but once we boarded our mood brightened.
  - temporary physical states:
    (d) By the end of the race, Yumi was **tired**.
- Unlike most stative passives, we can often modify adjective participles by using the intensifier *very*:
  (e) Eric is very **interested** in earthquake prediction.

Exercise 4

With reference to the example sentences in Focus 3:

1. Identify the verb *tenses* used with adjective participles in the example sentences. How does verb tense used with these participles compare with verb tenses generally used in stative passives? Can you explain the meaning differences that seem to account for this?

   EXAMPLE: *am delighted*

   am = present tense

2. As noted in Focus 3, one way to identify some (although not all) adjective participles is to see if they can be modified by *very*. Try this modifier test on the first four example sentences in Focus 3. Then try the same test on the dynamic and stative passive sentences in Focus 2. Compare your results.

   EXAMPLE: I am *very* delighted with the news.

Exercise 5

Identify each *be* + participle form in the following TV sports broadcast as either a stative passive or an adjective participle.

   EXAMPLE: is known—stative

> (1) Well, folks, it's another beautiful day for a baseball game here at Wrigley Field, which is known as the place everybody wants to be on a sunny Sunday afternoon in Chicago. (2) Well, almost everybody . . . I guess it's true that a few people might be found under beach umbrellas on the shores of Lake Michigan today. (3) But anyway, for those of you who are connected to your TV remote controls, don't change the channel because it's going to be a great game today! (4) The players say they are relieved to be at home again after five days on the road, and our fans in the stands are excited as always. (5) Check out the group that's positioned above home plate with the sign "Another World Series for the Cubs or What?" (6) We can only hope that they won't be disappointed.

Focus 4

Common Rhetorical Functions of Stative Passives

● Stative passive verbs have a number of **descriptive uses** in discourse. Note that many of the stative passives in the examples below are followed by prepositions: *in, with, by, for,* etc.

● **Describe location or position:**

(a) The Amazon River **is located** in Brazil.	*Located* is often used in geographical descriptions.
(b) The ratel, a fearless animal, **is found** in Africa and India.	*Found* typically describes plant and animal habitats.
(c) The Secret Service agents **were positioned** to protect the President if necessary.	*Positioned* often suggests placement. Other verbs: *placed, bordered (by), surrounded (by)*

● **Describe characteristics or qualities:**

(d) The sea horse's body **is covered** with small bony plates.	This type of description is common in science.
(e) *The Daily Scandal* **is filled** with untrue stories.	

● **Describe manner or method:**

(f) Temperature **is measured** in degrees.	This use is common in science and mathematics.

● **Describe part-whole relationships:**

(g) Tokyo **is divided** into prefectures.	Other verbs: *composed (of), organized (into)*
(h) Geology **is made up of** many subfields such as seismology and petrology.	

● **Describe purpose:**

(i) The Geiger counter **is used** for detecting radiation.	Other verbs: *designed, intended*
(j) Greetings such as "How are you?" **are used** to promote communication, not to get information.	These verbs may be followed by *for* + gerund (verb + *-ing*) or an infinitive *(to* + verb).

- **Describe connection:**

(k) Do you know the old song that begins: "The knee bone**'s connected** to the thigh bone?"	Other verbs: *attached (to), joined (to), separated (from), accompanied (by)*

- **Describe reputation or association:**

(l) El Greco **is** best **known for** his religious paintings.	Other verbs: *considered, regarded (as), remembered (for), thought to be*

- **Define or name:**

(m) The ratel **is** also **known as** the "honey badger."	Other verbs: *labeled, named, termed*
(n) Pants having legs that flare out at the bottom **are called** bellbottoms.	

Exercise 6

State the rhetorical function of stative passives in each of the following sentences, using categories from the chart above.

1. As an infant, man is wrapped in his mother's womb; grown up, he is wrapped in custom; dead, he is wrapped in earth. (Malay Proverb)
2. Hallucinations are often associated with abnormal mental conditions.
3. In the midwestern United States, soft drinks such as cola or root beer are referred to as "pop".
4. Natural geysers, which are found in Japan, New Zealand, and the United States, are sometimes classified as renewable energy.
5. The Special Olympics is meant to give disabled children a chance to compete in athletic contests.

Exercise 7

Each of the words or phrases in Column A below is rhetorically related in some way to one of the phrases in Column B. Match up the pairs and then write a sentence for each, choosing an appropriate stative passive to connect the word groups. Add other words or change word forms as necessary. For some groups, you may reverse the order of information, as shown in the Examples.

EXAMPLES: l,d. Language *may be defined* as the spoken or written means by which people express themselves and communicate with others.

The spoken or written means by which people express themselves and communicate with others *is called* language.

1. language
2. alcohol thermometers
3. hand
4. monuments to unknown soldiers
5. human brain
6. Sigrid Undset

a. Belgium, Britain, France, Italy, Portugal, and the United States
b. three parts: the hindbrain, the midbrain, and the forebrain
c. the author of *Kristin Lavransdatter*, a novel about medieval Norway, for which she won the Nobel Prize.
d. the spoken or written means by which people express themselves and communicate with others
e. structural specialization at the end of the arm, enabling grip and the fine motor tasks that characterize higher primates
f. measure very low temperatures

Focus 5

FORM

Stative Passives in Relative Clauses

FORM

- We also use stative passives in relative clauses:
  - as the verb in a clause beginning with *who, which,* or *that*:
    (a) Our English teacher, who **is regarded** as a brilliant instructor, won a national teaching award.
    (b) The tomato plants that **were covered** with burlap survived the autumn frost.
  - in a reduced relative clause (one in which *who, which,* or *that* is deleted). These stative passives have the form **past participle (without *be*)**:
    (c) The old man **known** as Joe would feed the pigeons in the park every day.
    (d) My school, **located** in the center of the city, is easy to get to by bus or subway.

Exercise 8

Each of the following sentences has one verb form error. Correct the errors.

1. The population of the inner city, now surround by suburbs, has decreased during the last decade.
2. Wilma Rudolph is regard as a great athlete.
3. Where is date palm trees found in the United States?
4. Uruguay, which is border by Argentina and Brazil, is one of the smallest countries in South America.
5. The long, narrow building join to the Engineering school is where the Department of Physics can be found.
6. That kind of animal called a herbivore because it eats only plant material.

Exercise 9

Edit the following paragraph to correct verb form errors.

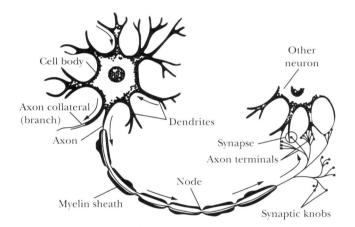

(1)Neurons, or nerve cells, often referred to as the building blocks of the nervous system. (2)They are not shape like blocks, though, but more like snowflakes. The human brain estimated to contain about one hundred billion neurons. (3)The neuron composes of three main parts: a cell body, dendrites, and an axon. (4)The cell body is shape like a sphere. (5)The dendrites, which look like branches of a tree, receive messages from other nerve cells. (6)The axon may regard as the tree's trunk; it sends messages away from the cell. (7)the larger axons found outside the brain.

Activities

Activity 1

Make up five word group sets like the ones in Exercise 7. Give your sets to another student to create sentences using stative passives. Check the responses and discuss whether you have agreed on the relationships between the word groups.

Activity 2

Find a text that has a number of passive verbs. (Science texts, instruction manuals, and texts that define or classify are good sources). Analyze the passives that you find. Are they mostly dynamic or stative passives? What rhetorical functions do the stative passives serve? Are there any that don't seem to fit the categories in this chapter?

Activity 3

Create your own trivial pursuit! Make up five sentences like the ones following, describing people, places, or things using stative passives, but don't reveal who/what they are; use pronouns or general terms for the subjects. (Pronouns create more of a challenge.) See if others can guess what you are describing.

Here are some examples. (Can you guess the answers?)

1. It is divided into nine innings.
2. It can be found in tacos, spaghetti sauce, and ceviche.
3. This dramatist and poet is known as the Bard of Avon.
4. They are also called twisters.
5. This country is bordered by Italy, Austria, Germany, and France.

Activity 4

Think of a famous person, either current or from the past: a politician, actor, novelist, athlete, etc. Write a brief description, giving information about what the person is known for. Have your classmates try to guess who it is.

> **EXAMPLE:** She is considered one of the great actresses in American film. She is known throughout the world for her role as Scarlett O'Hara in *Gone with the Wind*.
> (Vivien Leigh)

Activity 5

Draw a diagram or map of one of the following:

1. an area (your room, apartment or house, a neighborhood or commercial district, for example)
2. a machine or device
3. an invention of your own creation (a machine that writes your papers for you? a device that gets you out of bed in the morning?)

In your diagram/map, label at least four or five objects, parts, buildings, or whatever would be found there. Then write a paragraph describing the locations of objects or the ways in which you have divided your diagram/map into parts. Use stative passives in your descriptions.

Activity 6

Find out something new about geography. Most people have "geography gaps"; that is, they're not as knowledgeable as they might like to be about certain areas in the world. (Do *you* know what countries Iraq is surrounded by? Do you know where Lake Maracaibo is located?) Find an atlas at home or in a library and do some research on one or two geographical areas you don't know much about: a country, part of a country, or perhaps even a continent. Write a description of what you found out, using stative passives where appropriate.

6

Article Usage
Generic

Task

(1)The medical field has changed rapidly in the last century. (2)In the past, the family practitioner responded to all medical needs (e.g., childbirths, surgeries, diseases, etc.) and relied on natural remedies to alleviate pain but not necessarily to cure it. (3)The doctor's role was more of an onlooker as "nature took its course." (4)Today, doctors play a more active role in healing. (5)With their more specialized training, they are able to prescribe wonder drugs and perform sophisticated surgeries on patients who, in the past, would not have survived without this "technology."

(6)On the one hand, prolonging life has always been the ideal. (7)Yet, sometimes lifesaving/enhancing procedures come in conflict with certain well-established social, religious, and moral values. (8)Thus, there is a need for medical ethics. (9)This is a field that considers the ethical implications of medical procedures and argues the reasonable rights and limits that doctors should have in making decisions about improving, prolonging, or saving lives.

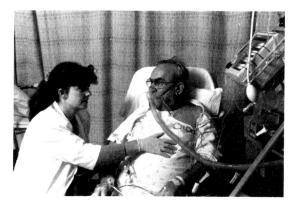

The following list summarizes several current or potential practices in the medical profession that are controversial. Discuss the pros and cons of several of these practices in class and come to your own conclusions about what is or is not ethical.

1. Researchers using animals (e.g., mice, cats, cows, etc.) to test toxicity of drugs or the effect of artificial organ implants.
2. Drug companies bribing doctors with vacations and other perquisites ("perks") to prescribe newly manufactured, less well-known drugs to their patients.
3. Machines sustaining lives of severely injured people who are in a vegetative state.

4. Childless couples using surrogate mothers to bear children, who may be genetically related to only one parent.

5. Engineering genetic changes in embryos to prevent birth defects or diseases.

6. Forcing birth control (e.g., abortions, contraceptives, etc.) on a population which for religious or cultural reasons does not desire it.

7. Parents conceiving a child in order to obtain a matching organ or tissue to save the life of another one of their children.

8. Poor people selling their own organs in order to make a living.

9. Requiring doctors to reveal the results if they have a positive AIDS test and to quit their active medical practices.

Focus 1

MEANING

Specific versus Generic

MEANING

- Generic reference relates to the general rather than the specific nature of something. Specific reference indicates one member of a class; generic reference indicates all or representative members of a class. Note in the following examples the specific and generalized meanings of *laser* in different contexts.

(a) Her doctor used a **laser** to treat her varicose veins.	specific reference
(b) The **laser** cured Paul's cataract problem.	specific reference
(c) The **laser** has been used in medicine since the 1960s.	generalization
(d) A **laser** can cut through soft tissue with a searing light.	generalization
(e) **Lasers** reduce the recovery period needed for ordinary operations.	generalization

Exercise 1

For each of the following pairs of sentences, check the option that makes a general versus a specific reference about the italicized noun phrase. Note that different references are only sometimes marked by different articles.

EXAMPLE: **a.** *An immunity* is a resistance to infection. ✔

b. I have *an immunity* to small pox.

1. **a.** There is *some medicine* in the cupboard.

   b. *Medicine* prevents, alleviates, and cures physical and mental illnesses.

2. **a.** *A cholera epidemic* is started by contaminated food or water.

   b. *A cholera epidemic* killed many people this year.

3. **a.** *A doctor* claimed to have discovered a miracle burn ointment.

   b. *A doctor* is trained to treat burns.

87

4. **a.** *Siamese twins* are born with parts of their bodies attached.

   b. *Siamese twins* were born to a couple in Germany.

5. **a.** There is no cure for *a cold*.

   b. I have had *a cold* for four weeks.

6. **a.** *The mouse* used in the experiment was injected with morphine.

   b. *The mouse* is an excellent research animal.

7. **a.** The patient will sit in *the wheelchair* until her daughter arrives.

   b. *The wheelchair* has improved the lives of the handicapped.

8. **a.** Angela has been playing *the saxophone* for three years.

   b. Angela has been playing *the saxophone* that was in the corner.

9. **a.** *People* have been waiting in the waiting room since 11:00 A.M.

   b. *People* kept alive only by machines should be allowed to die.

10. **a.** *Water* from springs contains minerals.

    b. *The water* from the spring cured my illness.

Focus 2

FORM ● MEANING

Abstract Generic versus Concrete Generic

FORM
MEANING

- The most common way to signal general reference in English is to use *the, a,* or ∅ before one of the following noun phrase types. (See Focus 3 for another less common option.)

definite article	= **the** laser (singular count noun)
indefinite article	= **a** laser (singular count noun)
zero article	= ∅ lasers (plural count noun)
	= ∅ blood (non-count noun)

- There are two types of generic reference:
  - **Abstract generic** reference uses the definite article *the* with singular countable nouns and non-count nouns to refer to certain well-defined, entire classes of entities. These entities are humans, animals, organs of the body, plants, complex inventions, and devices, but **not** simple inanimate objects.

    (a) **The dermatologist** specializes in skin care.

    (b) **The platypus** is an unusual creature.

    (c) The heaviest organ is **the skin**.

    (d) **The eucalyptus** is native to Australia.

    (e) **The computer** has revolutionized the workplace.

    (f) It is difficult to play **the harp**.

    (g) NOT: **The basket** is used for carrying.

    (h) NOT: **The towel** absorbs water.

- **Concrete generic** reference pertains to each or all of the representatives of a class rather than to the whole class. It uses a greater variety of forms than abstract generic reference does:
  - **Singular count nouns:** $a(n)$ + **singular count noun**
    - **(i)** **An operation** is stressful to one's body.
    - **(j)** NOT: **The operation** is stressful to one's body.
  - **Plural nouns:** ∅ + **plural noun**
    - **(k)** **Carriers** may pass infections on to others.
    - **(l)** NOT: **The carriers** may pass infections on to others.
  - **Non-count nouns:** ∅ + **non-count noun**
    - **(m)** **Ultrasound** can detect the sex of an unborn baby.
    - **(n)** NOT: **The ultrasound** can detect the sex of an unborn baby.

Exercise 2

In each set, select one noun that we can refer to with abstract generic *the*. Then, use it in a general sentence. Note that descriptive words before and after nouns do not affect the use of generic *the*.

EXAMPLE: tattered flag/California redwood/stepbrother

The California redwood is older than other trees.

1. lining of the coat/apartment made of brick/elephant of Africa
2. dust on the moon/illustration of the month/elevator for service personnel
3. fork/bench/liver
4. western barbeque/lung made of iron/rug from Persia
5. free love/fin of a fish/dusty rose
6. Hungarian embroidery/American automobile/Spanish tile
7. mortician/exception/door

Exercise 3

Underline all of the instances of generic reference in the first two paragraphs of the Task description.

EXAMPLE: <u>The medical field</u> has changed rapidly in the last century.

Exercise 4

Check the sentences in which *the* could be substituted for *a(n)*. Then explain why.

EXAMPLE: A transistor is used in computers. ✔

Because the transistor is a complex device, *the* is possible.

1. An X-ray machine is used in radiotherapy.
2. A solar eclipse lasts about 7.5 minutes.
3. An octopus has eight legs.
4. A sedative calms nerves.
5. A sprain is suffered when an ankle is wrenched.
6. A piano has 52 white keys.
7. A calculator adds, subtracts, multiplies, and divides.
8. A road is wider than an alley.
9. A telescope is required by astronomical researchers.
10. A human brain is larger than a bird brain.
11. A grammar book contains useful information.

Focus 3

USE

The + Plural Noun for General Reference

USE

- Sometimes, *the* may be combined with plural nouns when referring generally to
  - plant and animal groups that are the target of special attention.
    - **(a)** The Sierra Club is intent on saving **the redwoods**.
    - **(b)** We went to a fund-raising benefit for **the whales**.
  - social, political, religious, and national groups. (Note that *the* is optional here.)
    - **(c) (The) Nazis** propagate discrimination and hate.
    - **(d) (The) Republicans** believe in conservative values.
    - **(e) (The) Catholics** have large families.
    - **(f) (The) Swedes** live in the land of the midnight sun.
- (A few nationality words do not allow plural endings and require *the*: the Swedish, the Danish, the Finnish, the Polish, the Swiss, the English, the French, the Dutch, the Irish, the Welsh, the British.)

Exercise 5

Match up the following generalizations (or stereotypes) with the corresponding types of people. Select five generalizations you agree with and write them in complete sentences below.

EXAMPLE: (The) Italians eat a lot of pasta.
Criminals commit serious crimes.

Generalization	**People**
1. face racial discrimination	a. Swiss
2. want equality in marriage	b. Muslim
3. know many languages	c. professor
4. like to dance	d. racist
5. eat a lot of pasta	e. politician
6. like to loan money at high interest	f. Brazilian
7. discriminate against different races	g. criminal
8. must publish or perish	h. feminist
9. forget campaign promises	i. laborer
10. pray to Allah	j. African-American
11. want more than the minimum wage	k. Italian
12. commit serious crimes	l. banker

1. _____

2. _____

3. _____

4. _____

5. _____

Focus 4

Representatives of a Class

USE

- Singular concrete generics with *a(n)* describe generalized instances of something. This means that the noun class is being referred to one member at a time because of its relation to singular noun phrases within the sentence or context.

  (a) A policeman carries **a gun**.

  (b) A laser directs **a beam of light** to make incisions.

- In Focus 2, you learned that certain nouns can be abstract generic. These same nouns can optionally be preceded by *a(n)* if they are being referred to one member at a time.

  (c) The/A dermatologist uses **a special solution** to remove warts.

  (d) The/A kangaroo carries **its young** in a pouch.

  (e) NOT: **An elephant** is in danger of becoming extinct.

Exercise 6

For each of the following pairs, put an X above the underlined noun phrase that refers to a generalized instance of something and circle the related singular noun phrase in each sentence.

$$\overset{X}{}$$

EXAMPLE: a. A <u>computer</u> can only carry out tasks commanded by (a programmer).
    b. I have a <u>computer</u>.

1. **a.** A <u>dragon</u> is a mythical beast that breathes fire from its throat.

   b. A <u>dragon</u> killed the knight.

2. **a.** Please hand me <u>a wrench</u> from my toolbox.

   b. <u>A wrench</u> is an indispensable tool for a plumber.

3. **a.** A <u>person</u> needs a friend in troubled times.

   b. I see a <u>person</u> waiting at the door.

4. **a.** <u>A drill</u> easily makes a hole in wood or metal.

   b. <u>A drill</u> made a hole in the wood.

5. **a.** <u>A snail</u> carries its house on its back.

   b. We will use <u>a snail</u> in the experiment.

6. **a.** <u>An apartment</u> became vacant on 22nd Street.

   b. I would like to rent <u>an apartment</u> with a balcony.

7. **a.** We have <u>a deciduous tree</u> in our front yard.

   b. <u>A deciduous tree</u> sheds its leaves every fall.

8. **a.** <u>A prism</u> reflects a rainbow of colors.

   b. <u>A prism</u> fell to the floor.

9. **a.** <u>A race car</u> was parked outside the bank.

   b. <u>A race car</u> accelerates to great speeds during a Grand Prix event.

Exercise 7

Read the following text. Find all of the examples of concrete generic reference with *a(n)*. List each one below and identify the line number where it was found. You should be able to find at least ten more examples.

EXAMPLE: 4   an aid to navigation

HOW COMPUTERS WORK

1 **Background** The earliest computing device was the abacus used by the ancient Greeks and
2 Romans and is still in use in the East today. There are mechanical devices using sliding scales,
3 similar to the slide-rule, which date back almost two millennia, for performing various
4 kinds of calculation, usually as an aid to navigation. In 1642, the French philosopher-
5 mathematician Blaise Pascal built a mechanical adding machine, and in 1671, German
6 philosopher-mathematician Gottfried Leibniz built a machine to perform multiplication.
7 In 1835, British mathematician Charles Babbage designed the first mechanical computer, the
8 analytical engine. The work of another British mathematician Alan Turing, in the 1930s,
9 marked the next major milestone. He developed the mathematical theory of computation
10 and, in particular, showed how a machine could be conceived which could perform any
11 computation (the so-called Turing Machine). The digital computer is the direct descendant of
12 these ideas. In the 1940s, American mathematician John van Neumann developed the basic
13 design for today's electronic computers. Finally, with the development of the transistor in
14 1952 and the subsequent microelectronics revolution, the Computer Age was started.
15 **Basic system** A computer is a collection of various components. At the heart is the CPU
16 (central processing unit), which performs all the computations. This is supported by memory,
17 which holds the current program and data, and 'logic arrays', which help move information
18 around the system. A main power supply is needed and, in the case of a mini- or mainframe
19 computer, a cooling system. The computer's 'device driver' circuits control the peripheral
20 devices, or add-ons, which can be attached. These will normally be keyboards and VDU
21 (visual display unit) screens for user input and output, disc drive units for mass memory
22 storage, and printers for printed output.

23   A computer can only carry out tasks as commanded by the programmer, who translates
24 instructions written in everyday language into a program that is a coded form matching the
25 electronic coding within the computer's internal machinery. The program and data to be
26 manipulated—text, figures, images, or sounds—are input into the computer which then pro-
27 cesses the data and outputs the results. The results can be printed out or displayed on a VDU,
28 or stored in a memory unit for subsequent manipulation. Whatever the task, a computer can
29 function in only one of four ways: input/output operations, arithmetical operations (addition,
30 subtraction, multiplication, and division), logic and comparison operations (for example, is
31 the value of A equal to, less than, or greater than B), and movement of data to, from, and
32 within the central memory of the machine. The programmer's role is to devise a set of in-
33 structions, an *algorithm,* that utilizes these four functions in a combination appropriate to the
34 job in question.
35   **Types** There are four 'sizes', corresponding roughly to their memory capacity and pro-
36 cessing speed. *Microcomputers* are the smallest and the most common and are used in small
37 businesses, at home and in schools. They are usually single-user machines and are often re-
38 ferred to as home computers. *Minicomputers,* also known as personal computers, are generally
39 larger and will be found in medium-sized businesses and university departments. They may
40 support from a dozen to 30 or so users at once. *Mainframes,* which can often service several
41 hundreds of users all at once, are found in large organizations such as national companies and
42 government departments. *Supercomputers* are the most powerful of all. There are very few in
43 the world and are mostly used for special highly complex scientific tasks, such as analysing
44 the results of nuclear physics experiments and weather forecasting.

Source: *Hutchinson Pocket Encyclopedia.* London: Helicon, 1987

**Line
Number:**   **Example:**

1.

2.

3.

4.

5.

6.

7.

8.

9.

10.

Focus 5

Definitions

USE

- We can use both abstract generic and concrete generic structures in making definitions. Standard definitions (*X* is *Y* that *Z*) may emphasize a class, an example, or a group, as in the following:
  - **Abstract Generic**
    - **(a) The chicken** is an animal that lays eggs. (the chicken = a class)
  - **Concrete Generic**
    - **(b) A chicken** is an animal that lays eggs. (a chicken = an example = any members)
    - **(c) Chickens** are animals that lay eggs. (chickens = a group = all members)
    - **(d) Chicken** is a meat that is very moist. (chicken = all/any)
- Definitions can include classifications, attributes, comparisons, etc.
  - **(e)** The platypus is **a mammal** that lays eggs. (classification)
  - **(f)** A duck is a bird **that can swim.** (attribute)
  - **(g)** Vultures are birds **that are larger than rats.** (comparison)

Exercise 8

Write definitions using the words provided below. (Recall from Focus 2 that not all nouns can be referred to using abstract generic reference.)

> **EXAMPLE:** stegosaurus
>
> *A stegosaurus is a prehistoric animal that roamed the earth thousands of years ago.*

1. screwdriver
2. unicorn
3. bell-bottoms
4. stethoscope
5. eels

6. spatula
7. honey
8. violins
9. checkers
10. veal

Focus 6

FORM

Articles with Names of Illnesses

- The names of illnesses follow a range of noun patterns:

the + Noun	*a/an* + Noun		*(the)* + Noun + Plural
the flu	a cold	an ulcer	(the) bends
the gout	a hernia	a stroke	(the) mumps
the plague	a headache	an earache	(the) measles
	a heart attack	a sore throat	(the) chicken pox
			(the) hiccups

Non-Count Noun		∅ + Noun (with Final -s)
influenza	leukemia	diabetes
pneumonia	diarrhea	rabies
malaria	mononucleosis	herpes
arthritis	cardiovascular disease	AIDS
cancer	tuberculosis	

Exercise 9

Have you or anyone you know ever suffered from any of the illnesses/diseases listed in Focus 6? Write short paragraphs that describe the symptoms for at least one illness from each column.

EXAMPLE: *Usually, a cold starts with a headache. Sometimes a sore throat develops. Often, a fever and a cough follow.*

Exercise 10

Fill in a correct disease/illness that matches the information in the following blanks.

EXAMPLE: <u>*AIDS*</u> is caused by a blood-borne virus (HIV, Human Immunodeficiency Virus).

1. _____ ravaged Europe between 1347-1351.

2. _____ is the bulging out of a part of any of the internal organs through a muscular wall.

3. _____ is a contagious disease that causes red spots to appear on the skin.

4. _____ is caused by a parasite, which is transmitted by a female mosquito.

5. _____ is a form of cancer that is marked by an increase in white blood cells.

6. _____ is an inflammation of the lungs caused by bacteria or viruses.

7. _____ is a decompression sickness experienced in the air or the water.

8. _____ consists of sores on the skin or internal parts of the body and is often caused by stress.

9. _____ is a common name for a cerebral hemorrhage.

10. _____ is a sound caused by contractions of the diaphragm.

Focus 7

FORM

Articles with Body Parts

FORM

- We use three patterns for generic reference to organs, parts of the body, or body fluids:
  - Use *the* + noun for singular body parts.
    - **(a)** **The heart** can be transplanted.
    - **(b)** Cancer of **the bladder** has been linked to cigarette smoking.
  - Use *the* + non-count noun to refer to massive areas or parts of the body.
    - **(c)** **(The) blood** carries nutrients to body tissues.
    - **(d)** **(The) skin** is sensitive to ultra-violet rays.
  - Use *the* + noun + plural for plural or paired body parts.
    - **(e)** Excessive smoke inhalation damages **the lungs**.
    - **(f)** Regular exams of **the teeth** will prevent serious dental problems.
    - **(g)** **The veins** carry blood throughout the body.

Exercise 11

Study the following diagram and write sentences describing the location or function of at least eight of the following body parts.

EXAMPLE: *The brain controls all muscular movements of the body.*

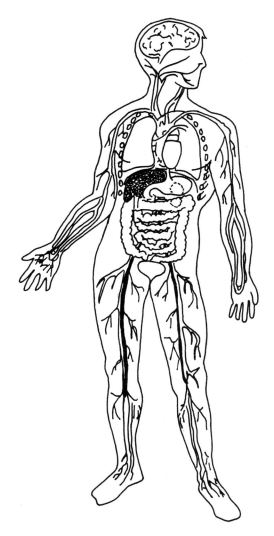

(Source: *Hutchinson Pocket Encyclopedia.* London: Helicon, 1987.)

Exercise 12

Fill in the following blanks with the correct article: *a(n), the*, or ∅. Don't forget to use *the* for second-mention referents.

(1) _____∅_____ syphilis is a sexually transmitted disease, which is easily cured with antibiotics if it is treated within the early stages of infection. (2)During the primary stage, a person may develop _____ chancre, which is an open lump or swelling, usually in the genital region. (3)After several weeks, _____ chancre will disappear, but the infection has entered _____ blood and it is being carried to all parts of _____ body.

(4)During the secondary stage, new symptoms will appear a few weeks to six months after the first infection. (5)Symptoms may include _____ skin rash, whitish patches on the mucous membranes in _____ mouth and _____ throat, and spotty, temporary baldness. (6)Other discomforts may include _____ low-grade fevers, _____ headaches, and _____ swollen glands. (7)Because the infected person may think he or she has only _____ cold at this stage, it is important to check with a physician if any of these signs appear.

(8)During the latent stage, all symptoms of _____ syphilis disappear. (9)The disease is hidden, but it is not gone. (10)Spirochetes, which are the spiral-shaped bacterium that cause _____ syphilis, are invading _____ heart and _____ brain. (11)In this stage, the infected individual appears disease-free.

(12)The late stage of syphilis generally begins ten to 20 years after the beginning of the latent stage. (13)In late syphilis, untreated patients may become incapacitated or develop _____ cardiovascular disease, _____ heart damage, _____ blindness, or _____ insanity.

(14)Fortunately, if _____ syphilis is treated early, the infection will not recur, providing it is not contracted again from an infected person.

Adapted from Ralph Grawunder and Marion Steinmann, *Life and Health, Third Edition*. New York: McGraw-Hill, Inc., 1980, pp. 300–301.

Focus 8

USE

Topic Focus in Discourse

USE

- Abstract generic forms (*the* + noun) have prominent status in discourse. They often occur in subject position of a sentence and are common in the introductory sections of an extended text (especially a technical or science text) where one general topic is being discussed.

Exercise 13

Reread the text in Exercise 7.

1. Underline all the instances of the word *computer* or *computer* with other prefixes (e.g., *micro-, super-,* etc.).
2. Examine each of these and then circle the abstract generic uses with *the* that you find.
3. Answer the following questions: Do they often occur in subject position of a sentence? Are they more prevalent in the introductory section of the text? Can you find any other abstract generic forms in the first paragraph?

Focus 9

Non-count Generic

- Various premodifiers such as adjectives, noun adjuncts, or participles can precede non-count nouns. Even though the modification limits the noun, it is still considered non-count generic and does not require an article.
  - **Unmodified: Oil** is an important resource.
  - **Modified:**
    - **(a)** Adjective: **Texan oil** has boosted the U.S. economy.
    - **(b)** Noun Adjunct: **Olive oil** is a major export of Spain.
    - **(c)** Pres. Participle: Lard produces a flakier pie crust than **cooking oil**.
    - **(d)** Past Participle: **Burned oil** creates a terrible smell.

Exercise 14

In class, state your preference for the following pairs and explain why. (Your teacher will call on you.)

EXAMPLE: Which do you prefer, rice vinegar or wine vinegar?
I prefer rice vinegar because it is milder.

Which do you prefer:
1. scrambled eggs or fried eggs?
2. brown rice or white rice?
3. blueberry muffins or corn muffins?
4. hot cereal or cold cereal?
5. salt-water fish or fresh-water fish?
6. cooking classes or dancing classes?
7. caffeinated or decaffeinated coffee?

Exercise 15

Review your knowledge of the ideas presented in this chapter by filling in the correct generic article in the blanks of the following text.

1. When (a) _____ laser was introduced to the medical profession more than thirty years ago, (b) _____ doctors felt that it might replace (c) _____ surgical scalpel in curing (d) _____ ailments. What they have found since then is that (e) _____ laser, which is (f) _____ short-pulsed, high-powered light beam, has increased the accuracy of (g) _____ surgical cuts and reduced (h) _____ recovery period following many operations. How can this be?

2. The cutting power of (a) _____ laser beam can be more accurate than (b) _____ surgeon's hand because (c) _____ beam is computer-controlled. Because (d) _____ cuts are more accurate, (e) _____ scarring is kept to a minimum. In the past, (f) _____ operation to remove (g) _____ gallstones required (h) _____ patient to stay in the hospital ten days. Now, this operation takes only a few hours on (i) _____ outpatient basis.

3. Besides cutting (a) _____ gallstones, (b) _____ lasers can treat a wide variety of other conditions affecting (c) _____ body as well. They can remove (d) _____ kidney stones, (e) _____ tumors, or (f) _____ cataracts. They can also provide relief to (g) _____ hemorrhoid sufferers and cure such common conditions as (h) _____ nearsightedness and (i) _____ farsightedness. Even (j) _____ tatoos can be removed by (k) _____ lasers.

4. Although (a) _____ doctor's hand will never be fully replaced by (b) _____ laser surgery, (c) _____ doctors must recognize the permanent place of these healing beams in (d) _____ hospitals and (e) _____ clinics.

Activities

Activity 1

A riddle is a puzzling question that often involves a play on words. Try to answer the following riddles, which require a concrete generic reference, and then create a riddle of your own.

   EXAMPLE: What is black and white and red all over? (a newspaper–"read")

1. What kind of fruit is always in trouble?
2. What is it that has a mouth that is bigger than its head?
3. What kind of man can truly be said to be immersed in his work?
4. When is a rock not a rock?
5. What vegetable is dangerous when found in a ship?

Activity 2

The field of medicine can vary in different cultures. Do research at the library or conduct interviews with other students to learn about the type of medicine you are least familiar with. What are the medical training, medicine, and techniques associated with that type of medicine? If you know less about the West, you might investigate synthetic drugs, surgical technology, CAT scans, etc. If you know less about the East, you might investigate natural herbal drugs, acupuncture, homeopathy, massage, osteopathy, etc. Once you have completed your research, write a short paper about your findings, incorporating correct use of the generic article.

Activity 3

Locate one chapter in an introductory science textbook (e.g., physics, chemistry, biology, etc.) that talks about general principles in that field. Note the frequency of use of abstract generic versus concrete generic articles in the chapter.

Activity 4

Discuss which types of political, social, or religious groups would disagree most with each of the medical practices mentioned in the Task. For example, would (the) Catholics be in favor of birth control? Would doctors be in favor of declaring positive AIDS tests results for themselves?

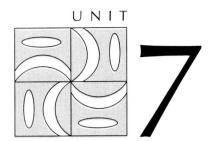

Reference

The, It/They,
Demonstratives
and Such

Task

Speakers of the same language often use language differently, based on differences in age, education, social status, gender, and so on. Such differences have been of great interest to sociolinguists, who study language variation.

In a book called *You Just Don't Understand: Women and Men in Conversation*, sociolinguist Deborah Tannen discusses female-male communication differences. Drawing most of her examples from American English speakers, she proposes that communication between men and women may be considered cross-cultural because in our society, boys and girls tend to be raised differently.

Below are some common situations discussed by Tannen and the ways that she believes women and men typically respond to them. After reading the situations and responses, discuss your opinions about the differences pointed out. Use the questions as a guide for your discussion. Then write a paragraph stating your individual opinion in response to one of the questions. Present evidence or explanation to support your view.

1. Do you agree that such responses are typical of men and women in the situations described?
2. Have you experienced any exceptions to these generalizations about male-female communication differences?
3. Do you see characteristics of women in general or of men in general that may help to explain the typical responses in all of these situations?
4. Do you think the gender-based communication differences described are common in cultures other than American culture?
5. Do you think that gender differences alone account for the different responses, or could some other variables account for them? What might such variables be?

Situation 1

TALKING ABOUT TROUBLES

Someone (male or female) has a personal problem. She or he is very upset and tells a friend about the problem.

The friend is female: She empathizes by telling the person that she knows how it feels to have the problem. She may provide an example of the same problem or a similar one from her own experience.

The friend is male: He offers advice about how to solve the problem.

Situation 2

ASKING SOMEONE TO DO SOMETHING FOR YOU

Someone who is in a position of authority in a workplace needs to get something done and wants to have a person she or he supervises do it.

The person is female: She does not state the request directly, but rather makes a suggestion that it be done. (For example: "You might finish this report this afternoon.")

The person is male: He states directly what it is he wants done. (For example: "Have this report finished this afternoon.")

Situation 3

EXPRESSING VIEWS

Someone expresses an opinion about a topic or presents his or her ideas on a topic.

The listener is female: She expresses agreement with the speaker or, if she disagrees, asks for clarification or further explanation.

The listener is male: He challenges the speaker's views and explores possible flaws in the argument or idea.

Situation 4

HAVING A CONVERSATION

A group of people at a social event, such as a party, are engaged in conversation.

The group consists of females: They will tend to view conversation as a way of making connections and sharing experiences among participants. They will seek to establish common bonds among the group in conversation.

The group consists of males: They will tend to regard the conversation as a way to get attention or to impart information. More so than women, individual men will try to maintain center stage by delivering monologues, telling jokes or lengthy stories, or giving long explanations. They will typically be more concerned with asserting their own status than with establishing common bonds in a conversation.

Focus 1

FORM

Review of Reference Forms

FORM

- Several kinds of reference are used in English to refer to information previously stated. This information is called **the referent**. The referent could be a word, a phrase, a sentence, or a longer stretch of discourse. In spoken English, the referent could be something the speaker has said earlier or something that another speaker has said.
- Reference is very important both in writing and in speech because it helps to make connections between parts of a discourse. The reference forms we will focus on in this unit include:
  - **Article *the* + noun phrase**
    (a) Ruth enjoys talking about *gender-based language differences*. She finds **the topic** a fascinating one.
  - **Pronouns *it/they/them***
    (b) Lin: Do you know much about *language variation?*
    Yumi: Not a lot, but I did read a little about **it** in my introductory linguistics course.
    (c) *Phonology and semantics* are subfields of linguistics. **They** are concerned with language sounds and meanings, respectively. I studied **them** a few years ago.
  - **Demonstrative pronouns and adjectives:** *this, that, these, those.* Pronoun and adjective forms are the same. Adjectives are used before noun phrases (e.g., *this* research).
    - *this*
      (d) Tannen says that *men tend to advise friends who come to them with troubles.*

      My experience supports $\left\{ \begin{array}{l} \textbf{this.} \\ \textbf{this claim.} \end{array} \right\}$

- *that*

  (e) Fred: Do you think *men resist asking for directions?*

  Yani: I would agree with $\left\{\begin{array}{l}\textbf{that.}\\\textbf{that generalization.}\end{array}\right.$

- *these*

  (f) *Two of the gender differences* seem especially true to me.

  $\left.\begin{array}{l}\textbf{These}\\\textbf{These differences}\end{array}\right\}$ will be the topic of my paper.

- *those*

  (g) George: I know *people who constantly give advice when it's not requested.*

  Lily: $\left\{\begin{array}{l}\textbf{Those people}\\\textbf{Those}\end{array}\right\}$ are the ones that I avoid!

- **Pro-form *such* + noun phrase**

  (h) I read several studies about *how young boys are often encouraged to be aggressive and competitive.* I think **such an upbringing** would influence a boy's behavior when he gets older.

  (i) I had never thought much about the influence of *age, social class, gender, etc.* on language use. However, I agree that **such variables** probably do affect greatly the ways in which we communicate.

Exercise 1

Underline the reference forms (*it, they, the* demonstrative and *such* reference) that refer to information in previous sentences. Put brackets around the referents. There may be more than one reference form in a sentence.

> **EXAMPLE:** We discussed [the responses to each situation].
> We didn't always agree that <u>such responses</u> were typical.

1. According to Professor Tannen, for women, talk is important for creating connections between people. For men, these connections tend to be formed more through activities than talk.

2. Men and women sometimes experience frustration with each other because of their different communication styles. The frustration may be especially great between men and women who spend a great deal of time together.

3. Tannen notes that women have a tendency to make suggestions rather than give commands when they want something done. She thinks this tendency may reflect women's sense of authority in certain situations.

4. Speakers use language differently depending on differences in age, education, social status, and gender. Such differences are of interest to linguists.

5. Pitch and volume are two aspects of speech. The way we use them in speech may affect how we are perceived by others in communication situations.

6. Women have higher-pitched voices than men do. This can be a disadvantage when they are trying to assert authority.

7. In some business contexts, women may regard personal questions, such as how a fellow worker spent the weekend, as a way of showing collegiality. Men may consider the questions inappropriate in these contexts.

8. Some studies show that men tend to dominate conversation in mixed (male-female) groups. Based on your experience, do you agree with that?

9. I agree with the idea that men and women should try to understand each other's different communication styles. It makes sense to me.

10. We could accept the communication differences we have with the "other gender," or we could try to negotiate different ways of communicating that would be more productive and less frustrating. These are two possible approaches to our differences in communication styles.

Exercise 2

The following passage, written by sociobioligist Lewis Thomas, describes the common habit of worrying. Discuss what you think the referent is for each underlined reference form.

Worrying is the most natural and spontaneous of all human functions. It is time to acknowledge <u>this</u>, perhaps even learn to do <u>it</u> better. Man is the Worrying Animal. <u>It</u> is a trait needing further development, awaiting perfection. Most of us tend to neglect <u>the activity</u>, living precariously out on the thin edge of anxiety but never plunging in.

Excerpted from Lewis Thomas, *The Medusa and the Snail*. New York: Bantam Books, 1979, p. 67.

Focus 2

FORM

The and Demonstrative Adjective Reference Forms

FORM

- When we use *the* + **noun phrase** reference or demonstrative adjectives *this, that, these,* or *those* + **noun phrase** reference, these reference forms may:
  - repeat all of the referent:
    (a) I liked *the books*, and I might even reread them sometime. I would probably recommend **the books** to anyone who is interested in Chinese history.
  - This type of repetition is most typical if the referent doesn't have adjective modifiers. Also, it is more common as a later reference rather than second mention.
- Demonstrative forms are usually not repeated in second mention of something, although it is possible to do so. Instead, pronouns *it* or *them* or *the* + **noun phrase** is used.
  (b) Oh, did you see *this book* in the children's section? You know, my sisters and I must have read **it** a hundred times when we were young.

- repeat part of the referent:

    (c) I read *two interesting studies about language differences between different age groups.*

    I have referred to $\left\{ \begin{array}{l} \textbf{the two studies} \\ \textbf{these two studies} \end{array} \right\}$ in my paper.

- be a synonym for the referent:

    (d) I read *one study about differences based on educational levels.*

    I did not, however, use $\left\{ \begin{array}{l} \textbf{the article} \\ \textbf{that article} \end{array} \right\}$ for my paper.

- be a classifier for the referent:

    (e) We went to see *Hamlet.* **The play** was performed outdoors at the city center.

    (f) I would like to take South American literature and the history of jazz next quarter. Several of my friends recommended **these courses.**

- paraphrase a clause or sentence referent:

    (g) Over the weekend, *you should revise your paper* and type it. **The revised paper** should be turned in on Monday.

    (h) *The aerosol is then sprayed into the mixing chamber where the water vaporizes.* **This vaporization process** is repeated.

- This type of reference is commonly used to refer to processes or other activities and the results of them.

Activity	Result
You revise a paper	the revised paper

- The paraphrase may repeat part of the referent and also use a classifying or descriptive noun such as *process* or *effects.* An example of this is (h) above.

Exercise 3

For each sentence pair, underline *the* and demonstrative references in the second sentences and put brackets around their referents in the first sentences. Then state what type of reference is used in relation to the referent: repetition of the entire referent, partial repetition, a synonym, or a paraphrase. The first one is done as an example.

1. Psychologists have distinguished [three dimensions of emotions]. <u>These dimensions</u> can be used to characterize differences in the ways cultures recognize and express emotions. *partial repetition*

2. One dimension distinguishes between what are called the primary emotions and what are termed the secondary emotions. The primary emotions are considered universal by some psychologists.

3. The primary emotions are also considered to be biologically based. These feelings include anger, grief, joy, and disgust.

4. The secondary emotions are blends of the primary emotions. These blended emotions, such as contempt (a blend of anger and disgust) are not universal.

5. Another dimension of emotions distinguishes pleasant emotions from unpleasant ones. The positive emotions are ones such as love and joy, whereas the negative emotions are ones such as sorrow and shame.

6. The last dimension classifies emotions based on intensity. This classification of feelings can distinguish worry from terror and sadness from depression.

7. All societies have what are called display rules regarding emotions. These rules dictate how and when people may express certain emotions.

8. For example, in some cultures, people would express grief by crying. In other cultures, this emotion might be expressed by silence.

Information source: C. Wade and C. Tavris, *Psychology* (New York: Harper & Row, 1987).

Exercise 4

Make up a sentence with *the* reference or demonstrative reference to follow and elaborate each of the sentences below. The referent is underlined. Try to use a variety of the reference types discussed in Focus 2. An example is given for the first. Think of another sentence you might use to elaborate that referent.

EXAMPLE: Everyone has negative feelings.

However, in some cultures, it is considered polite not to express **these emotions**.

1. Everyone has negative feelings.
2. Psychologists note that the smile does not have universal meaning.
3. Facial expressions are important signals of emotion.
4. Fury is a very intense emotion.
5. Nonverbal signals such as posture, gestures, and eye contact also express emotions.

Focus 3

USE

Personal Pronoun versus The Reference

USE

• Personal pronouns *it, they/them,* as well as *the* + **noun phrase**, can refer to previously given information.

I like *psychology*.

(a) $\left.\begin{array}{l}\textbf{It}\\\textbf{The subject}\end{array}\right\}$ is interesting to me.

Bill is planning to take *geology and political science.*

(b) $\left.\begin{array}{l}\textbf{They} \\ \textbf{The courses}\end{array}\right\}$ will satisfy general requirements for him.

(c) He'll take $\left\{\begin{array}{l}\textbf{them} \\ \textbf{the courses}\end{array}\right\}$ next fall.

- **They and them**, unlike **it** and **the + noun phrase**, refer only to plural noun phrases. They are not used to refer to more than one noun clause or larger parts of a sentence.

She said that *she had finished her paper* and that *she was going to turn it in today*, but *then her dog ate the paper.*

(d) Well, I for one, don't believe $\left\{\begin{array}{l}\textbf{it.} \\ \textbf{the story.}\end{array}\right.$

(e) NOT: Well, I don't believe **them**.

- The chart below shows some of the contexts in which a particular reference form would be used.

it, they, them	*the* + Noun Phrase
- **One possible referent** **(f)** I like *that book* a lot. I read **it** last year. **(h)** Kip is taking *math and English.* **They** are his most challenging subjects.	- **More than one possible referent** **(g)** I read *the book,* but I didn't see *the movie.* **The book** was good. **(i)** Kip is taking *math and English.* He is also taking art and history. **The first two** are his most challenging subjects.
it	
- **Only one possible referent.** - **Referent is a clause or sentence.** **(j)** Toni: There is *evidence that women tend to add more details to stories they tell than men do.* Rick: I believe **it**.	- **Referent might not be clear unless a noun phrase is used.** **(k)** To whom it may concern: I am returning *the enclosed cassette recorder.* The volume is jammed. Also sound quality doesn't seem very good. **The recorder** came with a one-year guarantee.
(l) Tom: *Song's chances of winning a gold medal at the summer Olympics are getting better every every day.* Lee: I don't doubt **it**. (It is possible to use *the* reference for some clause or sentence contexts; e.g., *I believe* **the** *evidence.* In many contexts, however, *the* reference would sound awkward or repetitive.)	- **Speaker wants to classify or characterize the referent.** **(m)** *Violence* is increasing in our society. **The problem** cannot be ignored.
	- **Speaker wants to paraphrase previous information in a sentence as a noun phrase.** **(n)** This medicine should not be taken when you are driving because *it can make you sleepy or it may affect your vision.* **The effects** are only temporary, but nevertheless, you need to be cautious.

Exercise 5

Decide whether *it, they, them,* or *the* + noun phrase is appropriate for each blank. Use a form of the verb in parentheses if a verb is needed. If *the* + noun phrase should be used, choose a noun phrase that fits the context.

1. I have to write a paper for my class about the sixties. I can't decide whether to write my paper about the Civil Rights marches in the early sixties or about the hippie movement in the late sixties. (a) _____ (appeal) to me because I'd like to find out more about the history of segregation in the South. (b) _____ (be) both interesting topics, however.

2. Sandro: Do you think it's true that men tend to be more direct about what they want than women do? Alicia: Oh, yes, I'm convinced of _____ .

3. I tried your suggestion to move the second paragraph of my essay to the beginning of the introduction. _____ (be) a good one; my teacher liked the revision also.

4. Plants break up water into hydrogen and oxygen with the help of sunlight. Sunlight that is caught by grains of chlorophyll in the plant splits the water molecules into hydrogen and oxygen. Most of the oxygen eventually passes out of _____ .

5. Scientists believe that there are more than five senses. The ear, of course, is the organ for the sense of hearing. However, in addition, _____ (have) receptors that help us to create a sense of balance.

Focus 4

Demonstrative Adjectives and Demonstrative Pronouns

MEANING
USE

- Demonstrative adjectives and pronouns *this, that, these*, and *those* tell the reader/listener whether a referent is singular (*this, that*) or plural (*these, those*) and whether it is near or far.
- The concept of distance may involve space or time.

	Near	Far
Space	**(a)** Take **this chair** right here. **(c)** I'll get two of **these**, please. And one melon.	**(b)** Can you see **that** tall **tower** in the distance? **(d)** **Those buildings** next to the tower are part of the new arts center.
Time	**(e)** Let's finish watching **this movie**. It's almost over. **(g)** **These** are difficult times because of the economy.	**(f)** I'd like to see **that** again. It was one of my favorite musicals. **(h)** **Those** were called the golden years because prosperity was widespread.

- The notion of distance may also be abstract. It may involve:
  - the distance in the discourse between the referent and the demonstrative.

	Near	Far
Discourse Distance	**(i)** *Age* is another factor affecting language use. **This influence** can be seen in slang.	**(j)** *The introduction to my thesis* provided background on my topic. It suggested several hypotheses addressing the issue. **That section** also presented an outline of my thesis.

- The "Far" example above illustrates discourse distance in two senses: First, the writer may consider the underlined referent distant from the reference form because the first mention is more than a sentence earlier in the text. Second, the referent could refer to an earlier and thus more "distant" part of the writer's paper. For example, the writer could be summarizing in a concluding chapter what she or he did in the introduction.
- In some contexts, a writer might use *this section* instead of **that** *section*. Keep in mind that it is the speaker's subjective attitude about distance that determines the demonstrative.

- The relevance of a referent to the speaker/writer.

	Near	Far
Relevance to Speaker/ Writer	**(k)** I'm going to use **this journal article** for my article for my paper. It has some good support for my opinion.	**(l)** I'm not going to use **that magazine article** for my paper. It's not very closely related to my topic.

- What a speaker has said herself or himself versus what another speaker has said.

	Near: Same speaker	Far: Other speaker
Location of Referent in Speech	**(m)** I favor gun control. I feel very strongly about **this**.	**(n)** Hal: I think gun control laws are needed. Tori: I agree with **that**.

- Demonstrative pronoun *that* is also often used rather than *this* in a concluding statement for a description or explanation.
    - **(o)** When Wilhelm Roentgen, a German Professor of Physics, discovered the X-ray in 1895, he did not completely understand the nature of these new rays. He called them X-rays because the letter *x* stands for an unknown quantity in mathematics. **That** is how the X-ray came to be named.
- **Demonstrative adjective + noun phrase reference**, like *the* reference, can point more explicitly to a referent than a demonstrative pronoun can. Therefore, we use it when a pronoun might not clearly signal the referent.
    - **(p)** When you do strenuous exercise, you should wear proper clothing and *you should warm up* first. **This warm-up** will help prevent injuries.
    ("**This** will help prevent injuries" does not clearly signal the referent. *This* could be interpreted as *both* wearing proper clothing and warming up.)
- **Demonstrative adjective** reference can also, like *the* reference, further describe or classify a referent:
    - **(q)** Before writing your draft, *you should try to brainstorm some ideas and then cluster your ideas into categories*. **These prewriting techniques** can help you get started.

Exercise 6

Put an appropriate demonstrative form in each blank: *this, that, these,* or *those*. If you think more than one might be appropriate, discuss in class the contexts (including speaker attitude) in which each might be used.

1. I spent my vacation last month in Costa Rica and had a wonderful time. The people

   were really friendly, the scenery was beautiful, and the weather was perfect. I also loved

   the food. You should visit ＿＿＿＿＿＿＿＿ country sometime; you'd love it there too.

2. Have you seen the entertainment section of the newspaper yet? There are a couple new movies at the theaters. (a) _____ movie based on Kazuo Ishiguro's novel looks good. I think I'll pass on the new James Bond film, though. I've never really liked (b) _____ movies.

3. Erin: Did you know that the Pope will be in town (a) _____ weekend?

   Victor: No, I hadn't heard (b) _____ .

4. Dear Senator Rotrosen: I am writing (a) _____ letter to urge you to do something about cleaning up our polluted lake. (b) _____ situation is disgraceful; people are afraid even to go swimming. I know that some officials have suggested closing the beach to swimming, but (c) _____ is certainly not the answer to (d) _____ problem.

5. Have you ever wondered how and why fireflies produce their twinkling lights? (a) _____ lights are created by special glands. At night, female fireflies sit on stems of grass while the males fly around, flashing their lights. The females flash back and, after signals are exchanged a few times, the male finds the female. (b) _____ is how fireflies mate.

Exercise 7

For the following contexts, use a demonstrative adjective and a classifying or descriptive noun to refer to the previous information that is underlined.

EXAMPLE: Before making gravy, put the flour in a baking pan and bake it for about five minutes.

This process will add to your preparation time, but it will keep your gravy from having a floury taste.

1. Exciting. Suspenseful. Amusing. _____ describe best the newest novel by Ira Dubrow.

2. If you spend too much time in the sun, you may get end up with skin damage and dehydration. _____ are not worth a suntan.

115

3. We'll be hearing a lot from our elected officials about <u>whether or not taxes should be raised.</u> _____ continues to be a widely debated one.

4. Before you turn in your essay, <u>you should correct any grammatical errors you see; you should also correct misspelled words.</u> _____ will improve the readability of your essay.

5. <u>Smiles, frowns, raised eyebrows, and shrugs of the shoulder</u> all convey emotions. _____ may have different meanings in different cultures, though.

6. <u>Women</u> sometimes <u>think men are being unsympathetic</u> when they give advice about a problem rather than share troubles. _____ stems from a difference between men and women in what they think is an appropriate reaction to such a situation.

Focus 5

Demonstratives versus *The* and *It* Reference

USE

- There are many contexts in which either demonstrative, *the* or *it* reference would be acceptable. The choice of reference form often depends on the speaker's or writer's intentions and on what the speaker/writer thinks the listener/reader knows.
- Use **demonstratives (adjectives or pronouns)** rather than *the* reference when greater emphasis on the referent is desired:

| I heard *a speaker* on campus this afternoon | |
Less Emphasis on Referent	**More Emphasis on Referent**
(a) The speaker was talking about the dangers of nuclear power. (Emphasizes the speaker's topic.)	**(b) This speaker** was the best I've heard regarding the nuclear power issue. (Emphasizes the speaker.)

- **Demonstrative pronouns** put greater emphasis on referents than *it* does in contexts where either might be used:

Less Emphasis on Referent	**More Emphasis on Referent**
(c) I'm not sure if I'll *type my paper myself.* If I do, **it** will probably take me all day! (Emphasizes the result of having to type: new information.)	**(d)** I'm going to hire someone to *type my paper.* I have more important things to do that **that**! (Emphasizes the act of typing: previous information.)

- **Demonstrative pronouns** are more concise than *the* + **noun phrase** when the referent is obvious and *the* + **noun phrase** would be needlessly repetitive. This is especially true when *the* reference would be a paraphrase of a clause or sentence.

  I asked my instructor if I needed *to include the bibliography with my draft.*

  (e) She told me **that** would not be necessary.

  (f) Repetitious: She told me **the inclusion of the bibliography** would not be necessary.

- *That* should be used rather than *it* in cases where *it* does not as clearly signal a clause or sentence referent:

  Did you know that *the ocean is only a block from your cabin* and that *there's a ferry to take you to the island?*

  (g) Yes, I was aware of **that**. (*That* refers to all of the italicized information. *It* might be ambiguous, because it could be interpreted as referring to the ferry.)

- As mentioned in Focus 2, we do not usually repeat demonstratives as second mentions. A second mention is typically some other form of reference, such as *it* or *the*:

  (h) *This paper* is one of the best I've written. I'm sure my classmates will enjoy reading **it**.

  (i) NOT: I'm sure my classmates will enjoy reading **this paper.**

  (j) *This attitude* is one I disagree with. In my opinion, **the attitude** is based on a lack of information.

  (k) NOT: In my opinion, **this attitude** is based on a lack of information.

Exercise 8

Put an appropriate reference form in each blank. The referent is underlined. Use *it, the* + noun phrase, a demonstrative adjective (*this, that, these,* or *those*) or a demonstrative pronoun + noun phrase. When a cue in parentheses is given, use it to choose a reference form. More than one choice might be possible for some blanks.

1. I've just finished a really good novel. _____ was about an American

   woman who goes to live in India. (Put focus on the theme of the novel.)

2. I also read a biography. _____ was the most interesting one I have ever

   read. (Put focus on the subject of the sentence.)

3. I just found out that Chinese, English, Spanish, Hindi, and Arabic are the languages

   with the most speakers. I didn't know _____ before.

4. The Danish linguist Otto Jespersen described several theories on the origins of language. One is called the 'ding-dong' theory. <u>This theory</u> proposes that speech arose as a result of people reacting to stimuli in their environment and making sounds to reflect it. _____ is not one that is believed by most linguists.

5. Another theory of the origins of language was termed <u>the 'pooh-pooh' theory</u>. _____ maintains that speech started when people made instinctive sounds caused by emotions.

6. You can eat most vegetables either raw or cooked. <u>If you cook them,</u> _____ may reduce the nutrients you get. (Emphasize the result.)

7. Nicholas is making sure that the spare tire for his car is well-inflated before he leaves for his business trip. During his most recent trip, <u>he got a flat tire and was stranded in the desert for hours.</u> _____ was the last thing he needed after a busy and exhausting week. (Emphasize the referent.)

8. We consulted the forest ranger as to whether we could <u>take our dog with us on our camping trip in the national park.</u> He said _____ would not be allowed.

9. <u>Five students</u> were singled out for awards at our end-of-the-year banquet. _____ had outstanding academic records and had participated in a number of community projects. (Emphasize the referent.)

Focus 6

FORM ● MEANING

Such Reference

FORM
MEANING

- *Such* + **noun phrase** reference is less common than the other forms of reference discussed so far. Nevertheless, we use it in many contexts, both spoken and written.
- *Such* in reference phrases occurs with singular count nouns, plural count nouns, and non-count nouns. With singular nouns, the article *a* or *an* always precedes the noun.

Such + Singular noun	**(a)** The police thoroughly investigated the *burglary*. They concluded that only experienced thieves could have accomplished **such a heist**.
Such + Plural Noun	**(b)** *Impatiens and fuchsia plants* need little sun. **Such plants** are good for shady areas of your garden.
Such + Non-Count Noun	**(c)** I can't believe *the things* they told us about their friends. In my opinion, they really shouldn't divulge **such personal information.**

- *Such* phrases with plural or non-count nouns often follow a list or series of things. The list represents examples of a class of items.
    - **(d)** You should try to eat more *fruits, vegetables, and whole grains*. **Such foods** are important for good health.
- Another form of **such** reference is (**number**) + **such** + **singular or plural noun:**
    - **(e)** *Several students* have demonstrated superior performance in the field of mathematics. **One such student** is Ruby Pereda.
    - **(f)** Now more than ever we need *forward-thinking candidates* for the city council. **Two such candidates** are Ben Ho and Ulla Teppo.
- The meaning of *such* in referring to previous context is usually similar to "like that" or "of that class/type of thing."
    - **(g)** Men and women often have different responses to the same situations. **Such responses may** result from the ways they have been brought up. (responses that can be classified as "different")
    - **(h)** We need a strong and honest leader. **Such a person** is Mario Baretta. (a person belonging to the type "good leader")
- As with other forms of reference, the referent of *such* + noun phrase may be:

A Single Word	**(i)** I admire your *attitude*. **Such an attitude** shows great respect for others.
A Phrase	**(j)** She has *a very positive attitude*. **Such an attitude** probably results from both her temperament and the way she was raised.
A Clause	**(k)** They said that *women should stay at home*. **Such an attitude** does not reflect the feelings of most Americans.
A Sentence	**(l)** *He believes the world owes him a living*. **Such an attitude** is not going to get him very far.
More Than One Sentence	**(m)** *My younger brothers think that girls should do all the housework. They also believe that the women in the family should serve them.* **Such an attitude** about the role of women is common in my culture, but it seems to be changing.

Exercise 9

Underline the *such* reference in each of the following groups of sentences or dialogues. Then state what the referent is. If you wish, you may paraphrase the referent.

> **EXAMPLE:** Men tend to view conversation as a way to assert status and to impart information.
>
> <u>Such attitudes</u> are not as common with women.
>
> *Referent*: Men's view that conversation is for asserting status and imparting information

1. The Italian composer Giuseppe Verdi wrote one of his greatest operas, *Falstaff*, when he was 80. To have created this brilliant musical work at such an advanced age is truly remarkable.

2. In the early decades of American filmmaking, Asians were often portrayed as servants, launderers, cooks, gardeners, and waiters. Such stereotypes denied the many achievements of Asian Americans at that time.

3. Child: Mom, is it really true that washing your face too much can make you really sick?

   Mother: Of course not! Where did you ever get such a silly idea, dear?

4. Lightning never strikes in the same place twice. Rattlesnakes intentionally give warnings to their victims by rattling their tails. The sap of a tree rises in the spring. Such beliefs, although common, are not supported by scientific evidence.

5. Some people who pursue physical fitness with a passion fill up their homes with stationary bicycles, rowing machines, and stair climbers. Each time a new exercise machine appears on the market, they rush to their local sporting goods stores. However, such equipment is not needed to become physically fit.

6. Van: Did you hear that our former English teacher has joined an expedition to climb Mount Everest?

   Rosa: Who would have ever thought she would do such a thing?

7. Although Jimmy Connors won many tennis championships, he often showed poor sportsmanship by yelling at the referees and throwing his racket down when he lost a match. Such displays of temper made him unpopular with many tennis fans.

8. We are now faced with a number of serious problems in our metropolitan areas. One such problem is how to best help the thousands of homeless people.

9. During the past year, Chi has won 5,000 dollars in the lottery and a vacation to Tahiti in a drawing at his local supermarket. I wish I had such luck.

10. When you have just met someone, what types of personal questions should you avoid asking? The answer depends on what culture you are in. For example, in some cultures it might be acceptable to ask a woman how old she is, how much money she makes, or even how much she weighs, but in many cultures such questions are considered impolite.

Focus 7

Such versus Demonstrative Adjectives

MEANING

- Because **such** refers to a class or type of thing, *such* reference usually has a more general meaning than the demonstrative adjectives *this, that, these,* or *those* before nouns.
  - When Mr. Contentious came to our restaurant, he complained about the location of his table, criticized the menu, insulted the waiter, and failed to leave a tip. We hope we never again have to deal with . . .

Specific	Type
(a) this person. (Mr. Contentious)	**(b) such a person.** (anyone who would act the way that Mr. Contentious did)

- Two types of dinosaurs with birdlike hips were stegosaurs and ankylosaurs.

Specific	Type
(c) These dinosaurs . . . (stegosaurs and ankylosaurs)	**(d) Such dinosaurs** . . . (dinosaurs with birdlike hips including stegosaurs and ankylosaurs)

. . . were herbivorous.

- In the United States, it has become common for the media to report every little ailment that the president suffers and every medical treatment, however minor, he receives. Does the public really need . . .

Specific	Type
(e) this information? (information about minor ailments and medical treatment)	**(f) such information?** (information of a personal and insignificant nature, including minor ailments and medical treatments)

Exercise 10

Answer the following questions based on the examples in Focus 7.

1. Which words after *such* (person, dinosaurs, information) repeat a word in the preceding context? Which do not? How can you explain this difference?

2. Can you think of words that might be substituted for those occurring after *such* in the examples? Are they more general or more specific than the words in the examples? How do they change the meaning?

   EXAMPLE: *such a person* ⟶ *such a grouch* (more specific; describes Mr. Contentious negatively)

3. Often a modifier can be used to make a "class" word more specific. For example, *advanced* in "at such an advanced age" makes it clear that reference is to those ages late in life. In the examples in Focus 7, what modifiers could be added to define more specifically the words following *such*?

Exercise 11

1. For each of the word pairs below, think of one or more general terms that you could use to classify or characterize them.

   EXAMPLE: Word pair: football, hockey
   General terms: sports, spectator sports, violent sports, popular sports
   (a) love, anger
   (b) drug trafficking, murder
   (c) earthquakes, hurricanes
   (d) backgammon, chess
   (e) your choice (list related words): _____

2. Now select one of your general terms for each word pair. Add to each pair other words or phrases that could be classified by this term.

   EXAMPLE: Violent sports: *soccer, boxing*

3. Write a statement (one or two sentences) for each topic above. Use *such* plus the classifier term you selected to refer to items already stated. (The items could be the word pairs or words you added.)

   EXAMPLE: I know many people who love to go to football and hockey games. However, I don't enjoy watching *such violent sports.*

4. Discuss the difference in meaning that would result if you replaced *such* in each statement with a demonstrative adjective (*this, that, these, those*).

   EXAMPLE: However, I don't enjoy *those* violent sports.
   "*Such* violent sports" refers to any sports that are especially violent; "*those* violent sports" refers only to football and hockey.

Exercise 12

Identify and correct the errors or stylistically inappropriate reference forms in each of the following sentences. There may be more than one way to correct errors.

1. What did you think about this research? I disagreed with a lot of this research.
2. Our math teacher gave us a surprise quiz. Can you believe he would be this unkind man?
3. Many modern cities have both buses and subways. Traffic congestion is certainly reduced by those public transportation.
4. This year I took both an English course and a Spanish course. It was quite easy for me because French is my native language, and the two languages are similar.
5. I have a friend who likes to wear only two colors of clothing: blue and purple. She dresses in such colors every day.
6. One study says that male children do not pay as much attention to female children as they do to other males. What do you think about it?
7. Some people insist on giving advice even when it's not requested. Such an advice is generally not appreciated.
8. I am keeping the blue shirt I ordered from you. This shirt fit fine. However, I am returning the striped shirt because this was much too small.
9. In this paper I plan to discuss two emotions that all cultures share. The two emotions that all cultures share are joy and grief.
10. Did you hear her boast that she never has to study for her courses? The student misses the point of what an education means.

Activities

Activity 1

In teams, make up lists of statements that include both amazing facts and "untruths." Good sources for hard-to-believe facts are reference books such as *The Guinness Book of World Records* or *Ripley's Believe It or Not* as well as almanacs. Mix in with the amazing facts some of your own statements that are *not* true. Each team should then read their list of statements to another group. The listeners must agree on which ones they believe and which they don't believe. Score a point for each correct judgment as to whether a statement is true or not.

Activity 2

Write a paragraph comparing the language use of different groups based on variables other than gender. Consider differences you are aware of based on age, social status, occupation, geographical location, or education.

Activity 3

Write a letter to either a) a business to complain about unsatisfactory service or merchandise or b) one of your political representatives (e.g., the prime minister, a senator, the President) to voice your opinions about an issue that is important to you. Exchange your letter with another classmate. The classmate should check your use of reference forms to see if they are appropriate and then write a response to your letter, playing the role of the company or person to whom you addressed it.

Activity 4

Imagine that you have set up business as a Dog Consultant. This does not mean that you consult with dogs, but rather that you give advice to potential canine buyers about what types of dogs would best suit their interests and circumstances. Based on the information in the chart, suggest one or more breeds for each of the clients described after the chart. Use at least one *such* reference phrase in your recommendation to express the idea that dogs of the same breed share certain characteristics.

	Dog	Size	Behavior with Children	Characteristics
	Akita	Large	Excellent	Affectionate; excellent guard dog; easily trained
	Airedale	Medium	Very good	Sound temperament; easy to train; needs lots of exercise
	Boston Terrier	Small	Good	Affectionate; intelligent; needs daily brushing
	Bulldog	Medium	Very good	Good-natured; loyal; good watchdog
	Dachsund	Small	Excellent	Loyal; affectionate; good watchdog

	Dog	Size	Behavior with Children	Characteristics
	Dalmation	Large	Good	Good-natured; loyal; easily trained; needs lots of exercise
	Doberman	Large	Good with own family	Brave; loyal; superb guard dog
	German Shepherd	Large	Good with older children	Intelligent; excellent guard dog; trains well
	Pekinese	Toy	Not good	Loyal; brave; good watchdog
	Poodle	Toy to Very Large	Very good	Very intelligent; playful; very trainable
	Shi Tzu	Toy	Excellent	Happy; affectionate; daily grooming needed

Reprinted with the permission of Macmillan Publishing Company from THE HOUSEHOLD CHARTALOG by UltraCommunications. Copyright ©1989 by UltraCommunications.

EXAMPLE: *Client:* Kenji Hayashi
Situation: Wants a watchdog; has two small children
Recommendation: I would suggest either a bulldog or a dachsund. Such dogs are better with small children than Pekinese are, and they make good watchdogs.

Client	*Situation*
1. Paul Meyers	Elderly, admits to being grouchy; wants a small affectionate dog; it doesn't have to be good with children since he isn't very fond of them either.
2. Sandy Cole	Preparing for a marathon; wants a dog to accompany her on daily runs; doesn't have much time or patience to train it, though.
3. Nina Strenski	Has been burglarized twice; has three young children; needs a guard dog.
4. Benny Bruiser	Regards himself as extremely intelligent; wants his dog to be pretty smart too.
5. Doris Florendo	Would like a watchdog as she lives alone; however, it can't be very big since she has a small apartment.

Activity 5

Choose one of the sentences below to develop a paragraph. Then write the rest of the paragraph, creating a context appropriate for including the sentence. (The sentence could occur anywhere in the paragraph after the first sentence.)

(a) Those subjects just aren't worth studying.

(b) Those TV programs should be taken off the air.

(c) Such advice should be helpful to anyone visiting _____. (Choose a city or country to fill in the blank.)

(d) Such a person is to be avoided whenever possible.

(e) Such bad luck shouldn't happen to anyone.

Activity 6

As you do reading for other courses or for your own interests, write down examples of *such* reference that you find in a notebook. Include the *such* phrase and the phrase(s) or sentence(s) to which each refers. Make a note of the context (e.g., an explanation of a chemical process, a comment on people's behavior, a description of a product in an advertisement). At some point, you may want to compare your findings with the class to see the ways in which *such* reference is used in written texts.

Object Complements

Task

What will the world be like as we enter the third millenium in the year 2000? In a book called *Megatrends 2000*, John Naisbett and Patricia Aburdene describe economic, political, and social forces that they believe will transform the world, or, in some cases, American culture in the first part of the twenty-first century. Here are some of the predictions they make:

1. The English language will become the world's first truly universal language.
2. Nations will regard war as an obsolete way of solving problems, especially the "superpower" countries.
3. Even as peoples of the world communicate more closely, individual cultures will increasingly find their unique qualities important and seek to preserve racial, linguistic, national, and religious traditions.
4. The arts will replace sports as American society's dominant leisure activity; Americans will consider alternatives to attending sports events such as football and baseball.
5. The trend of the future in the global economy is "downsizing": producing and using smaller, lighter, and more sophisticated products (e.g., smaller computers, lighter building materials, electronic impulses used for financial transactions instead of paper).
6. In the first decade of the third millenium, we will think it quaint that women in the late twentieth century were excluded from the top levels of business and politics.
7. The world's nations will increasingly cooperate to address global environmental problems.

Which of these predictions, if any, do you consider almost a certainty by the beginning of the twenty-first century? Which do you think probable? Which do you find unlikely developments? Discuss with your classmates current evidence for or against these predictions. Then write a paragraph stating your opinions about one of these predictions.

Focus 1

Subject and Object Complements

FORM
MEANING

- **Subject complements** are noun phrases, adjectives (or adjective phrases), and prepositional phrases that complete predicates with *be* verbs. They are called subject complements because they describe subjects:

Subject	*be* verb	Subject Complement
(a) Korea	is	**Noun phrase** a Pacific Rim nation.
(b) New products	will be	**Adjective phrase** smaller and lighter.
(c) The roles of women	are	**Prepositional phrase** in transition.

- With *be* verbs, the subject complements express what the speaker or writer believes are facts about the subjects.
- **Object complements** describe the grammatical objects of sentences:

	Object	Object Complement
(d) We can call	Korea	**Noun phrase** a Pacific Rim nation.
(e) Many consider	smaller products	**Adjective phrase** better in several ways.
(f) The authors find	women's roles	**Prepositional phrase** in transition.

- Object complements often reflect the subject's perspective, belief, or observation about the object. The information in the complement may not be factual, and the speaker may not agree with it. For example, some people make think smaller products are better, but the speaker could disagree.
- Complements used with verbs such as *consider* and *find* may often be paraphrased by infinitive phrases or *that* clauses:
  - **(g)** Many consider smaller products **to be better.**
  - **(h)** The authors find **that women's roles are in transition**.

Exercise 1

Identify and underline each of the object complements in the following passage. State the noun or noun phrase that each refers to.

EXAMPLE: <u>an unlikely future event</u>

referent: *Megatrend 2000's* prediction about the arts replacing sports

(1)I think *Megatrend 2000's* prediction about the arts replacing sports an unlikely future event, for the near future anyway. (2)The authors present statistical information that shows Americans increasingly interested in visiting museums and galleries or attending concerts. (3)It's not that these trend forecasters consider spectator sports in jeopardy, but they do believe that Americans' desire to attend sports events will diminish. (4)While I find their statistics intriguing and their lists of facts impressive, I also find their conclusion somewhat unconvincing. (5)Perhaps their prediction will be reality some day, but at the beginning of the twenty-first century? (6)I'd call that a bit premature!

Focus 2

USE

Noun Object Complements

USE

- Noun object complements are used
  - to express events that name or designate a title or characteristic for the object:

Verbs	Examples
call　　name christen　proclaim declare　pronounce label　　term	**(a)** My little brother **named** his goldfish **Charley**. **(b)** The judges **declared** her **the winner**.

- to qualify the object:

Verbs	Examples
believe　find consider　imagine deem　　think	**(c)** They **consider** their son **a genius**. **(d)** We **found** Prague **a beautiful city**.

- We tend to use these verbs for description in more formal English or in literature:
  - **(e)** Stanley **thought** the nightwatchman **a strange character indeed**.
  - **(f)** She **imagined** herself **the queen of an ancient nation**.

129

● to describe an attribute resulting from an event or action:

Verbs	Examples
appoint crown elect make	**(g)** Mel's roles in those two movies **made** him **a star.** **(h)** The City Council **appointed** Maria **the chairperson.**

Exercise 2

Imagine that you have a very limited English vocabulary, and must communicate with others who have the same vocabulary. You can, however, create new names for things by combining words. For example, if you didn't know the word *school*, but you did know the words *place, learn,* and *people,* you could call a school "a people–learning place." Given the vocabulary list below, what could you name each of the following numbered items?

In your responses, use your new terms as object complements.

Vocabulary: **verbs:**   *move, make, play*
                    nouns: *place, house, machine, people, food, animal, water*
                    adjectives: *hot, cold, soft, hard, small, large, red, white*
                    adverbs: *fast, slow*

EXAMPLE: air conditioner
                    We could call an air conditioner a *"making-house-cold machine."*

1. cat
2. cherry Popsicle
3. microwave oven
4. gymnasium
5. refrigerator

6. swimming pool
7. fireplace
8. mashed potatoes
9. hippopotamus
10. sports car

Exercise 3

State your opinion of the following people, places, and things, using a noun object complement.

EXAMPLE: Babe Ruth   *I consider Babe Ruth* **one of the greatest baseball players.**
                    Montreal   *I would call Montreal* **a good city to live in if you don't mind cold winters.**

1. football
2. Picasso
3. a relative
4. Florida
5. a book you've read (choose one)

6. your hometown
7. anchovies
8. John F. Kennedy
9. a subject you've studied (choose one)
10. country western music

Focus 3

Active versus Passive Structures with Noun Complements

USE

- Like other active sentences, active sentences with noun object complements put more emphasis on the **agent** (performer of the action) expressed as the subject and less on the receiver of the action:

Agent	**Receiver**	**Complement**
(a) The senior class elected	Solange	president.

- Passive sentences put greater emphasis on the receiver and the result of the action and less on the agent:

Receiver	**Complement**	**Agent**
(b) Solange was elected	president	by the senior class.

- In passive sentences, we often delete the agent when it is already known to the listener/reader or is unimportant:

(c) Solange was elected president.

Exercise 4

Change the emphasis from the receiver of action to the agent in sentence (b) of each sentence pair below. Restate each agentless passive sentence, making an active sentence with an agent as the subject. The agent is stated in parentheses.

> **EXAMPLE:** (a) At the end of *The Wizard of Oz*, the weary adventurers discover the great wizard is only human. (b) The wizard is proclaimed a fraud. (Dorothy)
> *Dorothy proclaims the wizard a fraud.*

1. (a) My family just bought a sailboat. (b) On Sunday, the boat will be christened *Shady Lady*. (my grandfather)
2. (a) The Nobel Prize Committee finished their selections. (b) A Czech poet was announced the winner of one of the prizes. (the committee)
3. (a) For six months, geologists for an oil company have been trying to find oil off the coast of Alaska. (b) Last week the exploration was declared a failure. (the oil company)
4. (a) Both the Democratic and the Republican conventions will be held later this summer. (b) Senator Kim is considered the leading Presidential candidate. (the Democratic party)
5. (a) Karen and Albert got married today at City Hall. (b) They were pronounced husband and wife at exactly noon. (the judge)

131

Focus 4

Complementation with *As* and *For*

- Some verbs can take noun or adjective object complements only with *as* or *for*:

accept (as)	*recognize (as)*
describe (as)	*mistake (for)*
regard (as)	*take (as/for)*

- The object comes between the verb and *as* or *for*:

	Verb	Object	Complement
(a) Naoko	**regards**	her music teacher **as**	one of the most patient people she knows.
(b) Just	**take**	that comment **as**	a joke.
(c) Ramon	**mistook**	the compliment **for**	an insult.

- The verb *consider* can take *as* optionally.
  - **(d)** I considered you (**as**) my friend.
  - **(e)** We considered that town (**as**) a possible vacation spot.

Exercise 5

Complete the following statements with your opinions or information about yourself. Share responses with your classmates.

EXAMPLE: I regard *honesty* as one of my best qualities.

1. I regard _____ as one of my best qualities.

2. I consider _____ as the best reason to get a good education.

3. I would describe my personality as _____.

4. I accept _____ as one of my shortcomings.

5. I regard _____ as a waste of time.

Exercise 6

Ask other classmates their opinions about five things that could be described with noun object complements. Use verbs from either Focus 2 or Focus 4 for responses.

EXAMPLE: What do you think of okra?

Response: I would **describe** it **as a slimy food**.

What's your opinion of the book *Megatrends 2000?*

Response: I **find** it **interesting speculation about the future**, even though I don't agree with it all.

Focus 5

Adjective Object Complements

- Adjective object complements usually describe perceptions, judgments, and observations about the sentence object:

Verbs	Examples
consider find imagine prove think	**(a)** Dr. Salazar **considered** the research findings **invalid.** **(b)** I **find** *Megatrends 2000's* predictions about English **believable**. **(c)** Time **has proved** some of the predictions in the book **wrong**.

- Adjective object complements occur with the verbs *discover* and *find* (in its sense as a synonym of *discover*):

  (d) The police **discovered** the stolen car **abandoned**.

  (e) She **found** her home **intact** after the tornado struck.

- Adjective complements also occur with *make* to describe qualities resulting from events or actions:

  (f) All the confusion **made** her uncomfortable.

Exercise 7

What do you think about each of the following activities or ideas? Use adjective complements in your answers. The example shows a range of possible responses. Share your opinions with your classmates.

> **EXAMPLE:** saving a little money every month
>
> I consider it **wise** because you never know when you might need extra money.
>
> I would call it **sensible and disciplined**.
>
> I'd describe it as **difficult** unless you have a good income.
>
> For me, I'd call it **unrealistic**!

1. skydiving (jumping from a plane with a parachute on)
2. studying English grammar
3. making school noncompulsory after the age of 12
4. riding a motorcycle without a helmet
5. banning smoking in all public places
6. spelunking (exploring caves)
7. making alcohol illegal
8. creating schools for profit rather than having public schools

Exercise 8

Make a comparative assessment about five or more of the following pairs, using either a noun phrase or adjective phrase object complement.

> **EXAMPLE:** Julia Roberts and Jodi Foster (actresses)
>
> *I consider Jodi Foster **the better actress**.* (noun complement)
>
> *I find Julia Roberts **less talented**.* (adjective complement)

1. soccer and football
2. the East Coast and the West Coast of the United States
3. biology and geology
4. sushi and hamburgers
5. Madonna and Barbra Streisand
6. English and some other language
7. classical music and jazz
8. city vacations and country vacations
9. American films and films from another country
10. dogs and cats

Exercise 9

How do you think each of the situations below would make the persons mentioned feel? Use an adjective object complement in your response.

> **EXAMPLE:** Your dog runs away.
> *That would make me **very upset**.*

1. Your best friend is invited to make a guest appearance on a popular television talk show.
2. You see someone you met just a few weeks ago and you can't remember her name.
3. Your teacher gets a ticket for jaywalking from a policewoman. (crossing in the middle of the street instead of at the intersection)
4. Someone tells you that you look just like your mother or your father.
5. Your family receives word that you have won an award for academic excellence.

Focus 6

USE

Prepositional Complements

USE

- Prepositional complements typically qualify or describe feelings, discoveries, or observations about the sentence object:

	Object	Prepositional Complement
(a) The contest judges considered even though it was a few minutes late.	my entry	**on time**
(b) Sharon discovered	her car	**with one tire missing.**
(c) The police found	the robbery victim	**in a state of panic.**

Exercise 10

Imagine that you have reached the scene of a car accident shortly after it happened. The numbered statements below are your notes about what you saw. Give a report of the accident with prepositional object complements to make clear that the statements are your observations. Start your sentences with I + one of the following verbs: *find, notify, observe, consider.*

> **EXAMPLE:** The driver of the station wagon was in tears when I arrived.
> Report: *I found* the driver of the station wagon in tears when I arrived.

1. The sports car was on the northeast curb.
2. A telephone pole was on the ground in between the two cars.

3. Most of the front windshield of the station wagon was in small pieces on the street.
4. Part of a cellular telephone was under the sports car.
5. From what I saw, the driver of the sports car was at fault.

Focus 7

Object + Noun Complements versus Indirect Objects

MEANING

- Objects with noun complements after them look similar to indirect objects followed by direct objects:

Indirect Object	Direct Object	Meaning
(a) I gave my teacher	the report.	I gave the report **to** my teacher.
(b) I bought my friend	a gift.	I bought a gift **for** my friend.
Direct Object	**Noun Complement**	**Meaning**
(c) I consider my teacher	a good communicator.	I think that my teacher is a good communicator.

Although the forms are the same, the meanings are different.
- In most cases, these different structures occur with different verbs. There are, however, a few exceptions:
  - *Call, find,* and *make* occur with indirect objects:

	Indirect Object	Direct Object	Meaning
(d) We called	**him**	a cab.	We summoned a cab **for** him.
(e) We found	**Nancy**	a new watch.	We got a new watch **for** her.
(f) They made	**her**	a cake.	They baked a cake **for** her.

  - *Call, find,* and *make* also occur with noun object complements:

	Direct Object	Noun Complement	Meaning
(g) We called	**him**	**a genius.**	We said that he was a genius.
(h) We found	**Nancy**	**an entertaining speaker.**	We thought that she was a good speaker.
(i) They made	**her**	**the chair of the committee.**	They appointed her to the position.

Exercise 11

The numbered sentences below are ambiguous. Which completion would make sense if the sentence had a noun object complement? Which would fit if the sentence had an indirect object? Discuss the sentences in class.

1. My great aunt found the elderly man a charming partner.
   a. However, he insisted that he wanted to be alone and asked my aunt not to play matchmaker.
   b. She happily accepted his invitation to go on a cruise.
2. I called him a bell attendant.
   a. However, to my embarrassment, I discovered he was the manager of the hotel.
   b. However, they were all busy carrying up other people's luggage, so he had to wait to get to his room.
3. We made my little sister a pumpkin for Halloween.
   a. She put a candle in it and set it out on the porch.
   b. She looked really cute in her costume, although it was hard for her to walk very fast when she went trick-or-treating.
4. We found him a fox.
   a. He seemed both clever and sly.
   b. He had always wanted one for a pet.

Focus 8

FORM

Word Order Variation of Object Complements

FORM

- So far in this unit, you have used the pattern **object + object complement**. If the object is a long phrase, you can reverse the order:

Object Complement	Object	
(a) We declared	the winner	the person who came closest to guessing the number of beans in the jar.
(b) I find	questionable	the prediction that English will be the universal language.

Exercise 12

If you were looking for a furnished apartment to rent and had a good income, what would you consider necessary to have in it? Desirable? Not worth high rent? Undesirable? State your opinion about each of the features below, using a noun or adjective object complement. Vary the order of the object and complement based on the length of the object. Make up your own items for the last three.

EXAMPLE: a yard with a swimming pool, jacuzzi, and hot tub
> *I'd consider a necessity* a yard with a swimming pool, jacuzzi, and hot tub.

1. a personal gym with weights, aerobic machines, and a sauna
2. a frost-free refrigerator that dispenses ice cubes and crushed ice
3. a large-screen color TV
4. a king-size waterbed with satin sheets
5. wall-to-wall pure white carpeting in every room
6. a dishwasher
7. an answering machine that lets you retrieve messages away from home
8. (your choice)
9. (your choice)
10. (your choice)

Activities

Activity 1

In England, they call an elevator "a lift" and the hood of a car "the bonnet." On the East Coast, they call a carbonated soft drink "a soda," but in the Midwest they call it "pop." What other examples do you know of regional or national differences in English vocabulary? Discuss some of the ones that come to mind with your classmates. You might also interview people from other regions or countries to find out differences they are aware of.

Activity 2

You have just been elected the mayor of a small town. You now have to appoint people for each of the positions listed below. You may choose either famous people or members of your class for each of the positions. Write a list of your appointments and, after each, a reason for your choice. If you wish, add other positions you'd like to include in your town.

> **EXAMPLE:** I'd appoint Zachary the small claims court judge because he has a lot of patience.

dogcatcher

head of sanitation department

divorce court judge

small claims court judge (small claims = cases about minor things such as a faulty car repair)

police chief

traffic control officer

justice of the peace (to perform marriages)

city sports director

entertainment director for official functions

speech writer

Activity 3

If you were going to create an ad for a "Personals" column (where people advertise for partners or companionship), what would you write about yourself? Using object complements, make up an ad that emphasizes your stellar qualities and that would attract the perfect person for you! Here's an example of this type of ad:

> Looking for that special person. I consider myself very charming, unusually intelligent, in excellent health, and overall quite fascinating. You would find me a good listener and an entertaining conversationalist.

Activity 4

This activity is a cross between two games: To Tell the Truth and Fictionary. In groups of three, find pictures of animals with names that you don't think others would know. Bird and fish guidebooks are good sources for this. One person on your team will tell the rest of the class (or another group) the real name of the animal, using an object complement structure. The other two persons in your group will make up names. Each of you will try to convince the others that your name is the correct one. After you've given your names, they have to guess which is the true name. Here's an example:

A: (Showing picture of a bird) We call this bird **a large-beaked mosquito eater.**

B: No, actually we call this bird **a yellow-bellied sap sucker**. (*B* is giving the real name.)

C: Well, the truth is that we call it **a bleary-eyed cactus climber**.

After the others have voted on who they believe is telling the truth, reveal the real name and give one point for a correct guess.

Activity 5

Which occupations do you consider glamorous? Which ones do you think are boring? Exciting? Lucrative? With some of your classmates, brainstorm a list of occupations. Then create adjective categories to classify them. Summarize your results for the rest of the class, using object complements.

> **EXAMPLE:** We found the following jobs exciting: [list]; we consider the next group of occupations hazardous to your health: [list]; we find ourselves unable to agree on these occupations: [list].

Activity 6

Make up five pairs of people, places, or things to compare, as was done for Exercise 8. Give your list to another classmate or group to write sentences comparing them. In your comparisons, use noun or adjective object complements and the following verbs: *find, consider, think, regard as, describe as.*

> **EXAMPLE:** English class and chemistry class
> Response: I consider English *more enjoyable.*
> solar energy and nuclear power
> Response: I regard solar energy as *a better way* to provide energy.

Activity 7

Write an opinion essay on one of the following topics:

(a) Elaborate one of the opinions you expressed about a prediction made in *Megatrends 2000.*

(b) State your opinion about two competing theories or ideas. Examples: creationism vs. evolution; strict vs. lenient regulations in high school; women should have equal job opportunities vs. women should stay at home.

(c) Describe your feelings about a person in your life you admire or appreciate.

Use object complements in expressing your opinions.

Relative Clauses
Modifying Subjects

Task

Inventions such as the refrigerator, vacuum cleaner, lawnmower, etc. have simplified life for many households. Not all inventions simplify, however. Rube Goldberg has created a few inventions that actually make life more complicated.

For this task, you will focus on one of these inventions—a postage stamp applicator. Pair up with a classmate and take turns describing the invention below.

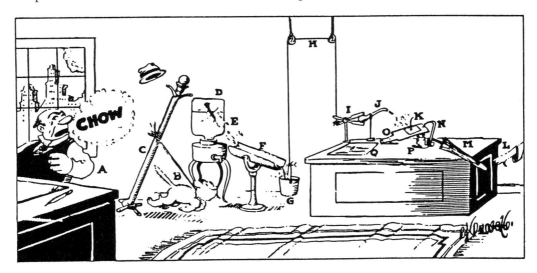

From Charles Keller, *The Best of Rube Goldberg*. 1979. Used by permission of the publisher: Prentice Hall/A Division of Simon and Schuster, Englewood Cliffs, N.J., 1979.

Here is some information that you will refer to in the description:

A man sneezes.

A dog is tied to a coat rack.

A water cooler container breaks.

Water spills from a trough into a bucket.

A nutcracker squeezes a bulb on a medicine dropper.

A woman grabs an umbrella.

A spring throws a paddle over on an envelope.

While either you or your partner looks at the invention and describes one stage of the operation, the other writes down what he or she hears. Here are a couple of sentences to get started:

1. The man who sneezes frightens a dog.
2. The dog that is tied to the coat rack runs when the man sneezes.

Your and your classmates should take turns describing the operation until the description is complete.

Focus 1

FORM

Review of Restrictive Relative Clauses

FORM

- A relative clause modifies a noun phrase in a main clause:

Noun Phrase	**Relative Clause**

that
The contract ~~the contract~~ was signed yesterday *is now valid.*

main clause

- In this example, the relative pronoun *that* replaces the noun phrase *the contract* in the relative clause. In other words, the subject of the relative clause has been embedded into the subject of the main clause. This makes the relative clause subordinate to the main clause.
- There are four general types of relative clauses. They may modify main clause subjects or objects. Relative pronouns may be subjects or objects in their own clauses.

Noun Phrase in Main Clause	Relative Pronoun in Relative Clause	Example
(a) Subject	Subject	S S *The contract* **that** was signed yesterday is now valid.
(b) Subject	Object	S O *The contract* **that** he signed yesterday is now valid.
(c) Object	Subject	O S I have not read *the contract* **that** was signed yesterday.
(d) Object	Object	O O I have not read *the contract* **that** he signed yesterday.

142

- This unit will focus on relative clauses modifying subjects in main clauses. These clauses can have various relative pronouns and functions:

Type of Noun in Main Clause	Relative Pronoun	Function of Relative Pronoun	Example
person	**(a)** who/that	subject	A person **who/that** sells houses is a realtor.
	(b) whom/that	object of verb	The broker **whom/that** she hired is very experienced.
	(c) whom	object of preposition	The employees **to whom** she denied a pay raise have gone on strike.
	(d) whose	possessive adjective	Clerks **whose** paychecks were withheld must go to the payroll office.
(thing or animal)	**(e)** that/which	subject	The mansions **that/which** were sold last week were expensive.
	(f) that/which	object of verb	The dog **that/which** they chose as their company mascot was a terrier.
	(g) whose	possessive adjective	The division **whose** sales reach the million-dollar point will win a bonus.

Exercise 1

The passage below describes another Rube Goldberg device. Underline all of the relative pronouns. Then, identify and write down the function of the relative pronoun in each relative clause (e.g., subject, object of verb, etc.). There may be more than one relative clause in a sentence.

EXAMPLE: Sentence (1) *that*—subject function

(1)A kerosene lamp <u>that</u> is set near the window has a high flame which catches on to the curtain. (2)A fire officer whom a neighbor calls puts out the flame with a stream of water which the officer shoots from outside the window. (3)The water hits a short man who is seated below the window. (4)He thinks it is raining and reaches for an umbrella which is attached to a string above him. (5)The string is attached to a wooden platform that is beside him. (6)The upward pull of the string on one side of the platform causes an iron ball that is resting on the other side of the platform to fall down. (7)The ball is attached to a second string that wraps around a pulley and connects to a hammer. (8)The downward pull of the ball on the second string causes a hammer to hit a plate of glass. (9)The crashing sound of the glass causes a baby pup that is in a cradle to wake up. (10)In order to soothe the pup, its mother rocks the cradle in which the pup is sleeping. (11)The cradle, to which a wooden hand is attached, is on a high shelf above a stool. (12)A man who is sitting on the stool below the shelf and whose back is positioned in front of the wooden hand smiles as the wooden hand moves up and down his back.

Here is a picture of the device that was just described. What do you think this device is used for?

Focus 2

Restrictive Relative Clauses Used for Specificity

MEANING

- A relative clause makes the meaning of the noun it modifies more specific.
  (a) Less Specific: A man walked into the office.
  (b) More Specific: A man who was wearing a pin-striped suit walked into the office.
  (c) Less Specific: The secretary can type 70 words per minute.
  (d) More Specific: The secretary whom Dolores hired yesterday can type 70 words per minute.

Exercise 2

You are starting a small business in which you produce solutions made from simple ingredients. Make a statement about each liquid's remarkable abilities, using the cues provided.

> **EXAMPLE:** hair rinse (lemon juice and camomile flowers)
>
> A rinse *that consists of lemon juice and camomile flowers* makes your hair shiny and silky.

1. hangover remedy (water and fruit juice)
2. invisible ink (cobalt chloride, gum arabic, and water)

3. perfume (English Lavender, alcohol, water)

4. tanning oil (tincture of iodine, olive oil)

5. facial masque (powdered milk, avocado)

Exercise 3

For each of the phrases below, write two sentences. Use a *who* relative clause for one and a *whose* relative clause for another.

EXAMPLE: will not get a job

A person who is not skilled will not get a job.

A person whose interview skills are poor will not get a job.

1. will not pass the course
2. will not win a beauty contest
3. will fail to make friends
4. can never take a vacation
5. is not prepared to run a race
6. should not drive a car

Exercise 4

Robert Thornton, in his book *Lexicon of Intentionally Ambiguous Recommendations* (New York: Meadowbrook, Inc., 1988), cleverly advises employers about how to write letters of recommendation for less than exemplary employees without offending them. To do this, he suggests writing lines that have double meanings. For example, a sentence like "He's a difficult man to replace" can mean that it is impossible to replace him because he is so good, or it can mean that he will resist if you even try to replace him.

Match the following ambiguous recommendations with their real meanings. Then follow the model to write sentences that clarify what the employer actually wants to say but has decided not to.

EXAMPLE: Recommendation: He's a man of great visions.

Real meaning: He hallucinates.

The employee ＿＿＿＿＿＿ is/does/did not really ＿＿＿＿＿＿ but ＿＿＿＿＿＿.

The employee who hallucinates on drugs does not really have great vision but could be a drug addict or crazy.

Recommendations

1. He's a man of many convictions.
2. A man like him is hard to find.
3. He's always trying.
4. She merits a close look.
5. Her input was always critical.
6. He's not the type to run away from responsibility.

Real Meanings

a. Don't let her out of your sight.
b. He'll get on your nerves.
c. She's never had a good word to say.
d. He'll walk very quickly, though.
e. He disappears frequently.
f. He's got a prison record a mile long.

Exercise 5

Today has been a very bad day for one business executive named Ann. The following sentences describe what went wrong. Change the second sentence in each pair to a relative clause introduced by *whom*.

EXAMPLE: The secretary made ten errors. Ann asked him to type the letter.
The secretary whom Ann asked to type the letter made ten errors.

1. The associate called in sick. Ann was working with him on a major project.
2. The graphic artist decided to quit. Ann hired her two years ago.
3. The accountant required extra receipts in order to file the claim. Ann telephoned her.
4. The lawyer lost the court case. Ann hired him to represent her.
5. The client canceled the appointment. Ann was supposed to play golf with him.
6. The banker denied her loan application. Ann deals with him.
7. The supervisor criticized the work of two new employees. Ann admires her greatly.

Focus 3

FORM

Review of Reduced Restrictive Relative Clauses

FORM

- We can reduce relative clauses in several ways:
  - We can delete relative pronouns if they function as objects in relative clauses.
    - **(a)** A letter (which) he sent was never received.
    - **(b)** The accountant (whom) he corresponded with was well qualified.
    - **(c)** NOT: The accountant with (whom) he corresponded was well qualified.
  - We can delete relative pronouns in relative clauses with *be* as an auxiliary verb in progressive or passive constructions. In these cases, both the relative pronoun and *be* are deleted.
    - **(d)** The cafeteria (which **is**) situated at the end of the hall is closed.
    - **(e)** The water (that **was**) left in the pitcher evaporated.
    - **(f)** The customer (who **is**) complaining to the manager is my aunt.
    - **(g)** A child (who **had been**) playing on the equipment was asked to leave.
  - We can delete relative pronouns in relative clauses with *be* + preposition phrases. Both the relative pronoun and *be* are deleted.
    - **(h)** Chairs (which **are**) in the conference room cannot be moved.
    - **(i)** A board member (who **was**) at the meeting decided to resign.

146

- In relative clauses with *be* + adjective, we can delete the relative pronoun and *be,* but the adjective must be moved before the noun in the main clause.

    (j) Clients ~~(who are)~~ (interested) will always return. = Interested clients will always return.

    (k) NOT: Clients interested will always return.

    (l) A girl ~~(who was)~~ (beautiful) stepped into the room. = A beautiful girl stepped into the room.

    (m) NOT: A girl beautiful stepped into the room.

- In relative clauses with *have (not)* (= possession or lack of possession), we can delete the relative pronoun and replace *have* or *have not* with *with* or *without.*

    (n) People ~~(who have)~~ credentials can be hired. *[with]*

    (o) The workers ~~(who did not have)~~ identification were asked to leave. *[without]*

Exercise 6

Look again at the diagram in the Task and analyze the operation of the stamp applicator. Look particularly at how the objects and the dog were affected during the process. Then write a sentence containing a relative clause with an object relative pronoun that has been deleted.

    EXAMPLE: (B) The dog (that) *the man frightened ran out of the room.*

1. (C) The hat rack ———————————————— .

2. (D) The ice-water container ———————————— .

3. (I) The nutcracker ————————————————— .

4. (J) The medicine dropper ————————————— .

5. (K) The postage stamp ————————————— .

6. (M) The umbrella ————————————————— .

Exercise 7

Reduce relative clauses in the following paragraphs where possible.

> **EXAMPLE:** A person who is assertive can develop great self-confidence.
>
> A person who has self-confidence can do anything.
>
> *An assertive person can develop great self-confidence.*
>
> *A person with self-confidence can do anything.*

1. It is easy to spot the person who is the decision-maker in an American business meeting. A person who is leaning toward the other members of the group and who is giving direct eye contact is usually the decision-maker.

2. Body language that is composed of many gestures can communicate 80% of a message. A voice that is friendly, a posture that is relaxed, and a handshake that is firm all convey assertiveness.

3. Anyone who has been working in the same position for a while will receive criticism at one time or another. Criticism that is unfair needs to be countered. Criticism that is constructive needs to be acknowledged.

4. A person who is dressing for success in an American business setting should worry about the material, color, and style of his or her clothing. Generally, a suit that is coordinated and that is made of an expensive wool appears most authoritative. Colors which are dark transmit more authority.

5. If you are someone who feels unsatisfied with your personality, do not be discouraged. Anyone who can develop a mental picture of what he or she wants to be can change. Anyone who has the determination to keep this image in his or her mind on a day-to-day basis will see his or her new personality become a reality.

Focus 4

USE

Informal and Formal Speech Modifications of Relative Clauses

USE

- The use or omission of object relative pronouns may vary according to formality:

Informal

↑

(a) The person he hired did not work out.
(b) The person *that* he hired did not work out.
(c) The person *who* he hired did not work out.
(d) The person *whom* he hired did not work out.

↓

Formal

- In formal written English, the preposition should always precede the object relative pronoun.

Informal

↑

Formal

(e) The coworker she listens to is not here today.
(f) The coworker **who** she listens *to* is not here today.
(g) The coworker **whom** she listens *to* is not here today.
(h) The coworker **to whom** she listens is not here today.

Exercise 8

Rewrite the following dialogue in a less formal style.

Luca: The accountant to whom we talked last month should be calling.

Maya: Is he concerned about the bank account which we closed in January?

Luca: No, he is calling about personal taxes that you haven't paid yet.

Maya: Oops! That's one person whose call I'd better not miss!

Exercise 9

Write responses to the following statements about your own life using *whom, which,* or *that.*

EXAMPLE: Describe the people with whom you have worked.
The people with whom I have worked are serious and diligent.

1. Describe a sport which you enjoy.
2. Describe a person with whom you have disagreed.
3. Describe a chore that you disliked when you were a child.
4. Describe a gift for which you are grateful.
5. Describe a person on whom you rely.
6. Describe a person whom you will see tomorrow.

Exercise 10

Imagine that you purchased some items at a store and then realized when you got home they were unsuitable. Explain your situation to a friend. Delete the relative pronoun in your statements.

EXAMPLE: *The suede shoes I purchased* last night are too tight.

1. curtains
2. cassette tape
3. electric blanket

4. color TV
5. raincoat
6. toothpaste

Exercise 11

Identify with a check mark the sentences for which the preposition should precede the object in formal usage. Then, embed each relative clause in a main clause of your own creation. The underlined part should be the identical noun in each case. ★Note that it is not possible to move particles in phrasal verbs such as *turn out, break down, come across*, etc.

EXAMPLES: The boss put off the meeting until Monday. (*off* is a participle, not a preposition)

The meeting that the boss put off until Monday is important.

We wrote to four employees last week. ✔

The four employees to whom we wrote last week will not be rehired.

1. She wrote for the associate editor at the publishing company.
2. The Chairman of the Board spoke to the Board of Directors.
3. The supervisor put down the rebellion.
4. I have learned about all of the company rules.
5. He put out his cigarette in the "No Smoking Area."
6. The secretary consulted with a supervisor.
7. The paycheck will be sent to the staff on May 1.
8. He brought up several good points at the meeting.
9. The salesperson handed in the report.

Exercise 12

Below you will find information about four homes which celebrities sold for various reasons. Write sentences about this information using as many relative clauses that modify subjects as you can. A few examples have been done for you.

EXAMPLES: The mansion that the oil tycoon sold for $2,000,000 has three fireplaces.

The penthouse whose owner was a world-renowned physician sold for $4,000,000.

VILLA

Owner: country western singer
Reason for sale: divorce
Price: $3,000,000

Enter through walled gates and find sophisticated hacienda. 2-acre home with horse corral. 6 bedrooms/8 baths. Pool, tennis, jacuzzi, spa.

PENTHOUSE

Owner: world-renowned physician
Reason for sale: death
Price: $4,000,000

Towering 20 stories above downtown. 3 bedrooms/4 bathrooms. Close to Music and Performing Arts Center. Modern design. 20 minutes from beach.

MANSION

Owner: oil tycoon
Reason for sale: bankruptcy
Price: $2,000,000

European chateau with exquisite detailing. 50 miles from the coast. 4 bedrooms/4 bathrooms. 3 fireplaces. View of lake. Very private acre far from bustle.

BEACHHOUSE

Owner: corporate executive
Reason for sale: job move
Price: $5,000,000

On the beach. 3 acres + private 120 ft. of beachfront. Bright and spacious. Pool room. 3 stories. State-of-the-art sound/video system. 5 bedrooms/4 bathrooms. Atrium library.

Activities

Activity 1

Define the following business-related terms, using relative clauses.

> **EXAMPLE:** per capita income
> The average annual income that a particular population earns is called "per capita income."

bankruptcy

sales commission

exchange rate

gross national product

prime rate

mortgage

Activity 2

Write a letter of complaint to a store or company about a defective item that you bought. Write at least two sentences with relative clauses modifying main clause subjects.

> **EXAMPLE:** Dear Sir:
> The toaster that I bought in your store last week is defective. The selector lever that determines how dark the toast will be is stuck...

Activity 3

The Task described an unusual invention—a postage stamp applicator. Try to draw a similar diagram for another device. Then describe the various features of the device in the same manner that you did in the Task. Choose one of the following ideas or one of your own.

fly swatter

door opener

pencil sharpener

cheese cutter

window washer

adjustable chair

Activity 4

Find an outline, chart, or flow diagram in a magazine, newspaper, or a textbook that has various levels or interdependent steps. Then try to describe the diagram using at least three sentences with relative clauses modifying main clause subjects.

> **EXAMPLE:**

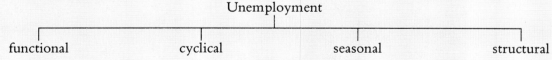

> Unemployment
>
> functional   cyclical   seasonal   structural

There are several types of unemployment. A person who is functionally unemployed has lost his or her job and is looking for another. A person who is a victim of a temporary downswing in the trade cycle is cyclically unemployed. A person who is seasonally unemployed means that he or she is not working during a particular season, e.g., the holiday season or the harvesting season. Someone who is permanently unemployed, and this is probably the most tragic, is a victim of a structural change in society which has made his particular field or skill obsolete.

Source: *Hutchinson Pocket Encyclopedia*. London: Helicon, 1987.

After you have written your description, reduce all of the relative clauses that can be reduced according to the rules discussed in this unit.

10

Relative Clauses
Restrictive Versus Nonrestrictive

Task

Imagine that you and your classmates are attending your English class reunion ten years from today. Break up into small groups and write skits about what you will say to each other. Think about what occupations (high fashion model, airline pilot, insurance salesperson, etc.) or activities (charity organizations, sports, clubs, etc.) you will be involved in at that time. Also consider what your marital status will be (married, single, or divorced). Make sure that each person in your group says at least three lines which contain some of the following types of information:

Information Types	**Examples**
1. Remind others about who you are or about who other people are.	"Hey, there's Ahmed, who used to sit in the back of the room."
2. Recall how you remember your classmates.	"Aren't you the one who was always clowning around?"
3. Wonder about people whom you do not recognize or who are absent from the reunion.	"Where's Paula, who used to get A's on all of the tests?"

153

4. Brag about your new job.	"Now I am working for Rothwell International, which incidentally is one of the biggest engineering companies in the world."
5. Impress others with your own or your spouse's accomplishments.	"My wife Delia is vice-president of a firm that markets pharmaceutical products worldwide."
6. Tell others where you are now living.	"I now live in Cali, which is in the northern part of Colombia."
7. Inject information about your spouse or family.	"My husband is at home taking care of our five children. He is a liberated man, which is what I like."

After you have finished writing, perform your skits in front of the class. Save your skits for a later exercise.

Focus 1

Restrictive versus Nonrestrictive Relative Clauses

**FORM
MEANING**

- Restrictive relative clauses are necessary to identify the head noun (the noun they describe).

(a) I admire **professors** *who lecture well.*	The relative clause limits the type of professors that are admired. Not all professors are admired—only the ones who lecture well.

- Nonrestrictive relative clauses add additional or incidental information.

(b) I admire **my professors**, *who lecture well.*	The relative clause does not aid in the identification of the professors. The possessive adjective *my* makes it clear which professors are being talked about. The relative clause gives supplementary information.

- In written English, one or more commas (or sometimes parentheses) set off nonrestrictive relative clauses from other parts of the sentence. In spoken English, a nonrestrictive relative clause is set off by pauses and a drop in pitch.
  - **(c)** The old cafeteria (which still looked the same) had been decorated with balloons and streamers.
  - **(d)** I was happy to see Professor Thompson (pause) who was my physics professor.

- Head nouns of nonrestrictive relative clauses are usually of the following types:
  - unique, unusual, or one-of-a-kind nouns:

    (e) When I return home to Chicago from Frankfurt, I will telephone **my mother**, who lives in Joliet.

  - proper nouns:

    (f) She will pick me up at **O'Hare**, which is the International Airport of Chicago.

  - previously mentioned nouns or nouns familiar by context:

    (g) She usually meets me at **the baggage claim**, which exits onto the street, rather than at the gate inside the building.

  - nouns that refer to all of a class or can be preceded by *any* or *all*:

    (h) It will be great to get home and taste Mom's home-cooked meals. I hate **airline food**, which is generally overcooked and unappealing.

Exercise 1

In the following pairs of sentences, punctuate the sentence that contains the nonrestrictive relative clause. Then, explain why the information contained in the nonrestrictive relative clause is additional or incidental to the meaning of the sentence.

EXAMPLE: **a.** The smog that covers Mexico City is very unhealthy.

b. Smog, which is a fog that has become polluted with smoke, is a pervasive problem in many large cities.
(This relative clause is nonrestrictive because it adds additional information to a general statement about all smog.)

1. **a.** The teacher who got married last year will not be returning this year.
   b. Your teacher who has studied English linguistics previously can help you with your grammar problems.
2. **a.** People who drink should not drive.
   b. People who require water to survive may someday run out of pure water.
3. **a.** Today I'm going to a church which is on 10th Street.
   b. Today I'm going to church which is on 10th Street.
4. **a.** The world which is actually pear-shaped was once thought to be flat.
   b. The world that our children will inherit will hopefully be a peaceful one.
5. **a.** Samuel Clemens who was a famous American author wrote *Tom Sawyer.*
   b. Samuel Clemens was the famous American author who wrote *Tom Sawyer.*
6. **a.** Yesterday we went to "The City" which is another way to say San Francisco.
   b. Yesterday we went to the city which is directly south of San Francisco.

Exercise 2

Reread the sample sentences in the Task. Write *N* next to the nonrestrictive relative clauses and *R* next to the restrictive relative clauses.

EXAMPLES: Aren't you the one who was always clowning around? *R*

I now live in Cali, which is in the northern part of Colombia. *N*

Then reread your group's skit and identify the restrictive and nonrestrictive clauses in the same way.

Focus 2

FORM

Positioning of Nonrestrictive Relative Clauses

FORM

- In Focus 1 in Unit 12, you learned that restrictive relative clauses may modify main clause subjects or objects. Nonrestrictive relative clauses can also modify main clause subjects or objects and they can have various relative pronouns and functions:

Subject of Main Clause	Subject of Relative Clause	
(a) *My tenth class reunion, which*		was held in Atlanta, was very entertaining.

Object of Preposition in Main Clause	Object of Relative Clause	
(b) I visited with *my old boyfriend,*	*whom*	I hadn't seen for ten years.

Object of Main Clause	Object of Preposition in Relative Clause	
(c) I also saw *my old biology teacher,* to	*whom*	I owe my love for science.

Subject of Main Clause	Possessive Adjective	
(d) *The former cheerleaders,*	*whose*	names I could not remember, led us all in some old football cheers.

- In nonrestrictive relative clauses, *which* (versus *that*) is used for nonhuman references.

  (e) Atlanta, which is in Georgia, is a great place for a reunion.

  (f) NOT: Atlanta, that is in Georgia, is a great place for a reunion.

Exercise 3

Put brackets around all of the nonrestrictive relative clauses and circle the head noun for each one.

(1)(*The Specialty Travel Index,*) [which is well known to travel agents], should be consulted more often by the layman as well. (2)Anyone who is interested in traveling to rare or exotic places will enjoy thumbing through this volume. (3)436 tour operators advertise in this index. (4)Entries are organized by subject matter and geographical emphasis and are cross-indexed for your convenience. (5)For example, if you want to visit Mauritius, which is an island in the Indian Ocean, you only need to look under *M* in the geographical index, which is alphabetically organized. (6)If you would like a tour which specializes in "soccer," "solar energy," "space travel," or "spectator sports," you only need to look under "S" in the subject index. (7)"Chocolate tours," "whale-watching tours," "holistic health tours," and "military history tours" are just a few more of the some 176 special interest tours that are listed in this index.

(8)Irma Turtle, who is one of the advertisers in *The Specialty Travel Index*, began her career in an interesting way. (9)Bored with her job in business, she decided to start a tour-guiding service. (10)Travelers on her first tour explored Algerian rock paintings, which had been discovered in the Central Sahara. (11)Today she leads other exciting tours. (12)For example, the tour of "Pantanal" of Brazil, which contains the world's largest wetlands, offers views of 600 species of tropical birds. (13)Another tour utilizes Berber guides to take travelers through the Atlas Mountains, which are in Morocco. (14)Finally, Jivaro Indians (whose ancestors were headshrinkers) now lead adventuresome tourists through the Ecuadorian Amazon.

(15)The next time you are planning a trip, don't forget to consult *The Specialty Travel Index*, which describes the unusual tours of Irma Turtle and other one-person travel operators.

Adapted from Arthur Frommer, *Arthur Frommer's New World of Travel*, 1988. Used by permission of the publisher: Frommer Books/Prentice Hall Press/A Division of Simon & Schuster, New York.

Exercise 4

Read the following story. Circle the relative pronouns, and add commas where needed.

EXAMPLE: Last year I took an airline trip from Frankfurt, (which) is in Germany, to Chicago, (which) is in Illinois.

(1) The trip which lasted 15 hours was the longest trip I had ever taken. (2) Seated on my left was a lady who had a baby. (3) The lady whose name was Mary talked nonstop to me and the man on her left the entire 15 hours. (4) Apparently, she was going to visit her husband whom she hadn't seen for quite a long time. (5) Her husband who is in the army is stationed in Frankfurt. (6) The last time that he was home was two years before when he came home for the Christmas holiday. (7) Mary told us that her husband had never even seen the baby whose name was Billy. (8) Although Mary was very nice, I did get very tired of her chatter which did not seem to end. (9) My one break occurred when the movie *Found in Space* which is a science-fiction film was shown on the screen in front of us. (10) The man who was sitting on Mary's left side and I gladly watched the whole picture from start to finish with our earphones firmly in place!

Exercise 5

You are a tourist visiting Vancouver, British Columbia, on your own. To entertain yourself, you took several tours listed below. Describe the tours you took in a letter to a friend. Use as many as nonrestrictive relative clauses as you can.

EXAMPLE: March 4, 19____

Dear Owen,

I've really been enjoying myself in Vancouver. I've already spent more than $400 on tours, but it has been worth it. First, I took the City of Vancouver Tour, which was a five-hour tour of important sights around the city. . . .

Regards,
Your Name

Name: City of Vancouver Tour
   Price: $35.00
   Description: five-hour bus tour of important points of interest: Stanley Park, Queen Elizabeth Park, Capilano Suspension Bridge
Name: Dinner Theatre Evening
   Price: $70.00
   Description: bus transportation, six-course dinner, tip, and ticket to play "A Streetcar Named Desire"

Name: Victoria City Tour
  Price: $75.00
  Description: 12-hour bus ride to the capital of British Columbia, ferry toll included, world famous Butchart Gardens
Name: Whistler Resort
  Price: $100.00
  Description: one day of skiing at world-class resort, lunch, ski rentals not included
Name: Fishing Trip
  Price: $175.00
  Description: half-day of fishing on Pacific Coast, private boat, guide, tackle, bait, license, lunch

Focus 3

USE

Nonrestrictive Relative Clauses in Definitions

USE

- Nonrestrictive relative clauses are often used for defining terms in sentences.

  Pink eye, *which is an eye inflammation*, is contagious.

  In order to join components of an electronic circuit, you need **to solder**, *which involves applying a soft metal that melts.*

Exercise 6

Imagine you are a travel buff and write sentences describing your standard equipment. Use a nonrestrictive relative clause with a subject relative pronoun for each item.

EXAMPLE: lap-top

I always bring a lap-top, *which is a portable computer.*

1. luggage cart
2. money belt
3. travel iron
4. adapter

5. travel calculator
6. detergent
7. a Swiss army knife
8. book light

Focus 4

Comment on Whole Proposition

USE

- Some nonrestrictive relative clauses comment on a whole proposition in the main clause. These are used most often in informal conversation.

    (a) Last week I returned from a three-week cruise, which was a relief!

    (b) I had eaten too much food, which was a big mistake.

Exercise 7

Tell your friends about some of your travel mishaps, using nonrestrictive relative clauses. In your comments, use one of the following adjectives:

disappointing	frightening	painful
exasperating	tiring	embarrassing

> **EXAMPLE:** When my brother and I were traveling in Mexico City, we got stuck in a traffic jam, *which was very exasperating*.

1. My friend and I wanted to save money in Venice, so we walked from the train station

   all the way to our hotel, _____ .

2. While hiking in the Sierra Nevada Mountains, I almost fell off a mountain trail, _____

   _____ .

3. On my bike tour of Canada, I fell down and broke my leg, _____

   _____ .

4. Once I left my traveler's checks in my hotel room and did not have any way to pay

   my bill at an expensive Tokyo restaurant, _____

   _____ .

5. On my last trip to Paris, I had to wait three extra hours to catch my return flight

   home, _____ .

Focus 5

Quantifying Expressions

FORM
USE

- Some nonrestrictive relative clauses comment on head nouns that describe an entire group or a portion of a group of persons or things. These are formed by combining quantifiers (such as *all of, most of, none of, many of, each of, two of,* etc.) with a nonrestrictive relative pronoun in the clause.

  (a) I have five phone calls to make, **all of which** should be done immediately.
  (b) I need three volunteers, **one of whom** must be very strong.

Exercise 8

You are packing clothes to take on a trip. Comment on the present state of your wardrobe, filling in relevant information and using quantifiers in each nonrestrictive relative clause below.

EXAMPLE: I have *two* pairs of shoes, *one pair of which* must be repaired.

1. I have _____ shirts, _____ are in good condition.

2. I have _____ sweaters, _____ could be too heavy for traveling.

3. I have _____ pairs of stockings, _____ might need mending.

   Can you mend them?

4. I have _____ pairs of pants, _____ might be suitable for traveling.

5. I have _____ suits, _____ will be versatile enough for day and

   evening wear.

Exercise 9

In order to get information about hotels on Matland Island, which you are going to visit, you consult a travel guide that contains the following table. In pairs, discuss which hotels have certain features. (An X indicates that the hotel has this feature. An O indicates that the hotel does not have this feature.) Use as many nonrestrictive relative clauses as possible.

EXAMPLE: Matland Island features three hotels, all of which accept credit cards.

Hotels	Matland Hotel	Overlook Lodge	Green Tree Inn
accepts credit	X	X	X
has TV	X	X	O
has suites	O	O	X
has pool	O	O	O
has refrigerators	O	X	X
has room fans	X	O	X
has ocean views	O	X	O

Activities

Activity 1

In groups of three, name three facts that are common knowledge about the following people. Then, create one or more sentences that contain relative clauses about these individuals.

John Lennon

Abraham Lincoln

Marilyn Monroe

Joan of Arc

Winston Churchill

Mahatma Gandhi

Mother Teresa

Fidel Castro

EXAMPLE: John Lennon (lead singer of the Beatles, born in Liverpool, England, was killed in New York) John Lennon, *who was the lead singer of the Beatles,* was born in Liverpool, England.

Activity 2

In one paragraph, describe the location, dates, people, and activities associated with a reunion you have attended. Use as many nonrestrictive relative clauses as possible.

EXAMPLE: Last summer I attended my family reunion, *which was held on a ranch in Montana* . . .

Activity 3

Interview five members of your class about various aspects of their native countries. Record that information below.

Name	Native Country	National Foods, Sports, Dances, etc.
1.		
2.		
3.		
4.		
5.		

Write several sentences about your classmates that incorporate this information.

EXAMPLE: Nicola, who is from Brazil, likes to dance the samba.

Activity 4

You are preparing to be a tour guide of your hometown or the city you are presently living in. Think of five sights that are in a two-mile radius and write the script you would use, incorporating as many details as possible about the sight, such as historical origin, age, unique aspects, etc.

EXAMPLE: We are now looking at Lafayette Park, which is one of the best-groomed parks in Washington, D.C. Straight ahead is the White House, whose construction began in 1792. To our right is the Treasury Building, which was built near the White House so that a former President, Andrew Jackson, could "keep his eye on those handling the cash..."

Activity 5

Reread the text on computers in Exercise 7, Unit 6. Look for as many examples as you can of nonrestrictive relative clauses used for defining terms. Hint: one example appears at the beginning of the second paragraph.

11

Relative Adverbials

Task

How much do you know about the city and region where you live? Consult with your classmates to see who can provide the following information:

HISTORY:

- the year or decade when the city was founded (or century if your city is very old)
- the places where people first settled, created neighborhoods, or developed commercial centers
- the reasons why people settled in your area, both in its earliest stages as a community and later during its development

NOW:

- the location of buildings where the city government operates
- the places where you think visitors would most like to go
- the reasons why you think visitors would enjoy spending time in your city or area
- the times when buses or other public transportation start and stop running each day
- the times when rush hour begins and ends if you live in a city with lots of traffic
- the areas where traffic is usually heaviest
- how most people get to work in your area (public transportation, car, bicycle, etc.)
- the areas where the most people live
- the places where it's fun to go shopping
- the places where you can go for a picnic
- the places where you can find peace and quiet outdoors
- the restaurants where you can get the best food
- how to get to the nearest airport from your school
- how a tourist could get information about sightseeing in your area

Focus 1

Relative Adverbs versus Relative Pronouns

MEANING

- Relative adverbs *where, when, why,* and *how* can replace prepositions + relative pronoun *which* when these prepositions convey meanings of place, time, reason, or manner.

Meaning	Relative Adverb	Replaces Prepositions
place	**where**	*at, in, to, from*
time	**when**	*in, on, during* + *which*
reason	**why**	*for*
manner	**how**	*in*

(a) A spa is a place $\left\{ \begin{array}{c} \textbf{to which} \\ \textbf{where} \end{array} \right\}$ you can go either to exercise or to relax.

(b) Summer is the season $\left\{ \begin{array}{c} \textbf{during which} \\ \textbf{when} \end{array} \right\}$ many people take vacations.

(c) A reason $\left\{ \begin{array}{c} \textbf{for which} \\ \textbf{why} \end{array} \right\}$ some people move to large cities from small towns is to find job opportunities.

(d) I don't really understand the way $\left\{ \begin{array}{c} \textbf{in which} \\ \textbf{how} \end{array} \right\}$ you solved this equation.

- *Where, when,* and *why* can all follow the head nouns they modify. If *how* replaces *in which,* however, the noun must be deleted in standard American English:

(e) Correct: I like **how** you wrote your paper.

(f) NOT: I like **the way how** you wrote your paper.

Exercise 1

Substitute relative adverbs for prepositions + *which* whenever possible. Make other necessary changes. The first one has been done as an example. Discuss why in some cases a relative adverb cannot replace a relative pronoun.

1. The beginning of a new year is a time during which many Americans decide to make changes in their life-styles.

   Substitution: The beginning of a new year is a time *when* many Americans decide to make changes in their life-styles.

2. On January 1, the day on which resolutions for the new year are often made, we hear people vowing to lose weight, quit smoking, or perhaps change the way in which they behave toward family or friends.

3. Those who want to shed pounds may go to weight-loss centers; these are places which offer counseling and diet plans.

165

4. Others may join a health club at which they can lose weight by exercising.

5. Still others choose a less expensive way to lose weight: they just avoid situations in which they might snack or overeat.

6. People who want to quit smoking may contact organizations that can help them to analyze the times at which they have the greatest urge to smoke and to develop strategies to break the habit.

7. Those who decide to change their behavior toward others may also seek professional help, to find out the reasons for which they act in certain ways.

8. Most people are sincere about their promises at the time at which they are made; however, by February, many New Year's resolutions are just a memory!

Focus 2

FORM

Relative Adverbials Following Head Nouns

- One form of clause with relative adverbs has a **noun** before the adverb. This noun is called a **head noun** because it is the head of the clause which follows and describes it:

Head Noun +	**Relative Adverb** +	**Clause**
a place	where	you can go to exercise

- **The head noun** is often a general word such as *place, time,* or *reason,* but it can also be a more specific one, especially for places and times.

  (a) <u>**A place**</u> **where we can get good ramen** is just around the corner.

  (b) Elba is <u>**the island**</u> **where Napoleon was exiled.**

  (c) I'll always remember <u>**the day**</u> **when astronauts first landed on the moon.**

  (d) We read about <u>**the period**</u> **when plagues spread throughout Europe.**

  (e) <u>**One reason**</u> **why the hummingbird needs such a speedy metabolism** is that it loses body heat rapidly.

  (f) Do you know <u>**the reason**</u> **why a character weakness is called "an Achilles heel"**?

- Note that the head noun can be definite (*the* + noun) or indefinite (*a, one* + noun):

Definite	**Indefinite**
the day when **the reason** why	**a place** where **one reason** why

- As stated in Focus 1, when *how* is used, you must delete the head noun (e.g., *the way*) — so *how* adverbial clauses may only follow one of these patterns in standard English:

  (g) Citizens of a country should learn $\left\{ \begin{array}{c} \textbf{the way} \\ \textbf{how} \end{array} \right\}$ their government functions.

  (h) NOT: Citizens of a country should learn **the way how** their government functions.

Exercise 2

Identify each of the head nouns in Focus 1. What other phrases could you substitute for these head nouns? Are your substitutions more general or more specific in meaning than the original ones?

EXAMPLE: A spa is *a kind of health club* where. . . .
(more specific)

Exercise 3

A. Match each of the time periods in the first column with an event in the second column. Then make sentences, using relative adverbials + an appropriate head noun.

EXAMPLE: 1887   Sir Arthur Conan Doyle wrote the first Sherlock Holmes story.

1887 was *the year when* Sir Arthur Conan Doyle wrote the first Sherlock Holmes story.

1. 1961	**a.**	Whitcombe L. Judson invented the zipper
2. August 10	**b.**	most people are fast asleep
3. 3:00 A.M.	**c.**	many couples get married in the United States
4. Mesozoic Era	**d.**	Russian cosmonaut Yuri Gagarin orbited the earth.
5. 1891	**e.**	Ecuadorians celebrate Independence Day
6. June	**f.**	dinosaurs roamed the earth

B. Now match places with events. Again, make sentences using an adverbial clause with an appropriate head noun. Try to use nouns other than *place* if possible.

EXAMPLE: Florida, Missouri   Mark Twain was born here.

Florida, Missouri, is *the city where* Mark Twain was born.
(Note that *here* is deleted.)

1. Ankara	**a.**	You can get a pastrami sandwich here.
2. the kidneys	**b.**	Bats can often be found here.
3. New Zealand	**c.**	Turkey moved its capital here from Constantinople.
4. basement	**d.**	Maori is spoken here.
5. deli	**e.**	Junk is often stored here.
6. caves	**f.**	The water in your body gets regulated here.

C. For this part of the exercise, match reasons to statements. Again, give a sentence for each match.

> **EXAMPLE:** Crime   Many people move from large cities because of this.
>
> Crime is *one reason why* many people move from large cities.

1. aerobic exercise
2. surprise endings
3. the chance to "turn over a new leaf"
4. computer malfunctions
5. beautiful foliage
6. allergic reactions

a. People look forward to the New Year for this reason.
b. Some people avoid shellfish because of this.
c. Many love autumn for this reason.
d. People enjoy the stories of Guy de Maupassant because of this.
e. People take up jogging or bicycling to get this.
f. Students sometimes don't get papers in on time for this reason.

D. Finally, match processes or methods in the first column to statements in the second. Make sentences for your matches, using the head noun *way* or the relative adverb *how*.

> **EXAMPLE:** Adding an *-ed*   This is the way you form the regular past tense in English.
>
> Adding an *-ed* is the way you form the regular past tense in English.

1. studying history
2. journeying by covered wagon
3. an opinion poll
4. repeating commands and giving rewards
5. not smoking
6. talking with stones in his mouth

a. You teach a dog to lie down in this way.
b. You can help to prevent heart disease by doing this.
c. Most early American pioneers made the trip West in this way.
d. The Greek orator Demosthenes learned to speak clearly in this way.
e. People survey the attitudes of large populations in this way.
f. You can prepare for a career as a lawyer in this way.

Exercise 4

Complete each of the blanks with appropriate words or phrases about yourself.

> **EXAMPLE:** <u>The shoreline</u> is a place where <u>I go to watch the birds.</u>
>
> <u>Starting with my conclusion</u> is the way I <u>often begin to write a draft for a paper.</u>

1. _____ was the year when I _____ .

2. _____ is the place where I _____ .

3. The reason why I don't like _____ is _____

_____ .

4 The way I get to school/work is _____ .

5. _____ is a/the day when I _____ .

6. _____ is a reason why I _____ .

7. A _____ where I _____ is _____ .

8. _____ is how I _____ .

Focus 3

FORM

Relative Adverbs without Head Nouns

FORM

- Another pattern with relative adverbs has no head noun:

	Relative Adverb +	**Clause**
(a) This is	where	we will meet tomorrow.
(b) That was	when	I decided to go to bed.
(c)	Why	she left is a mystery.
(d) She explained	how	to change a tire.

Exercise 5

Restate each of the sentences you made in Exercise 3 without the head nouns (except for the ones in Part D for which you used *how*).

EXAMPLE: 1887 was when Sir Arthur Conan Doyle wrote the first Sherlock Holmes story.

Focus 4

Head Nouns without Relative Adverbs

**FORM
USE**

- Another pattern uses only the head noun and its modifying clause:

Head Noun	+	Clause
the time		I get up in the morning

(a) Conran's is **a store I go to for kitchen supplies.**

(b) November 1 is **the day most Catholics celebrate All Saint's Day.**

(c) **The reason spiders can spin perfect webs** is based on their instincts, not learned behavior.

(d) Public transportation is **the way many city dwellers get to work.**

- With specific head nouns expressing **place**, you must often include a direction preposition:

(e) Dominic's is the restaurant I go **to** for pizza.

(f) NOT: Dominic's is the restaurant I go for pizza.

(g) Denver is the city I live **in**.

(h) NOT: Denver is the city I live.

- The preposition is often optional in informal English with the head noun *place*:

(i) Dominic's is the place I $\begin{Bmatrix} \textbf{go} \\ \textbf{go to} \end{Bmatrix}$ for pizza.

Exercise 6

Restate the sentences you made in Parts A, B, and C of Exercise 3, using the pattern in Focus 4: head noun + adverbial clause. Add or delete words as necessary.

EXAMPLE: Florida, Missouri, is *the city Mark Twain was born in.*

Focus 5

Contexts for Relative Adverb Patterns

USE

- It is not yet clear in what contexts native speakers of English use the relative clause patterns that have been outlined in this unit. We can, however, note some tendencies to use one pattern over another in certain contexts. The following are some general guidelines.

- In standard English, use a head noun when the clause is the object of a preposition:

  (a) We celebrated our anniversary at **the place** where we first met.

- The pattern **head noun + relative adverb + clause** tends to be used:

  - to focus on or emphasize the time, place, reason, or manner:

    (b) Today is **a day when** all nations will want to join in prayers for peace in the world.

    (c) This is **the place where** most of my family lived at one time or another.

  - when the meaning of the head noun is specific:

    (d) I know **a nursery where** you can get beautiful orchids.

  - when the context is more formal (such as written versus spoken English):

More Formal	Less Formal
(e) Barton's is **a store where** one can find expensive cameras discounted.	**(f)** Barton's is **where** you can get a fantastic deal!

  - when the head noun is the subject of a sentence rather than part of the predicate:

Subject	Predicate
(g) A place where you can buy film is at the intersection of Hammond and Belknap.	**(h)** The corner of Hammond and Belknap is **where** we usually meet.

  In the example (g), *a place where* helps to introduce new information.

- We tend to use the pattern **relative adverb + clause** (omitting the head noun) when:

  - the head noun phrase has a general meaning rather than a specific one:

General Meaning	More Specific Meaning
the place the time the reason	the building the first day the primary reason
(i) I know **where** you can get help with your writing. **(k)** She told us **when** to show up.	**(j)** I saw **the building where** the fire started. **(l)** I remember **the first day when** I arrived in the United States

- you can infer the head noun from context or from general knowledge:

    (m) Greece is **where** the Olympics **started.** (Inferred: the country)

    (n) 551 B.C. is **when** Confucius **was born.** (Inferred: the year)

- the context of speaking or writing is informal:

Informal	More Formal
(o) Why she did that is a mystery to me!	**(p)** Let us examine **the reasons why** language loss may occur.

These examples show how the degree of formality may overrule the tendency for head nouns to appear in the subject position and to be omitted in predicate position.

- We tend to use the pattern **head noun + clause** in contexts similar to ones for head noun + relative adverb + clause:

    - head nouns with more specific meanings

        (q) Let us know **the day you will arrive.**

    - more formal contexts such as written English

        (r) Please state **the reason you are seeking this position.**

    - subject position

        (s) A **place you can get information** is across the street.

This pattern, however, has less emphasis on the information introduced than the pattern with both head noun and relative adverb.

Exercise 7

Decide whether the form given in (a) or (b) would be more typical or appropriate for each context, even though both may be grammatically correct. Use the guidelines given in Focus 5. Explain your choices.

1. Ethel: Max! What did you just turn off that light for?
   Max: Dear, if you'll wait just a minute, you'll find out _____

   (a) the reason why I did it.

   (b) why I did it.

2. _____ was one of the happiest days of my life.

   (a) The day I got married

   (b) When I got married

3. _____ is right across the street.

   (a) A place where you can get a great cup of coffee

   (b) Where you get a great cup of coffee

4. Oh, no! Can you believe it? I forgot _____

   (a) the place where I put my keys again.

   (b) where I put my keys again.

5. _____ is that they don't have enough spare time.
   (a) One reason many people feel stress
   (b) Why many people feel stress
6. I would now like all of you in this audience to consider _____
   (a) the many times your families offered you emotional support.
   (b) when your families offered you emotional support. It's hard to count them all, isn't it?
7. Let me show you _____
   (a) the way this compact disc player works.
   (b) how this compact disc player works.
8. Ms. Cordero just told us _____
   (a) the time when we should turn in our papers.
   (b) when we should turn in our papers.
9. Last year my family took a trip to see _____
   (a) the house where my great-grandfather grew up.
   (b) where my great-grandfather grew up.
10. _____ an etching is produced is by using acid to "bite" lines into a metal plate, which is then printed.
   (a) The way
   (b) How

Focus 6

USE

Relative Adverbs in Descriptions of Time and Place

USE

- We often use relative adverbs in descriptions of places and periods of time. These descriptions sometimes appear at the end of sentences, set off from the main clause by a comma, because they are non-restrictive.
  - Sometimes we repeat the head noun or a form of it in the part set off by a comma:
    (a) It was a beautiful April **day, a day when** wispy clouds raced across the shoreline and signs of spring were everywhere.
  - A general noun before the relative adverb may refer to the noun in the main clause:
    (b) They left the war-torn **city, a place** where they had never known peace.
  - In other cases, we use only the noun of the main clause. This is similar to a nonrestrictive clause with a relative pronoun:
    (c) I'll always remember with fondness my old **neighborhood, where** folks sat out on their front porches on long hot summer nights, sipping cool drinks, telling tales about the past, and listening to the music of the crickets.

Exercise 8

Complete the following sentences with descriptions based on your experiences. Use the information in parentheses for some blanks.

1. A very important day for citizens of my country is ———————— , a day when

——— .

2. One of my favorite places is ————————————————————————— ,

   a place where ——————————————————————————————————————

   ——— .

3. I'll never forget (day/year) ———————— , when ———————————————— .

4. To me, one of the most beautiful places in the world is ———————— , where

——— .

Exercise 9

Imagine that you run a travel agency that is currently offering special fares to the cities in the chart below. Based on the information in the chart, write sentences that offer your opinions on where and/or when the following people should travel. Use relative adverbs *where* or *when* in giving your advice. Two examples are given for the first one.

1. Mr. Wallace wants to vacation in an Asian country that is warm in the winter.

   Advice: I'd recommend Singapore, where the average high temperature in January is 86 degrees Fahrenheit.
   OR If Mr. Wallace doesn't like cold weather, he should avoid Tokyo in January, when the average high temperature is 47 degrees Fahrenheit.

2. Mr. and Mrs. Lu are planning to take a trip to Buenos Aires sometime this year. They'd like to go when it's cool; they hate hot weather.

3. Ms. Simms wants a Christmas vacation in a warm place but not one with a high elevation because she has trouble breathing at high altitudes.

4. The Valencia family wants to know when the best time of the year to visit Moscow is.
5. Mr. and Ms. Brinton want to know where they could go to find cool temperatures in July.

City	Country	Elevation (ft.)	Average High Temperature (Fahrenheit)	
			January	July
Auckland	New Zealand	89	73	56
Buenos Aires	Argentina	505	85	57
Mexico City	Mexico	7,340	66	74
Moscow	Russia	505	21	76
Nairobi	Kenya	5,971	77	69
Reykjavik	Iceland	92	36	58
Singapore	Singapore	33	86	88
Tokyo	Japan	19	47	83

Source: *The World Almanac and Book of Facts 1990*, New York: Pharos Books

Activities

Activity 1

Did you know that some parts of your tongue can be more sensitive to certain tastes than other parts? The picture below shows sensitive areas for the four basic tastes: salty, bitter, sweet, and sour. In a paragraph, describe the sensitivity location for each taste; use at least two relative adverb clauses.

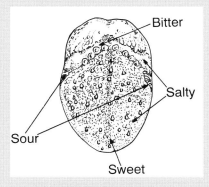

Activity 2

How would you complete statements that begin as follows?

I'd like to know the date (day, year, century, etc.) when. . . .
I 'd like to find out the place (country, city, etc.) where . . .
I wish I knew the reason(s) why . . .
I am interested in finding out how . . .

Generate a list of statements, using each of the relative adverbs above (with or without head nouns) to express things you'd like to know. Use the patterns given to begin your sentences. Share your statements with others in your class to see if anyone can provide the answers.

Activity 3

Make lists of places and times/dates as was done in Exercise 3, either individually or in teams. Then present the items on your list one by one to others who must define or identify the word or phrase in some way with a relative adverb phrase. (If you prefer to do this as a competitive game, you could set time limits for responses and award points.) The following are a few examples of items and responses.

Place/Date/Time	Possible Response
February 14	That's a day when people exchange valentines.
Switzerland	It's a country in Europe where skiers like to go because of the Alps.
Trattoria	It's a restaurant where you can get Italian food.

Activity 4

With a classmate, take turns interviewing each other about dates and places that have been important or memorable in your lives. These could be times and locations of milestone events such as birth and graduation, but they could also include a few humorous incidents or dates/places that may not seem so important now but were when you were younger. (For example, 1982 was the year when I broke my leg playing Frisbee; I'll never forget a trip to Florida, where I first saw the ocean.) Make a list of your interview findings and report a few of them orally to the class, using relative adverb clauses in some sentences. (In addition to *when* and *where,* you might also use relative adverb *why* in giving reasons why a date or place was important.)

Activity 5

Create a booklet providing information for tourists or new students about the city where you now live. Use some of the categories provided in the Task as headings for your guide (For example, "Places Where You Can Go for Entertainment") and/or make up others you think would be useful (For example, "Places Where You Can Get the Best Pizza"). You could divide the project so that individuals or small groups would each be responsible for a section or two of the guide.

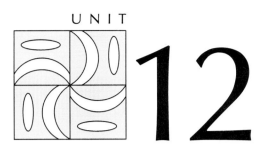

12

Reference Adjectives and Adverbials

Task

Study the following picture sequence.

Tell or write a story about the sequence, using at least eight of the following phrases. When you are finished, compare your narrative with the one found in Exercise 13.

monthly paycheck   identical bill
responsible parent   single bill
mere child   remorseful child
northeastern city   distant skyline
commercial ship   principal diet
rightful owner

> **EXAMPLE:** It was payday. Before coming home, a father cashed his monthly paycheck and...

Focus 1

MEANING

Attributive versus Predicative Adjectives

MEANING

- Consider the position of the adjective *red* in the following sentences:
  (a) The dress that is **red** is beautiful.
  (b) The **red** dress is beautiful.
- These two sentences have about the same meaning. However, the adjective in the first sentence is predicative (follows the noun), and the adjective in the second sentence is attributive (precedes the noun).
- Most adjectives (of size, shape, condition, age, and color) can appear in either position.
  (c) The fruit that is **ripe** should be picked. The **ripe** fruit should be picked.
  (d) Put the pieces that are **round** in the jar. Put the **round** pieces in the jar.
- A few adjectives change meaning when positioned predicatively versus attributively.

Example	Meaning
(e) The child is **sorry**.	The child is apologetic.
(f) The **sorry** child is dressed poorly	The condition of the child is unfortunate.
(g) The guardian is **responsible** for the mishap.	The guardian should take the blame and is accountable for what happened.
(h) The **responsible** guardian waited patiently.	The guardian is trusted or depended upon.

Exercise 1

Read the following pairs of sentences and discuss the difference in meaning of the identical adjectives.

EXAMPLE: **(a)** I would like to meet a particular woman.

(b) I would like to meet a woman who is particular about her appearance.

The first option means that you want to meet a specific woman that you have in mind. The other option means that you want to meet a woman who tries to maintain a nice appearance.

1. **(a)** Each car has individual compartments.
   (b) The inn has an art deco room and an early American room. In fact, each room in the inn is individual.
2. **(a)** Tom is the regular milkman.
   (b) Tom is a milkman who is regular about his deliveries.
3. **(a)** We have bought the basic plan.
   (b) We have bought the plan which is basic to our success.
4. **(a)** He has a certain disposition.
   (b) He is certain about what he saw.
5. **(a)** The proper owner has arrived.
   (b) The owner is proper when he converses with the tenants.
6. **(a)** The whole team applauded his return.
   (b) The team feels whole again.
7. **(a)** I'm looking for a specific book.
   (b) Most books about how to write a novel are too general. I'd like a book that is specific.
8. **(a)** There was an apparent misunderstanding.
   (b) There was a misunderstanding that was apparent to everyone there.

Focus 2

MEANING

Reference Adjectives: Showing Rank

MEANING

- Most adjectives can be both attributive and predicative. A small set of adjectives is only attributive, however. These are called **reference adjectives.** One group of reference adjectives shows the importance or rank of the noun.

His $\begin{cases} \textbf{main} \\ \textbf{prime} \\ \textbf{principal} \\ \textbf{chief} \end{cases}$ occupation was engineering, but he enjoyed inventing gadgets on the side.

Exercise 2

Discuss with your classmates the main activity of the following workers. Try to use a variety of ranking adjectives from Focus 2.

EXAMPLE: Fumigator

A fumigator's chief activity is to kill insects and other pests in people's homes.

1. lifeguard
2. taxidermist
3. appraiser
4. pediatrician
5. sanitary engineer
6. clown
7. contractor

Focus 3

MEANING

Reference Adjectives: Showing Lawful or Customary Relationships

MEANING

- Another group of reference adjectives shows that something or someone is recognized by law or custom.

(a) The $\left\{\begin{array}{l}\textbf{lawful}\\\textbf{legal}\end{array}\right\}$ heir does not deserve the inheritance.

(b) The devoted housekeeper is the $\left\{\begin{array}{l}\textbf{rightful}\\\textbf{true}\end{array}\right\}$ heir.

Exercise 3

Ask a classmate the following questions.

> **EXAMPLE:** What type of legal identification do you carry?
> I carry my driver's license.

1. What is your legal date of birth on your birth certificate?
2. What is the true name of Mark Twain?
3. What are the lawful responsibilities of a judge?
4. Who is the rightful heir to the British throne?
5. What legal action has someone you know (or a well known person) taken against someone else?
6. What is the true name of "The Big Apple"?

Focus 4

MEANING

Reference Adjectives: Time Relationships

MEANING

- The following reference adjectives qualify the time reference of the noun:

(a) The $\left\{ \begin{array}{l} \text{original} \\ \text{previous} \\ \text{latter} \\ \text{former} \\ \text{present} \\ \text{future} \end{array} \right\}$ occupant lived in New York for ten years.

(b) The **late** owner died of cancer this year.

Note that *late* has a different meaning here than not being on time. It refers to someone who has recently died.

Exercise 4

Imagine that you have just purchased a home designed by a famous architect, who originally lived in the house. Since then, the house has had several different occupants. Make sentences about the present and former occupants of the house, according to the information in the following chart.

> **EXAMPLE:** The original occupant of the house was Franklin Sperry, who incidentally also designed the house.

Dates	Occupant	Occupation
1965–1970	Franklin Sperry	Architect
1970–1971	Jessica Sperry(Sperry's daughter)	Student
1971–1980	Jean Londa	Movie Star
1980–1981	Jessica Sperry-Green	Interior Designer
1981–1990	Forest Green (Jessica's now deceased husband)	Sculptor
1990 to present	You	Your occupation

Focus 5

Reference Adjectives of Frequency

MEANING

- Some reference adjectives relate to frequency.

I subscribe to a(n) {
Sunday
daily
weekly
quarterly
yearly
annual
} journal.

Exercise 5

Identify and write down the usual frequency of the following types of publications.

EXAMPLE: professional journal
It's usually a quarterly publication.

1. telephone book
2. fashion magazine
3. newspaper

4. news magazine
5. tabloid
6. college yearbook

Focus 6

Reference Adjectives: Showing Location

MEANING

- Another group of reference adjectives gives the geographical reference of the noun:

The {
rural
urban
Southern
} condition is worsening.

Exercise 6

Discuss the native foods and specialties of the various regions of the United States in class, using the information in the following chart. Which region's food are you most familiar with? Which region's specialties appeal to you most? Which three regions have one native food in common? If you could choose one region to live in because of the food, which would it be?

> **EXAMPLE:** I like the vegetables and seafood of the Southern region.

Native Foods and Specialties of Regions in the United States		
Region	**Native Foods**	**Specialties**
The West	artichokes, olives avocados, figs, dates, lemons chili peppers pinto, kidney, and navy beans	enchiladas, tacos Caesar salad chowmein, chop suey chicken-fried steak
The Northwest	wild berries and fruits wild honey bay shrimp, wild game nuts (walnuts, hickory nuts)	pancakes sourdough bread roast beef oxtail stew
The Midwest	freshwater fish wild game corn, beans, and squash wild rice	sauerkraut and dumplings sausages and pot roast hot dishes rice pudding
The Northeast	maple sugar and syrup wild game (turkey and duck) cranberries soft-shell crab	corned beef sandwiches baked beans apple pie clam chowder, boiled lobster
The South	yams, black-eyed peas greens (turnips, kale, collard) peanuts, pecans crab, shrimp, crawfish	key lime pie jambalaya and gumbo grits and spoon bread creole chicken

Focus 7

Reference Adjectives: Relating to Uniqueness

MEANING

- Other reference adjectives show the uniqueness of the noun:

  (a) She was the { **only** / **sole** } survivor of the shipwreck.

  (b) Fortunately, a **single** life jacket buoyed her to shore.

  (c) From that point on, she lived a **solitary** life on the island.

Exercise 7

Sometimes comparisons can be made between two seemingly different objects or ideas. Write your own comparisons for the following noun phrases below.

    EXAMPLE: solitary death

        A solitary death *is like a leaf falling to the ground with no one to catch it.*

1. single candle
2. single heart
3. only child
4. sole right

5. solitary existence
6. sole survivor
7. only hope

Focus 8

Reference Adjectives: Showing Previous Mention

MEANING

- Another group of reference adjectives is used to show previous mention of a noun.

  (a) first mention   I saw a funny *television show* on Monday.

  (b) second mention   The { same / very / exact / self-same / identical / precise } *television show* was replayed on Tuesday.

Exercise 8

Most people can recall a coincidence where something happened which they were not expecting. The pictures in the Task referred to such an event—it was a coincidence that the very bill the little boy lost turned up in the belly of the fish he was to eat. The following statements will help you recount coincidences from your own life to your classmates. Use as many different adjectives from the previous exercise as you can.

> **EXAMPLE:** You and someone else bought or wore the same outfit.
>
> I wore a beautiful blue satin dress to the school prom. I was really surprised when my best friend showed up wearing the identical blue dress.

1. You had just enough money to buy something.
2. You or someone else discovered you had a name in common.
3. You discovered you were related to someone else.
4. You discovered that you or someone else had an unusual hobby in common.
5. In a faraway place, you met someone from your hometown.
6. The timing of one event coincided well with the timing of another event.
7. Some other coincidence from your own experience.

Focus 9

MEANING

Reference Adjectives Used for Identification

MEANING

- Some other reference adjectives give you identifying information about the noun.
    - **(a)** **Environmental** law is a relatively new field.
    - **(b)** NOT: Law that is environmental is a relatively new field.
    - **(c)** He is an **atomic** scientist.
    - **(d)** NOT: He is a scientist that is atomic.
    - **(e)** John just entered a **medical** school.
    - **(f)** NOT: John just entered a school that is medical.

Exercise 9

Answer the following questions with an *adjective + noun* occupation, field, or place.

EXAMPLE: Who cleans teeth?
A *dental hygienist.*

1. What field investigates electrical circuitry?
2. Who designs automobile engines?
3. Where can people with mental problems get help?
4. What field investigates political issues?
5. Who helps patients restore movement after an accident or illness?
6. Where can people learn a trade?
7. What field investigates the origin of different customs and cultures?
8. Who trains future movie stars to act?
9. Where can students apply for loans at a university?

Exercise 10

Define the following terms.

EXAMPLE: dental school
This is a school where people train to be dentists.

1. environmental design
2. social work
3. professional athlete
4. psychiatric aide
5. administrative office
6. theological school

Focus 10

MEANING

Reference Adjectives
Used as Intensifiers

MEANING

- Some reference adjectives intensify or emphasize the noun in the following ways:

(a) That is an **utter** disaster.	= absolute, entire
(b) He was a **total** stranger.	= complete, entire
(c) It is a **mere** coincidence.	= only, nothing more than
(d) I have never seen such a **sheer** fraud.	= undiluted, pure

Exercise 11

Fill in *utter, total, mere,* or *sheer* in the following sentences about a trip. In some cases, more than one choice is possible.

EXAMPLE: Our guided tour of Spain turned out to be a(n) <u>utter</u> disaster last summer.

1. Because our tour guide was a(n) _____ novice, he was a(n) _____ bore and we missed some of the best sights.

2. It was _____ coincidence that we ran into our neighbors, the Whites, in Barcelona and they gave us some better suggestions for the remainder of the trip.

3. Because our guide was a(n) _____ fool, we decided to take off on our own.

4. Fortunately, with a(n) _____ phone call to the travel company, we recovered half of our expenses of the trip.

5. The second half of our trip was a(n) _____ contrast to the first part.

6. It was _____ genius to rent a car.

7. Where we had gotten a(n) _____ glimpse of the scenery, we now had a(n) _____ feast for our eyes.

8. Where we had been scheduled to stay a(n) _____ day in a city, we could now stay as long as we wanted.

9. It was a(n) _____ challenge to make all our own decisions about when and where we wanted to go.

10. The _____ truth of this story is that making our own travel plans was well worth the effort.

Focus 11

Using Adverbs to Minimize or Approximate

MEANING

- Some adverbs function like adjectives when they precede the noun phrase.
  - Some adverbs minimize or downgrade the noun.

(a) I did not realize that he was $\begin{cases} \textbf{just} \\ \textbf{merely} \\ \textbf{only} \\ \textbf{simply} \end{cases}$ a boy.

- Other adverbs show approximation or lack of completion.

(b) But she is $\begin{cases} \textbf{almost} \\ \textbf{nearly} \\ \textbf{practically} \end{cases}$ a woman.

Exercise 12

Engage in short dialogues with your classmates, following the pattern provided. Complete the response to the question with one of the adverbs in the previous Focus.

EXAMPLE: Q: Why can't he bring me my bill?
A: He's just the busboy.

1. Why is she acting so crazy?
2. Why can't he get more work done?
3. Why hasn't that doctor found a cure for my illness?
4. Why won't you wear that emerald ring?
5. Why won't they talk to us?
6. Make up your own question.

189

Exercise 13

The following story describes the pictures in the Task. Rewrite the story, replacing each numbered blank with a different adjective and noun. Try to use as many adjectives from this unit as possible.

It was payday. Charles Dawson, a (1)<u>nuclear physicist</u>, cashed his (2)<u>monthly paycheck</u> and came home with a gift for his son Homer—a brand-new dollar bill. Being a (3)<u>responsible parent</u>, he only gave Homer a (4)<u>single bill</u>, as Homer was a (5) <u>mere child</u> of 6 years old.

Homer gazed in wonder at the bill, thinking about what he would buy. Just then a strong breeze blew through a nearby window. It blew the bill right out of Homer's hand and out the window. The (6)<u>remorseful child</u> felt sorry that he had not held on to the bill more tightly.

Soon Homer lost sight of the dollar, as it blew across the (7)<u>distant skyline</u> of a large (8)<u>northeastern city</u> and over the hulls of two (9)<u>commercial ships</u>. When it finally landed in the ocean, a large tuna, whose (10)<u>principal diet</u> was usually smaller fish, gobbled it down for supper.

Two days later, the Dawson family had the shock of their lives. Mrs. Dawson had prepared a baked tuna for dinner. When Mr. Dawson slit it across the backbone, lying inside was the (11)<u>identical bill</u> that Homer had lost. The gypsy bill had returned to its (12)<u>rightful owner</u>.

Activities

Activity 1

Search in a newspaper or magazine for examples of the different types of reference adjectives and adverbs discussed in this unit. The following categories will serve as a review:

law or custom   location/position/place

time/frequency   former identification

geography   identifying information

uniqueness   intensification

Bring in these examples to share with your classmates.

Activity 2

Haiku is a type of Japanese poetry which often takes its inspiration from nature themes. Here is an example:

The silence of dusk
A single star in heaven
Sings a plaintive song

Can you identify the reference adjective in this poem? What does it mean? What does the poem mean?

Haiku is always constructed in the following manner:

Line One - 5 syllables
Line Two - 7 syllables
Line Three - 5 syllables

Write a haiku poem, using at least one reference adjective or adverb phrase in one of the three lines, as in the example above (a single star). If you need help, here are a few suggested phrases:

previous spring   true maple
Oriental shell   sole snowflake
identical shadow   mere frog

Compare your poem with those of several classmates. Can you identify the reference adjective or adverb in each one? Try paraphrasing each poem.

Activity 3

If you were shipwrecked on a desert island with only one other person, who would you choose to be your sole companion? In groups, study the following chart and discuss your choice. Clarify why this person would be preferable to the others.

Person	Age	Place of Birth	Occupation	Hobby
Ann	9	rural	student	fishing
Sue	45	urban	cultural anthropologist	Polynesian dance
Chong	24	urban	financial planner	bird-watching
Mike	17	rural	audiovisual technician	swimming
Juana	28	rural	dramatic coach	poetry reading

Activity 4

Select a residential building that you know something about or would like to know more about. This could be your own home or apartment or someone else's. Do some research to find out about the original owners or tenants. Who were they? What were their main occupations? Were any of the previous owners or tenants related to the original owners or tenants? Share the results of your research with other members of the class.

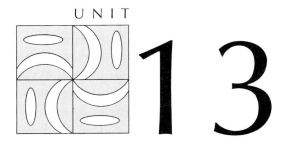

13

Correlative Conjunctions, *Respectively*

Task

Pair up with a classmate and play the roles of a student and a Registration Advisor at New World Alternative College. Together, you will make a plan for a four-semester, 15-course schedule.

STUDENT ROLE:

You want to complete your Associate degree in two years. Referring to the general list of requirements on page 193, try to find out from the Registration Advisor the specific course offerings you can choose to fulfill these requirements. Also find out when these courses are offered.

REGISTRATION ADVISOR:

Referring to the list of specific course offerings on page 194, (which the student does *not* have), help the student plan his/her schedule for a two-year associate degree. Find out which courses the student would like to take and inform him/her of when they are offered. As decisions are made, fill in the Study Plan provided on page 193. Here are some examples of student questions and advisor responses:

Student: I need to take an English composition course. What options do I have?

Advisor: You can take either Expository Writing or Technical Writing. They are offered both semesters.

Student: I'd like to take a foreign language in the spring of my first year.

Advisor: No, that's not possible. You'll have to take it in the fall. Neither Spanish nor French is offered in the spring.

Student: When can I take a math course?

Advisor: Both General Mathematics and Computer Science are offered in the fall only.

Student: For my social science requirement, I want to take Communication Studies and Anthropology. I can't take them both during the same semester, can I?

Advisor: Yes, you can. Not only Communication Studies but also Anthropology is offered every semester.

Student Information Sheet
New World Alternative College
Associate Degree Requirements

Required Courses

English Composition (1 course)
Mathematics (1 course)
Humanities (2 courses)
Social Sciences (2 courses)
Life Sciences (2 courses)
Physical Sciences (2 courses)
Environmental Studies (4 courses)

Elective Courses (1 course)

Foreign Language
History

New World Alternative College
STUDY PLAN

	Fall	Spring
Year 1		
Year 2		

Advisor's List
Course Schedule
New World Alternative College

Unless stated, all courses are offered all semesters.
Prerequisites are also listed.

English Composition

Expository Writing
Technical Writing

Humanities

(prerequisite: one English
   Composition course)
Linguistics
Philosophy
Religious Studies

Social Sciences

Anthropology
Communication Studies
Economics (Fall only)
Geography(Fall only)

Physical Sciences

Astronomy
Physics
Geology (Spring only)

Mathematics

General Mathematics
   (Fall only)
Computer Sciences
   (Fall only)

History

U.S. History (Spring only)
World History (Spring only)

Foreign Language

Spanish (Fall only)
French (Fall only)

Life Sciences

Psychology
Biology

Environmental Studies

(prerequisite: one Life
   Science course)
The Greenhouse Effect
Air Pollution
Garbage Disposal
Hazardous Waste
Acid Rain
Endangered Wildlife

Focus 1

Correlative Conjunctions

FORM
USE

- Correlative conjunction pairs are
  both/and   neither/nor   either/or   not only/but also
- Correlative conjunctions join two noun, verb, adjective, adverb, or preposition phrases:

Phrase Type	Example
Noun	**(a)** Neither **Chinese** nor **Japanese** will be offered at Corona College this semester.
Verb	**(b)** Mary will not only **complete** her coursework but also **write** her Master's thesis by June.
Adjective	**(c)** Mrs. Thomas was both **surprised** and **jubilant** that her daughter finished her degree.
Adverb	**(d)** Daniel worked both **fast** and **hard** to finish his project by the due date.
Prepositional Phrase	**(e)** Mark usually studies either **at home** or **in the student lounge.**

- *Either/or* can also join two clauses.
  - **(f)** Either **the teacher has to slow down the lecture pace** or the students need to take notes faster.
- *Not only/but also* can join two clauses as well. The clause following *not only* has an inverted subject with:

Verb	Example
be	**(g)** Not only **was Mr. Jones strict** but he was also unfair.
Modal Verbs	**(h)** Not only **could she sing** but she could also dance.
Auxiliary Verbs *be, have* and *do*	**(i)** Not only **is she taking Chemistry** but she is also taking Biology. **(j)** Not only **has she visited New York** but she has also visited Boston. **(k)** Not only **did he teach Economics** but he also sold real estate.

- Note that *also* usually appears before a main verb or after modal verbs, *be*, or auxiliary verbs *be, have,* and *do* in the second clause.
  - **(l)** Not only did he pass Geology but he **also passed** History.
  - **(m)** Not only is she tired but she **is also** sick.
- *Neither/nor* can join clauses but only in literary or very formal contexts. The clauses following *neither* and *nor* both have inverted subjects.
  - **(n)** Neither **did Elizabeth speak** nor **did she move** when the soldiers marched by the bridge.
- *Both/and* cannot join clauses.
  - **(o)** Both **the advisor** and **the student** discussed the study plan.
  - **(p)** NOT: Both **the advisor listens to the student** and **phe student listens to the advisor.**

- *Neither/nor* is preferred over *both/and* + *not* to show things that are excluded.
  - **(q)** The library building is neither **attractive** nor **inspiring**.
  - **(r)** NOT: The library building isn't both **attractive** and **inspiring**.

Exercise 1

Underline the correlative pairs in the sample conversations in the Task.

EXAMPLE: You can take <u>either</u> Expository Writing <u>or</u> Technical Writing.

Exercise 2

Think of a couple you know very well, such as your parents, an aunt and uncle, or married friends. With a partner, orally discuss how the couple's appearance, personality, preferences, habits, household responsibilities, or other features coincide using correlative conjunctions.

EXAMPLE:	Appearance	Both my mother and my father have black hair.
	Personality	My mother and my father are neither sociable nor friendly around strangers.
	Preferences	On weekends, my parents like to go either to restaurants or to the movies.
	Habits	My parents neither smoke nor drink.
	Household Responsibilities	Not only does my mother vacuum every weekend, but my father also vacuums on Wednesdays.

Focus 2

USE

Parallelism; Conciseness

USE

- In formal usage, the two phrases that correlative conjunctions join must be the same grammatical structures. If they are not, the sentence will not be parallel and should be rephrased.
  - **(a)** Not Parallel: Not only **was he an honors student** but also **a scholarship recipient.** (clause/noun)
  - **(b)** Parallel: He was not only **an honors student** but also a **scholarship recipient.** (noun/noun)
  - **(c)** Not Parallel: Both **gaining work experience** and **to earn academic credit** are important benefits of an internship. (gerund/infinitive)
  - **(d)** Parallel: Both **gaining work experience** and **earning academic credit** are important benefits of an internship. (gerund/gerund)

(e) Not Parallel: The dean of the college is neither **knowledgeable** nor **is he articulate**. (adjective/clause)

(f) Parallel: The dean of the college is neither **knowledgeable** nor **articulate**. (adjective/adjective)

(g) Not Parallel: She said either **that she would meet us at the post office** or **wait for us here**. (clause/verb phrase)

(h) Parallel: She said that she would either **meet us at the post office** or **wait for us here**. (verb phrase/verb phrase)

- In formal usage, parallel structures should be concise, without unnecessary repetition.

  (i) Repetitious: She knew either **that she needed an A** or **that she needed a B** to pass the course.

  (j) Concise: She knew that she needed either **an A** or **a B** to pass the course.

  (k) Repetitious: Not only **was John disqualified for poor attendance**, but **Betty was also disqualified for poor attendance**.

  (l) Concise: Not only **John** but also **Betty** was disqualified for poor attendance.

  (m) Repetitious: Debbie both **will attend classes in the fall** and **will attend classes in the spring**.

  (n) Concise: Debbie will attend classes both **in the fall** and **in the spring**.

Exercise 3

Read each sentence. Write *OK* next to sentences that are well-formed, parallel, and not repetitious. Rephrase the rest for concise, formal style.

EXAMPLES: I cannot stand to eat either liver or raw fish.   *OK*

Not only is Maria tired but also sick.

Maria is not only tired but also sick.

1. Not only *The New York Times* carried but also *The Los Angeles Times* carried the story of the train disaster in Algeria.
2. Juanita will both major in English and in Sociology.
3. The Boston Red Sox either made the finals in the baseball competition or the Detroit Tigers did.
4. Suzuki neither found her watch nor her wallet where she had left them.
5. The Smith family both loves cats and dogs.
6. Mr. Humphrey thinks either that I should cancel or postpone the meeting with my advisor.
7. Not only am I going to the dentist but also the barber tomorrow.
8. Mary is going to either quit her job or rearranging her work schedule to take Astronomy.
9. I hope that the honor students are both prepared and that they are ready to take Calculus.
10. Todd neither saw or talked to his roommate Bill.
11. Both bringing traveler's checks and cash is necessary for any trip.
12. Nor my two daughters nor my son wants to take an aisle seat on the airplane.

Exercise 4

The following paragraphs contain several examples of nonparallel, inconcise structures with correlative conjunctions. Identify and rephrase them for formal style.

(1)In the last 40 years, family life trends have changed dramatically in the United States. (2)In the past, it was expected that everyone would get married in their early 20's. (3)Now having to choose either between a family or a career, many are opting for the career and remaining single. (4)Others are postponing first marriages until their 30's or 40's.

(5)If and when couples decide to marry, many are deciding to limit their family size. (6)Not only couples are having fewer children, but they are also deciding to have no children at all. (7)On the other hand, some singles are deciding to either have children by themselves or to raise their own or adopted children with same sex partners.

(8)In the past, women worked either for personal satisfaction or to earn extra money for luxuries. (9)Today both husband and the wife must work in order to survive. (10)Because of this, husbands and wives do not always adhere to traditional sex roles. (11)Now either the husband might do the cooking and cleaning or the wife might do the cooking and cleaning.

(12)Both because of the greater stress of modern life and the greater freedom that each partner feels, divorce is becoming more and more common. (13)Neither the rich are immune nor the poor. (14)In some states, the divorce rate approaches 50 percent. (15)But marriage cannot be all bad, though. (16)Not only many people get divorced but these same people also get remarried one or more times throughout their lifetimes.

Focus 3

MEANING ● USE

Correlative Conjunctions for Emphasis

MEANING
USE

- We use correlative conjunctions, instead of simple conjoined phrases, for emphasis.
  - *both/and*
    - **(a)** A: I hope Pablo and Karl come to the party.
      B: You are in luck! Both Pablo and Karl are coming to the party.
  - *either/or*
    - **(b)** A: I only have two openings left. You can come either on Wednesday or on Friday.
      B: I'll come on Friday.
  - *neither/nor*
    - **(c)** A: My mother and father wouldn't miss my graduation.
      B: Really? Neither my mother nor my father can attend mine.
- *Not only/but also* shows greater emphasis than *both/and*. *Not only* usually comes before already known information, and *but also* introduces new or surprising information in a sentence.
  - **(d)** A: I'm so glad that Donna entered the math contest.
    B: Not only did she enter, but she also won the contest.

Exercise 5

Imagine that you are planning an annual potluck-dinner office party, and you have jotted down the following notes about assignments. Your supervisor has asked you the following questions to get a progress report on the party. How would you answer these questions to show that everything is under control? Use as many correlative conjunctions as possible. (Don't forget to review the rules for subject/verb agreement with correlative conjunctions in Unit 2.)

> **EXAMPLE:** Who will decorate for the party?
>
> *Neither* Mario *nor* Penny have time, so I will ask someone else.

1. Who can bring a salad?
2. Who's planning to make the main dish?
3. Who can bring the alcoholic beverages?
4. How will you keep the drinks cold?
5. Have you tried to get a portable tape player?
6. Who's going to bring the bread?
7. Have you had any luck in locating someone to bring an ice-cream maker?

Food	Guest
wine and beer	Abraham and Julio
soft drinks	Amy
main dish (lasagne)	Nancy and Janet
salad	John and Betty
French bread	Thinh or Saddam
vegetable dish	Charlene
homemade ice cream	Still looking for someone with an ice-cream maker— already asked Joseph and Tina
Other	
ice chest	Marcy or Tanya
portable tape player	Felipe and Noriko don't have one— keep asking
decorations	Mario and Penny— ask someone else

Exercise 6

Answer the following questions with correlative conjunctions for emphasis. Write your answers below.

EXAMPLE: Spain doesn't border Portugal or France, does it?
Yes, it borders *both* Portugal *and* France.

1. Cameroon and Algeria are in South America, aren't they?
2. Martin Luther King and Jesse Jackson were prominent Black lawyers, weren't they?
3. Honey or sugar can be used to sweeten lemonade, can't it?
4. Whales and dolphins are members of the fish family, aren't they?
5. Niagara Falls is situated in Venezuela and Colombia, isn't it?

Exercise 7

Using the information in parentheses, respond to the following statements with *not only/but also.*

EXAMPLE: I heard that Samuel has to work on Saturdays (Sundays).
Samuel has to work *not only* on Saturdays *but also* on Sundays.

1. Shirley Temple could dance very well. (sing)
2. The language laboratory is great for improving pronunciation. (listening comprehension)
3. Nola should exercise twice a week. (go on a diet)
4. Becky has to take a test on Friday. (finish a project)
5. Thomas Jefferson was a great politician. (inventor)
6. The dictionary shows the pronunciation of a word. (part of speech)
7. The International Student Office will help you to locate an apartment. (a part-time job)
8. It rained all day last Tuesday. (last Wednesday)

Focus 4

Respectively

**MEANING
USE**

- *Respectively* changes the meaning of sentences that have two phrases joined by *and*.

    (a) Wanda and Harry cooked and cleaned.
    (Both Wanda and Harry did both activities.)

    (b) Wanda and Harry cooked and cleaned, respectively.
    (Wanda cooked and Harry cleaned.)

    (c) Martin and Yoshiko write screenplays and direct movies.
    (Both Martin and Yoshiko do both activities.)

    (d) Martin and Yoshiko write screenplays and direct movies, respectively.
    (Martin writes screenplays and Yoshiko directs movies.)

- We cannot use *respectively* with only one conjoined phrase.

    (e) NOT: Wanda cooks and cleans, respectively.

- We cannot place *respectively* after the first or second pair of joined phrases in more formal speaking or writing.

    (f) Hussein Daoud and Mita Meschi are an engineer and a doctor, respectively.

    (g) Hussein Daoud and Mita Meschi, respectively, are an engineer and a doctor.

    (h) Howard Bates and Ann Fonner were hired in June and August, respectively.

    (i) Howard Bates and Ann Fonner, respectively, were hired in June and August.

Exercise 8

Combine the following two sentences with *respectively*.

> **EXAMPLE:** Winston Churchill was the Prime Minister of England. Golda Meier was the Prime Minister of Israel.
>
> *Winston Churchill and Golda Meier were the Prime Ministers of England and Israel, respectively.*

1. Paraguay is a landlocked country in South America. Chad is a landlocked country in Africa.
2. Babe Ruth hit 60 home runs in one season. Josh Gibson hit 84 home runs in one season.
3. In 1989, the per capita income in California was $19,740. In 1989, the per capita income in Alabama was $13,679.
4. Washington, D.C., is the capital of the United States. Ottawa is the capital of Canada.
5. Monet painted impressionist paintings. Picasso painted Cubist paintings.
6. Lucille Ball had a child when she was 42. Audrey Hepburn had a child when she was 41.

Exercise 9

Create sentences using *respectively* in different positions, using the following word pairs as prompts.

> **EXAMPLE:** Your father and your mother
>
> My father and mother are from Holland and Indonesia, *respectively.*
>
> My father and mother, *respectively,* are from Holland and Indonesia.

1. Your eye color and your hair color
2. You and your best friend
3. Your grandmother and your grandfather
4. Your doctor and your dentist
5. Your kitchen and your bedroom
6. Your writing skills and your speaking skills

Activities

Activity 1

Imagine that you are a supervisor for a company which allows fairly flexible hours for its part-time employees. Your boss recently called you to find out which day and time would be most convenient for each employee's evaluation conference. In order to help you in your decision, you asked the four workers you are supervising to indicate on the following blank schedule forms which hours they are available. An *A* indicates that a worker is available during a particular hour.

Conference Availability Charts

Pepita

	M	T	W	Th	F
9-10	A		A		A
10-11	A	A			
11-12		A	A	A	
12-1					
1-2			A		A

Tuan

	M	T	W	Th	F
9-10					
10-11					
11-12		A	A	A	
12-1	A	A	A	A	A
1-2			A		A

Tom

	M	T	W	Th	F
9-10					
10-11	A	A			
11-12			A		
12-1	A	A	A	A	A
1-2		A		A	

Laleh

	M	T	W	Th	F
9-10	A		A		A
10-11					
11-12			A		
12-1					
1-2		A		A	

Now respond to the following memo your boss has sent to you detailing who is and who is not available at the following times. Try to use the words *both, either,* or *neither* in your responses.

*** Memo ***

DATE: March 6

TO: Bob Masters

FROM: Robert Umeda

I am free at the following times for the end-of-the-year conferences. Please tell me who is also available at the following times.

Monday

9-10 _Both Pepita and Lalen are available. (Neither Tom nor Tuan can come.)_ _____

10-11 _____

12-1 _____

Tuesday

11-1 _____

12-1 _____

1-2 _____

Thursday

11-12 _____

1-2 _____

Friday

9-10 _____

12-1 _____

Activity 2

Imagine that you have two children, and both you and your spouse have to work outside the home, which leaves little time for keeping a household running. In the chart below, choose which chores you would like to do and which chores you would like your spouse to do by marking an X under the appropriate column. If you feel that any of the tasks should be shared, write B (for both) under each column. Discuss your choice of respective duties with a classmate, using as many of the expressions you have learned in this unit as possible.

	My Chore	My Spouse's Chore
cook meals		
wash dishes		
vacuum floors		
dust furniture		
decorate the house for holidays		
care for the yard		
bring in the mail		
shop for food		
shop for clothes		
get the car repaired		
pay bills		
clean toilets and fixtures		
do laundry		
take out garbage		
take children to day care		
attend community meetings		
read bedtime stories to children		

Activity 3

Listen carefully to a television program (e.g., a cooking program or a sports program) and jot down the statements you hear which contain *both/and, not only/but also, either/or,* or *neither/nor*. Bring your notes to class and discuss which types of correlatives were used more often and whether they were used to show emphasis or not.

Activity 4

THE CORRELATIVE GAME
PREPARATION FOR THE GAME

1. Divide the class into two teams. Each team should create a set of 18 cards that contain difficult True/False statements, that will hopefully stump the other team. You should pattern these statements after the structures you have learned in this lesson. For example:

    1. Jackie Kennedy and Marilyn Monroe were a President and a movie star, respectively. (F, Jackie Kennedy was the wife of a President)
    2. Neither South Africa nor Argentina has a northern seaport. (T)

2. On a second set of cards, each team will write the names of team members on the opposite team, using the following constructions:

    Either *Mary* or *Sam* (six cards with other names)
    Both *Tony* and *Maria* (six cards with other names)
    Neither *Thanh* or *Vivian* (six cards with other names)

RULES OF THE GAME

1. Teams should exchange sets of cards. Each team will have 18 T/F Cards and 18 Name Cards.
2. One member of the first team reads the name card first, for example:

"Either Mary or Sam"	This means that only one of these two students can answer the question.
"Both Tony and Maria"	This means that both Tony and Maria can help each other answer.
"Neither Thanh nor Sam"	This means that Thanh or Sam cannot answer the question, but the rest of the members of the team can.

    If the first card is chosen, Mary or Sam decides who will take a guess. For the sake of example, presume Mary decides to try.
3. Next, the member of the first team reads the T/F statement. If Mary can answer it correctly, she gets one point and the same team continues. If she answers it incorrectly, it is the other team's turn.
4. The team with the most points at the end of the stack of True/False cards wins the game.

Activity 5

Based on the Task at the beginning of this unit, write a 10- to 15-line dialogue between a college advisor and a student in which various course/schedule options are being discussed. Try to use *either/or, neither/nor, both/and,* and *not only/but also* at least once each.

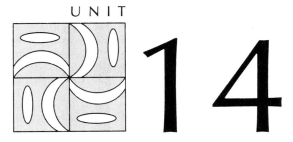

UNIT

14

Logical Connectors

Task

Stories play an important role in the traditions and everyday life of cultures throughout the world. In all cultures, people use stories to explain the mysteries of life, to illustrate values and truths, to share feelings and ideas, and, of course, to entertain and delight. Whether whispered by one person to another or told before a huge audience, stories are one of the most common ways that people of all cultures communicate ideas.

One type of story found in cultures all over the world is the creation myth, which explains how the universe and life on Earth came to be. Two creation myths, one from Finland and one from Micronesia, are summarized below; they describe how the sun, the moon, and first people on Earth came to exist.

After you read the stories, write a paragraph pointing out their similarities and differences. In comparing the stories, consider the following questions:

1. What existed at the beginning of creation?
2. In what order were things created?
3. Who was responsible for creating the universe and the first people and how were they created?

From Finland:

In the beginning there was only Water, Air and Air's daughter, Ilmatar. Ilmatar spent her time wandering around the world. One day Ilmatar sank down to rest upon the ocean's face as she was very tired. When she lay down, the seas rolled over her, the waves tossed her and the wind blew over her. For seven hundred years, Ilmatar swam and floated in the sea. Then, one day while she lay floating with one knee up out of the water, a beautiful duck swooped down and landed on her knee. There it laid seven eggs. As the days went by, the eggs grew hotter and hotter until Ilmatar could no longer endure the heat and pulled her knee into the water. Because of this, the eggs rolled into the ocean and sank to its bottom. Eventually, one of the eggs cracked. From the lower half of its shell, the earth was formed. From the egg's upper shell, the sky formed over the land and sea. From the yolk of the egg, the sun rose into the sky. From the white of the egg, the moon and stars were created and took their place in the heavens. Later, Ilmatar gave birth to the sea's child, whom she called Vainamoinen. For seven years Vainamoinen swam the seas. Then he went ashore and became the first person on earth.

From Nauru, Micronesia:

In the beginning there was only water and the creator, Areop-Enap, who lived in a mussel shell in the sea. It was very dark in the sea and also in the shell; as a result, Areop-Enap couldn't see very well. He could, however, feel around in the dark. Thus it was that he discovered a large snail and a small snail who were occupying the shell with him. Areop-Enap used his power to change the small snail into the moon and put it at the top of the shell. Then, by the light of the moon, Areop-Enap spotted a worm in the shell. He got the worm to separate the upper and lower parts of the shell. The lower part became the sky, while the upper part became the earth. Because of all this work, the poor worm died of exhaustion. Its sweat, dripping into the lower shell, became the salty sea. After the sky and the earth had been created, Areop-Enap placed the big snail into the sky to be the sun. Finally, from stones he made the first people to hold up the sky.

(Adapted from Maria Leach (1956), *The Beginning: Creation Myths around the World*, New York: Funk & Wagnalls.)

Focus 1

FORM ● MEANING

Logical Connectors in English

FORM
MEANING

- When you express ideas, there are many types of meaning relationships that can exist between one idea and another. For example, some relationships between ideas involve:
  - Reason–result:

    (a) Ilmatar was very tired. She lay down on the ocean's face.
  - Time sequence:

    (b) Areop-Enap created the moon. He put it at the top of the shell.
  - Contrast:

    (c) In the Micronesian myth, the sun was a snail. In the Finnish myth, the sun came from an egg yolk.
  - Generalization—Clarification:

    (d) In the Finnish myth, everything in the heavens was created from an egg. The sun came from the yolk and the moon and stars came from the white of the egg.
- In many cases, you want to make explicit what the meaning relationships between ideas are so that a listener or reader can more easily understand the connections. To do this, you can add words and phrases that signal the relationships.

  (e) Ilmatar was very tired, **so** she lay down on the ocean's face.

  (f) **After** Areop–Enap created the moon, he put it at the top of the shell.

  (g) In the Micronesian myth, the sun was a snail, **whereas** in the Finnish myth, the sun came from an egg yolk.

  (h) In the Finnish myth, the universe was created from an egg. **That is,** the sun came from the yolk, and the moon and stars came from the white of the egg.
  - As the examples above show, words and phrases not only express a variety of meaning relationships, but they also connect ideas in different ways.

208

- **Coordinating conjunctions, or coordinators,** such as **so,** connect the ideas in two independent clauses. In written English, we usually express these clauses as one sentence joined by a comma. They may also be separate sentences.

Independent Clause	Independent Clause
(i) Ilmatar lay down on the ocean's face,	**for she was tired.**
(j) Ilmatar kept the eggs on her knee,	**but** eventually they got too hot.

- Coordinating conjunctions are a small set of connectors. They include *and, but, yet, so, or, nor,* and *for* (meaning "because").

- **Subordinating conjunctions,** or **subordinators,** such as *after* and *whereas,* connect ideas within a sentence. They show the relationship between an idea in a dependent clause and an idea in an independent clause. The subordinating conjunction is what makes a clause dependent:

Independent Clause	**Independent Clause**
(k) Areop-Enap put the snail in the sky.	Areop-Enap made people.
Dependent Clause	**Independent Clause**
(l) After Areop-Enap put the snail in the sky,	he made people.
Independent Clause	**Dependent Clause**
(m) Areop-Enap put the snail in the sky	**before** he made people.

You are probably familiar with most of the subordinating conjunctions in English. Some other common subordinators include *since, if, unless, although,* and *while.*

- **Sentence connectors,** or **adverbials,** such as *that is,* usually indicate meaning relationships between two or more independent clauses. The independent clauses may be separate sentences. They may also be in the same sentence, joined by a semi-colon.

Independent Clause
(n) Areop-Enap discovered two snails living in the shell with him.

Independent Clause
In addition, a worm inhabited the shell, as he later found out.

Independent Clause
(o) Ilmatur could not endure the heat from the eggs; **consequently,**

Independent Clause
she put her knee back into the water.

There are many sentence connectors in English that signal meaning relationships. This unit will review types of meaning relationships expressed by these connectors, and it will focus on aspects of these connectors that may be particularly challenging for advanced students of English. We use many of the sentence connectors primarily in written English.

Exercise 1

For each of the sentence pairs below, write down what the relationship of the second sentence is to the first: an added idea, an example, a similarity, a contrast, or a result.

1. In Greek mythology, Ares, the god of war, was often violent and belligerent. The goddess Athene was a peacemaker.
2. Novels entertain us. They help us to understand human behavior.
3. The myths of many cultures include a god of thunder. The Mayan god of thunder was Chac.
4. Ancient civilizations did not know the scientific explanations for natural phenomena such as storms. They made up stories to explain these events.
5. Jason, the Greek leader of the Argonauts, went on a long sea voyage to get the Golden Fleece. The Greek hero Odysseus embarked on a long voyage.

Focus 2

FORM

Punctuation of Sentence Connectors

FORM

- We can use many of the sentence connectors at the beginning, the middle, or the end of a sentence or independent clause. The punctuation surrounding a sentence connector depends on where it appears in a sentence:
  - If the connector begins a sentence, use a period before it (ending the previous sentence) and a comma after it:
    (a) Apollo is the god of the sun in Greek mythology. **Similarly,** Balder is the sun god in Norse myths.
  - If the connector begins an independent clause after another independent clause in the same sentence, use a semicolon before it and a comma after it.
    (b) Balder was much loved by the other gods; **however,** he was accidentally killed with a mistletoe dart by one of them.
  - If the connector is in the middle of a sentence or independent clause, it is usually separated from the rest of the sentence or clause by commas.
    (c) Many mythological characters have more than one name. Some, **in fact,** have several name variations.
- We do not usually use commas with *also* when it is in the middle of a sentence, nor do we use a comma before *as well* when it follows a verb.
  - **(d)** Aphrodite is the Greek goddess of love. She is **also** the goddess of beauty.
  - **(e)** Balder died from his dart wound. His wife Nanna died **as well,** having suffered a broken heart.

- If the connector comes at the end of the sentence, punctuation is usually not necessary except for *though* and *however:*

  (f) The gods were grief-stricken when Balder died. The mortals reacted **in the same way.**

  (g) Tu, known in Polynesian myths as the angry god, was quite belligerent. He could sometimes be very kind, **however.**

Focus 3

MEANING

Sentence Connectors: Signaling Addition and Alternatives

MEANING

- Additive connectors signal information that in some way adds to or elaborates what has been previously stated. The following charts list some of the most common types of additive sentence connectors.

  - **Simple additive** connectors have the general meaning of *too* or *also.*

Meaning	Connector	Example
Show simple addition	*also*	**(a)** You can pay your fees by credit card. You can **also** write a check.
	in addition	**(b)** Ming has to register for classes today. **In addition,** he has to pay his course fees.
	furthermore	**(c)** This plant requires sun all day. **Furthermore,** it needs rich soil.
	moreover	**(d)** As your mayor, I promise to make this city safe for all. **Moreover,** I will create new jobs.

- **Emphatic additive** connectors signal an idea that stresses some aspect of what has been previously stated. They have a meaning similar to "Not only **that** (what I just said), but also **this** (what I'm saying now)."

Meaning	Connector	Example
Show emphatic addition	*what is more*	**(e)** We have succeeded in cleaning up the river. **What is more,** we have made it the cleanest in the entire state.
	as well	**(f)** Ricardo won the award for athletic achievement. He received academic honors **as well.**
	besides (this)★	**(g)** My brother goes to school fulltime. **Besides this,** he manages to work 20 hours a week.

★In this example and others in the unit, *this* means what has been previously mentioned. *This* will often be a demonstrative pronoun (*this, that, these,* or *those*), a demonstrative adjective + noun phrase, or *the* + noun phrase reference.

- We often use simple additive and emphatic additive connectors in similar contexts. The difference in use reflects the attitude of the speaker toward events and the degree to which he or she wants to emphasize the added statement:

I think I would be an excellent person for this job. My background in computers is extensive.

Simple Addition	Emphatic Addition
(h) I **also** have excellent writing skills.	(i) I have excellent writing skills **as well**.

Either connector would be appropriate in this context. The emphatic connector, however, puts greater stress on the range of the applicant's skills, implying that she is especially qualified.

- **Intensifying additive connectors** signal that the added idea will strongly support or help to verify a previously mentioned idea.

Meaning	Connector	Example
Show intensifying addition	*in fact* *as a matter of fact* *actually*	(j) Spokane has a lot of rain lately. **In fact**, it has been raining all week. (k) You can take the rest of the pie with you. **As a matter of fact**, I wish you would, since I'm on a diet. (l) Gretchen has never cared for the color magenta. **Actually**, it's one of her least favorite colors.

- Intensifying additive connectors often add an elaboration of an idea just stated rather than adding another, related idea as emphatic connectors do:
This weekend is going to be very busy. I have a lot of schoolwork to do.

Emphatic Addition	Intensifying Addition
(m) **Besides that,** I have to finish moving to my new apartment. (adds another activity that will be done; emphasizes how busy the weekend will be)	(n) **In fact,** I have to write three papers. (adds a statement to support the idea of having a lot of schoolwork)

- **Alternative connectors** signal a special kind of addition. They indicate a possibility in addition to the one just mentioned.

Meaning	Connector	Example
Other possibility	*on the other hand* *alternatively*	(o) I may work this summer. **On the other hand**, I may take a long vacation. (p) You could take the history course you eventually need this semester. **Alternatively**, you could complete your schedule with a science course.

- *On the other hand* and *alternatively* have very similar meanings. We use *on the other hand* in both spoken and written English. *Alternatively* is a somewhat more formal connector, and we don't commonly use it in conversational English.

- The "other possibility" expressed by the alternative connectors could be various parts of the previously mentioned idea:

   Washington, D.C., might be fun to visit this summer.

	Other Possibility	Part Changed
On the other hand,	(q) it might be too crowded.	fun
	(r) Minneapolis might be a better place to visit.	Washington, D.C.
	(s) it might be better to go there in the fall.	this summer

Note that the idea expressed in the alternative clause is usually a paraphrase or shortened form of the idea in the first clause. Repeating all of the first clause would be overly repetitious in most cases:

(t) NOT: Washington, D.C., might be a good place to visit this summer. On the other hand, Washington, D.C., might be a good place to visit in the fall.

- Some of the additive connectors, such as *in fact* and *on the other hand,* may signal other meanings; these meanings will be explained later in the unit.

Exercise 2

Use an appropriate sentence connector from the list below to signal the addition relationship expressed in the last sentence of each pair or group of sentences. More than one connector could be appropriate for most contexts. Try to use each connector once.

also	what is more	in fact
in addition	as well	as a matter of fact
furthermore	besides	actually
moreover		

> **EXAMPLE:** Leonardo da Vinci was a painter and sculptor.
> He was an architect and a naturalist.
> He was an architect and a naturalist *as well.*
> (Other possible connectors: all simple addition and emphatic addition connectors)

1. The poinsettia is a beautiful plant, but be careful with it around animals. It is poisonous.
2. Jerry has plenty of sunscreen if you'd like to use some when we go to the beach. He has four different kinds.
3. I can't go skating because I have to work on Saturday. I need to get a new pair of skates.
4. The Aztec deity Quetzalcoatl was the god of the sun and the air. He was the god of wisdom and a teacher of the arts of peace.

5. Ladies and gentlemen of the jury, I will show you that the defendant could not possibly have committed this crime. This is an innocent man before you! I will reveal who really should be on trial today.

6. Our teacher asked us if we had ever read *El Cid*. I hadn't. I had never even heard of it.

7. Gina is very talented musically. She plays the flute with the symphony orchestra. She occasionally plays bass violin with a jazz group.

8. Potassium maintains fluid balance in body cells. It controls nerves and muscles.

9. You have an error in article usage in the third paragraph of your report. You need to correct a typographical error in that paragraph.

10. Well, I admit I ate a lot of the cookies that were in the kitchen. I probably had about a dozen.

Exercise 3

Make up two sentences for each of the following directives. Use one of the addition sentence connectors to link the ideas between the sentence.

> **EXAMPLE:** I enjoy sailing because I like being outdoors.
> *In addition,* it's exciting to participate in races.

1. Give two reasons why you enjoy something you often do in your spare time.
2. Give two reasons why you like one movie or television show you've seen better than another.
3. State two advantages of flying over driving when a person goes on a long trip.
4. State two uses for computers.
5. Give two reasons why people tell stories about themselves.
6. Give two reasons why you should study English.
7. State two differences between English and your native language.
8. Give two reasons why someone should visit a particular city or country.
9. Give two reasons why someone should get to know you.
10. State two things that you are very good at doing.

Exercise 4

Add a sentence after each sentence below that would express another possibility. Use *on the other hand* or *alternatively* to signal the connection.

> **EXAMPLE:** I could get a job this summer.
> On the other hand, *I could take a few courses in summer school.*

1. I could stay home this weekend.
2. You might want to get a cat for pet.
3. The theory of the big bang, explaining the origins of the universe, could be correct.
4. If you're looking for a used car to buy, you could check the classified ads in the newspaper.
5. Outlawing the possession of guns in the United States could help to decrease crime.

Exercise 5

After each of the statements below, add three alternative statements by focusing on different parts of the statement. Use *on the other hand* or *alternatively*.

EXAMPLE: It could be fun to get a job making pizzas this summer.

On the other hand, { it could get boring after a while.
it might be more interesting to get a job at a television studio.
it would probably be more fun to eat the pizzas!

1. Hong Kong might be a good place to go for our Christmas vacation.
2. Advanced composition could be a good course for me to take next quarter.
3. It might be fun to go shopping on Saturday.
4. We might want to explore this cave tonight.

Focus 4

MEANING

Addition Sentence Connectors: Exemplification, Identification, and Clarification

MEANING

- Another set of addition sentence connectors signal that a statement will provide examples, identify further an idea already mentioned, or clarify a previously mentioned idea.
- **Exemplification** connectors signal examples of what has been mentioned. Some of these connectors, such as *for example,* indicate that what follows will be a representative example. Others, such as *in particular,* indicate a special member of a set. Still others, such as *to illustrate,* may introduce an example.

Use	Connector	Example
Exemplify a typical member	*for example*	**(a)** Reactions to bee stings can be severe. **For example**, a person could experience breathing difficulty.
	for instance	**(b)** Some sports involve considerable body contact. Take, **for instance**, football.
Exemplify an important or the most important member	*especially*	**(c)** Violence in movies seems to be increasing. Action films **especially** appear to be getting more violent.
	in particular	**(d)** Learning the rules for article usage in English can be difficult. **In particular**, the use of articles with generic nouns may be confusing.
Introduce an example	*to illustrate*	**(e)** The steps for saving your computer file are quite simple. **To illustrate,** we will save the file you have just created.
	as an example	**(f)** Many great composers have had their share of misery. **As an example,** consider the life of Mozart.

- **Identification connectors** signal that something will be more specifically identified.

Use	Connector	Example
Identify something mentioned or implied	*namely*	**(g)** There is a very important issue before us; **namely,** we need to decide how to reduce the budget by one fourth.
	specifically	**(h)** I have a question about connectors. **Specifically,** when do you use *in fact?*

- **Clarification connectors** signal that something will be clarified or rephrased.

Use	Connector	Example
Clarify or rephrase something already mentioned	*that is*	**(i)** The garlic should be minced; **that is,** you chop it into very small pieces.
	in other words	**(j)** You can't go on with this hectic life-style. **In other words,** you need to learn to relax.
	I mean	**(k)** I can't go to that play. **I mean,** $70 is just too much for me to spend in one evening.

We use connectors *that is* and *in other words* in both spoken and written English. *I mean* is informal; although we use it in some written contexts, we generally do not use it in formal academic English to clarify a statement.

Exercise 6

Use an exemplification, identification, or clarification connector from the list below that would be appropriate for each blank.

for example	especially	to illustrate	that is
for instance	in particular	as an example	in other words

1. Many words in English have origins in Greek myths. *Chaos,* _____ , is a word the Greeks used to describe the unordered matter that existed before creation.

2. Some natural objects have English names that derive from Roman words for mythological characters. Planets (a) _____ have been given such names. (b) _____, here are a few of them. Jupiter is named after the god of the sky. Neptune, in Roman mythology, was the god of springs and rivers. And Saturn was a god of agriculture.

3. Some names for metals in English also derive from myths. The metal uranium, _____ , comes from the Latin *Uranus* (the god of the sky). The metal tellurium comes from the Latin *Tellus* (the goddess of the earth).

4. Sometimes we may refer to an idea as *chimerical*; _____ , it is unrealistic or fanciful. This word comes from the name for a Greek monster, the Chimaera, which had a lion's head, a goat's body, and a dragon's tail.

5. Some English names for bodies of water also derive from Greek words. This is true (a) _____ in the case of oceans. (b) The name for the Arctic Ocean, _____ , comes from the Greek word for *bear*, *arkto*. The name for the Atlantic Ocean derives from *Atlantides*, who were sea nymphs. And the word *ocean* itself comes from *Oceanus*, the oldest member of the mythological race, the Titans.

6. Some governments are known as *plutocracies*; _____ , they are governments run by the wealthy. The word *plutocracy* comes from *Plutus*, the god of wealth.

Exercise 7

Add an identification statement after each of the following sentences to further specify information conveyed. Use *namely* or *specifically* to indicate its relationship to the sentence before it.

EXAMPLE: There is one thing I really like about you.
Namely, you never blame other people when something is your fault.

1. I see two major problems with the essay you wrote.
2. There is one habit I wish I could break.
3. There are a few things I would like to know more about regarding English grammar.
4. I wonder if you'd help me with something.
5. There are several things you might do to improve your financial situation.

Exercise 8

Below is a list of words along with their definitions. Make up one sentence using each word. Then for each, add an independent clause that explains the word. Use *in other words, that is,* or *I mean* to signal the relationship between the clauses. Use a semicolon to punctuate them.

> **EXAMPLE:** intractable   difficult to manage or get to behave
> Our new labrador puppy is intractable; *in other words,* it is hard to make him behave.

1. ichtyhologist (noun)   someone who specializes in the study of fishes
2. polychromatic (adj.)   having many colors
3. terriculous (adj.)   living in the ground
4. carnivore (noun)   meat-eating animal
5. digress (verb)   to stray from the main topic in speech or writing
6. captious (adj.)   tending to find fault with things and to make petty criticisms
7. xenophobic (noun)   having a fear or dislike of strangers or foreigners

Focus 5

FORM

Placement of Exemplification Connectors

FORM

- Connectors that introduce examples usually begin sentences. We may place the other exemplification connectors in different parts of a sentence, depending on what is being exemplified. The connectors *for example, for instance, especially,* and *in particular* can follow examples expressed as noun phrases.
- Myths around the world have similarities.

Scope of Example: Sentence	Scope of Example: Noun Phrase
(a) For example, **in many creation myths, only water and air exist in the beginning.**	**(b)** Let us consider **creation myths,** for example.
(c) In many creation myths, for example, **only water and air exist in the beginning.**	**(d)** Let us consider, for example, **creation myths.**

- I'm really having trouble using verb tenses.

Scope of Example: Sentence	Scope of Example: Noun Phrase
(e) In particular, **I'm not sure when to use the present perfect instead of the simple past tense.**	**(f) The future perfect tense,** in particular, **is troublesome.**

Exercise 9

Column A below has a list of general statements about clouds. Column B presents examples for each statement. Some examples, indicated in parentheses as "typical," are representative. Others, indicated in parentheses as "special," express the most important member. Make a sentence for each of the examples in Column B, using an appropriate connector.

EXAMPLE: Cumulus clouds, *for example,* are tall, whereas cirrus clouds are featherlike.

Column A	Column B
1. Types of clouds are distinguished by height.	cumulus clouds are tall, while cirrus clouds are featherlike (typical)
2. They are also distinguished by altitude.	stratus clouds hover only a few hundred feet above ground, whereas cumulonimbus clouds may be found upward to 50,000 feet (typical)
3. Some clouds are very thin.	cirrus and stratus clouds are quite wispy (special)
4. Clouds also differ in color.	stratocumulus clouds are dark, altostratus are gray or blue, and cirrocumulus are white (typical)
5. Some clouds are signs of rain.	cirrostratus and cumulonimbus clouds may signal an advancing storm (special)
6. Not all clouds produce rain.	stratocumulus clouds are usually not rain producers (typical)

Focus 6

FORM ● MEANING

Abbreviations Signaling Examples and Clarification

FORM
MEANING

- In written English, we commonly use and sometimes confuse two abbreviations: **e.g.** and **i.e.**
  - The connector *e.g.* (from Latin *exempli gratia*) is an abbreviation for **for example.**
    - **(a)** Native American myths often feature animals; **e.g.,** the Coyote appears frequently in these myths.
  - The connector *i.e.* (from Latin *id est*) is an abbreviation for *that is.*
    - **(b)** Dogs are quadrupeds; **i.e.,** they have four feet.
- Note that as with *for example* and *that is,* a comma follows these connectors.

Exercise 10

Some of the sentences below use *i.e.* or *e.g.* correctly; some do not. Identify which ones are incorrect and explain why.

EXAMPLE: There are many kinds of fruit trees that grow in my state; i.e., there are orange, pear, and peach trees.

Incorrect — The second clause presents examples.

1. The caterpillar underwent a metamorphosis; i.e., it became a butterfly.
2. Cows are herbivores; e.g., they do not eat meat.
3. American folktales often use exaggeration for humor; i.e., in the story of Paul Bunyan, his pancake griddle was so big that to grease it, men had to skate across it with bacon on their skates.
4. Many vegetables are good sources of vitamins; e.g., broccoli has a lot of Vitamin C.
5. *Young* and *old* are antonyms; i.e., they are opposite in meaning.
6. Some words in English can be spelled several ways; i.e., *theater* can also be spelled *theatre*.
7. Adolf Hitler was a megalomaniac; e.g., he believed he had unlimited power.

Focus 7

MEANING

Sentence Connectors Signaling Similarity

MEANING

- Sentence connectors expressing similarity signal that two or more ideas, events, or situations are alike.

Meaning	Connector	Example
Show similarity	*similarly*	**(a)** The lungs of vertebrates absorb oxygen from the air. **Similarly,** gills, the respiratory organs of many aquatic animals, take in oxygen from water.
	likewise	**(b)** If you study, you will probably do well on the exam. **Likewise,** if you don't study at all, you will probably not do very well.
	in the same way	**(c)** Learning to play a musical instrument well requires practice. **In the same way,** learning to speak a second language fluently cannot be accomplished without practice.

- Some things to note about similarity sentence connectors:
  - The clause introduced by a similarity connector should usually paraphrase or condense some information from the first clause, not just repeat all of it.
    (d) Blake likes to collect stamps. Likewise, this has been one of Karen's favorite hobbies for years.
    (e) NOT: Blake likes to collect stamps. Likewise, Karen likes to collect stamps.

- The similarity relationship often involves more than one different constituent.

   (f) Football players try to carry a football across their goal line. Similarly, soccer players try to kick a soccer ball across their goal line.

   Comparison: football players   soccer players
                      carry   kick
                      football   soccer ball

- *Likewise* and *in the same way* often suggest greater similarity, or sameness, than *similarly* does.

   (g) Patrice bought some new clothes when we went shopping.

   (h) Likewise, Mary bought a few new outfits.

   (i) The spots on leopards help to camouflage them in the jungle. **Similarly,** spots on fawns help to hide them in the woods.

- We usually place all three connectors at the beginning of a sentence. We can, however, use them in other positions in a sentence, especially when the point of similarity is expressed in the verb phrase.

   (j) Dogs may *get excited during an electrical storm.* Cats may react **in the same way.**

   (k) Constance *turned in her paper on Friday.* Jamal did **likewise.**

   (l) A man in the audience *started to heckle the speaker.* Others behaved **similarly.**

Exercise 11

Sometimes the difficult aspect of using similarity connectors, especially *likewise* and *in the same way,* is avoiding too much repetition of information from the first sentence in the second sentence. In the sentence pairs below, the second sentence is repetitious. Rephrase or condense the information in these sentences and add a similarity sentence connector.

> **EXAMPLE:** The best way to cook a chuck arm beef steak is to braise it. One of the best ways to cook cubed steak is to braise it.
>
> *Revised: Likewise,* braising is one of the best ways to prepare cubed steak.
>
> After an earthquake, you should check for gas leaks and electrical problems.
>
> After a hurricane, you should check for gas leaks and electrical problems.
>
> *Revised: In the same way,* these possible dangers should be checked after a hurricane.

1. If you have an ink stain on your carpet, dry-cleaning solvent can remove it. If you have crayon marks on your wallpaper, dry-cleaning solvent can remove them.

2. During a thunderstorm, avoid standing on a hilltop. During a tornado, avoid standing on a hilltop.

3. In the United States, the availability of grapes is low during the winter months. The availability of apples and pears is low during the early summer months.

4. To save energy used for heating water, you can wash your clothes in cold water. To save energy used for lighting, you can turn off the lights when you leave your house.

5. To celebrate a couple's 25th wedding anniversary, the traditional gift is something silver. To celebrate a couple's 50th wedding anniversary, the traditional gift is something gold.

Exercise 12

The chart below gives information about myth and folklore spirits in western Europe. Imagine that you are a professional folklorist, and that you have been asked to write a summary of the ways in which these spirits are similar. As preparation for your summary, use the information in the chart to make at least five pairs of sentences expressing similarity. Use a similarity connector with the second sentence of each pair.

EXAMPLE: Pixies enjoy playing tricks on humans; elves *likewise* enjoy fooling people.

Name of Spirit	Fairy	Pixie	Brownie	Elf
Where Found	Ireland, England, Scotland	England	Scotland	Scandinavian countries
Typical Residence	forests, underground	forests, in a rock	humans' houses, farms	forests
Appearance	fair, attractive, varied size	handsome, small	brown or tawny, small, wrinkled faces	varied: some fair and some dark
Visibility to Humans	usually invisible; visible by use of a magic ointment	usually invisible	usually invisible	usually invisible; visible at midnight within their dancing circle
Clothing Color	green, brown, yellow favorite: green	always green	brown	varied
Favorite Pastime(s)	dancing at night	dancing at night; playing tricks on humans	playing tricks on humans	dancing at night; playing tricks on humans
Rulers	fairy king and queen	pixie king	none	elf-king

(Information from: Herbert Robinson and Knox Wilson, *Myths and Legends of All Nations,* Totowa, New Jersey: Littlefield, Adam & Co., 1976.)

Focus 8

Sentence Connectors Signaling Contrast and Concession

MEANING

- Contrast connectors show that two ideas differ or are not compatible.

Meaning	Connector	Example
Show contrast	*however*	**(a)** In some creation myths, the sun exists before people do. In others, **however**, people create the sun.
	in contrast	**(b)** The characters in legends may be based on people who actually lived. **In contrast**, the characters in fables, often animals, are fictional.
	on the other hand	**(c)** The proposed new hotel complex will benefit our city. **On the other hand,** it will create serious problems with increased traffic.
	though	**(d)** This lake is not very good for fishing. It's great for swimming and water skiing, **though.**
Contrary to previous statement	*in fact*	**(e)** Early civilizations thought the earth was the center of the universe. **In fact**, the earth revolves around the sun.
	however	**(f)** Some people think that whales are fish. **However**, these animals are mammals.

223

- **Concession sentence connectors** signal a reservation about something: The first statement is true, but the second statement is also true or needs to be considered. The second statement may express surprising or unexpected information.

Meaning	Connector	Example
Show reservation without contradicting previous claims	*even so*	**(g)** New York is beset with many urban problems. **Even so**, it is still a great city.
	however	**(h)** Most of my meal was excellent. The vegetables, **however**, were slightly overcooked.
	nevertheless	**(i)** Native Americans have had to struggle to preserve their traditions. **Nevertheless**, many of the old stories are still passed down to the new generations.
	nonetheless	**(j)** I know mountain climbing can be dangerous. I'd like to try it **nonetheless**.
	despite (THIS)	**(k)** Chifumi has to get up at 5:00 A.M. to get to school on time. **Despite this,** she has never missed a class.
	in spite of (THIS)	**(l)** The day was cold and rainy. **In spite of the inclement weather**, we decided to take a hike.
	on the other hand	**(m)** Learning a new language can be fun. **On the other hand**, it can also be frustrating.

Exercise 13

Look again at Exercise 9. Restate the information in 1, 2, and 4 of Column B as sentence pairs with a contrast sentence connector.

Exercise 14

Use the information in the chart from Exercise 12 to make up five sentence pairs expressing differences between the various European folklore spirits.

EXAMPLE: The favorite pastime of fairies is dancing at night. Brownies, in contrast, enjoy playing tricks the most.

Exercise 15

The chart below gives information about people who had remarkable achievements in the face of adversity. Use the information to make up sentence pairs linked by a concession connector. Use a variety of connectors.

EXAMPLE: Hellen Keller was deaf and blind. *In spite of these difficulties,* she became an eloquent communicator.

Person	Difficulty	Achievement
Helen Keller	was deaf and blind	became an eloquent communicator
Martin Luther King	encountered racial prejudice	preached nonviolence toward adversaries
Beethoven	became deaf	continued to write symphonies
Charles Dickens	grew up in poverty	became a famous novelist
Stephen Hawking	is confined to a wheelchair by Lou Gehrig's disease	became an internationally acclaimed physicist
Jim Abbott	has only one arm	played professional baseball as a pitcher

Exercise 16

As you have seen in this unit, some of the sentence connectors may signal more than one meaning relationship. These include *on the other hand* (alternative, contrast, concession), *in fact* (intensifying addition, contrast), and *however* (contrast, concession). Review these connector meanings in Focus 2 and Focus 7. Then write down which relationship each signals in the sentences below.

1. Driving to Denver will take you 16 hours. On the other hand, you can fly there in less than two hours.
2. The mechanic told me the fuel pump needed to be replaced. In fact, the fuel pump was fine.
3. Your essay is very good. It could use some more variety in vocabulary, however.
4. I might take biology next quarter. On the other hand, I may take geology.
5. In the distance, the next city looked fairly close. However, as it turned out, it wasn't very close at all.
6. That television is expensive. In fact, it costs triple what my old one cost.
7. The newspaper weather forecast predicted heavy rain all weekend. On Saturday, however, there was not a cloud to be seen anywhere.
8. This soup has a good flavor. On the other hand, it could use a little salt.
9. Nylon is a very light material. It is, however, also very strong.
10. I'm having a hard time following these directions. In fact, it seems impossible to figure them out.

225

Focus 9

Sentence Connectors Expressing Causal Relationships

MEANING
USE

- We use sentence connectors that signal cause/effect or reason/result relationships with statements of effects and results. Connectors before statements of causes or reasons are subordinators (such as *since, because, because of, due to the fact that*) rather than sentence connectors.

Meaning	Connector	Example
Show result	*as a result*	**(a)** English spelling rules can be confusing. **As a result,** some have proposed simplified spelling.
	as a result of (THIS)	**(b)** Some people suffer from acrophobia. **As a result of** this phobia, they avoid heights.
	because of (THIS)	**(c)** Canvas is strong material. **Because of its strength**, it is used for tents.
	due to (THIS)	**(d)** A megaphone is a hollow cone. **Due to its shape,** it can amplify sound.
	consequently	**(e)** John couldn't get to the library. **Consequently,** he wasn't able to finish his research.
	therefore	**(f)** The plot of this book is not very original. The ending, **therefore**, is easy to predict.
	thus	**(g)** Spring water is filtered through permeable rocks. **Thus,** it is usually fairly clean.
	hence	**(h)** Fluorocarbons have stable carbon–fluorine bonds; **hence,** they are inert and heat-resistant.

- These reason-result (or cause–effect) connectors differ mainly in degrees of formality. We use connectors *as a result (of)*, *because of*, and *due to* in both spoken and written English. We use the connectors *therefore, consequently, thus,* and *hence* more in written English, with *thus* and *hence* being the most formal. To express reason-result relationships in conversation, speakers tend more to use subordinators like *because* and *since*.
- In addition to effect/result connectors, purpose connectors express causal relationships.

Meaning	Connector	Example
Show purpose	*in order to* (DO THIS)	**(i)** We'll test your cholesterol tomorow. **In order to test it,** we must ask you not to eat anything for four hours.
	with this in mind	**(j)** Catherine needed to go grocery shopping after work. **With this in mind,** she took her grocery list to work.
	for this purpose	**(k)** The house needs to be painted. **For this purpose,** we're now scraping the old paint off.

Exercise 17

The two charts below give information about various characters from myths and legends. Use the information from Chart A to make sentence pairs expressing reason–result relationships. Use Chart B to make sentence pairs expressing purpose relationships. For all sentence pairs, use an appropriate sentence connector.

EXAMPLE: The Norse Gods believed nothing could harm Balder, the sun god. *Consequently,* they thought it fun to hurl weapons at him.

CHART A

Character(s)	Event/Situation	Result
1. Norse gods	believed nothing could harm Balder, the sun god.	thought it fun to hurl weapons at him.
2. Con, relative of Pachacamac, Incan god of fertility	was defeated in battle by Pachacamac.	left Peru and took the rain with him.
3. William Tell	refused to salute the Austrian governor during the Swiss War of Independence	was sentenced to shoot an apple from his son's head with his bow and arrow.
4. Paris, Trojan hero	wanted the beautiful Helen of Troy for his wife.	awarded Aphrodite a golden apple in a contest between her and two other goddesses.

CHART B

Character(s)	Action/Event	Purpose
1. Robin Hood	robbed the rich	help the poor
2. Haokah, Sioux god of thunder	used the wind as a drumstick	create thunder
3. The Pied Piper of Hamelin	played his musical pipe so the rats would follow him out of town	rid Hamelin Town of rats
4. The Pied Piper	rid Hamelin town of rats	wanted the children of Hamelin to follow him

Activities

Activity 1

Look at the paragraph or paragraphs you wrote comparing the two creation myths in the Task. Rewrite your comparison, using some of the sentence connectors in this unit.

Activity 2

In groups, create a list of ten facts or opinions on different topics. Below each fact, leave several spaces. Then pass the list to another group. The members of that group have to add another fact to each statement, using an addition sentence connector to signal the relationship. When they finish, they should pass the list to another group who will do the same thing until several groups have added sentences to the list.

> **EXAMPLE:** Group 1: Tomatoes are very good for you.
>
> Group 2: In fact, they are a good source of vitamins.
>
> Group 3: In addition, they taste good.
>
> Group 4: Furthermore, you can use them in a lot of different ways, such as in making sauces or salads.
>
> Group 1: San Francisco is a beautiful city.
>
> Group 2: It also has great restaurants.
>
> Group 3: It's a book lover's city as well.
>
> Group 4: What's more, you can go sailing in the bay.

Activity 3

Make a list of five words that you think others in the class might not be very familiar with. Use a dictionary if necessary. Try to find words that could be useful additions to someone's vocabulary. Exchange lists with one of your classmates. Each of you should look up the word in the dictionary to see its range of meanings. Then write one sentence using the word in a context and add a statement defining the word, using one of the clarification sentence connectors (*that is* or *in other words*) as was done in Exercise 8. If you wish, you can connect the sentences with a semicolon to show their close relationship.

> **EXAMPLE:** The word *right* is **polysemous**; that is, it has several meanings depending on the context.

Activity 4

Turning point is a term used to describe an event that has changed or influenced someone in an important way. Consider three turning points in your life. Write an essay in which you explain how each turning point has changed your life. Use reason-result sentence connectors in your explanations.

> **EXAMPLE:** One of the major turning points in my life was when my family left Vietnam for the United States. Because of this, we had to start a new life and adjust to an entirely different culture.

Activity 5

Pair up with another classmate. Your task is to find out six things that you have in common and six things that are different about you. The similarities and differences should not be things that are apparent (e.g., not similarities or differences in physical appearance, the similarity of both being in the same class, etc.). Consider topics such as goals, hobbies, travels, language learning, families and various likes and dislikes (foods, sports, courses, books, movies, etc.). As you discover the similarities and differences, make a list of them. Then each of you should write six sentence pairs expressing your discoveries, using similarity and contrast connectors. Divide the task equally so that each of you states three similarities and three differences. Share some of your findings with your classmates.

EXAMPLE: Sven started learning English when he was 12. *Similarly,* I first started taking English courses when I was 13.

Kim loves to read science fiction. *In contrast,* I read mostly nonfiction books.

I love math. Tina, *on the other hand,* hopes she never has to take another math course in her life.

Activity 6

Visit a library and look up some other creation myths from different countries. Write an essay describing what similarities they have and how they differ.

UNIT

15

Discourse Organizers

Sequential Connectors;
There + Logical Sequential
Connectors; Rhetorical
Questions

Task

What national or global issues do you feel strongly about? Perhaps they include the increasing pollution of our environment, the plight of homeless people, or the need for more racial tolerance. Next, consider some of your concerns on a more local or personal level. Does your school lack certain facilities you think you should have? Is crime a problem in your community? Do you feel that some people don't understand members of your age group or ethnic group?

Choose one national or global issue that interests you and one personal or local one. Then, for the two issues you choose, explore each by writing at least five questions about it. Here is an example for the issue of overpopulation:

1. Is overpopulation becoming a more serious problem?
2. How should the problem of overpopulation be dealt with in developing countries?
3. Does anyone have the right to tell others how many children they should have?
4. What are the religious, cultural, and individual factors that need to be considered in addressing the population problem?
5. Can we ever solve the problem of overpopulation?

After you have written your questions, choose one question for each issue and write a paragraph in response to each, answering the question to the best of your knowledge. Do not write the number of the questions in front of your responses. Save your paragraphs for exercises later in this unit. The example below is a response to question 4.

There are a number of factors that may influence people's desire to have large families. One is the conviction that parents should have many children to take care of them in their old age. Also, in some cultures, children provide labor for a family farm or business and help the family maintain steady income. A third factor is that in places where infant mortality is high, couples may have large families because not all the children will survive. Religious beliefs that are opposed to birth control are a fourth factor affecting family size. A fifth is the belief that a large family is a sign of prosperity and health. Finally, there are those who just love having lots of children around. In summary, all these factors need to be considered and addressed in any program designed to deal with the population problem in a given location.

Focus 1

Sequential Connectors: Chronological and Logical Sequence

MEANING
USE

- Sequential connectors may be chronological, logical, or either.
  - **Chronological sequential connectors** signal sequence of events in time, such as in a story or the steps of a process:
    - **(a) At first**, the lake seemed very cold. **Later**, after we had been swimming for a while, it seemed warmer.
  - **Logical sequential connectors** organize the sequence of topics in parts of discourse, such as the parts of a speech or an essay:
    - **(b)** I have several items of business to share with you at this meeting. **First**, I will report on our latest expenditures. **Then**, I will present a proposal for our next ad campaign. **Lastly**, I will tell you about our Christmas party plans.
- The chart below presents some of the most common sequential connectors.

Chronological		
Beginning	*at first*	**(c) At first**, Fred didn't like his new neighbor.
Continuation	*eventually*	**(d)** Eva was running slowly in the race at first. **Eventually** she pulled ahead, though.
	subsequently	**(e)** Our first destination was Seoul, Korea. **Subsequently**, we went to Bangkok, Thailand.
Conclusion	*at last*	**(f) At last** they reached Vancouver, where they planned to spend the night.
	in the end	**(g) In the end**, both our hero and his adversary died.

Chronological and Logical			
		Chronological	**Logical**
Beginning	*first* *first of all* *to start with*	**(h) First**, turn on the ignition. **(j) First of all**, check the gas level. **(l) To start with**, Matt went to Costa Rica.	**(i) First**, let's consider the main issues of this debate. **(k) First of all**, I will discuss the arguments against the construction of a new subdivision. **(m) To start with**, the developers have not done an environmental impact study.
Continuation	*next* *then*	**(n) Next**, he flew to Venezuela. **(p) Then**, he traveled to Brazil. Note that with continuation connectors, one can follow another. A statement with connector *then* could follow a statement with *next*, or one with *next* could follow one with *then*.	**(o) Next**, I will explain my opponent's stand on this issue. **(q) Then**, I will summarize the main points of this debate.
Conclusion	*finally* *lastly*	**(r) Finally**, he spent a few weeks in Argentina. **(t) Lastly**, check the oil level.	**(s) Finally**, I will evaluate the various arguments. **(u) Lastly**, drug abuse is associated with low self-esteem.

Logical		
Beginning	*to begin with* *the first* + noun *one* + noun *in the first place*	**(v) To begin with**, air pollution is the type of pollution most seriously affecting our city. **(w) The first type of pollution** I'd like to discuss is that caused by automobiles. **(x) One cause of prejudice** is ignorance. **(y) In the first place**, we need to get more legislation to help the disabled.
Continuation	*secondly* *the second (third, fourth, etc.)* + noun *a second (third, fourth, etc.)* + noun *in the second place*	**(z) Secondly**, we also have a problem with noise pollution. **(aa) The second point** concerns the issue of whether schools should tell students what they can or cannot wear. **(bb) A second question we might ask** is who should take responsibility for the homeless? **(cc) In the second place**, we need to change our attitudes.
Conclusion	*the last* + noun *a final* + noun *to conclude* *in conclusion*	**(dd) The last reason** is one I am sure everyone is aware of. **(ee) A final question** might be where we will get the funds we need. **(ff) To conclude**, pollution is obviously getting worse in our city. **(gg) In conclusion,** parents must take a more active role in schools.

Exercise 1

Make up a sentence with a beginning sequential connector that could follow each of the sentences below. Try to use a variety of connectors.

> **EXAMPLE:** My family is very special. *In the first place*, my father and mother have worked very hard to provide all of us an education.

1. My family is very special.
2. Learning to ride a bicycle is easy.
3. I appreciate many of the things my friends do for me.
4. Smoking can cause a lot of health problems.
5. Foods with too much fat should be avoided.
6. We need to start taking major steps to save our planet.
7. When I started learning English, it was hard.

Exercise 2

For the sentences below, write a list of ideas that could follow, using beginning, continuation, and concluding sequential connectors in your list. Try to use a variety of connectors.

EXAMPLE: I can think of several things I don't have that I'd like to have. *To start with, I'd like to have a really good camera. Next, I wouldn't mind having a new car. Lastly, I'd love to have my own house.*

1. I can think of several things I don't have that I'd like to have.
2. Our school could use a few improvements.
3. I have a few gripes about _____ (You pick the topic.)
4. I think I have made progress in several areas during the past few years.
5. My home (apartment/room) is a comfortable place for several reasons.
6. Several world problems seem especially critical to me.
7. I wouldn't want to move from where I live for several reasons.
8. I have several goals for my future.

Exercise 3

Look at the paragraphs you wrote for the Task. Did you use sequential connectors? If so, which ones? If not, could you have used some to organize your ideas?

Focus 2

FORM ● USE

The Use of *There + Be* to Introduce Classifications

FORM
USE

- We often use *there* as a discourse organizer when we discuss a topic by dividing it into parts. ***There* + verb** introduces a classification.
  - The verb used is a form of *be* or a modal + *be*:
    (a) There are three ways to get to the freeway from campus.
    (b) There were four principal causes for the recession.
    (c) There could be several explanations for this child's behavior.

234

- Noun phrases that follow the *be* verb include a number or quantifier and, generally, an abstract general noun:

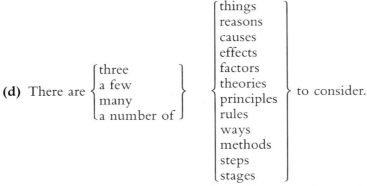

(d) There are $\left\{\begin{array}{l}\text{three}\\ \text{a few}\\ \text{many}\\ \text{a number of}\end{array}\right\}$ $\left\{\begin{array}{l}\text{things}\\ \text{reasons}\\ \text{causes}\\ \text{effects}\\ \text{factors}\\ \text{theories}\\ \text{principles}\\ \text{rules}\\ \text{ways}\\ \text{methods}\\ \text{steps}\\ \text{stages}\end{array}\right\}$ to consider.

- Another common type of noun phrase following *there + be* is:
  (number or quantifier) + *types/kinds* + *of* + **plural noun**
    (e) There are **three kinds of rhetorical questions**.
    (f) There are **several types of students**.
- To organize and introduce subtopics that follow, you may use sequential logical connectors. These sequential connectors were presented in Focus 1. We use the following sequential connectors most often for subtopics after *there + be* introducers.

Beginning	Continuing	Ending
first	*second, third,* etc.	*last*
first of all	*secondly*	*finally*
to start with	*next*	*lastly*
the first + noun	*the second, the third,* etc. + noun	*the last* + noun
one	*a second, a third,* etc.	*the last*
one + noun	*a second* + noun, etc.	*a final* + noun
in the first place	*in the second place*	*finally*

EXAMPLE: (g) **The first** rule of the road is to be courteous.
   (h) In **the first stage** of the process, water is drawn into a tube.
   (i) **A second** cause of teenage crime is lack of hope about the future.
   (j) **Lastly**, pollution can be decreased by driving our cars less.

- In the list above, note that parallel forms of connectors are given for beginning, continuing, and ending. It helps the reader or listener when sequential connectors used to organize texts are of similar types:

  The first rule is . . .
  The second is . . .
  NOT: One rule is. . . . Secondly, . . .

- Composition reference books often caution writers that *there is/there are* can be wordy and therefore should be eliminated in many contexts. That is good advice. Note, however, that *there is* and *there are* as discussed in this unit have rhetorical functions as introducers.

Exercise 4

Fill in the blanks with appropriate words or phrases from Focus 2. Use different forms of connectors for each passage. Add commas where needed.

1. _____ two _____ of twins. _____ is called identical. _____ is called fraternal.

2. _____ four _____ that our teacher has for turning in assignments. _____ we have to use white, lined paper. _____ the paper cannot be torn out of a notebook. _____ we need to use a pen, not a pencil. _____ all papers need to be turned in on time.

3. _____ three main _____ in the process of making rayon, a fabric produced from soft woods and other vegetable materials. _____ the material is pulped. _____ it is treated with caustic soda, nitric acid, and other substances until it turns into a liquid. _____ it is forced through tiny holes in metal, forming liquid filaments which solidify into threads.

    (Information source: *Science and the World around Us*, Chicago: Rand, McNally & Company, 1968.)

4. _____ of pasta, with a great variety of shapes. _____ macaroni, which is a curved tube. _____ fettucine, which looks like a thin ribbon. Capelletti is_____; it is shaped like a hat. _____ is ravioli; it is square-shaped and stuffed with cheese or meat. _____ rotini, which has a corkscrew shape. And these are only a few of them!

Exercise 5

Look again at the paragraphs you wrote for the Task. Did you use a *there+* **verb** introductory phrase? If so, read your sentence to the class. If not, make up a *there* sentence that might be used to develop one of your questions.

Exercise 6

Write a sentence with *there* + **verb** to introduce a classification for each topic below. Then write at least two or three sentences that could develop the topic.

EXAMPLE: *There are three grammar points we will cover this week. One is relative clauses. A second is generic articles. The last is the conditional form of verbs.*

1. Types of books you like the best
2. Things that you think make a good movie or TV program
3. Topics that you are covering in a particular class for a specific amount of time (e.g., a week, a quarter, a semester)
4. Steps for performing a procedure that you know how to do (e.g., replacing a computer ribbon, solving a math problem, studying for an exam, parallel parking)
5. Professions or careers that would be good for someone who likes people
6. A topic of your choice

Focus 3

MEANING
Summary Connectors

MEANING

- Summary connectors also help to organize discourse. Some of these connectors signal that the ideas expressed summarize what has been said before.

Meaning	Connector	Example
General summary	*in summary* *to summarize*	**(a) In summary**, drug abuse is a major problem today. **(b) To summarize**, we should all exercise our right to vote.
Review of main idea	*as has been previously stated/mentioned*	**(c) As has been previously stated**, many people did not consider AIDS a serious problem at first.

- Some summary connectors may be used either after statements to summarize or before them to introduce what will be discussed.

Meaning: Summary of Points		
Connector	Link to Preceding Discourse	Link to Following Discourse
all in all	**(d)** From my talk, I hope you will agree that, **all in all**, our experiments have been successful.	**(e)** I have been asked to report on our recent experiments. **All in all**, they have been very successful.
overall	**(f)** From the evidence presented in this essay, it appears that, **overall**, the quality of television seems to be declining.	**(g) Overall**, the quality of television seems to be declining. For example, the news is getting more like entertainment.

Meaning: Condensation of Points		
Connector	Link to Preceding Discourse	Link to Following Discourse
briefly	**(h) Briefly**, so far I have discussed three of the arguments for gun control.	**(i) Briefly**, the arguments for gun control can be summed up in this way. (Description follows.)
in short	**(j) In short**, as I have shown, the arguments against euthanasia are mostly religious ones.	**(k) In short**, the arguments against euthanasia, which I will discuss next, are mostly religious ones.

Exercise 7

Write a summary statement for each of the sentences or brief passages below. Use the summary connector indicated in parentheses. For statements that will introduce topics, make up any sentence that fits the context.

> **EXAMPLE:** My paper will discuss the problem of overpopulation. (briefly)
>
> Summary statement: *Briefly, overpopulation is a serious threat to the survival of all life on Earth.*

1. Today, I'd like to talk about something I know every one of you is concerned about. (briefly)
2. By hooking a computer into a national electronic system, you can communicate and get information in a number of ways. For example, you can send and receive messages from others who have subscribed to the system or get the weather report for the day. You can take courses or play computer games. You can make travel reservations or look up information in an encyclopedia. (all in all)

3. Without iron, the body wouldn't have hemoglobin, which is an essential protein. Hemoglobin, found in red blood cells, carries oxygen to the rest of the body. A deficiency of iron can cause headaches and fatigue. (in short)

4. Good friendships do not develop easily; they require effort. You need to make time for your friends. You should be prepared to work out problems as they arise, since things will not always go smoothly. You shouldn't expect perfection from your friends. (in summary)

5. So far, I have discussed several of the causes and effects of divorce. (as has been previously mentioned)

6. There are several things to keep in mind if you want to train a dog to obey you. First you need a lot of patience. Secondly, you should not punish your dog for misbehaving but rather correct the inappropriate behavior. You should never hit a dog unless it is threatening to bite someone. Finally, remember to praise your dog for behaving properly. (all in all)

7. Fellow classmates: We have finally reached this proud moment, when we will receive our diplomas as testimony of our many achievements. In my speech to you this afternoon, I would like to stress what I believe is one of the most important purposes of education. (briefly)

8. In many American cities, it's difficult to get much real news from the local television news programs. For example, the local news on a typical hot summer day might feature interviews with people who are complaining about the weather and perhaps a look at this season's swimwear fashions. You may find out how much money a blockbuster movie made at the box office over the weekend. Another "news" segment might tell you about some new product that you can buy. (overall)

Focus 4

Overview of Rhetorical Question Functions

USE

- Rhetorical questions, unlike other questions, are not asked to get information. We can use them in discourse to introduce topics, to focus on key points, and to signal topic changes.

- As a special focusing device for important parts of a written text or a speech, rhetorical questions can help to create reader/listener involvement with your topic and your ideas about it:

  (a) Statement: Overpopulation is becoming a more serious problem.

  (b) Rhetorical Question: Is overpopulation becoming a more serious problem?

  (c) Statement: No one has the right to tell others how many children they should have.

  (d) Rhetorical Question: Does anyone have the right to tell others how many children they should have?

- Rhetorical questions invite the reader to think about an issue with the speaker or author:

  (e) We learn, as we say, by "trial and error." Why do we always say that? Why not "trial and rightness" or "trial and triumph"?

  From Lewis Thomas, "To Err is Human," *The Medusa and The Snail*, (New York: Bantam Books, 1979), p. 30.

Exercise 8

Write a question that might be used to begin a written essay or a speech for at least eight of the following topics. Ask a classmate to tell you which ones he/she finds the most intriguing.

EXAMPLE: Language learning: *Can chimpanzees really learn to talk about bananas?*

1. Gangs
2. Television commercials
3. Pollution
4. Education
5. Computers
6. Teenage pregnancy
7. Language learning
8. Professional athletes
9. Drugs
10. Movies
11. The sixties
12. Prejudice

Exercise 9

Which of the questions that you wrote for the Task do you think might create the most interest for a reader? Exchange your list with one or more class members and get their opinions.

Focus 5

Uses of Rhetorical Questions: Introducing Topics and Background, Focusing on Key Points, Signaling Topic Shifts

USE

- The straightforward, or **direct**, rhetorical question is often used to **introduce topics**. This type of question guides the reader toward answers to be discovered in the text. It may be either a wh-question (*what, why, when, who,* etc.) or a yes-no question.

   (a) How does nitrogen circulate?

   (b) Can the Congress save the budget?

   (c) Is aggression a part of human nature?

   (d) What are the most common causes of fatigue?

- Titles of books, articles, essays, and speeches also use rhetorical questions to introduce their topics.

   (e) "What is a University?" by John Henry Newman

   (f) "Are Women Human?" by Dorothy Sayers

   (g) "Were Dinosaurs Dumb?" by Stephen Jay Gould

- Direct rhetorical questions may also **introduce background information** for a topic.

   (h) Remember the great flouride debate?

   (*Newsweek*, February 5, 1990, p. 61)

   This question introduces background information about the flouride controversy in the 1950's before presenting the main topic—current research on the effects of drinking flouridated water. Note that this question leaves off the first two words, "Do you," of the full question form.

- A second kind of rhetorical question, the **leading question,** is used to focus on the main points of a topic. Leading questions imply a "Yes" answer. In other words, according to the writer's or speaker's intentions, they are incapable of receiving a negative answer:

Rhetorical Question	**Writer/Speaker Viewpoint**
(i) Haven't we had enough wars?	We have.
(j) Don't divorced fathers as well as mothers have rights to their children?	They do.
(k) Isn't English hard enough to learn without all those different article usage rules?	It is.

- Although these questions have negatives, the implication is positive. They can be paraphrased as negative tag questions. For example:

   (l) We've had enough wars, haven't we? (= We have.)

- Another type of rhetorical question that focuses on key points may be characterized as not taking "yes" for an answer. While leading questions have positive implications, this type of question has negative implications:

Rhetorical Question	Writer/ Speaker Viewpoint
(m) What kind of solution is that to our problem?	It is **no kind** of solution, or it is a bad solution.
(n) How much longer can we ignore signs of global warming?	We **can't** ignore them much longer.
(o) Who was more committed to nonviolence than Ghandi?	**No one** was more committed.

- Finally, we often use rhetorical questions in argumentative texts (e.g., editorials, opinion essays) to signal changes from one subtopic to another:
  - **(p)** So far we have looked at the some of the causes of teenage gangs. But what are the effects on the communities in which they thrive?

Exercise 10

The excerpts below are from the beginning paragraphs of books, articles, or essays. For each, predict what the rest of the text might be about.

1. What do we know about the universe, and how do we know it? Where did the universe come from, and where is it going? Did the universe have a beginning, and if so, what happened **before** then? What is the nature of time? Will it ever come to an end?
2. Are you as white knuckled as I am when traveling as an air passenger? What's it worth to save a buck?
3. Do you believe that the more you diet, the harder it is to lose weight because your body adapts and turns down your rate of burning calories—your metabolism?
4. Why is it that when newspapers are confronted with a story that has anything to do with sex, they often screw it up?
5. Who in the world—in his right mind—would ever pick Mike Donald to win a U.S. Open?*

*The U.S. Open referred to here is a golf championship.

Exercise 11

Exchange the two paragraphs you wrote for the Task with a classmate who has not seen your list of questions about the issues. Write a rhetorical question that might introduce the information for each of your classmate's paragraphs. If necessary, you may change the lead sentence that your classmate wrote to eliminate any repeated information.

> **EXAMPLE:** *What makes couples reluctant to limit the size of their families? There are a number of factors.*

When you have finished, read each other's questions to see if they accurately reflect the paragraph topics.

Exercise 12

Write a leading question to express each of the following opinions. More than one form is possible, and some ideas may need to be rephrased, not just transformed into a question. State the positive implication of each in parentheses.

> **EXAMPLE:** Opinion: We've gone far enough in the space race.
>
> Possible questions and implications:
>
> *Isn't it time to stop the space race? (It is.)*
>
> *Haven't we gone far enough in the space race? (We have.)*
>
> *Shouldn't we consider stopping the space race? (We should.)*

1. Our senior citizens deserve more respect.
2. We need to start thinking more globally.
3. Our school already has too many required courses.
4. Women deserve the same job opportunities as men.
5. All people should have a place to live.

Exercise 13

State the negative implications of the following rhetorical questions taken from various published texts. The thesis for each is given in parentheses. Which of the questions do you find most effective in making their points? Which question has the form of a declarative sentence (an uninverted question)?

1. How many Americans can afford a $45,000 Mercedes Benz? Should auto safety be reserved only for the wealthy?
   (Thesis: Auto safety devices such as air bags need to be put in all cars.)
2. Fair-minded people have to be against bigotry. How, then, can fair-minded people ignore, condone, or promote discrimination against divorced fathers—100 percent of whom are men—and make believe it isn't discrimination?
   (Thesis: In child custody cases, the courts often discriminate against divorced fathers.)
3. I am, I hope, a reasonably intelligent and sensitive man who tries to think clearly about what he does. And what I do is hunt, and sometimes kill. . . . Does the power that orchestrates the universe accord a deer more importance than a fly quivering in a strip of sticky tape?
   (Thesis: People should not be against hunters because everyone kills living things.)

4. One of the more popular [comic book] characters is Wolverine, a psychopath with retractable metal claws embedded in his hands and a set of killer instincts that make him a threat to friend and foe alike. This is a proper model for children?
(Thesis: The themes and characters in modern comic books are not appropriate for children.)

5. In 1977, the federal government spent twice as much on dental research as it did on alcoholism research. How many murders and fatal accidents are accounted for by impacted wisdom teeth or unsightly overbite?
(Thesis: More research on alcoholism is needed.)

6.

(Thesis: Everyone needs a moisturizer!)

Exercise 14

The following excerpts from an essay by Isaac Asimov use rhetorical questions to develop an argument about the need to control the world's population. Identify the rhetorical questions. Then discuss how the author uses them to develop his ideas. Which ones signal topic shifts? What is the overall effect of the questions? Do you think they are effective in involving you as a reader in the topic?

LET'S SUPPOSE....
by Isaac Asimov

Suppose the whole world became industrialized and that industry and science worked very carefully and very well. How many people could such a world support? Different limits have been suggested, but the highest figure I have seen is 20 billion. How long will it take before the world contains so many people?

For the sake of argument, and to keep things simple, let's suppose the demographic growth rate will stay as it is, at two per cent per annum.... At the present growth rate our planet will contain all the people that an industrialized world may be able to support by about 2060 A.D....

Suppose we decide to hope for the best. Let us suppose that a change *will* take place in the next 70 years and that there will be a new age in which population can continue rising to a far higher level than we think it can now.... Let's suppose that this sort of thing can just keep on going forever.

Is there any way of setting a limit past which nothing can raise the human population no matter how many changes take place?

Suppose we try to invent a real limit; something so huge that no one can imagine a population rising past it. Suppose we imagine that there are so many men and women and children in the world, that altogether they weigh as much as the whole planet does. Surely you can't expect there can be more people than that.

Let us suppose that the average human being weighs 60 kilogrammes. If that's the case then 100,000,000,000,000,000,000 people would weigh as much as the whole Earth does. That number of people is 30,000,000,000,000 times as many people as there are living now.

... Let us suppose that the population growth-rate stays at 2.0 per cent so that the number of people in the world continues to double every 35 years. How long, then, will it take for the world's population to weigh as much as the entire planet?

The answer is- not quite 1,600 years. This means that by 3550 A.D., the human population would weigh as much as the entire Earth. Nor is 1,600 years a long time. It is considerably less time than has passed since the days of Julius Caesar.

Do you suppose that perhaps in the course of the next 1,600 years, it will be possible to colonize the Moon and Mars, and the other planets of the Solar system? Do you think that we might get many millions of people into the other world in the next 1,600 years and thus lower the population of the Earth itself?

Even if that were possible, it wouldn't give us much time. If the growth-rate stays at 2.0 per cent, then in a little over 2,200 years—say by 4220 A.D.—the human population would weigh as much as the entire Solar system, including the Sun.

(From *Earth: Our Crowded Spaceship*, 1974)

Activities

Activity 1

Choose one of the issues you focused on for the Task or some other issue you are interested in. Perhaps one of the topics in Exercise 1 might be of interest. Write an essay using sequential connectors to organize your topics.

Activity 2

Think of a topic that can be classified into parts or aspects (kinds of things, steps in a process, etc.), a topic that your classmates would know something about. Write a sentence for the topic using *there are*.

> **EXAMPLE:** *There are* lots of things you need to be aware of when you're driving.
>
> *There are* several ways to get from campus to the airport.
>
> *There are* many kinds of students at this school.

Exchange papers with another classmate and write one thing/way/kind, etc., that could develop the topic. When you are through, exchange again with a different student and add something to another paper. Use appropriate connectors. Continue exchanging papers until each has at least three or four sentences that develop the topic. Read some of the results aloud.

Activity 3

Expand one of the following topics into an essay:

There are a number of things a new student to this campus should be told when he/she gets here.
There are several (or many) goals I have for the future.
One of the topics you developed for the task.

Activity 4

Look through magazines and newspapers for evidence of rhetorical questions in advertisements. Discuss the kinds of questions that are used to sell products. Then create your own ad for a product, either a written one that might be used in a magazine or a script that could be used for a TV or radio commercial. Share your creations with the class; if possible, perform the commercials.

Activity 5

Along with cautions about overuse of *there*, composition textbooks often warn writers to use rhetorical questions sparingly. While this is generally good advice, some writers and speakers use them quite liberally in argumentation. The following are two examples of this. Discuss whether you think they are effective in getting their points across.

One by one, human failings have been redesignated as diseases.... Do you find yourself lacking energy? Are you accomplishing less than others think you should? Could you be suffering from that 19th-century imperfection called laziness? Not a chance; you've got hypoglycemia, the most deadly epidemic since the plague.... Remember the old days when you thought they called it work because it was difficult, unpleasant, and boring? Those days are over. Remember when drug or alcohol abuse was a product of some combination of hedonism and foolishness? That era has ended too. Now you're an addict.

(Rex Julian Beaber, "Stress and Other Scapegoats" *Newsweek*, April 4, 1983, p. 13.)

Suppose there were no critics to tell us how to react to a picture, a play, or a new composition of music. Suppose we wandered innocent as the dawn into an art exhibition of unsigned paintings. By what standards, by what values would we decide whether they were good or bad, talented or untalented, successes or failures? How can we ever know that what we think is right?

. . . .

Purpose and craftmanship end—and means—these are the keys to your judgment in all the arts. What is this painter trying to say when he slashed a broad band of black across a white canvas and lets the edges dribble down? Is it a statement of violence? Is it a self-portrait? If it is *one* of these, has he made you believe it? Or is this a gesture of the ego or a form of therapy? If it shocks you, what does it shock you into?

And what of this tight little painting of bright flowers in a vase? Is the painter saying anything new about flowers? Is it different from a million other canvases of flowers? Has it any life, any meaning, beyond its statement? Is there any pleasure in its forms or texture?

(Marya Mannes, "How Do You Know It's Good?" from *But Will It Sell*, J. P. Lippincott, 1962.)

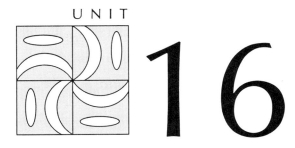

UNIT

16

Conditionals
Only If/Unless Even Though/Even If

Task

"When I was young, we didn't speak unless we were spoken to! We were allowed to go out only if we had done all the housework." Sound familiar? Part of the process of growing up is listening to your parents, grandparents, or other older relatives tell you how things were different "back then" or "when we were your age." What have your parents, grandparents, aunts, or uncles told you about the way life was for them when they were young or before you were born? Write brief answers to as many of the following questions as you can:

1. How did they get around from place to place?
2. What did they do for entertainment?
3. What family rituals or celebrations did they observe?
4. What rules did they have to obey as young children or teenagers?
5. What hardships did they have to endure?

Share your responses with your classmates. In general, do you think your older relatives had a harder life than you do now or an easier one? Do you think their lives were more complex or simpler? Discuss your views with others in your class.

Focus 1

Exclusive Conditions:
Only If and *Unless*

MEANING

- Use *if* to indicate conditions for an event in the main clause:

Main Clause	Condition
(a) As a girl, my grandmother went shopping every Saturday afternoon	**if** she had finished all of her assigned chores at home.

- To emphasize the **only condition** under which an event will or should take place, use *only if* or *unless.*
  - Use *only if* when the main clause is affirmative; it means "only on the condition that":

Main Clause	Condition
(b) My grandmother went shopping	**only if** she had finished her assigned chores.

  - Use *unless* when the main clause is negative; it means "except on the condition that":

Main Clause	Condition
(c) My grandmother didn't go shopping	**unless** she had finished her assigned chores.

- You can also use *unless* with affirmative main clauses. The implication is negative, however:

Main Clause	Condition
(d) As a girl, my grandmother stayed home on Saturday	**unless** she had finished her homework.

Implication: As a girl, Grandmother **didn't** go anywhere on Saturday if she hadn't finished her homework.

- Summary

Main Clause	Subordinator
Affirmative	*only if* *unless* (negative implication)
Negative	*unless*

Note that for hypothetical situations, use the subjunctive form *were:* Nowadays, my grandmother would spend the day shopping only if she **were** bored.

Exercise 1

Decide whether *if, only if,* or *unless* should be used in each blank.

When We Were Your Age...

As each generation ages (or should we say, matures), it tends to judge the younger generations as somehow not quite measuring up to those of the past; the new generation may be regarded as a bit lazier, less disciplined, or less imaginative. My family was no exception. "Drive to school?" my father would exclaim to my siblings and me. "Why, when we were your age, we walked everywhere (1) _____ there was a blizzard. And if we couldn't walk, we went by car (2) _____ the buses weren't running." The meal options were generally fewer for my parents' generation also: "(3) _____ we didn't like what was served for dinner," my mother would remind us, "we had to eat it anyway." According to my parents, entertainment was more active before television-watching became the main leisure pursuit, and obligations more strictly followed. As children, they usually played games outside (4) _____ the weather was dreadful. And that, of course, was allowed (5) _____ all homework had been completed. Later, dating in high school wasn't permitted (6) _____ grades were acceptable, and then (7) _____ the parents had met the potential date.

Perhaps people shouldn't talk about the past (8) _____ they promise not to make the present sound so much worse than the past. Or they could make comparisons (9) _____ they admit that some aspects of the past weren't so great. On the other hand, glorifying the past and complaining about the present may be an inalienable right of the older generations.

Exercise 2

Make each of the following a negative condition by using *unless* instead of *only if* and making other changes as necessary.

> **EXAMPLE:** When I was your age, we went to the movies *only if* it was a holiday.
>
> When I was your age, we *didn't go* to the movies *unless* it was a holiday.

1. Back in the old days, we locked our houses only if we were going on a vacation.
2. We could have ice cream for dessert only if it was a special occasion.
3. We could go out after dinner only if we had cleaned up the kitchen.
4. In high school, we were permitted to stay overnight at our friends' houses only if all the parents had met each other.
5. We were allowed to go to house parties only if they were chaperoned by adults.

Exercise 3

Look again at the list of answers you made for the Task. Did any items on your list have conditions? Make up an *only if* or *unless* condition for some of the items on your list and share them with the class.

> **EXAMPLE:** My great-grandfather milked the cows every morning at 6:00 A.M. *unless* he was ill.

Focus 2

FORM ● USE

Subject/Verb Inversion with Fronted *Only If* and *Not Unless* Emphasizers

FORM
USE

- You can use *only if* or *not unless* at the beginning of a sentence to emphasize a condition. When they begin a sentence, the first verb (auxiliary or copula *be*) and the subject of the main clause are inverted.

Condition	Main Clause
(a) **Only if** our parents approved	**could we go** out on a date.
(b) **Not unless** a party is chaperoned	**will my parents allow** me to attend.

- The subject and verb are not inverted if the sentence begins with *unless*. A comma separates the condition from the main clause:

Condition	Main Clause
(c) Unless my parents give permission,	**I can't go** on the weekend trip.

Exercise 4

Express these statements from a course syllabus more emphatically by beginning the sentence with *only if* or *not unless*. Make any changes you think are needed (e.g., change pronouns to nouns).

1. You may not turn in papers late unless you are ill.
2. Assignments may be handwritten only if they are daily homework exercises.
3. Students will receive credit for this course only if they attend at least two-thirds of the class sessions.

Focus 3

MEANING

If . . . Not versus Unless

MEANING

- In statements expressing **hypothetical or future events**, *unless* and *if . . . not* have roughly the same meaning:

Future Main Clause	Future Conditional Clause
(a) Juana will take a math course	**if** it does **not** conflict with her work schedule. **unless** it conflicts with her work schedule.
(b) She won't take a science course	**if** it does **not** satisfy a requirement. **unless** it satisfies a requirement.

- In statements expressing **past conditions**:
  - a conditional clause with *if . . . not* is contrary to fact. The main clause is also contrary to fact:

Contrary to Past Fact Main Clause	Contrary to Past Fact Conditional Clause
(c) Violeta couldn't have passed her Latin exam (Violeta **did** pass her exam.)	**if** she had**n't** had a tutor. (She **did** have a tutor.)

251

- in a conditional clause with *unless*, two meanings are possible:

Main Clause	Conditional Clause
(d) Violeta couldn't have passed her Latin exam	**unless** she'd had a tutor.

Possible Implications:

1. Violeta **did** have a tutor. She **did pass** the exam. (Both clauses are contrary to fact, the same as with *if . . . not* conditional statements.)
2. Violeta **did not have** a tutor. She **did not pass** the exam. (Only tutoring might have prevented her from failing.)

- In statements with main clauses that are contrary to present fact, use only *if . . . not* in the conditional clause:

Contrary to Present Fact Main Clause	Contrary to Present Fact Conditional Clause
(e) Cho and Ben wouldn't have so much homework this term (They have a lot of homework.)	**if** they were **not** enrolled in the calculus course. (They are enrolled in the calculus course.)
(f) They would have a lot of spare time (They don't have much spare time.)	**if** they were **not** in that class. (They are in the class.)

- **(g)** NOT: Cho and Ben wouldn't have so much homework **unless** they were enrolled in the calculus course.
- **(h)** NOT: They would have a lot of spare time **unless** they were in that course.
- Use the expression *if it weren't (hadn't been) for* + noun with contrary to fact main clauses:

Conditional Clause	Contrary to Fact Main Clause
(i) If it weren't for you,	I would still be working at that horrible place. (I am no longer working at that place.)
(j) If it hadn't been for Pham's English-speaking friends' encouragement	she wouldn't be so fluent in English. (Pham is fluent in English.)

- *Unless* is not used in this way:
  - **(k)** NOT: **Unless** it were for you . . .
  - **(l)** **Unless** it had been for her English-speaking friends' encouragement . . .

Exercise 5

Complete each of the blanks by forming a negative conditional statement with the cues in parentheses, which give conditions that are contrary to fact. Use *if . . . not* or *unless* as appropriate. In cases where both are possible, use *unless*. Add any words or phrases you think are needed.

> **EXAMPLES:** Sandy needs two more courses in chemistry to graduate. He's glad now that he took a chemistry course last year because _____ .
>
> (not complete Chemistry I/not be able to enroll in Advanced Chemistry this term)
> Completion: *unless he had completed Chemistry I, he wouldn't have been able to enroll in Advanced Chemistry this term.*
>
> Gabriela is really good at calculus. I know that she is because _____ .
>
> (be not/not be able to get perfect scores on all her exams)
> Completion: *if she weren't, she wouldn't be able to get perfect scores on all her exams.*

1. Randy's advisor was concerned that Randy had decided not to take a typing class.

   Randy explained that _____

   _____ .

   (not drop the typing class/not be able to work at the the pharmacy last month)

2. Earl has been complaining all term about the amount of reading he has to do for his

   courses. He says that the history class is the worst. In fact, _____

   _____ .

   (not take a history course/ have only light reading right now for his classes)

3. Rita is glad that she tape-recorded her grandfather talking about his childhood. _____

   _____ .

   (not record his reminiscences/not know about this part of her family history.)

4. Natasha took a TOEFL preparation course. She told me that _____

   _____ .

   (not take the course/be much more worried about the exam)

5. I just read about the thousands of acres of forest land that are destroyed by fires every

year. People need to take better care of natural resources. _____

_____ .

(not so careless with the environment/be able to enjoy its beauty more)

Exercise 6

Complete the following sentences with a statement about yourself.

EXAMPLE: If it hadn't been for my parents,
I might not have gone to college.
I would have considered a different profession instead of joining the family business.

1. If it hadn't been for my parents,
2. If it weren't for my friends' support,
3. If it hadn't been for my English teacher,
4. If it weren't for (name) _____ 's good advice,

Focus 4

MEANING

Emphatics: *Even Though* and *Even If*

MEANING

- We use both *even though* and *even if* to emphasize conditions. However, their meanings are different:
  - *Even though* is an emphatic form of *although*. It means "despite the fact that." The condition after *even though* is a reality:

Main Clause	Actual Condition
(a) My uncle walked to work	**even though** his job was five miles away.

- *Even if* is an emphatic form of *if*. It means "whether or not." The condition after *even if* may or may not be a reality.

Main Clause	Condition Actual or Not
(b) My uncle will walk to work	**even if** it is raining. (He walks when it rains as well as when it doesn't rain.)

254

- With past tense and habitual present conditions, *even if* can mean "even when":

   (c) My uncle $\begin{Bmatrix} \textbf{walks} \\ \textbf{used to walk} \end{Bmatrix}$ to work **even if** it $\begin{Bmatrix} \textbf{rains.} \\ \textbf{was raining.} \end{Bmatrix}$

- *Even* cannot be used by itself as a substitute for *even though* or *even if*:

   (d) NOT: **Even** it rains tomorrow, I'll walk to school. (Use *even if*.)

   (e) NOT: **Even** it was raining, I walked to school yesterday. (Use *even though*.)

Exercise 7

Choose the correct form—*even though* or *even if*—for each blank.

1. Fran's mother was never without a car. However, she would often walk three miles to the market _____ she could have driven if she had wanted to.

2. _____ Duane's grandfather had a daytime job, he also worked every evening for many years.

3. Our family had a rule for dinner: We had to eat at least a few bites of each kind of food. _____ the food was something we had tried before and didn't like, we still had to eat a mouthful.

4. Last Christmas Eve, _____ the temperature dropped to below zero, my father insisted we take our traditional stroll through the neighborhood singing Christmas carols.

5. We'd love for you to spend the holidays with us. It would be wonderful if you could stay at least a week. But _____ it's only for a day or so, we hope you'll plan to come.

Exercise 8

Complete each of the blanks below with information about your efforts to achieve current goals and your dreams for the future. Share your responses with your classmates.

1. Even though I don't like to _____ , I do it anyway because _____
   _____ .

2. I try to _____ even if _____
   _____ .

3. Even though _____ , I hope I can _____
   _____ .

4. Even if I never _____ , I still _____
   _____ .

5. I would like to _____ even though _____
   _____ .

Focus 5

USE

Giving Advice

USE

- We often use the connectors in this unit in statements of advice that include conditions:
  - **(a)** Don't make reservations at the Four Seasons restaurant **unless you're prepared to spend a lot of money.**
  - **(b)** Take a foreign language course **only if you're willing to do homework daily.**
- We sometimes use humorous conditions with advice statements to make a point indirectly; the condition is not to be taken literally:
  - **(c)** Don't go to see the movie *Last Alien in Orlando* **unless you need a nap.**
    (Implication: The movie is boring.)
  - **(d)** Take English 4 **only if you have nothing to do on the weekends**.
    (Implication: The class is difficult; you'll have a lot of homework.)

Exercise 9

The columns below are draft notes for an unfinished travel guidebook, *Making Your Way Around the U.S.: Dos and Don'ts.* The rather eccentric author separated the advice from the conditions on note cards, as shown in the two columns below. Decide which condition in the second column matches each piece of advice in the first column.

Advice

1. Visit Fairbanks, Alaska, in January
2. Don't attempt to sprint to the top of the 110-story Sears Tower in Chicago
3. Don't pass up the delicious deep fried Cajun crawfish in New Orleans.
4. Resist feeding the bears in Yellowstone Park, Wyoming
5. Plan your trip to Florida's Disneyworld on a holiday
6. Pack plenty of insect repellent for your summer vacation to Bangor, Maine
7. Don't order the Wiener schnitzel at Helmut's Gasthof in Milwaukee, Wisconsin
8. Take an umbrella to Seattle
9. Get on the Los Angeles freeway during rush hour
10. Don't plan to get into the trendiest nightclubs in New York City

Condition

a. even if they offer you a tour of Old Faithful Geyser
b. only if you enjoy taking naps while you're driving.
c. even if they offer you a fine bottle of German wine to accompany your meal.
d. unless you are fond of mosquitoes and other pesky little creatures.
e. even though your travel agent assures you that the rainy season is over.
f. only if you've wondered what it's like to run around in seven layers of clothing.
g. unless you've recently won an academy award, been on the cover of *Vanity Fair*, or are on a first-name basis with the doorman.
h. even though your cholesterol level approaches the number of days in a year.
i. only if you believe that waiting in long lines is a wonderful way to develop patience.
j. unless you've been in training for a marathon.

Exercise 10

Make advice statements by combining information in the Conditions and Advice Columns. Use an appropriate conjunction: *if, only if, unless, even if, even though.* Make any changes necessary. The condition statements can either begin or end your sentences.

EXAMPLE: Condition   **Advice**

     you have plenty of water   take a hike in Death Valley

     Unless you have plenty of water, don't take a hike in Death Valley.

     Take a hike in Death Valley *only if you have plenty of water.*

Condition

1. you don't have a wet suit to keep you warm.
2. you are in Cody, Wyoming
3. you have exact change for the busfare.
4. you love spicy food.
5. the doorman at your hotel calls a cab for you.
6. you like leisurely trips.
7. you don't mind climbing a lot of stairs
8. your budget is limited.

Advice

a. order the Kung Pao chicken at the Panda Inn.
b. take a riverboat cruise on the Mississippi River.
c. walk to the top of the cathedral in Seville, Spain.
d. get on a bus in New York City
e. treat yourself to a good meal in Paris.
f. don't go swimming off the Oregon Coast in winter.
g. be sure to visit the Buffalo Bill Museum of the Wild West.
h. don't forget to tip him.

Exercise 11

The paragraph below has five errors involving the conditions focused on in this unit. Identify and correct them.

HOW TO EVALUATE HEALTH NEWS

(1) These days we are constantly hearing and reading about biomedical studies concerned with factors that affect our health. (2) Even these studies often present results as general "facts," the conclusions are not always true. (3) Only if multiple studies have been done it is wise to generalize results to a larger population. (4) Furthermore, you shouldn't be too quick to believe a study unless the number of subjects involved isn't large because generalizations cannot be made from a small sample size. (5) Even the sample size is big enough, the results may not be statistically significant. (6) In other words, a statistical difference between two factors may be important only the difference could not happen by chance.

Activities

Activity 1

Make a list of five things that you are reasonably sure you want to do or will do in the future (e.g., graduate from college in three years; spend Saturday parachuting). For each item, write a sentence that includes a necessary condition. Use *if* for each condition.

> **EXAMPLES:** I'll graduate from college in three years *if I can take four courses each term.*
>
> I'm going parachuting on Saturday *if it doesn't rain.*

Exchange your sentences with a classmate. Rewrite each of your classmate's sentences, changing each condition to an exclusive condition. Use either *even if* or *unless* as appropriate.

> **EXAMPLES:** I'll graduate from college in three years *only if I can take four courses each term.*
>
> I'm going parachuting on Saturday *unless it rains.*

Check each other's rewrites for accuracy. Then discuss whether or not any of the rewrites changed the meanings of the statements.

Activity 2

Most of us have some strong opinions or beliefs about things that we would never do or that we would be very unlikely to do. For example, a person might believe that she would never accept a job that she hated, or would never live in a very cold climate. Similarly, we may believe we *would* probably do certain things under most circumstances, such as studying for final examinations or keeping in touch with our families. Make a list of five things that you believe you would be very unlikely to do. For each item on your list, imagine a circumstance under which you might change your mind or be forced to behave differently and write it down as a possible exception. Use either *unless* or *only if*. Here is an example.

> I wouldn't live in a very large city.
> *Exception*: I would do it *only if* I could be chauffeured wherever I wanted to go.

Make another list of five things that you usually do or that you would do under most circumstances. For each, imagine a situation that might cause you to behave otherwise and label it as a possible exception. Here is an example:

I watch either football or baseball games every weekend.

Exception: I watch them every weekend *unless I am out of town*.

Compare your responses with those of your class members.

Activity 3

Here's a chance to share your knowledge. Either individually or as a collaborative project with some of your classmates, create one of the following guides.

1. A guide that informs students which courses at your school to avoid or which to take only under certain conditions.
2. Advice about what to do or not to do in your hometown or country.
3. A guide of your choice

For as many items as possible, use condition statements with *only if, unless, even if*, or *even though*. Your conditions could be humorous or serious.

Activity 4

Imagine that you can run your school or city for a year. You can make any rules/laws you wish, and everyone will have to obey them. Make a list of the regulations you will enforce, using conditional statements where they might be needed.

Activity 5

Write an essay describing the life of one of your older relatives or friends from information you have heard about him/her. Use at least a few conditional statements in your description.

Activity 6

Discuss the attitudes of different cultures toward advice given by the oldest members of their societies. Do the cultures you know about respect and try to follow the words of wisdom offered by their senior citizens? What differences in attitudes have you observed among cultures?

U N I T

17

Adverbial Clause Reduction/Participles

Task

On one of your hiking trips to Rowland's Ridge, you unearthed an old diary with a few sparse notes scrawled in it. Apparently, a lonely traveler had kept a record of his travels some 100 years ago. Using your map (provided below), trace the traveler's steps. Then, orally discuss his route and what occurred along the way in class. Use as much of the diary information as you can.

> **EXAMPLE:** Discouraged by poor crops and having no cash, the traveler left Springton in order to find work.

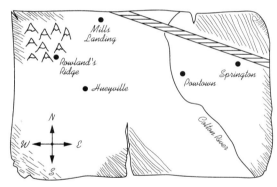

Jan. 30: Discouraged by poor crops. No cash. Left Springton to find work.

Feb. 4: Today searched for job in Powtown. No luck. All jobs require skills I don't have.

March 15: Crossed the Colton River but raft turned over. Lost everything except diary and my watch. Walked to Hueyville.

March 18: No work in Hueyville. Met kind woman in Hueyville. Told me about vacant house abandoned by miners near Rowland's Ridge

March 21: Sold my watch for supplies. Hiked to Rowland's Ridge. Found shack and moved in.

March 27: Days and days of rainy weather. Decided to fix up place. Borrowed tools to fix roof, walls, and floors.

March 29: Hammering floorboards. Saw red bag. Opened it. Eureka! A bag full of money. I am rich.

April 8: Guilty conscience. Worry about possible owner. Hiked to Mills Landing and ask Sheriff what to do. Says the money is mine because money left long ago. No one will ever claim.

April 10: My troubles are over! Back to Springton by train!

Focus 1

Temporal Adverbial Clauses

FORM
MEANING

- We can reduce temporal adverbial clauses that contain the words *after, before, while, when,* and *since* to participial phrases containing *-ing.* This is only possible if the subject in the adverbial clause is the same as the subject in the main clause.

Full Adverbial Clause	Reduced Adverbial Clause	Temporal Meaning
(a) While *we* were hiking last summer, we admired the scenery around us.	**(b) (While) hiking last summer,** we admired the scenery around us.	A time overlapping with the time expressed in the main clause.
(c) After *we* had hiked around half of the canyon rim, we were exhausted.	**(d) (After) having hiked around half of the canyon rim,** we were exhausted.	A time preceding the time expressed in the main clause.

Note that for each of these reduced temporal adverbial clauses, the adverb is optionally included.

Exercise 1

Complete the following sentences about the out-of-doors. Give advice, using an imperative.

> **EXAMPLE:** After getting lost in the woods, <u>look for familiar landmarks such as hills or trees</u>.

1. While treading along a narrow ridge, _____ .

2. When hiking in an area with poisonous snakes, _____ .

3. After getting frostbite, _____ .

4. Before entering mosquito country, _____ .

5. When washing dishes in the wilderness, _____ .

6. Before lighting a fire in the woods, _____ .

Exercise 2

Review your responses in the Task and write at least five sentences containing reduced temporal adverbial phrases like those shown in the focus box.

> **EXAMPLE:** After having returned to Springton with a bag of money, the lonely traveler was much happier than before.

Focus 2

FORM

Reduced Causal Adverbial Clauses with -*ing*

FORM

- We can also reduce causal adverbial clauses containing *because, since,* and *as* to -*ing* phrases. Again the subject in the main clause must be the same as the subject in the adverbial clause.

Full Adverbial Clause	Reduced Adverbial Clause
(a) Since/Because they enjoyed company, they invited us to visit.	**(b) Enjoying company,** they invited us to visit.
(c) As I had never gone skiing, I decided to take lessons.	**(d) Never having gone skiing,** I decided to take lessons. (Note that in the reduced form, a negative word like *never* or *not* precedes the auxiliary verb *have*.)

- Note that these reduced causal adverbial clauses cannot optionally include the adverb as the temporal adverbial clauses had done (i.e., It is not possible to say "Because enjoying company, they invited us to visit."). Also, these reduced adverbial clauses show both cause and ongoing action.

Exercise 3

Referring back to the Task, complete the following sentences.

EXAMPLE: Not having had a good harvest, <u>the man left Springton.</u>

1. Having no luck in Powtown, _____ .

2. Knowing he had no place to stay, _____ .

3. Selling his watch, _____ .

4. Being depressed by days of rainy weather, _____ .

5. Being blessed by good fortune, _____ .

6. Feeling guilty about the money, _____ .

Exercise 4

Imagine that you received a letter from a friend who is having a difficult time adjusting to life at a university in the United States. She is making excuses for several of her actions. Give her advice, using a reduced causal adverbial clause.

EXAMPLE: Because I arrived at my first class late, I waited outside the room and missed the entire lecture.

Having arrived to the class late, you should have quietly entered the room and sat down.

1. Because I have no typewriter, I do not type my papers.
2. Since my roommate plays loud music, I do not do my homework.
3. As I cannot understand my instructor, I have stopped going to class.
4. Because I do not know anyone, I sit alone in my room for hours.
5. Since I hate the food on campus, I go out for dinner every night and now I'm almost broke.

Focus 3

Reduced Causal Adverbial Clauses with -ed

- We can also reduce other adverbial clauses that contain past participles -ed and have causal meaning. Again, the subject in the adverbial clause must be the same as the subject in the main clause.

Full Adverbial Clause	Reduced Adverbial Clause	Meaning
(a) Because we were exposed to the elements, we got sun and wind burn.	**(b) Exposed to the elements,** we got sun and wind burn.	The adverbial clause gives a reason for the result in the main clause.
(c) Since we were being whipped by the cold wind, we zipped and buttoned our jackets more snugly.	**(d) Being whipped by the cold wind,** we zipped and buttoned our jackets more snugly.	The progressive aspect emphasizes the reason or cause for the result in the main clause.
(e) As we had been burned by the sun, we applied a soothing ointment to our faces.	**(f) Having been burned by the sun,** we applied a soothing ointment to our faces.	The action in the participle is completed and is the reason for the activity in the main clause.

Exercise 5

Tony and Maria have had several mishaps on their camping trip. Suggest a cause for each mishap by adding a reduced adverbial clause to each sentence below.

> **EXAMPLE:** They got lost on their hike.
>
> *Not having brought a map,* they got lost on their hike.

1. Tony was bitten by mosquitoes.
2. They were very thirsty.
3. They were very hungry.
4. Maria jumped in fright.
5. Maria was shivering.
6. Tony rubbed his blisters.

Focus 4

Ambiguity of Participial Phrases; Punctuation of Participial Phrases

FORM
MEANING

- Some reduced adverbial clauses before or after the main clause subject resemble reduced nonrestrictive relative clauses. Because of this, not all reduced clauses are adverbial. Sometimes they are adjectival.

Reduced Clause	Adverbial Function	Adjectival Function
(a) The miner, **living in poverty,** returned the money.	**(b)** The miner, (while he was) living in poverty, returned the money.	**(c)** The miner, (who was) living in poverty, returned the money. (The relative pronoun + *be* are deleted in the nonrestrictive relative clause.)
(d) The miner, **camped for the night on the Colton River,** began to write in his diary.	**(e)** The miner, (because he was) camped for the night on the Colton River, began to write in his diary.	**(f)** The miner, (who was) camped for the night on the Colton River, began to write in his diary.

- Reduced adverbial clauses (participial phrases) may appear at the beginning, middle, or end of a sentence. (The middle position is the least frequent.) Commas are needed in all positions, except the sentence-final position with the adverb included.
  - Position
    - **Initial:**
      - **(g)** Hiking alone in the mountains, Diane always carries water and a compass.
      - **(h)** Having signaled for help, all they could do was wait.
    - **Mid:**
      - **(i)** The men, fearing an attack, formed a circle with their wagons.
      - **(j)** The doe, having been frightened by the noise, disappeared from the clearing.
    - **Final:**
      - **(k)** The mountain climbers cheered, having reached their destination before sunset.
      - **(l)** The trackers waded across the river, holding tightly to the reins of their horses.
      - **(m)** The trackers waded across the river **while** holding tightly to the reins of their horses.

- Reduced adjectival clauses can be confused with reduced adverbial clauses only when they appear in beginning or middle position near the nouns they modify.
  - **Adverbial or Adjectival:**
    - (n) *Swimming vigorously,* **the horses** were able to cross the raging river.
    - (o) **The boys,** *covered with mud,* swam in the lake.
  - **Adverbial only:**
    - (p) **The horses** were able to cross the raging river, *swimming vigorously.*

Exercise 6

Fill in the following table with reduced adverbial or adjectival clauses. The first one has been done for you.

EXAMPLE: *Feeling reckless,* she sped along a winding road.

Reduced Clause   **Main Clause**

1. _____ she sped along a winding road.

2. _____ she beeped loudly at the car in front of her.

3. _____ she slammed into a tree.

4. _____ she hit her head on the windshield.

5. _____ a policeman came to the scene.

6. _____ she was taken to the hospital.

7. _____ she paid for the damages out of her own pocket.

Exercise 7

Peter Matthiessen, in his book *The Snow Leopard* (New York: Viking Penguin, Inc., 1978) uses reduced clauses extensively. Underline these clauses in the following excerpts. Which clauses have a clear adverbial function? Which ones have a clear adjectival function? Which ones could have either?

1. Awaiting the line of porters that winds through the paddies, I sit on the top level of the wall, my feet on the step on which the loads are set and my back against a tree. (Adverbial)

2. Glowing with nut grease, a squirrel observes our passing from its perch in a cotton tree (Bombax) in immense red blossom.

3. Hunched in a cold and soggy sleeping bag amongst the puddles, I have envied the owner of the crisp blue tent next door.

4. We live on an isle of canvas tenting spread between the lines of leak, and spend most of a dark day in sleeping bags, propped up against the wall.

5. In his first summers, forsaking all his toys, my son would stand rapt for near an hour in his sandbox in the orchards, as doves and redwings came and went on the warm wind.

6. Leaving the river, we climb toward the northwest.

7. But he interrupts himself, dropping to one knee and pointing upward, even as he digs into his rucksack for binoculars.

8. Having pitched our tents again, we set off up the steep mountain, which has open grass on these lower slopes due to south exposure.

9. On the east face of each edifice is a rough niche for offerings, and one cairn is decorated with fresh marigolds, no doubt placed there by the folk met earlier along the trail.

10. Yesterday morning, having stalled for two hours before departure to insure themselves three short days rather than two long ones on the trail, they stopped constantly to rest, and now this morning one man is complaining, and stirring up the others to protest their loads.

Exercise 8

Match the following main clauses and participial phrases. Then, rewrite the two clauses, inserting the participial phrase correctly.

    EXAMPLE: Praising its taste, Marco Polo consumed tea during his visit to China. (7-f)

Participial Phrases
1. Having healed numerous individuals from malaria,
2. Conquering American tropical lands,
3. Marketed either for consumption raw or for conversion into juice or syrup,
4. Upsetting the natural order of climate and ecology,
5. Inciting explorers to embark on long voyages,
6. Grown almost year-round,
7. Praising its taste,
8. Extracting the sugar from the sugarcane,
9. Dried,

Main Clauses

a. agriculture and industry have ruined tropical lands.

b. bananas are available in every season.

c. the natives sucked on the tender green shoots.

d. pineapple has been an important cash crop.

e. pepper was a prize commodity in the Middle Ages.

f. Marco Polo tasted tea during his visit to China.

g. the Spaniards were introduced to cocoa and chocolate.

h. quinine is a very useful medicinal plant.

i. cinnamon rolls up into small sandy-brown cigarette shapes.

Focus 5

MEANING

Emotive Verbs

 MEANING

- Reduced adverbial clauses containing emotive verbs can be quite challenging for non-native speakers of English to use correctly.
  - **Emotive Verbs**

amuse	*confuse*	*frustrate*	*please*
annoy	*embarrass*	*interest*	*puzzle*
bewilder	*excite*	*intrigue*	*shock*
bore	*frighten*	*irritate*	*surprise*
captivate			

- If we use the *-ed* participle, the focus is on the one experiencing the emotion. If we use the *-ing* participle, the focus is on the one/thing causing the emotion.

-ed Participle Refers to the Experiencer	*-ing* Participle Refers to the Actor(s)
(a) Captivated by photography, Toby took a course.	**(b)** Captivating the spectators, the fashion models posed for the photographers.
(c) Pleased by his photos, Toby submitted his best one to a photography contest.	**(d)** Pleasing the photographers, the good weather held out.
(e) Annoyed that he did not win the contest, Toby decided to try again next year.	**(f)** Annoying the cameraman, one model refused to smile.

Exercise 9

Circle the correct option.

      EXAMPLE: Nick jumped, _____ by the lightning.
           a. frightened
           b. frightening

1. The hikers, _____ , gazed at the lovely waterfall.
   a. surprised and bewildered
   b. surprising and bewildering

2. _____ and hot in her sleeping bag, Sue could not sleep.
   a. Bothered
   b. Bothering

3. The movie, while _____ and sensational, was inappropriate for children.
   a. intrigued
   b. intriguing

4. _____ that the bears had invaded the camp, the family left.
   a. Irritated
   b. Irritating

5. _____ by the lecture, many students fell asleep.
   a. Bored
   b. Boring

6. _____ in Indian artifacts, Martin collected arrowheads.
   a. Interested
   b. Interesting

7. They walked north instead of east, _____ their directions.
   a. confused
   b. confusing

Focus 6

USE

Dangling Participles

USE

- Native and non-native speakers of English sometimes incorrectly reduce an adverbial clause that has a different subject from the main clause. We call this type of clause a dangling participle. The effect can be quite humorous, as the following sentences illustrate.

Dangling Participles	Meaning as Worded
(a) Carrying a flashlight, the path was more visible.	The path was carrying a flashlight. **Reword:** Carrying a flashlight, I could see the path.
(b) Using binoculars, the pond was clearly defined.	The pond was using binoculars. **Reword:** Using binoculars, I could see the pond clearly.
(c) Enclosed in a waterproof can, the hikers kept the matches safe.	The hikers were enclosed in a waterproof can. **Reword:** Enclosed in a waterproof can, the matches were kept safe by the hikers.

Exercise 10

Sometimes while hiking in the woods in some parts of the world, a person may encounter a skunk and be unexpectedly sprayed. The following sentences relate to Jane's experience with this, but some of them contain dangling participles. Identify which sentences are incorrect, write down why they are humorous as they are presently stated, and come up with the correct form.

> **EXAMPLE:** Hiking in the woods, a skunk crossed Jane's path.
>
> *This sentence is humorous because it suggests that the skunk, not Jane, was hiking in the woods. The appropriate form would be "While Jane was hiking in the woods, a skunk crossed her path."*

1. Having been sprayed by a skunk, she screamed loudly.
2. Frightened and humiliated, we walked Jane back to the campground.
3. Having returned to the campground, we looked for some catsup.
4. Applying a thick coat of catsup all over her body, the skunk smell was neutralized.
5. Soaking her clothing for 30 minutes in vinegar and water, the smell diminished.
6. Having been victimized by a skunk, we were informed by Jane that she will think twice about hiking in the woods again.

Exercise 11

Correct the dangling participles in the following sentences.

EXAMPLE: After having been bitten by mosquitoes, the ointment felt soothing to her skin. (*After having been bitten by mosquitoes, she rubbed a soothing ointment onto her skin.*)

1. James pet the dog, while barking.
2. Water, while having a bath, leaked over the sides of the tub.
3. The hurricane terrified people, being driven from their homes.
4. Slithering along the path, I spied a snake.
5. Nearly suffocated by the heat, the room was packed with people.

Activities

Activity 1

We often use reduced adverbial clauses in giving directions for carrying out some procedure. Consider something you know how to do very well that requires several motions (e.g., making beef jerky, changing a tire, operating a video camera). Then, write the directions to do this activity, using at least two reduced adverbial clauses.

EXAMPLE: Before making beef jerky, cut strips of lean beef about one half inch thick. Then, hang these strips on a wood framework about four to six feet off the ground. Building a smoke fire, allow the meat to dry in the sun and wind.

Activity 2

The Old West has been a popular theme of many books, movies, and television programs. Action-packed scenes show men and women of the frontier fighting against excessive temperatures, hunger, wild animals, and outlaws. Read a western story or watch a western show on TV or at a theatre and try to summarize several impressive scenes. Use at least four reduced adverbial clauses in your summary.

EXAMPLE: Hearing that 50 head of cattle had disappeared from the Parker Ranch, the sheriff organized a tracking party to try to recover the animals. Twelve men were assembled, chosen for their riding skill and speed. Rising early in the morning, the tracking party began their search. Following the tracks of the cattle, the men located all 50 head at the base of a ravine before noon. They also located the three rustlers who had stolen them. Riding back to the Parker Ranch, the trackers were relieved that the outlaws had been captured.

Activity 3

Relax, close your eyes, and listen attentively as your instructor reads the following descriptions. Each one is unfinished as written. Use your imagination to create a visual image that completes each piece. Then write your ideas in complete sentences below.

A. Swish, zoom, zoom. The propeller turning and the engine roaring, the plane is ready for takeoff. The pilot radios the control tower for permission to move toward the runway. You are going for your first ride in a small plane. Your heart pounds as the wheels leave the ground, and you clutch your seat more tightly. Ascending higher and higher, you see nothing but white fog in every direction. Finally, the fog clears and you are astounded at the sight below. (Complete the description.)

B. Hiking for hours, you feel exhausted. Your mouth is dry and sweat is running down your forehead. You thought for sure you would be there by now. Hadn't they said to take the trail up to Conrad's peak and then head eastward for two miles? Shouldn't you be there by now? Sitting down, you lean back on a dusty rock and take a swig of water from your canteen. You close your eyes momentarily, but you are awakened by a sound off to your right. (Complete the description.)

Activity 4

Using the information in the Task (and your own embellishments), write a paragraph about the lonely traveler's journey. Include at least three reduced adverbial clauses in your description.

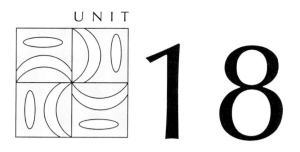

UNIT

18

Gerunds and Infinitives as Objects

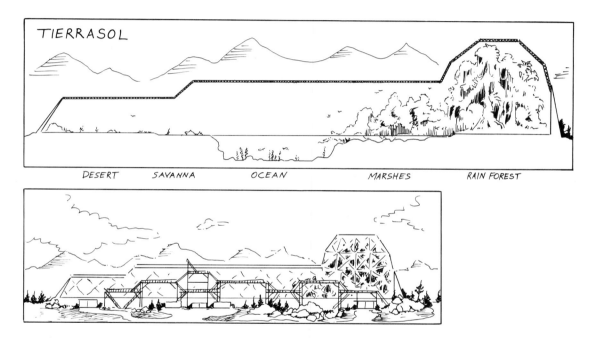

TIERRASOL

DESERT   SAVANNA   OCEAN   MARSHES   RAIN FOREST

Task

You and your classmates have been asked to review the final 10 applicants for "Tierrasol," an experimental space station located in the Arizona desert in the United States. This station is important because it will test on Earth the feasibility of establishing inhabited space stations on Mars. It is an airtight, greenhouse-like structure that contains miniature deserts, marshes, oceans, savannas, and rain forests. Various plants typical of each region will be grown, and the environment will be stocked with insects, fish, fowl, and small mammals in order for the inhabitants to be self-sustaining. All Tierrasolians will have their own individual apartments and laboratories. The group will share a library, a computer center, and communications facilities. They will also be able to receive newspapers, mail, and television broadcasts from within their glass-and-steel structure.

From among the following 10 finalists, only five will be chosen for this two-year assignment. It is your responsibility to consider the applicants' backgrounds based solely upon the descriptions provided and then rank them from 1 (=most desirable) to 10 (=least desirable). Choose carefully, as this is a very expensive project and future implementation will be based on the success or failure of it. In making your decision, remember to discuss with your classmates what might be the appropriate mix of males and females, whether married couples or singles are preferable, what skills and abilities are most essential, what compatibility factors should be considered, etc.

Computer engineer, female, 25 years old

Microbiologist, husband of computer engineer, 35 years old

Police Officer, male, 45 years old

Waste Management Specialist, wife of police officer, pregnant, 41 years old

Former Peace Corps health worker, female, 52 years old, single

Medical intern, female, 24 years old, single

Farmer, male, 43 years old, widowed

Ecologist, male, 23 years old, single

Astronaut, female, 36 years old, married

Politician, male, 58 years old, divorced, three children

After the discussion, answer the following questions: Who have you chosen to be the top five finalists? How did you get around to making a decision? Was there any candidate the group hesitated to eliminate? Were any of your classmates persuaded to select someone that he or she had not originally selected? Did you enjoy discussing the applicants with your classmates? After you have finished your discussion, save your ordered list for a future exercise.

Focus 1

FORM

Review of Gerund and Infinitive Complements

 FORM

- A gerund or infinitive complement is a reduced form of a sentence that has various functions in a base sentence:

Function	Examples
Subject	**(a) To know many languages** would thrill me. **(b) Speaking English** is fun.
Subject Complement	**(c)** His dream was **to sail around the world.** **(d)** Her hobby is **weaving baskets.**
Complements of Adjectives	**(e)** I am sad **to inform you of the delay.** **(f)** The children will be happy about **opening their presents.**
Direct Object	**(g)** Paco hopes **to see the play.** **(h)** Carol remembered **mailing the package.**

- The focus in this unit will be on gerund and infinitive complements as direct objects. Typically we can predict the form of the complement (either gerund or infinitive) by the choice of verb in the base sentence.
  - An infinitive must follow *want, need, hope, promise,* and *appear* (and other verbs in List A at the end of this unit).
    - **(i)** Scientists **appear** to be getting closer to an explanation.
    - **(j)** NOT: Scientists appear being getting closer to an explanation.
  - Some verbs from List A (like *desire, hate, like, love,* and *prefer*) may optionally include the preposition *for* with the infinitive complement when a second subject is present.
    - **(k)** Juan **hates (for) Isabel** to worry.
  - *Advise, convince, invite,* and *warn* (and other verbs in List B) must have a second subject and we can only use them with infinitive complements.
    - **(l)** Einstein **convinced other scientists** to reject Newtonian physics.
    - **(m)** NOT: Einstein convinced to reject Newtonian physics.
    - **(n)** NOT: Einstein convinced other scientists rejecting Newtonian physics.
  - *Appreciate, avoid, postpone, risk,* and *quit* (and other verbs in List C) take only gerunds.
    - **(o)** Einstein **risked** introducing a new theory to the world.
    - **(p)** NOT: Einstein risked to introduce a new theory to the world.
  - When a second subject of a gerund is stated, it should be possessive, especially when it is a pronoun.
    - **(q)** They couldn't understand **her forgetting** the appointment.
    - **(r)** The man didn't like **the committee's stealing** his idea.

Exercise 1

As you read the following text, circle all gerund complements and underline all infinitive complements. (Not every sentence may have one.)

EINSTEIN'S EARLY EDUCATION

(1) Albert Einstein was born in Ulm, Germany, in 1879. (2) Because he learned to speak at a late age, his parents feared that he was retarded. (3) Modern observers prefer to say that he was a daydreamer. (4) When he was five years old, Einstein began to attend a Catholic school. (5) One instructor was especially critical of his abilities and told his parents that it did not matter what field young Albert chose because he would not succeed in it. (6) In 1889, Einstein transferred to a very strict German school called the Luitpold Gymnasium. (7) The rigid structure forced Einstein to distrust authority and become skeptical.

(8) At age 12, Einstein picked up a mathematics textbook and began teaching himself geometry. (9) By 1894, Einstein's father's business had failed to prosper, and the family moved to Italy. (10) Einstein, however, remained behind and began feeling lonely and unhappy. (11) Consequently, he paid less attention to his studies and was finally asked by one of the teachers to leave. (12) He joined his family in Italy but was not able to matriculate at a university because he did not have a diploma. (13) When he heard that a diploma was not necessary to enter at the Swiss Polytechnique Institute in Zurich, he decided to apply.

(14)Einstein traveled to Switzerland but did not pass the entrance examination. (15)He was not prepared well enough in biology and languages, so he enrolled in the Gymnasium at Aarau to prepare himself in his weaker subjects. (16)Albert enjoyed studying in Aauru more than at the Lietpold Gymnasium because the teachers wanted to teach students how to think. (17)He took the exam again and was finally permitted to matriculate into a four-year program. (18)Einstein did not excel during these years at the Institute. (19)In fact, he rarely attended the lectures. (20)He read his books at home and borrowed his classmates' notes to pass tests.

(21)When Einstein graduated in 1900, he failed to obtain a position at the Institute. (22)His professors did not intend to reward Einstein's lackadaisical attitude toward classes with a position. (23)Because he did not get an academic appointment, he worked at the Swiss Patent Office. (24)He worked there for several years until he was offered an appointment as Associate Professor of Physics at the University of Zurich. (25)It was there that Einstein's revolutionary theories of space-time began to take hold and threatened to destroy the reputations of other colleagues who had built their careers on Newton's ideas of a clockwork universe.

Which type of complements are more common? Is the "to-verb" structure always a complement? What other meaning can it have? (Hint: Review sentence #20)

Exercise 2

Complete the following sentences based on the passage in Exercise 1. Use *to*-verb or verb + *-ing*. The first one has been done for you.

EXAMPLE: As a baby, Einstein appeared *to be* retarded.

1. As a young child, he failed _____ his teachers.

2. At age 10, Einstein decided _____ himself geometry.

3. Einstein neglected _____ his homework.

4. When Einstein's family left for Italy, he quit _____.

5. Because of this, one teacher advised him _____ school.

6. Without his family, he couldn't help _____ lonely.

7. He didn't mind _____ his family in Italy.

8. Unfortunately, he couldn't begin _____ at a university without a diploma.

9. He tried _____ into the Swiss Polytechnique but could not pass the entrance exam.

10. He regretted _____ the entrance exam the first time.

11. Professors at the Polytechnique declined _____ Einstein a position because of his lackadaisical academic performance.

277

12. As a clerk at the Swiss Patent Office, he continued _____ about physics.

13. The University of Zurich invited Einstein _____ a faculty member.

14. Many professors couldn't help _____ Einstein's unusual ideas.

15. Soon he began _____ well-established professors with his revolutionary theories.

Focus 2

MEANING

Gerunds versus Infinitives

MEANING

- Sometimes the choice of an infinitive or gerund does not affect meaning or minimally affects the meaning of a verb complement.

    (a) I prefer to eat fish every day. = **(b)** I prefer eating fish every day.

- With certain types of verbs (verbs of emotion and verbs of completion/incompletion), we affect meaning by the choice of infinitive or gerund. We often use gerunds to describe a real, vivid, or fulfilled action. We often use infinitives to describe potential, hypothetical, or future events.

- **Verbs of Emotion:**

Actual Event	Potential Event
(c) Did you **like** *dancing* last night? You seemed to be having a good time.	**(d)** Do you **like** *to dance*? I know a good nightclub.
(e) Tim **hates** *quarreling* with his wife over every little thing.	**(f)** Tim **hates** *to quarrel* with his wife, so he avoids it as much as possible.
(g) I **preferred** *studying* astronomy over physics.	**(h)** I **prefer** *to study* physics next year.

- **Verbs of Completion/Incompletion:**

Actual Event	Potential Event
(i) I **started** *doing* my homework. Question #1 is especially hard.	**(j)** Did you **start** *to do* your homework? I couldn't because I got sick.
(k) Did you **continue** *watching* the program yesterday after I left?	**(l)** Will you **continue** *to watch* the program after I leave?
(m) He **began** *speaking* with a hoarse voice that no one could understand.	**(n)** He **began** *to speak*, but was interrupted by the lawyer.
(o) She **stopped** *listening* whenever she was bored.	**(p)** She **stopped** *to listen* to the bird that was singing.(Note: *to* means "in order to" when it follows *stop*.)

- *Finish* is an exception to the preceding rule. It always requires a gerund.

  (q) They **finished reading** the book.

  (r) NOT: They finished to read the book.

- Besides the real event and potential event meanings, *remember, forget,* and *regret* signal different time sequence meanings when we use a gerund or an infinitive.

(s) Tom remembered **closing** the door.	First: Tom closed the door.
	Then: Tom remembered that he did so.
(t) Tom remembered **to close** the door.	First: Tom remembered that he needed to close the door.
	Then: Tom closed the door.
(u) I regret **telling** you what happened.	First: I told you what happened.
	Now: I feel sorry.
(v) I regret **to tell** you what happened.	First: I feel sorry.
	Now: I am about to tell what happened.

Exercise 3

In the Task, you and your classmates made decisions about who should be chosen to live in Tierrasol. At the last minute, the media released new information about the candidates based on several confidential interviews. Read and select the correct verb in each of the quotes that follow. In some cases, both verbs may be correct. If so, explain why.

EXAMPLE: Microbiologist: I would like (to go/going) only if my wife could go. (*To go* is preferred because the situation is hypothetical.)

1. Microbiologist: I would dread (to live/living) in Tierrasol without my wife.

2. Computer Engineer: I love (to smoke/smoking). As a matter of fact, I smoke three packs of cigarettes a day.

3. Police Officer: I like (to carry/carrying) a gun. In fact, I don't go anywhere without it.

4. Waste Management Specialist: I mean (to stay/staying) in Tierrasol only until the baby is born.

5. Former Peace Corps health worker: I hated (to work/working) under stressful conditions. That's why I returned early from my assignment.

6. Medical intern: I intend (to pass/passing) the Medical Boards Exam this fall, although I have already failed it twice.

7. Farmer: I loathe (to live/living) in closed spaces. I have claustrophobia.

8. Ecologist: I regret (to inform/informing) you that I am not optimistic about the Tierrasol experiment.

9. Astronaut: I will continue (to benefit/benefiting) from this experience in future space missions, even after Tierrasol.

10. Politician: Did I remember (to tell/telling) you that funding for future Tierrasol projects will be one of my major campaign issues once this project is finished?

Exercise 4

Would the information about the applicants included in Exercise 3 affect any of the decisions you made during the Task? Would you still rank your choices in the same way? Discuss why or why not in class, using as many gerunds or infinitives as you can.

> **EXAMPLE:** I wouldn't mind seeing the computer engineer be in the group if she could stop smoking so much.

Exercise 5

Read the following sentences. Write *NO* beside the incorrect sentences and make all necessary corrections.

> **EXAMPLE:** <u>*NO*</u> He agrees ^*to* speak at the convention.

1. _____ I expected him to see me from the balcony, but he didn't.

2. _____ They intended interviewing the ambassador the last week in November.

3. _____ I regretted to tell her that she had not been sent an invitation to the party.

4. _____ Patty has chosen attending the University of Michigan in the fall.

5. _____ Have you forgotten to fasten your seat belt again?

6. _____ Would you please stop to talk? I cannot hear the presenter.

7. _____ Did he suggest us go to a Japanese restaurant?

8. _____ She can't stand to do her homework with the radio turned on.

9. _____ Mr. and Mrs. Hunter forced their daughter's joining the social club against her will.

10. _____ Please remember working harder.

11. _____ Mary tends to exaggerate when she tells a story.

12. _____ I don't mind Tai to arrive a little late to the meeting.

13. _____ Would you care have a drink before we eat dinner?

14. _____ John neglected going to the dentist for three years.

15. _____ They can't afford taking a trip to the Caribbean this year.

Focus 3

FORM

Gerund Complements with Verbs + Prepositions

FORM

- Gerunds generally follow verbs + prepositions such as *agree to, look at, worry about,* etc.

  The Tierrasol committee could not agree to the farmer's *being* on the list of finalists. The members argued about *keeping* the police officer and the Peace Corps worker as well.

- An exception to this is when the preposition is *for* with such prepositional verbs as *ask for, ache for, care for, hope for, long for,* etc. In this case, use a second subject and an infinitive.

  The teacher asked for *the committee to make* a decision within 20 minutes. She hoped for *them to make* their announcement by 4:00.

Exercise 6

Since the beginning of time, human beings have tried to understand who they were and where they came from through religious beliefs, theories, and rituals. Write general statements about these ideas, using the prompts below. Include verb + *-ing* or *to*-verb in each response.

EXAMPLE: people   believe in   (human beings evolved from apes)
Some people believe in human beings' *having* evolved from apes.

1. religions	insist on	(God having created living things)
2. cultures	call for	(people have dietary restrictions)
3. cultures	think about	(their ancestors are pleased or displeased with them)
4. people	hope for	(relatives are reunited in an afterlife)
5. members	wait for	(God returns to the chosen people)
6. believers	complain about	(other people don't believe)
7. religions	argue about	(priests have proper authority)
8. members	agree to	(follow the laws and ordinances)

Focus 4

Gerund Complements with Phrasal Verbs

FORM

- Complements with phrasal verbs (e.g., *carry on, get over, take up*, etc.) and phrasal verbs followed by prepositions (e.g., *cut down on,* **look forward to**, *do away with,* etc.) always take the gerund (versus infinitive) form.

> Nutritionists are very curious about exploring the daily eating routines of the inhabitants of Tierrasol. Will the inhabitants be able to **carry on** *eating* at regular mealtimes? Will they **get over** *not having* the variety that they had outside of Tierrasol? Will they **give up** *ingesting* such large quantities of food? Will they **cut down on** *eating* so much meat? Will they **give up** *eating* beef? Will they **look forward to** *returning* to regular eating patterns once the experiment is over?

Note that *to* is not an infinitive marker in this last example but is a preposition in the phrasal verb *look forward to*.

Exercise 7

Complete the following dialogues with a sentence, using one of the following phrasal verbs and verb + *-ing*. Note that we usually consider the phrasal verbs more informal than the regular verbs.

carry on = continue
cut down on = reduce
give up = stop, surrender
go through with = perform a difficult act as planned
look forward to = anticipate
put off = postpone
put up with = tolerate
take up = start

> **EXAMPLE:** How much longer can you stand living in Buffalo?
> *I can't put up with living in Buffalo one more day.*

1. I'll bet you're going to have a wonderful time in Hawaii.

   _____ .

2. I have had a terrible headache for several days, but I don't have time to see a doctor.

   _____ .

3. When did you start playing golf?

_____ .

4. I notice you're not smoking anymore.

_____ .

5. Perry almost decided not to climb Mount Everest. Then do you know what happened?

_____ .

6. Will you continue to go to a new city each year for the rest of your life?

_____ .

7. Why haven't you touched your dessert?

_____ .

Focus 5

FORM

Gerund Complements of Verbs + Adjectives + Prepositions

FORM

- We also use gerunds in complements following verb + adjective + preposition combinations such as *be content with, be surprised at, be annoyed by,* etc.

    Church authorities were surprised at Galileo's **claiming** that the earth revolved around the sun. They were not used to **thinking** that the sun was the center of the universe. These theories made the Catholic Church suspicious of Galileo's **being** a loyal Christian.

Exercise 8

Read the following notes about important figures in scientific history. Write sentences about each person, using one of the following expressions: *be celebrated for, be famous for, be good at, be proficient in, be renowned for, be skillful in,* or *be successful in.*

EXAMPLE: Aristotle, Greek philosopher, laws of motion

Aristotle was a Greek philosopher who was famous for developing theories about motion.

1. Ptolemy, Egyptian philosopher and astronomer, made charts and tables from an observatory near Alexandria, Egypt
2. Descartes, French philosopher, developed a theory of knowledge by doubting, believed intuition was the key to understanding
3. Copernicus, Polish astronomer, concluded that the sun was at the center of the universe
4. Kepler, German astronomer and mathematician, realized that planets travel in ellipses rather than circles
5. Galileo, Italian astronomer and physicist; improved the telescope; wrote *The Starry Messenger*, which refuted the prevailing theory of an earth-centered universe
6. Newton, English mathematician, determined general laws of motion and the laws of gravity
7. Einstein, German physicist, published the Special Theory of Relativity and the General Theory of Relativity, introduced the concepts of gravitational fields and curved space

Exercise 9

Additional information about prospective Tierrasol inhabitants has been uncovered. Paraphrase the following quotes of the applicants with gerunds.

EXAMPLE: Waste Management Specialist: I would feel content to sit and sleep all day.

She would feel content with *sitting* and *sleeping* all day.

1. Microbiologist: I'm afraid of bad sunburns.
2. Computer Engineer: I am sorry to announce that I have contracted a life-threatening disease.
3. Police Officer: I am annoyed that my wife won't stay the full two years.
4. Former Peace Corps Health Worker: I am concerned that my first assignment was not successful, but this one will be.
5. Medical intern: I am embarrassed that I don't enjoy reading newspapers or watching TV.
6. Farmer: I will be delighted to form new relationships at Tierrasol.
7. Ecologist: I am disgusted that this project was not better planned.
8. Astronaut: I am fit to live in Tierrasol because I have already traveled on three space missions.
9. Politician: I am a little upset that I won't be able to do any campaigning for two years.

Exercise 10

Fill in the following blanks with verb + -*ing* or *to*-verb.

After taking off on the last Mercury mission, Gordon Cooper settled in for a good night's sleep halfway through his journey. Compared with most of the duties of spaceflight, it seemed (a)*to be*_____ (be) an easy enough undertaking. But Cooper ended up (b) _____ (have to wedge) his hands beneath his safety harness to keep his arms from (c) _____ (float around) and (d) _____ (strike) switches on the instrument panel.

Since Cooper's flight, (e) _____ (sleep) in space has become a routine matter—maybe too routine. When carrying out an especially boring or tiring task, some astronauts have nodded off—only they didn't really nod; they simply closed their eyes and stopped (f) _____ (move). There are none of the waking mechanisms that we would expect (g) _____ (have) on earth—one's head (h) _____ (fall) to one side or a pencil (i) _____ (drop) to the floor.

Space crews have also found that they don't need handholds and ladders to get around; they quickly learn (j) _____ (push off) with one hand and float directly to their destinations. (k) _____ (eat), use a computer, or do some other stationary task, astronauts now slip their stockinged feet into loops or wedges attached to the floor. Similarly, a single Velcro head strap suffices (l) _____ (keep) sleeping astronauts from (m) _____ (drift out) toward the ventilation ducts.

A favorite recreation in space is (n) _____ (play) with one's food. Instead of carrying food all the way to their mouths with a utensil, some experienced astronauts like (o) _____ (catapult) food from spoons. Although (p) _____ (drink) coffee seems like the most natural thing on Earth, in space it won't work. If you tried (q) _____ (tip) the cup back to take a drink, the weightless coffee would not roll out. One astronaut offers the following advisory: "Don't let your curiosity tempt you into (r) _____ (explore) a larger clump of liquid than you're prepared (s) _____ (drink) later." If you don't start (t) _____ (drink) your blob with a straw, it eventually attaches itself to the nearest wall or window.

Although spaceflight has its irritations, these are necessary if astronauts are to soar. The whole idea of airborne testing is to make (u) _____ (live) and (v) _____ (work) in weightlessness easy and unremarkable for ordinary folk.

Adapted from: Stewart, D. The Floating World at Zero G. *Air and Space.* August/September 1991, p. 38.

Activities

Activity 1

Reanalyze all of the data from this unit about the ten Tierrasol applicants. Considering *all* of the information, who would the top five applicants be? Write an explanation of how you came to your final decision, citing evidence from this unit.

Activity 2

You are a news reporter called to interview a visitor from another planet. Although this creature looks very much like a human being and speaks English, you find that it has some very different characteristics. Describe what you learned from the alien as a result of your interviews. You might include some information about what the alien is accustomed to, annoyed at, capable of, concerned about, desirous of, incapable of, interested in, suited for, susceptible to, sympathetic toward, and weary of. Use at least five gerund complements in your report.

EXAMPLE: The alien has a very unusual diet. It is used to eating tree bark and grass.

Activity 3

According to Einstein's special theory of relativity, astronauts who make a round-trip journey to a nearby star at a speed near the speed of light might age only a year or so. However, when they return to earth, they would find everyone else a great deal older. This type of "time travel" to the future is possible. Would you consider volunteering for such a mission? What would be the consequences of doing so? When you returned, would you continue to love your spouse or partner even though you would no longer be the same ages? What would you arrange to do on your first day back? Would you enjoy accepting future space mission assignments? Discuss these questions with your classmates.

Activity 4

With a partner, write a 15-item quiz which you can give to another pair of classmates to test their knowledge of gerund and infinitive complements.

> **EXAMPLE: 1.** I am interested in _____ (fly) to Tahiti.
> **2.** The teacher needs Tom _____ (ask) his parents for permission

Activity 5

You have decided that you would like to be included in the Tierrasol project. Write a letter to the Tierrasol selection committee, explaining why you feel you are qualified for the project. Try to be as persuasive as you can while using at least two gerund complements and four infinitive complements in your writing.

List A

to-verb complementation

> **EXAMPLE:** Julia hates to be late.

VERBS OF EMOTION

care	loathe
desire	love
hate	regret
like	yearn

VERBS OF INITIATION, COMPLETION AND INCOMPLETION

begin	manage
cease	neglect
commence	start
fail	try
get	undertake hesitate

VERBS OF MENTAL ACTIVITY

forget	know how
remember	learn

VERBS OF CHOICE OR INTENTION

choose	hope
decided	intend
expect	mean

VERBS OF CHOICE OR INTENTION (CONT'D)

need	propose
plan	want
prefer	wish
prepare	

VERBS OF REQUEST AND THEIR RESPONSES

offer	threaten
promise	vow
swear	

INTRANSITIVE VERBS

appear	seem
happen	tend

OTHER VERBS

continue	afford
	(can't afford)

List B

object + *to*-verb complementation

EXAMPLE: She reminded us to be quiet.

VERBS OF COMMUNICATION

advise	permit
ask	persuade
beg	promise
challenge	remind
command	require
convince	tell
forbid	warn
invite	urge
order	

VERBS OF INSTRUCTION

encourage	teach
help	train
instruct	

VERBS OF CAUSATION

allow	get
cause	hire
force	

OTHER VERBS

expect	trust
prepare	

List C

verb + *-ing* complementation

EXAMPLE: Trihn enjoys playing tennis.
We enjoyed his telling us about his adventures.

VERBS OF INITIATION, COMPLETION AND INCOMPLETION

avoid	postpone
begin	quit
cease	start
delay	stop
finish	try
get through	

VERBS OF ONGOING ACTIVITY

continue	keep
help	keep on
(can't help)	practice

VERBS OF EMOTION

appreciate	miss
dislike	prefer
enjoy	regret
hate	stand
like	(can't stand)
love	resent
mind	tolerate
(don't mind)	

VERBS OF COMMUNICATION

admit	mention
advise	recommend
deny	suggest
discuss	

VERBS OF MENTAL ACTIVITY

anticipate	remember
consider	see (can't see)
forget	understand
imagine	

19 Perfective Infinitives

Task

Have you ever wished you could go back in time and meet famous people from past eras, see things that no longer exist in the world, or participate in exciting historical events?

Consider the following statements. Which ones reflect things you'd like to have been able to see, hear, or do? Which sound less appealing or perhaps not appealing at all? Rank the statements from 1 through 10, with 1 representing your first preference and 10 your last.

I would like . . .

to have seen Michelangelo painting the Sistine chapel.

to have watched Rocky Marciano win the heavyweight boxing championship in 1952.

to have attended a performance by the famous blues singer, Billie Holiday.

to have been at Waterloo when Napoleon surrendered.

to have observed dinosaurs before they became extinct.

to have seen Anna Pavlova, the Russian ballerina, dance in Tchaikovsky's "Swan Lake" ballet.

to have walked through the Hanging Gardens of Babylon.

to have spoken with Confucius, the great Chinese philosopher.

to have heard the Greek epic poet Homer recite *The Iliad* or *The Odyssey*.

to have taken a cruise on the Nile River in Queen Cleopatra's barge as the sun was setting.

Compare your ratings with those of a few of your classmates.

Write five statements of other things that you'd like to have done in the past. Share a few with some of your classmates and then save them for exercises later in the unit.

Focus 1

FORM

Review of Perfective Infinitive Structures

FORM

- Perfective infinitives have the form *to* + *have* + past participle (verb + *-ed* or irregular form):

	Perfective Infinitive	
(a) I'd like	**to have seen**	the first football game ever played.
(b) She claimed	**to have been**	at home all evening.
(c) I expect	**to have finished**	my paper tomorrow.

- Like other infinitives, we use perfective infinitives in a number of clause types in sentences:
  - Subject noun clauses:

    (d) To have won the Boston marathon was a dream come true for her.
  - Subject noun clauses after introductory *it*:

    (e) It is useful **to have reviewed the chapter** before you attend the lecture.
  - Object complement clauses:

    (f) I would love **to have seen his face** when he opened the present.
  - Adjective clauses:

    (g) The question **to have been debated** was whether the union should go on strike.

    (h) That is a good course **for you to have taken.**
  - Degree complement clauses:

    (i) Benjamin is **too young to have known better.**

    (j) Those pants were **big enough to have fit a giant!**

Exercise 1

Complete the blanks with perfective infinitives, using the verb in parentheses.

EXAMPLE: She was happy _to have broken_ (break) the record for the 100 yard dash.

1. (a) The octogenarian next door considers himself _____ (be) quite a romantic fellow in his younger days. (b) He claims _____ (write) passionate love letters to more than a dozen women. (c) Not all of his letters got the responses he had hoped for, but in his opinion, it truly was better _____ (love) and lost than never _____ (love) at all.

2. David: (a) It was really nice of Hector _____ (give) us his car for our weekend trip. Alana: (b) Oh, he was happy _____ (be able to) help you out. (c) I'd really like _____ (go) with you on your trip, but my cousins were visiting that weekend.

3. (a) Jeanne is too smart _____ (believe) the story Russ told her the other day. (b) His story was outlandish enough _____ (convince) her that it was far from the truth.

4. (a) Dear Fran: Accepting that job offer was a wise decision for you _____ (make). (b) We're glad _____ (have) you as our office mate for the past three years. (c) Good luck! With your talent, we expect you _____ (receive) a big promotion before the end of the year.

MEANING

Perfective Infinitives Used to Express Past Events

MEANING

- Perfective infinitives signal past time in relation to present, past, and future moments of focus. Use them to express:
  - **past events relevant to the present moment of focus:**

Example	Meaning
(a) Miles is happy **to have finished** his report on Friday so he can go out tonight.	Miles is happy that he has finished his report. Now he can go out.

- Some verbs that commonly take perfective infinitive complements, such as *claim* or *consider*, express beliefs or attitudes. The event in the infinitive clause may or may not have actually happened:

Example	Meaning
(b) The driver claimed **to have stopped** for the traffic light before the accident.	The driver said that he stopped for the light before the accident occurred. (It may or may not be true that he stopped.)

- **unfulfilled past events:**

Example	Meaning
(c) Dr. Yamada wanted **to have completed** her research before the year ended. However, her funds for the project ran out.	Dr. Yamada wished that she had completed her research before the year ended.

- **past events that continue to the present time:**

Example	Meaning
(d) Ben considers his wife **to have been** his best friend ever since he got married five years ago.	In Ben's opinion, his wife was his best friend in the past and she still is.

- **past events relative to future events (future time before another future time):**

Example	Meaning
(e) Winona expects **to have made** all of her plane reservations by next week.	Winona expects that she will have made her reservations by next week.

We also commonly convey this meaning by nonperfective infinitives:

(f) Winona expects **to make** all of her plane reservations by next week.

When the **main clause verb** is **past tense,** speakers often use nonperfective infinitives in the complement clause to express the same meanings as perfective ones:

Nonperfective

(g) It was nice of you **to send**   me a birthday card.

Perfective

(h) It was nice of you **to have sent** me a birthday card.

- When the **main clause verb** is **present tense,** however, we need a perfective infinitive to signal past meaning:

Perfective: Past	Nonperfective: Future
(i) It **is** nice of you **to have sent** me a birthday card. (You have already sent it.)	**(j)** It **is** nice of you **to send** me a birthday card. (You said you will send one.)

Exercise 2

Which type of past meaning does each of the following sentences express: past relative to the present, to the past, or to the future?

1. The Castenadas plan to have toured most of the East Coast by the end of August; they have been traveling in the United States all summer and have only two weeks left.

2. They intended to have visited all of their West Coast relatives before the end of June, but because of car trouble they didn't see all of them until mid-July.

3. Four-year-old Ruby Castenada says that she would like to have stayed at Disneyland for the entire summer.

4. So far, Mr. and Mrs. Castenada consider the highlight of their vacation to have been their camping trip in Michigan.

5. At first, Tracy, their teenage son, was upset to have left all his friends for the summer.

6. However, now he admits that he would like to have toured even more of the country and hopes to do it again.

7. The Castenadas' goal is to have visited all of the continental United States before Tracy goes off to college.

Exercise 3

Restate the infinitives in the following quotations as perfective infinitives. If you had to choose one of them for a class motto, which one would you select? Which would you select for an epitaph? Can you think of any other sayings that use perfective infinitives?

> **EXAMPLE:** To win one's joy through struggle is better than to yield to melancholy. (Andre Gide, French author)
>
> *To have won* one's joy through struggle is better than *to have yielded* to melancholy.

1. What a lovely surprise to finally discover how unlonely being alone can be. (Ellen Burstyn, American actress)
2. To endure what is unendurable is true endurance. (Japanese proverb)
3. I would prefer even to fail with honor than to win by cheating. (Sophocles, Greek dramatist)

Exercise 4

Exchange the five statements you wrote for the Task with another classmate. Report one or more of your classmate's statements to the rest of the class or a small group, using a "that" clause with a past perfect verb.

> **EXAMPLE:** I would like to have heard Jimi Hendrix play the American National Anthem.
>
> Paraphrase: *Elena wishes that she could* have heard Jimi Hendrix play the American National Anthem.

Note that in the paraphrase, *could* is used as the modal with *wish* as the main clause verb.

Focus 3

FORM

Subjects of Perfective Infinitives

FORM

- The subject of a perfective infinitive object clause may be the same as the main clause subject.
  - When the main clause and infinitive clause subject are the same, we omit the infinitive clause subject after most main clause verbs:

Example	Meaning
(a) Mimi would like **to have flown** with the Wright Brothers on their first flight.	Mimi wishes that **she** could have flown with them.
(b) I am happy **to have been** able to help you.	I am happy that **I** have been able to help.

- With main clause verbs *believe, consider, find,* and *report,* we use a reflexive pronoun for the perfective infinitive clause if the main clause and infinitive subjects are the same:

Example	Meaning
(c) St. Augustine considered **himself** to have been a great sinner in his youth.	St. Augustine believed that **he** was a great sinner.
(d) They believed **themselves** to have been unjustly accused.	They believed that **they** were unjustly accused.

- The subject of the perfective infinitive may also differ from the main clause subject:

Main Clause Subject		Infinitive Subject	
(e) The jury	believes	**the defendants**	to have been at the scene of the crime.
(f) The lawyers	judged	**the evidence**	to have been very incriminating.

- Pronoun subjects of perfective infinitive clauses must be in the objective case (*me, him, her, us, them*):

  (g) The teacher considers **us** to have been capable of getting *A*s on the exam.

- When the subject of the infinitive clause has a general meaning such as "anyone," "someone," "everyone," or generic "we," or when it is known to the listener/reader, we often omit the subject:

Example	Meaning
(h) To have lost so many lives in the war is a tragedy.	It is a tragedy that **we/they/everyone** lost so many lives in the war.
(i) It is a shame **to have wasted** all that water during the drought.	It is a shame that **someone** wasted all that water during the drought.

The understood subject of the infinitive clause will, of course, depend on the context.

- Subjects of infinitive clauses may also occur after *for* with some verbs, especially when the main clause has a *be* + adjective or *be* + noun phrase:

  (j) For them to have lost so many lives in the war is a tragedy.

  (k) It is a shame **for someone** to have wasted all that water.

  (l) Our teacher plans **for us** to start a new unit tomorrow.

Exercise 5

Who or what is the subject of each perfective infinitive clause below? Underline your choice.

1. Ronald Reagan believes himself to have been a successful President.
2. Many people consider Indira Gandhi to have been a great leader.
3. The Secretary of Defense claimed to have been out of town when the scandal broke.
4. The State Assembly seems to have adjourned earlier than it did last session.
5. Some Americans believe Martin Luther King Jr.'s assassination to have been a conspiracy.
6. Crime appears to have become one of the most important political issues in the recent election.
7. The Congress planned to have voted on President Clinton's proposal yesterday.
8. For so many nations to have signed the environmental protection treaty was encouraging.

Focus 4

FORM

Passive and Progressive Forms of Perfective Infinitives

FORM

- So far the perfective infinitives in this chapter have been active, nonprogressive:

    to + *have* + **past participle**

- The **progressive** form of the perfective infinitive is
    - *to* + *have* + *been* + **verb** + *-ing*

	To Have Been **Verb** + *-ing*	
(a) I'd like	to have been watching	when Bart received his award.
(b) Mr. Park believed the police	to have been guarding	his store when the robbery occurred.

- The **passive** form of the perfective infinitive is
    - *to* + *have* + *been* + **past participle**

	To Have Been **Past Participle**	
(c) Bart would like me	to have been sent	a ticket to the ceremony.
(d) Mr. Park believed himself	to have been given	false information by the police.

Exercise 6

Rewrite each of the following clauses (*that*, *O-that*, or *when* clauses) as a perfective infinitive clause. Make any word changes that are necessary.

EXAMPLES: Josef wishes he could have discovered the Cape of Good Hope with Diaz.
Josef *would like to have discovered* the Cape of Good Hope with Diaz.
Veronica *believes that she was shortchanged.*
Veronica *believes herself to have been shortchanged.*

1. Our English teacher expects that we will finish our oral reports on our favorite celebrities by the end of next week.

2. Henri would prefer that he be the last one to present, but unfortunately for him, he is scheduled to be first.

3. Hideto claims that he was working on his report all weekend.

4. Isela believes she was greatly misinformed by one of her interview subjects.

5. We wish we could have heard more about Shaun's talk with Michael Jackson. (Change *wish* to *would like*)

6. Jocelyn hoped she would be given a chance to interview her favorite author, but the interview didn't work out.

7. Sandra claims that she was sent an autograph from a "major motion picture star," whose identity she is keeping a secret.

8. Gerard reported that Meryl Streep, his favorite actress, had been sitting in front of him at the symphony when he went to a concert last weekend.

9. Ty thinks that he has gotten the most interesting interview with a celebrity. (Use *consider* for the main verb.)

10. My teacher advised that I complete all of my research by Monday.

11. I will be relieved when I have presented my report, because the idea of getting up in front of others makes me anxious.

Focus 5

Negative Forms of Perfective Infinitives

FORM
USE

- Negative forms (*not, never,* etc.) are put before the infinitive verb in formal written English:

  (a) The three nations were right **not to have signed** the agreement until they could discuss it further.

  (b) **Not to have been contacted** for a job interview was a great disappointment to Daniel.

  (c) During his entire term, Representative Bolski appears **never** to have voted in favor of extra funds for child care.

- In less formal English, speakers sometimes put negative forms after *have*:

  (d) **To have not been invited** to the party made her upset.

  (e) I seem **to have not brought** the book I meant to give you.

  (f) That woman claims **to have never seen** the money that turned up in her purse.

Exercise 7

Rewrite each of the following sentences so that it contains a negative perfective infinitive clause. Use the pattern for formal written English.

> **EXAMPLE:** It appeared that Dr. Moreau had not been in Marseilles the last weekend in April.
>
> Dr. Moreau appeared *not to have been* in Marseilles the last weekend in April.

1. In reviewing evidence gathered for the murder trial, Detective Armand believed that the facts had not supported Dr. Moreau's claims of innocence.

2. It was quite strange, Armand mused, that Dr. Moreau had not told his housekeeper he would be away the weekend the murder occurred. (Replace *that* with *for* + noun.)

3. Furthermore, the doctor did not seem to remember much about the inn he claimed he had stayed in that weekend. How very odd!

4. Also, the doctor claimed that he had never known the victim, Horace Bix; yet Bix's name was found in his appointment book.

5. All in all, Detective Armand believed that Dr. Moreau had not given the police truthful answers to a number of questions.

Focus 6

Using Perfective Infinitives to Express Likes, Preferences, and Dislikes: Contrary to Past Fact

USE

- We use the following phrases, with **would** + **verb** to express likes, dislikes, and preferences with perfective infinitives. Alternative forms of these sentences, with perfective main clause verbs and nonperfective infinitives, appear in parentheses:
  - *would like*
    - **(a)** We **would like to have spent** the class period reviewing for the exam.
      (We would have liked to spend the class period reviewing for the exam.)
  - *would love*
    - **(b)** My parents **would love to have joined** us for dinner.
      (My parents would have loved to join us for dinner.)
  - *would prefer*
    - **(c)** I **would prefer not to have had** an early morning class.
      (I would have preferred not to have an early morning class.)
  - *would hate*
    - **(d)** **Wouldn't** you **hate to have been** in that crowded room?
      (Wouldn't you have hated to be in that crowded room?)
- Native English speakers often use perfective forms for both clauses in speech:
  - **(e)** We **would have liked to have spent** the class period reviewing for the exam.

  Although this pattern would sound fine to many native English speakers, it is not considered standard English.

Exercise 8

Use the cues below to make sentences expressing a past wish that did not materialize or an unpleasant event that was avoided. Use the standard English pattern of *would like, would love, would prefer,* or *would hate* followed by a perfective infinitive. Make any changes that are necessary, including any needed verb tense changes.

EXAMPLE: be asked to present my report first
I would like to have been asked to present my report first.

1. take all of my final exams on one day
2. forget the answers to the test questions
3. go to the movies instead of taking the exam
4. be the only one in class without the assignment
5. be given true-false questions for the entire test
6. study geology instead of biochemistry
7. walk into the classroom and find out the teacher was absent
8. be watching music videotapes all afternoon
9. not know that class was canceled
10. present an oral report rather than a written one

Focus 7

FORM ● USE

Using Perfective Infinitives to Describe Other Emotions and Attitudes

- In addition to statements about past wishes and preferences, statements expressing other emotions and attitudes have perfective infinitives. The most common structures are

- *be* + **adjective** + **perfective infinitive:**

		Be	**Adjective**	**Perfective Infinitive**
(a)	I	am	sorry	to have missed your party.
(b)	We	are	delighted	to have learned of your marriage.
(c)	They	were	shocked	to have been treated so rudely.

- *it* + *be* + **adjective** + (*of* + **noun**) + **perfective infinitive:**

	It	*Be*	**Adjective**	(*Of* + **Noun**)	**Perfective Infinitive**
(d)	It	was	generous	of you	to have lent us your car.
(e)	It	is	annoying		to have been waiting so long for our ticket.
(f)	It	is	nice	of Pamela	to have picked up her friends at the airport.

- *it + be + noun phrase + perfective infinitive*:

	It	*Be*	Noun Phrase	Perfective Infinitive
(g)	It	is	a pleasure	to have met you after all these years.
(h)	It	was	a miracle	to have found the contact lens in the swimming pool.

- *for + noun + perfective infinitive*:

	For	Noun	Perfective Infinitive
(i) It was fortunate	for	us	to have discovered the mistake.
(j) It strikes me as odd	for	him	to have driven all that way for a can of anchovies.
(k)	For	Kurt	to have had three plane delays in one day was very unlucky.

- You may also use modals before *be* with many of the expressions:

  (l) It **must be exciting** to have lived in so many countries!

  (m) It **would be a disappointment** to have missed the parade. I'm glad we made it on time!

Exercise 9

Give sentences with perfective infinitive clauses, using the cues. Use a variety of structures. If you wish, add descriptive words or phrases to expand the sentences.

EXAMPLES: Be foolish. . . . think that no one would notice

John must be foolish to have thought that no one would notice he had taken the dangerous chemicals.

It was foolish of us to have thought no one would notice we were missing from class.

1. Be a tragedy . . . lose so many homes in the volcanic eruptions.
2. Be unwise. . . . build a home so close to the volcano.
3. Be terrified. . . . see so much destruction.
4. Be pleased. . . . hear about your promotion to vice-president of the company.
5. Be kind. . . . donate your time to volunteer work.
6. Show up at the party together. . . . . be astounding. (Start with *for* + noun.)
7. Be impossible. . . . imagine a more unlikely pair.
8. Wear jogging shorts for the occasion . . . was considered improper.

Focus 8

Expressing Uncertainty about Past Events with Perfective Infinitives

USE

- Perfective infinitive clauses after the verbs *seem* and *appear* express uncertainty about past events based on present evidence:

  (a) I **seem to have forgotten** my homework assignment. Oh, wait, here it is in my notebook!

- Sometimes the "uncertainty" is actually a hedging device we use to avoid directly accusing or criticizing someone:

  (b) This assignment **appears to have been written** rather hastily.

  (c) Hmmm . . . someone **seems to have eaten** all the ice cream!

Exercise 10

Make up a sentence with *appear* or *seem* followed by a perfective infinitive for each of the following situations.

1. You go for a job interview. The interviewer asks to see your application form. You realize you must have left it at home. Respond to the question.

2. You are a teacher. One of your students looks as if she is on the verge of falling asleep. Make a comment to her.

3. As you are getting ready to leave the classroom, you discover that you no longer have your notebook, which you were carrying when you entered the room. Make a comment to the class as they are walking out.

4. You have just finished reading a novel that is the worst one you have ever read. Make a comment to a friend about the author of the book.

5. When the teacher starts going over the homework assignment, you realize that you did the wrong one. The teacher calls on you for an answer. Give an appropriate response.

Focus 9

Expressing Obligations, Intentions, and Future Plans with Perfective Infinitives

USE

- Perfective infinitives also occur with some verbs that express obligations and intentions. To express past obligations or plans that were unfulfilled, they may follow phrasal modals *be supposed* or *be to:*

  (a) The engineers **were supposed to have checked** all the controls before the shuttle was launched.

  (b) Caroline **was to have spent** the entire summer sculpting, but she ended up working at a bank for a month.

- Perfective infinitives express future time before another future time with verbs such as *plan, intend, hope,* and *expect.*

  (c) Do you **plan to have written** your report before Sunday?

  (d) The weatherman **expects** the rains **to have ended** by the weekend.

Exercise 11

Complete the following sentences with information about yourself; use a perfective infinitive clause in each.

EXAMPLE: By tomorrow, I intend *to have bought my sister a birthday present.*

1. By next week, I plan _____ .

2. I intend _____ within the next five years.

3. I was supposed _____ ,

   but I didn't because _____ .

4. I expect _____

   before _____ .

5. By _____ ,

   I hope _____ .

303

Focus 10

Perfective Infinitives in Degree Complement Clauses with *Enough* and *Too*

USE

- We use perfective infinitives, like nonperfective ones, in a variety of degree complement clauses.
  - With *enough* complements, perfective infinitives often express an event that could have happened in the past but did not actually happen:

Adjective + *Enough*	*Enough* + Noun
(a) The earthquake was powerful enough **to have destroyed** a whole city. (The earthquake could have destroyed a city.)	**(b)** I got enough homework on Friday **to have kept** me busy for a week. (The homework could have kept me busy for a week.)

- With *too* complements, perfective infinitives often indicate an event that did not occur or the speaker's disbelief that an event did occur. The main clause gives a reason:

Too + Adjective	*Too* + *Many/Much* + Noun
(c) We were too tired **to have gone** anywhere last night. (We didn't go anywhere last night because we were too tired.)	**(d)** She has too much intelligence **to have done** so poorly on the exam. (She did poorly, but I am surprised because she is so intelligent.)

Exercise 12

Use the phrases below to create sentences about past possibilities, using perfective infinitives.

EXAMPLE: poison.... strong enough

The poison that the child accidentally swallowed was strong enough to have killed her, but fortunately she recovered completely.

1. the noise... loud enough
2. ate enough popcorn
3. fireworks... bright enough

4. wind... strong enough
5. the weather in Moscow... cold enough
6. heard enough bad news

Exercise 13

The following sentences express disbelief about an event or explain why something didn't happen. Combine the ideas in each pair of sentences into one sentence, using a perfective infinitive clause.

> **EXAMPLE:** She couldn't have done well in the marathon last fall. She had sustained too many minor injuries.
>
> Combined: She had sustained too many minor injuries *to have done well* in the marathon last fall.

1. My brother couldn't have cheated on a test. He is too honest.
2. You couldn't have stopped taking piano lessons! You have too much talent.
3. Stan couldn't have bought that wild tie himself. He is too conservative.
4. Charmaine didn't stay at that low-level job. She has too much ambition.
5. They couldn't have taken on any more debts. They have too many already.

Activities

Activity 1

Interview ten people about regrets—either their greatest regrets or most recent ones. Then write the results of your survey, using statements with perfective infinitives. Share the results with your classmates. Here are some examples of paraphrases:

Jack's regret:	that he stopped dating Shirelle.
Paraphrase:	Jack is sorry *to have stopped* dating Shirelle.
Risa's regret:	that she didn't go to Vienna for her vacation.
Paraphrase:	Risa is sorry *not to have gone* to Vienna for her vacation.
Blanca's regret:	that she never learned Spanish from her mother.
Paraphrase:	Blanca is sorry *never to have learned* Spanish from her mother.

Activity 2

Interview one or more classmates about things that they hope or expect to do or have by the end of the next five years. Here are examples of some categories you might consider. Think of others that might be interesting to find out about. (Dates they hope to have had? Classes they expect to have passed? New foods they hope to have tried?)

Places you hope to have visited

Hobbies you hope to have engaged in

Educational degrees you expect to have received

Possessions you hope to have obtained

Books you'd like to have read

Skills you hope to have learned or developed

Present some of your findings in a brief oral report to the class.

Activity 3

A "tall tale" is a story that contains a great deal of exaggeration for a humorous effect. Imagine that you are at a Tall Tales Convention in which people compete to make up the funniest exaggerations. You have entered the "Enough is Enough Category." For this competition, you must make come up with statements like "The sidewalk was hot enough last weekend to have fried an egg on it" or "We made enough food last night to have invited the state of Texas for dinner." Either individually or in teams, make up entries for the competition. Have others vote on the best ones.

Activity 4

Write an imaginary interview or dialogue between you and a famous person who is no longer living. (It could be someone you mentioned in the Task.) In your dialogue use some perfective infinitive phrases. For example, you could ask the person what she or he might like to have done differently if circumstances had been different or if the person had lived at a different time. Or you might have the person comment on what he/she was happy/sorry to have done or how exciting/frustrating, etc., it was to have experienced certain events. Read your dialogue to class members without telling them who the famous person is. See if they can guess the person's identity.

20

Adjectival Complements in Subject and Predicate Position

Task

Human beings and animals have existed side by side since the dawn of history. More often than not, however, human beings have dominated animals. This does not mean that human beings have not admired or even revered animals for their intelligence, beauty, loyalty, and strength. But it does mean that human beings have generally been willing to kill animals in order to feed or clothe themselves. At the very least they have been willing to intrude on natural habitats or interrupt natural life cycles of animals in order to obtain useful by-products, such as eggs for food, shells for implements, and feathers for decoration.

The following table contains a list of terms that generate positive and negative associations concerning the relationship between human beings and animals. Jot down your ideas for as many terms as you can, then discuss your ideas in groups. After your discussion, write down statements about several of the terms. Here are some sample statements about *animal research,* the first term:

> It is unethical for animals like gorillas and chimpanzees to be used in medical research. That these primates are similar in some ways to human beings is undeniable. But researchers' blindly generalizing the findings from these experiments to human beings does not make sense. In addition, injecting and killing these animals during experiments is inhumane.

Term	Positive	Negative
animal research	provides a way to test the safety of drugs and cosmetics	animals dissected, injected, and killed in experiments
fur coat		
zoo		
oil tanker		
veal		
ivory		
pesticide		
campground		
bullfight		
hunting		
highway construction		

Focus 1

FORM

Overview of Adjective Complements

FORM

- Adjective complements are of three types: *that* clauses, infinitives, and gerunds. These complements can appear in subject position in front of linking verbs (such as *appear, be, become, look, remain, seem*) and adjectives.

Type	Example
that clause	**(a) That the blue whale is becoming extinct** seems sad.
infinitive (*for/to*)	**(b) For campers to pollute streams** is irresponsible.
gerund	**(c) Bulls' being killed in bullfights** appears brutal.

- A few adjectives (such as *ready, anxious, happy, eager,* etc.) take infinitive complements directly following them. In general, these adjectives show positive expectation and follow animate subjects.

  (d) Joshua is ready **for the hunting season to begin.**

  (e) Michelle is eager **for Joshua to shoot a fox.**

- If the main subject and the complement subject are alike, we delete the *for* clause.

  (f) Michelle is eager to have a fox coat.

  (g) NOT: Michelle is eager for herself to have a fox coat.

Exercise 1

In the following short texts, complete the adjective complements.

    EXAMPLE: Elizabeth Mann Borghese, who was the daughter of the writer Thomas Mann, taught her dog to take dictation on a special typewriter. That her dog *could type* is amazing.

1. Once a woman was thrown off a yacht and three dolphins rescued her and led her to a marker in the sea. Another time, several fishermen were lost in a dense fog, and four dolphins nudged their boat to safety. Dolphins' _____ is well-documented.

2. Mrs. Betsy Marcus' dog Benjy was known to sing "Raindrops Keep Fallin' on My Head." For a dog _____ is incredible.

3. At one time, passenger pigeons were very numerous. Now there are none because of massive hunting and the destruction of their natural forest home. Passenger pigeons' _____ is sad.

4. Jaco, an African gray parrot, could speak German. When his master left the house alone, he said, "God be with you." When his master left with other people, he said, "God be with you all." Jaco's _____ was extraordinary.

5. The dwarf lemur and the mountain pygmy possum were considered extinct. However, in recent years, these animals have reappeared. For extinct animals _____ is inspiring.

6. Washoe, a female chimpanzee, was taught sign language. She was able to make up words like *drink-fruit* (for watermelon) and *water-bird* (for swan). That Washoe _____ is intriguing.

Exercise 2

Imagine that you are an animal instead of a human being. What would make you happy if you were one of the following pets? Write your answers in first person and use one of the adjectives: *anxious, eager, happy, or ready.*

EXAMPLE: cat
I would be *eager* for my owner to feed me a tuna casserole.
I would be *happy* to lie around in the sun.

1. horse
2. parrot
3. dog
4. mouse
5. goldfish
6. snake

Focus 2

FORM ● USE

Adjective Complements in Subject and Predicate Position

FORM
USE

- In subject position, adjective complements usually contain a known idea, either previously mentioned or assumed through context.
  (a) I am sorry to say that certain businesses that sell sculptured ivory objects have hired poachers to kill elephants for their tusks. **For poachers to take the tusks from live elephants** is alarming. **That they sell them** is abominable. Worst of all, **elephants' becoming an endangered species because of this** is criminal.
- When *that* clauses and infinitives contain new information, they will more commonly appear in predicate position. We move the *that* clause or the infinitive to the end of the sentence and add *it* at the beginning.
  It + linking verb + adjective + adjective complement
  (b) It is interesting **that medical researchers have made important medical discoveries through animal research.** They need **to continue this work.**
  (c) It is neccessary **for protesters to call for a moratorium on animal testing.** Animals have rights too!
- Gerund complements do not normally occur with *it* constructions.
  (d) NOT: It is abominable poachers' killing elephants.

Exercise 3

Comment on the following facts found in the *Book of Lists 2* (Wallace et al., New York, William Morrow & Co., 1980) using a *that* clause in subject position.

> **EXAMPLE:** Tigers do not usually hunt humans unless they are old or injured. However, a tigress, the Champawat man-eater, killed 438 people in the Himalayas in Nepal between 1903 and 1911.
>
> *That so many people were killed in Nepal by a tiger* is tragic.

1. Black bears do not usually hurt humans unless they are hungry. When the Alaskan blueberry crop was poor in 1963, black bears attacked at least four people, one of whom they killed, because no other food was available.

2. In the central provinces of India, leopards have been known to enter huts and kill humans. One famous leopard, the Panawar man-eater, is reputed to have killed 400 people.

3. On March 25, 1941, the British ship *Britannia* sank in the Atlantic Ocean. While the 12 survivors sat in a lifeboat, a giant squid reached its arm around the body of one of them and pulled him into the ocean.

4. In South America, people have reported losing fingers, toes, or pieces of flesh while bathing in piranha-infested waters.

5. In 1916, four people were killed as they were swimming along a 60-mile stretch of the New Jersey coast. The culprit was a great white shark.

Exercise 4

Consider each of the following nouns that describe people and determine one characteristic which would be odd/ surprising/ unexpected/ impossible/ strange about the noun if it were true or if it had been true. Write a sentence that expresses your idea.

> **EXAMPLE:** Eskimos   Eskimos' living in grass huts would be *strange*.
>
> OR Their living in grass huts would be *strange*.

1. dictators
2. busybodies
3. bus drivers
4. procrastinators
5. Napoleon
6. Mohatma Gandhi
7. the ancient Greeks
8. your mother
9. your friend's father
10. our class

Exercise 5

Consider your responses during the Task and create dialogues with facts about animals, using a *that* clause and the adjective provided.

EXAMPLE: shocking   Q: What's so shocking?

                     A: It is shocking *that the oil from the grounded oil tanker killed thousands of innocent animals.*

1. irresponsible
2. encouraging
3. sad
4. important
5. outrageous
6. fortunate

Focus 3

MEANING

Infinitive, Gerund, and *That* Clause Adjective Complements

MEANING

- Infinitive, possessive gerund, and *that* clause adjective complements have different meanings. *That* clauses and possessive gerunds refer to factual information. Infinitives refer to future ideas or potential events.

Factual	Many zoos have instituted stricter laws regarding the care of their animals. **That zoos protect their animals/Zoos' protecting their animals** is important.	= Zoos actually protect their animals.
Potential	Many zoos have reported higher numbers of animals dying in captivity. **For zoos to protect their animals** is important.	= Zoos potentially can protect their animals (but they don't necessarily do so).

Exercise 6

What would be unexpected or unusual for the following people to do? Write a sentence that expresses your idea.

EXAMPLE: poachers   *For poachers to get permission to hunt animals would be unusual.*

1. bullfighters
2. zookeepers
3. oil magnates
4. lumberjacks
5. medical researchers
6. off-road motor bikers
7. sport hunters
8. commercial farmers

Exercise 7

Circle the best option and explain your decision.

EXAMPLE: (a.) It is interesting that Mary's rabbit only had one bunny.
(Most rabbits can potentially have more than one bunny. It seems here that the comment is about a specific rabbit that produced one bunny.)

b. It is interesting for Mary's rabbit to have only one bunny.

1. **a.** It is heartening that the Body Shop of London has refused to test its products on animals since its establishment.

   b. It is heartening for the Body Shop of London to refuse to test its products on animals since its establishment.

2. **a.** After an oil spill, it will be important that animals are rescued.

   b. After an oil spill, it will be important for animals to be rescued.

3. **a.** It is uncommon that members of the National Rifle Association are in favor of gun control.

   b. It is uncommon for members of the National Rifle Association to be in favor of gun control.

4. **a.** It is shocking that fishers have almost exterminated the blue whale.

   b. It is shocking for fishers to almost exterminate the blue whale.

5. **a.** It is true that dolphins catch diseases from humans at dolphin recreational swim centers.

   b. It is true for dolphins to catch diseases from humans at dolphin recreational swim centers.

6. **a.** It is strange that lemmings' commit suicide.

   b. It is strange for lemmings to commit suicide.

7. **a.** Companies' cutting down the Amazonian rain forests will lead to ecological disaster.

   b. For companies to cut down the Amazonian rain forests would lead to ecological disaster.

Activities

Activity 1

Research several animals that are becoming extinct. Understand how they are dying or being killed. Then, write a short paragraph, giving your feelings and opinions about *one* of these animals. Several suggestions are given below.

> California condor
> Arabian oryx
> orangutan of Borneo
> blue whale

Activity 2

What do rosary beads, pistol grips, and dice have in common? They are all made of ivory, sometimes illegally obtained. Hunters cut the tusks from elephants with chainsaws, sometimes while the animals are still alive. Then they sell the tusks to business people who smuggle them out of the country in gas tankers, cargo trucks, or personal luggage. Often political officials collaborate in the crime by issuing false import permits. Great profits are made all around at the elephant's expense.

Imagine that you have bought an ivory figure for $1000 and later learned that the ivory had been illegally obtained. Write a letter of complaint to the company from which you bought the figure. Use statments such as, "I have just learned that the figure I bought from you was made of illegally obtained ivory. Your selling me such an item is outrageous."

Activity 3

Find out how animals have been used in research of the following diseases: polio, diphtheria, mumps, hepatitis, diabetes, arthritis, high blood pressure, and mental illness. As a result of your research, express your opinions in a short oral report on the use of animals in furthering medical progress. Do you feel that it is important or unneccesary?

EXAMPLE: It is important for researchers to use animals in their research...

Activity 4

Michael W. Fox in his book *Inhumane Society: The American Way of Exploiting Animals* (New York: St. Martin's Press, 1990, p. 146) has expressed his opinion on modern zoos in the following way:

> Today's zoos and wildlife safari parks are radically different from the early iron and concrete zoos. It takes money to run a modern zoo, and zoo directors realize that they must compete with a wide variety of leisure-time activities. Concession stands, miniature railroads, and other carnival amusements, as well as dubious circuslike shows with performing chimps or big cats, lure many visitors to some of our large zoos and wildlife parks. What tricks and obedience the animals display are more a reflection of the power of human control than of the animals' natural behavior. Performing apes, elephants, bears, big cats, dolphins, and "killer" whales especially draw the crowds. Man's mastery over the powerful beast and willful control over its wild instincts is a parody of the repression and sublimation of human nature and personal freedom.

Do you agree with Fox? What statements do you feel are true? What statements do you feel are questionable?

314

U N I T

21

Noun Complements Taking *That* Clauses

Task

How good are you at explaining natural phenomena? Would you be able to explain why the North American and South American eastern coastlines and the Eurasian and African western coastlines appear to be mirror images of each other?

One account for this phenomenon is the theory that all of these continents once formed a single continent and subsequently moved apart.

Discuss some of the following questions with your classmates:

a. What explains the observation that shooting stars speed across the sky?
b. What explains the fact that there are oases in the desert?
c. What accounts for the fact that some rainbows are partial and some are full?
d. What could illustrate the idea that physical activity is difficult at high altitudes?
e. What could illustrate the law that heat flows from a warm place to a cooler place?
f. What fact could explain why the sun and moon appear larger near the horizon?
g. What fact could account for a person's reflection in a spoon appearing upside down?

Now add a few questions of your own about other intriguing natural events that you are curious about. Once you have written your questions, see if your classmates know the facts which explain them.

Focus 1

Overview of Noun Complements

**FORM
MEANING**

- Noun complements are of two types: *that* clauses and infinitives.

    (a) *That* clause: The theory **that water expands when it is frozen** is testable.

    (b) Infinitive: The requirement **for workers to wear safety goggles** is important.

- Both types of complements follow abstract nouns.

+ *That* Clause			+ **Infinitive**		
answer	*news*	*request*	*advice*	*possibility*	*request*
appeal	*notion*	*statement*	*command*	*plan*	*reminder*
axiom	*proposal*	*suggestion*	*instruction*	*preparation*	*requirement*
fact	*reason*	*theory*	*motivation*	*proposal*	*suggestion*
hypothesis	*reply*	*thesis*	*order*	*recommendation*	*tendency*
idea			*permission*		

- Noun complements may appear in subject or object position.
    - Subject:

        (c) **The fact** *that students must pay higher tuitions* disappoints us.

        (d) **The proposal** *for cities to fluoridate their water* was not well received.

    - Object:

        (e) The residents ignored **the appeal** *that they stay inside during the curfew*.

        (f) Most people understood **the recommendation** *for each citizen to make an effort*.

Exercise 1

Underline each noun complement. Circle the abstract noun that precedes it.

EXAMPLE: Early scientists believed (the notion) that matter could be divided into four basic elements: earth, water, air, and fire.

1. The tendency for liquids to turn into gases is well-known.
2. Moisture in the air provides the catalyst for industrial fumes to react and form acid rain.
3. Galileo proposed the hypothesis that all falling bodies drop at the same constant speed.
4. The possibility for a sailor to get lost at sea is low if he or she has a compass.
5. In 1913, Neils Bohr made the suggestion that electrons spin around the nucleus in orbits.
6. The idea that people can survive without light is preposterous.
7. The fact that overhead cables sag on a hot day proves that solids expand when heated.

Exercise 2

Summarize the information from the text by completing the statements which follow.

SOLAR RAYS AND OUR SKIN

(1) The increase of hydrofluorocarbons in the atmosphere is dangerously depleting the earth's ozone layer. (2) The effect of this is that people are having greater exposure to ultraviolet light rays. (3) Can these solar rays increase the chances of skin cancer? (4) Yes, in fact, they increase the cases of malignant melanoma–the deadliest type.

(5) According to The American Cancer Society, hundreds of thousands of new cases of skin cancer will be diagnosed in the United States each year. (6) About five percent of these will be malignant melanoma. (7) To prevent more cases, many doctors say that people should stay out of the sun altogether. (8) This is especially true for redheads and blonds with freckled skin. (9) At the very least, a person should cover up and wear a sunscreen with a high sun-protection factor (15, 25, or 30) during the periods of the day when ultraviolet rays are strongest.

(10) A good example of an anti-skin cancer campaign comes from Australia. (11) Lifeguards in the state of Victoria wear T-shirts with the slogan "SLIP! SLOP! SLAP!" which means slip on a shirt, slop on some sunscreen, and slap on a hat. (12) Although these hints may not please all sunbathers on beaches around the world, they might very well save their lives.

EXAMPLE: The news that *hydrofluorocarbons are depleting the earth's ozone layer* is having serious health consequences.

1. The appeal that _____ could save the lives of blonds and redheads.

2. The fact that _____ is evidence that ultraviolet rays can cause skin cancer.

3. The doctors' recommendation that _____ is not very popular.

4. The amusing idea that _____ has changed the sunbathing habits of people

   in Australia.

Exercise 3

Reread the questions in the Task and answer them, using a noun complement in object position.

EXAMPLE: What explains the observation that "shooting stars" speed across the sky?
Bits of interplanetary matter entering the earth's atmosphere and burning up explains the observation that "shooting stars" speed across the sky.

Focus 2

That Clause Noun Complements versus Restrictive Relative Clauses

MEANING

- For the rest of this unit, you will focus on noun complements taking *that* clauses. *That* clause noun complements resemble restrictive relative clauses, yet they have a different meaning. *That* clause noun complements define an idea, whereas restrictive relative clauses limit one.

Noun Complement	Meaning
(a) The story that she opened a restaurant is untrue.	*Opening a restaurant* is the story. The sentence still makes sense even if *the story* is deleted. In this sentence, *which* cannot replace *that*.

Restrictive Relative Clause	Meaning
(b) The story that/which she told was untrue.	The story in this sentence relates to a particular story, to the one that she told. The sentence will not make sense if *the story* is deleted. In this sentence, *which* can replace *that*.

Exercise 4

Which sentence in each of the following pairs contains a noun complement? Circle your choice.

EXAMPLE: ⓐ The idea that they question the witnesses is necessary.
　　　　　　b. The idea that he had was exciting.

1. **a.** Many people dispute the fact that human beings evolved from apes.
   b. Many people accept the fact that he mentioned.
2. **a.** The suggestion that she included in the letter will never be followed.
   b. The suggestion that a person should warm up before jogging is important.
3. **a.** The reply that she did not need help came as a surprise.
   b. The reply that contained important information was received too late.
4. **a.** I believe the theory that opposites attract.
   b. I believe the theory that my uncle proposed.
5. **a.** The news that was relayed on Thursday was disappointing.
   b. The news that the war had started depressed everyone.

Focus 3

That Clause Noun Complements in Subject Position

- *That* clause noun complements in subject position contain known or implied information. The predicates comment upon the facts or ideas contained in *that* clauses following *the fact/idea/news* etc.

  (a) Harry had to write many papers in college. He never learned how to type. **The idea that Harry graduated from college without knowing how to type** astonishes me.

  (b) When Teresa was diagnosed with cancer, everyone thought that she would not survive. Then, after several months of chemotherapy, the doctor said he could see no trace of the disease. **The fact that she was cured for good** is a miracle.

Exercise 5

The following paragraphs describe amazing facts about famous people. Make observations about each set of facts using a *that* clause following *the fact/idea/news* etc.

> **EXAMPLE:** When Beethoven was 28 years old, he became deaf. In spite of this, he was still able to compose music.
>
> *The fact that Beethoven composed music while he was deaf is amazing.*

1. Marie Antoinette and Louis XVI ate very well, while their Parisian subjects could not afford bread. When hearing of this, the unsympathetic queen is reported to have said, "Why, then, let them eat cake."

2. U.S. President Richard Nixon resigned from office in 1974 after a very serious governmental scandal. His associates who were interested in having him reelected had installed wiretaps at the headquarters of the Democratic National Committee at the Watergate Hotel. Rather than being honest, Nixon tried to cover up the scandal and this led to his downfall.

3. In 1919, Rudolph Valentino, a famous American movie star, married Jean Acker. In his silent films, he played the part of the great lover. But, on his wedding day, Acker ran away and Valentino never consummated his marriage with her.

4. For years, athletes did the high jump by jumping sideways or straddling over the bar. Then, Dick Fosbury discovered that he could break world records by going over head first, flat on his back. This technique is now called the Fosbury Flop.

5. The Japanese had long revered their emperor as divine. However, Emperor Hirohito destroyed this image by announcing to his people in 1946 that it was a false conception that he was descended from God. In fact, even at the early age of 14, Hirohito had doubted his own divinity.

Focus 4

Overuse of *The Fact*

MEANING
USE

- *The fact that* clause noun complements (in a and c below) are similar in meaning to the *that* clause verb complements (in b and d below); however, we generally consider them less formal.
  - **(a) Less formal: The fact** *that she refused the money* shows her sense of pride.
  - **(b) Formal:** *That she refused the money* shows her sense of pride.
  - **(c) Less formal:** People generally acknowledge **the fact** *that Japan must find alternate ways to use its space.*
  - **(d) Formal:** People generally acknowledge *that Japan must find alternate ways to use its space.*
- In writing, overuse of *that* clauses in object position with *the fact* can lead to wordiness. In most cases, we prefer the simple *that* clause.
  - **(e) Wordy:** He believed the fact that his daughter had been kidnapped, and he understood the fact that he would need to pay a ransom.
  - **(f) Concise:** He believed that his daughter had been kidnapped, and he understood that he would need to pay a ransom.
- Certain verbs (such as *accept, conceal, discuss, dispute, disregard, hide, overlook, support,* etc.) require the use of *the fact that* clauses in object position, however.
  - **(g)** The detectives concealed the fact that they had searched the room.
  - **(h)** The soldiers accepted the fact that they had been defeated.
  - **(i)** The police officers disregarded the fact that they needed a search warrant.
  - **(j)** NOT: The police officers disregarded that they needed a search warrant.

Exercise 6

The following text about toxic wastes contains too many *the fact that* clauses. Underline instances of *the fact* in the text. Then, cross out those that do not seem necessary or are incorrect.

(1) Citizens may believe ~~the fact~~ that they are safe from hazardous wastes, but they are misled. (2) Hundreds of chemical companies say the fact that they are disposing of toxic wastes, yet they conceal the fact that they are illegally dumping them or improperly disposing of them. (3) The tragic result is the fact that dangerous wastes are seeping into the water supply. (4) Although many manufacturers do not want to accept the fact that they need to find alternate means of disposal, environmental agencies are forcing them to do so. (5) Unfortunately, it has been too late in some cases. (6) The fact that residents who live near toxic waste sites often have greater chronic respiratory and neurological problems than people who do not support the fact that toxic waste is a major health issue. (7) Chemical companies can no longer overlook the fact that something must be done. (8) Experts claim the fact that landfills having double liners is one solution. (9) Companies also need to accept the fact that recycling and substituting hazardous chemicals for safer ones in their products will greatly improve the situation for their communities.

Focus 5

FORM

Noun Complements Following Transitive Adjectives and Phrasal Verbs

FORM

- When noun complements follow transitive adjectives (adjectives taking a preposition + a noun phrase) and phrasal verbs, they must be *the fact/news/idea/theory etc. that* clauses rather than simple *that* clauses.

Transitive Adjectives	Phrasal Verbs
disappointed in	*boast about*
worried about	*long for*
proud of	*give in*
sick of	*face up to*
tired of	*put up with*

(a) He is tired of **the fact that she refuses to see him**.

(b) NOT: He is tired of that she refuses to see him.

(c) He boasted about **the news that his team won**.

(d) NOT: He boasted about that his team won.

Exercise 7

Imagine that a very wealthy entrepreneur has just lost his fortune. Comment upon the circumstances of his condition using the words below and *the fact/idea/news, etc. that* clauses.

EXAMPLE: wealthy man (face up to)

The wealthy man had to face up to *the fact that he had lost his millions.*

1. his mother (worried about)
2. negligence (account for)
3. his creditors (weary of)
4. his employees (indignant at)

5. his wife (put up with)
6. the lawyers (bring up)
7. daughter (conscious of)

Exercise 8

Suppose you saw people doing the following strange actions. What would you remind them of in order to help clear up their confusion? Write a sentence about what you would say. The first one has been done for you.

EXAMPLE: driving a car without a license

I would remind them of the fact that they need a license to drive a car.

1. not leaving a tip for the waiter
2. washing the dishes with laundry detergent
3. making lasagne without cheese
4. playing soccer with a baseball
5. reading a book upside down
6. taking pictures without film in the camera
7. spelling the word *receive* with *i* before *e* after *c.*

Exercise 9

The following sentences review the structures learned in this unit. Correct those which contain errors. Write OK next to those that are correct.

EXAMPLE: The teacher overlooked the fact that Hung had not done his homework. *OK*

The fact that she made a confession $\overset{was}{\wedge}$ untrue.

1. Tom believes the fact that light travels faster than sound.
2. The suggestion which she take off her hat was not followed.
3. The fact that the automobile increased the distance a person could travel made it possible for a person to live and work in different places.
4. She is tired of that she always has to wash the dishes.
5. We are concerned about that there will be no more food.
6. I am grateful for the fact that the doctor assisted me in my decision.
7. Did the glasses help to conceal the fact that he had a scar on his left eyelid?
8. The fact that Mary finished her homework.
9. The fact that 20 million Russians died during World War II is tragic.
10. The request that we ignore the crime was considered unacceptable.
11. Do you agree the statement that blonds have more fun?
12. That Jerome passed the bar examination made it possible for him to practice law.

Activities

Activity 1

Homo sapiens have not always been good stewards of the earth. In fact, numerous environmental problems can be attributed to human beings' irresponsiblity. Discuss in class the specific reasons behind some of the following environmental problems which humans have created:

pollution of cities	burning of tropical rain forests
extinction of animals	oil slicks
toxic waste	acid rain

> **EXAMPLE:** The fact that people have continued to drive gasoline engines has created the pollution problem in cities.

Activity 2

In the Task, you discussed certain natural facts. Investigate one or more issues mentioned there (meteorites, rainbows, oases, lightning, eclipses, etc.) or one of your own and write a short report explaining what facts give them the unusual properties that they have. Use at least three noun complements in your report.

> **EXAMPLE:** Some people say that lightning never strikes the same place twice. However, the fact that we cannot predict when or where lightning will strike refutes this idea . . .

Activity 3

Select someone who you feel has an interesting job. Then interview him/her about it, e.g., find out the preparation required, daily activities, social contacts, equipment used, salary, etc. Then, describe the interesting facts you learned to a classmate. Use as many noun complements as you can.

> **EXAMPLE:** I was surprised by the fact that lawyers earn six-digit salaries.
>
> I was interested in the fact that it takes from five to seven years of schooling to become a professor.

Activity 4

Watch a mystery or detective program on TV or at the movies with your classmates. After the movie is over, discuss why the protagonists or detectives were not able to solve the mystery or crime sooner than they did. What facts were concealed, disregarded, or overlooked as the plot evolved? What facts finally led the protagonists or detectives to solve the mystery?

> **EXAMPLE:** The mother concealed the fact that Tony had a twin brother.
>
> The fact that Tony had a twin brother made the police finally realize that it was Tony's twin Jimmy who was guilty.

Activity 5

Read several editorials or opinion essays. Then write your own view of the ideas in the essays by using noun complements.

> **EXAMPLE:** The idea that people should not be allowed to own weapons makes sense.

U N I T

22

Verbs, Nouns, and Adjectives Taking Subjunctive Complements

Task

It is not uncommon for two different parties to disagree about the rightness of an issue or the solution to a problem. Often another person who is not biased toward either side will be called in to serve as an arbitrator. For this task, one or more classmates should role-play each side of the following issues. One other person, as the arbitrator, should listen, ask questions, and give recommendations to the two parties (e.g., I suggest that _____ , I recommend that _____ , I propose that _____ , etc.).

CASE #1

A young woman would like to attend an all-male college. The president of the college wants to maintain the 100-year tradition of an all-male campus.

CASE #2

A girl was in a serious car accident one year ago. She has been in a coma ever since and is not expected to recover. The doctors want to keep her alive. The girl's mother sees that there is no hope for her recovery and would like to remove her from the life-support system.

CASE #3

A father keeps his children at home rather than sending them to school because he feels children are being taught ideas counter to his religion. The school board feels it is unlawful to prevent children from getting a well-rounded education.

CASE #4

A supervisor fires a worker because the supervisor believes he is often late, undependable, and disrespectful. The worker denies these charges and claims that he is overworked and berated by his supervisor.

Focus 1

Subjunctive Verbs in *That* Clause Complements

FORM
USE

- *That* clause complements of verbs of advice and urging must contain a present subjunctive verb in North American English.

  (a) The arbitrator recommended that Susan not **be** hesitant.

  (b) It was stipulated that he **abandon** the plans.

- Verbs of advice and urging that require subjunctive complements are

advise	*move*	*recommend*
beg	*order*	*request*
command	*pledge*	*require*
demand	*pray*	*stipulate*
determine	*prefer*	*suggest*
insist	*propose*	*urge*

- The subjunctive verb in the complement is the base form of the verb: *be, go, take,* etc. We use the base form for all singular and plural subjects.

  (c) Her father demanded that he/they **be** back by 12:00.

  (d) That Mary/they **follow** all of the instructions was stipulated.

- For a similar yet less formal effect, we can use *should* + base form instead of the subjunctive.

  (e) Formal: The president insisted that the meeting **begin** on time.

  (f) Informal: Jody requested that we **should eat** at 6:00.

Exercise 1

During the Task, what were some of the recommendations that the arbitrator made to the conflicting parties?

EXAMPLE: He suggested that the president reconsider the all-male policy.

325

Exercise 2

Use the following base sentence to make comments about each of the situations in items 1 through 6. Fill in the first blank with the correct form of the verb in parentheses and the second blank with a subjunctive verb or *should* + base form, whichever is more appropriate.

Base sentence: She (or he) _____ that he (or she)_____ call her (or him) tomorrow.

> **EXAMPLE:** A boss to her employee (recommend)
> She _recommends_ that he _call her_ tomorrow.

1. A friend who wants to give another friend some information (insist)
2. An actor to a director who may offer him a part in a play (suggest)
3. A doctor to a patient who might have a deadly disease (require)
4. A neighbor to another neighbor who is too busy to talk (propose)
5. A father to an unsuitable companion for his daughter (forbid)
6. A salesperson to a customer (urge)

Focus 2

USE

Subjunctive Verbs in Noun Complements

USE

- Nouns that come from verbs of advice and urging may also take a noun complement with a subjunctive verb. Some of these nouns are *command, decision, demand, order, pronouncement, recommendation, request, suggestion,* etc.
  - (a) Suggest: **The suggestion that he be fired** was met with resistance.
  - (b) Request: She didn't listen to **his request that she take a sweater**.
  - (c) Advise: **His advice that she be set free** was unwise.

Exercise 3

Imagine that you live in an apartment complex surrounded by some very disagreeable neighbors in apartments 4A through 4F. Answer the following questions, using the prompts provided and a subjunctive complement.

> **EXAMPLE:** What did 4A do when you told him his music was too loud?
> ignore/suggestion
> *He ignored my suggestion that he turn off the stereo.*

1. What did 4B do when you asked her to return your watering can?
   not heed/proposal
2. What did 4C do when you wanted him to stop being a Peeping Tom?
   laugh at/demand

3. What did 4D do when you told her to stop stomping around?
   not listen to/demand
4. What did 4E do when you asked him not to come home drunk?
   refuse to pay attention to/request
5. What did 4F do when you advised him to give his dog away?
   ignore/advice

Exercise 4

Imagine that you have a friend Yang, and his family has given him a great deal of advice about how to succeed on his new job as a computer programmer. Which advice of Yang's family do you think was useful and which wasn't? Write a sentence that expresses your opinion of each family member's suggestion.

EXAMPLE: Uncle/flirt with the secretaries

His uncle's advice that he flirt with the secretaries was not appropriate.

Note: Try to use as many advice or urging nouns as you can.

Family Member	Advice
Uncle	flirt with the secretaries
Grandfather	be accurate in your math
Mother	be friendly
Sister	bring your boss coffee every day
Brother	be in good physical condition
Aunt	work overtime without pay
Father	act confident

Focus 3

FORM

Subjunctive Verbs in Adjective Complements

FORM

- Adjective complements can sometimes take subjunctive verbs. This is true when advice adjectives like *advisable, desirable, essential, imperative, important, mandatory, necessary, requisite, urgent,* and *vital* are in the main clause.

  (a) That he type is essential.
  (b) It is essential **that he type**.
  (c) That she be punctual is important.
  (d) It is important **that she be punctual**.

Exercise 5

A. Using the information from the following job advertisements, fill in the following statements with "that" clauses containing subjunctive verbs.

        EXAMPLE: It is important *that the accounting applicant be bilingual in Chinese and English* (accountant).

Accountant
An accounting firm seeks individual w/ min 2 yr exp. Requires good communication skills & ability to assist clients. Must be biling in Chinese. Previous exp in CPA firm is plus.
Call Mr. Tang 213-627-1409

File Clerk
Require at least 1 yr exp in law firm file rm. Knowledge of ofc equipment. Ability to work without supervision. Good command of English for switchboard relief.
Mrs. Jacobsen 310-395-6662

Chemist
Stable, fast-growing company is seeking chemist for formulation of industrial products. Must have BS degree in chemistry and at least 5 yrs exp. Non-smoker preferred. Xlent benefits. Redex Co
Redex Co. 714-773-2221

Manager
10 new Asst. Managers for marketing & sales needed. No exp. necessary. We train. Must be 18 & older. Must have car. Work in a wild & crazy office.
Super's 818-774-8234

Drivers–Shuttle
AIRWAY Shuttle needs outstanding drivers for day and eve shifts. Must be clean-cut, highly ethical, energetic. Great benefits and friendly environment.
AIRWAY 818-775-8156

Nurse
For career-minded nurse. Participate in clinical trials. & oversee needs for patients on daily basis. Need good track record of exp, be able to learn fast, self-starter. If interested call Westside Hospital 213-454-6210.

---

1. _____ is essential. (chemist)

2. It is mandatory _____ . (shuttle driver)

3. _____ is desirable. (file clerk)

4. It is imperative _____ . (manager)

5. It is necessary _____ . (nurse)

B. Create five more of your own sentences with information in the ads.

Activities

Activity 1

The owner of a factory has been losing a great deal of money, and he realizes that he must let five of his employees go. You, the company's personnel manager, must review the performance of the ten most problematic employees and make a decision as to which five to fire and which five to retain. The following list summarizes the problems with these ten employees. Put an X in either the "Fire" or "Retain" column, depending upon what you have decided. Then write a short report to the owner of the factory, explaining your decision.

Name	Problems	Fire	Retain
Mina A.	disagreeableness		
Homer O.	lack of ambition		
Gunnar F.	criminal background		
Sang S.	incompetence		
Fern M.	laziness		
Sherry B.	alcohol problem		
Maggie W.	clumsiness		
Ly P.	dishonesty		
Dawn M.	absenteeism		
Ann K.	loose morals		

EXAMPLE: Dear Mr. Johnson,

Related to your last request, I have determined which five employees should be dismissed. I suggest that Dawn M. be fired because she has missed 30 days of work during the last three months . . .

Activity 2

Read at least five advice columns in the newspaper such as "Ann Landers," "Dear Abby," "Miss Manners," etc. Summarize the problems and the advice given to persons requesting the advice.

EXAMPLE: A man had attempted many times to quit smoking. Counseling, nicotine chewing gum, and "cold turkey" were all ineffective. Abby suggested that he try acupuncture.

Activity 3

Have you or any of your classmates ever paid for something that was defective or did not work (e.g., a piece of clothing, a gadget, a machine, etc.)? Or have you ever paid for a service which you discovered later had not been performed (e.g., had your car fixed, your computer repaired, your watch cleaned, etc.)? How did or would you request the salesperson or service provider to correct these mistakes? Summarize your own and your classmate's responses here.

> **EXAMPLE:** Jocelyn suggested that the saleswoman replace the sweater because of the unravelling yarn.

1.

2.

3.

4.

5.

Activity 4

Read and summarize articles from the newspaper that describe political, environmental, or civic problems. Note particularly the solutions and suggestions that citizens, politicians, or organizations make to solve these problems. Use some subjunctive complements in your summary.

Activity 5

Over a thousand years ago, Anglo-Saxon and Scandinavian wizards and magicians used the power of runes to divine their future. Runes are alphabetic characters used much like tarot cards or I-Ching ideograms to obtain divine guidance on life's questions. You will have a chance to test the power of runes as a guide in the following activity.

1. Form groups of three or four students.
2. Think of a question you would like answered about some area of your life (e.g., work, relationships, travel, money, etc.).

   EXAMPLE: How will I get home for the holidays?

3. Point to one of the runes on the following chart (page 334).

   EXAMPLE: Yr.

4. Choose a number between 10 and 30 and move your finger clockwise the number of spaces you selected.

   EXAMPLE: 13

5. The rune you land on is your oracle. Read the text about this rune.

   EXAMPLE: Hagal

6. Share your question with your classmates and paraphrase your rune's "advice."

   EXAMPLE: It suggested that I be on my guard because my prospects may change unexpectedly, and it urged that I be cautious and patient.

THE SELF: This rune symbolizes a human being. It counsels you to exhibit your generosity, friendship, and altruism. It represents your positive character traits, those which you must draw upon to improve yourself.
Advice: You possess genuine power over events and you will find the solution to your problem within yourself. Only within yourself.

PARTNERSHIP: This rune signifies collective effort. It speaks of exchanges in an atmosphere of generosity and peace. In your job, teamwork will pay off. In love, it's an omen for a solid relationship, a meeting of minds and hearts.
Advice: Be warned against hesitation or selfishness. It's by thinking of others, by offering a gift, or simply by giving pleasure that you will be fulfilled.

GROWTH: This is the symbol of achievement, the completion of a project. It also signifies fertility, birth, completion, and renewal. An end or a beginning.
Advice: You are on the brink of a new departure. Have faith.

CONSTRAINT: The rune of the master of us all: time. Now is the moment to free yourself of material things and cultivate the life of the mind. Be patient, careful, and resolute. Thought is preferable to action.
Advice: The mind rules. Don't be grasping in your pursuit of success. Don't rush things. Wisdom alone will lead you to accomplishment.

FLOW: This is the quintessential female rune. It augurs well for everything that touches on artistic creativity, summoning up your reserves of intuition and imagination. Talents that are hidden will come to the fore. Work with them!
Advice: Don't give in to doubt. Let your deepest desires express themselves. Don't question your abilities.

TIR

WARRIOR: This is an arrow shot into the air. In your work life, this means you should get a project rolling and have both a competitive spirit and a will to win. In love, it suggests passion, sex, and fertility.

Advice: Act firmly and positively. Rely only on yourself, your energy, and your desires. It's simple: motivate yourself.

HAGAL

DISRUPTION: This rune is like a disruptive hailstorm. It represents the random in life—its problems and everyday frustrations.

Advice: Be on your guard: your prospects may change unexpectedly. Only caution and patience will lead you to success, because the final decision is out of your hands.

WYRD

THE UNKNOWABLE: This mysterious oracle reserves the right to remain silent and to withhold all advice.

SIGNALS: This rune deals with knowledge and learning. It is telling you that some sort of test awaits, one in which you may need the help of someone who is an expert.

Advice: Study the situation thoughtfully. Express your wishes but don't decide anything off the top of your head.

OS

FERTILITY: This especially concerns the family. It predicts the birth of a child, a marriage, or the improvement of life in the home. In matters of health, it foresees a healing process.

Advice: Tenderness and care will bring about growth. You're only just at the beginning, but soon the results will be visible.

ING

INITIATION: This is an enigmatic sign that speaks of hidden happenings. It stresses the importance of mystery, the revelation of a secret, and the possibility of finding something or someone. It's the rune of second chances.

Advice: Follow your intuition. The solution to the problem lies not in what you can see but in what you can feel.

PEORTH

SEPARATION: This rune suggests a change concerning material goods, cultural heritage, legacies, or money in general. Professionally, efforts must be made to stabilize a certain situation.

Advice: Expect some difficulties or delays. Good things come to those who wait. Avoid flighty behavior, doing too many things at once, or spending too much.

ODAL

JOURNEY: This signifies a journey or a major move. It can indicate the arrival of good news or an important change. Professionally, your activities are successful—plans may change and any negotiations will end favorably for you.

Advice: Be prepared to change course, to travel, to be more open-minded.

RAD

PROTECTION: A very positive rune. It speaks of being protected by an important person, whether at work or in love. You have a lot of self-confidence because this is a splendid time for you.

Advice: Positive change is in the offing. Control your emotions and be ready to meet all challenges.

EOLH

OPENING: An optimistic sign, a good omen of beginnings (or renewals). If you are ill, this rune signifies a healing or cure. In affairs of the heart, it indicates the start of an intimate relationship.

Advice: The time is for action, not surrender. In love, it promises good times.

KEN

UR

DAEG

THORN

YR

SIGEL

FEOH

JARA

IS

EH

WYN

STRENGTH: Growth and rewarding change, especially in your professional life. You should act energetically, for new responsibilities are yours for the taking. Your abilities will be put to the test.

Advice: Act with determination and do your best. Your work conditions may noticeably improve.

BREAKTHROUGH: Another positive rune that signifies prosperity and improvement. It represents the light after darkness, and triumph over adversity.

Advice: Take full advantage of opportunities when they arise. Remain serene and upbeat.

GATEWAY: You will soon receive good news that may change your life. But you will have to make a decision that will require a lot of thought.

Advice: Learn to listen to the opinions of others. Seek out help and wait for the right moment to act. If you don't have enough self-confidence, hold off.

DEFENSE: This rune involves danger that can, and should, be overcome. In fact, the goal you wish to attain is within reach, but you have to become more flexible and change your way of seeing things.

Advice: This is just a warning. You can improve the situation by questioning the way you think and changing the way you act.

WHOLENESS: This represents luck, victory, and the fulfillment of your hopes. In all areas of your life (work, love, health, etc.), energy is on the upswing.

Advice: Take advantage of it.

POSSESSIONS: This is very positive, an omen of increased wealth. New financial opportunities are the order of the day. It's also a symbol of victory, struggle, and an obstacle overcome.

Advice: Consolidate your gains and persevere along your path. Material reward will soon follow.

HARVEST: This rune symbolizes what has been sown and will soon be reaped. Thus, it speaks of work, perseverance, and patience. The earth has a natural cycle: planting and harvesting.

Advice: You are on the right path, the one that leads you to a reward. Don't stop halfway. But don't forget, things take time.

STANDSTILL: This involves obstacles, a cooling in your relations with others. At work, it can mean a loss of motivation. Passivity may get the better of you. In love, a relationship may lose passion and ardor.

Advice: For the moment, put your plans on hold. Before you act, wait for the situation to improve on its own.

MOVEMENT: This motion can involve a change of job, a business trip, a long journey, or a new home. This rune is a source of progress, demanding that you keep an open mind.

Advice: Be prepared to take control and get ready to adapt. Your horizons are broadening. Get rid of your hang-ups and throw yourself into an adventure.

JOY: You'll get pleasure from your work. Your artistic talents or manual skills will be unleashed. Joy will be found in your love life, through emotional and physical fulfillment. A change is coming, if your enthusiasm doesn't flag.

Advice: Use your creative gifts and your intuition to achieve your goals. Everything depends on how much fun you get out of accomplishing things.

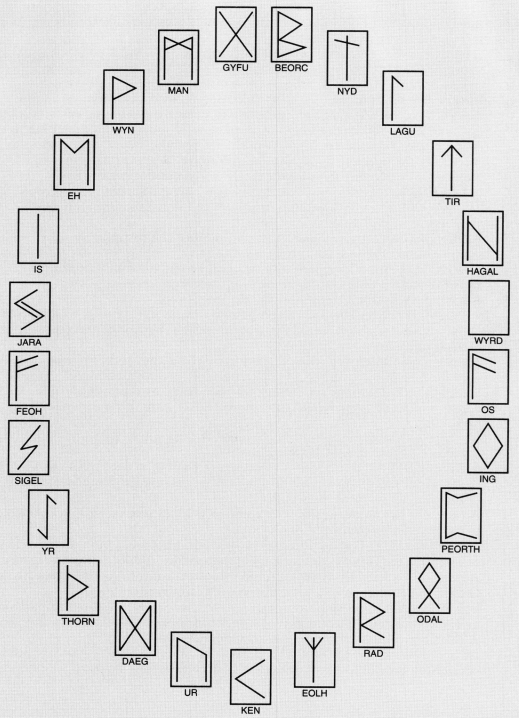

GYFU BEORC NYD LAGU MAN WYN TIR EH HAGAL IS WYRD JARA OS FEOH ING SIGEL PEORTH YR ODAL THORN RAD DAEG EOLH UR KEN

Thorsons, an imprint of Harper Collins Publishers Limited Extracts and material from THE RUNIC WORK-BOOK by Tony Willis.
Layout reprinted with permission from ELLE Magazine © 1991 ELLE Publishing L. P.

23 Complex Passives and Raised Structures

Task

What do you think the following statements have in common?

The first dream in a new house or under a new blanket or quilt is likely to come true.

Entering a house with the left foot first tends to bring bad luck.

Sneeze on Monday, sneeze for danger;
Sneeze on Tuesday, kiss a stranger;
Sneeze on Wednesday, get a letter;
Sneeze on Thursday, something better;
Sneeze on Friday, sneeze for sorrow;
Sneeze on Saturday, see your lover tomorrow.

If you guessed that they are all superstitions, you're right. Almost every culture seems to have beliefs and practices that are thought to bring good luck or misfortune or that help us to predict or control our future. Some practices have become so traditional that we don't think of them as superstitions. An example is the custom of throwing rice on a newly married couple; today, most of us don't regard this as a practice to ensure fertility for the newlyweds!

Here are some other superstitions from around the world:

Many centuries ago in Egypt, it was believed that a roasted mouse was beneficial to eat if one had a fever.

In parts of China, embroidering a cat on a child's shoe was thought to make the child as surefooted as a cat.

In Europe and other places, the word *abracadabra* was said to be a charm against sickness.

In Scotland, it was believed that tying knots in an apron would protect against accidents.

Think of superstitions you have heard and make a list of them. Consider the following categories: the weather, food, health, love, marriage, money, animals, bad luck, good luck, protection from evil, and any others you can think of. Share some of the ones you thought of with the class. Do you know the origins of any of them?

Focus 1

FORM

Structure of Complex Passives

FORM

- We call passive constructions followed by *that* clauses or infinitive clauses (*to* + verb) **complex passives**.
- Complex passives with *be* verbs generally have one of two forms:

Introductory *It* +	Passive +	*That* Clause
(a) It	is believed	that primates first appeared on the earth about 69 million years ago.
(b) It	is said	that the number 13 is bad luck.
(c) It	was reported	that a hijacker was arrested this morning.

- In some cases, the *that* clause may occur as the subject:
  (d) That a pot of gold lies at the end of a rainbow was believed by many of us when we were children.
- We generally use this form for special emphasis. With some verbs (e.g. *said*), the *that* clause cannot be the subject. In many cases, a subject *that* clause in the initial position would sound awkward.

Subject Other Than Introductory *It* +	Passive +	*To* Infinitive Clause
(e) Primates	are believed	to have first appeared on the earth about 69 million years ago.
(f) Thirteen	is said	to be an unlucky number.
(g) A hijacker	was reported	to have been arrested this morning.

- We derive this second type of complex passive from the first type in the following manner.
  - raise the subject of the *that* clause to the position of subject of the main clause:

    It is believed that **primates** —> **Primates** are believed

    Note that the verb changed to plural to agree with the subject.
  - the *that* clause, now missing its subject, changes to an infinitive clause:

    that first appeared on the earth about 69 million years ago —>
    to have first appeared on the earth about 69 million years ago.

    Note that the infinitive here is a perfective one because the main clause verb is present tense, but the *that* clause verb is past tense.

Exercise 1

Rewrite at least five of the superstitions your class thought of in the Task, using complex passive forms.

    EXAMPLE: *It is said that* if a picture falls in the house, someone will die.

             A red string tied around a finger on your left hand *is believed to help* your memory.

Exercise 2

The columns below have information about superstitions related to body parts. Match the descriptions or events in the first column to the results in the second column to form superstitions. Then make a statement for each match, using a complex passive.

    EXAMPLE: *It is believed that if you have a mole on your neck, you will get money.*

1. if your foot itches
2. if your eyebrows meet
3. if your nose itches
4. if your front teeth are set wide apart
5. if your cheeks suddenly feel flushed
6. if you can touch the fore-finger and the little finger of your left hand over the back of your hand
7. if you kiss your elbow

a. you will kiss a fool
b. you will turn into a member of the opposite sex
c. you will be a good cook
d. you will be lucky in money matters all your life
e. you will be traveling to a new land
f. someone is talking about you
g. you will be lucky in love

Exercise 3

In the following passage, identify the complex passive sentences. Underline the main clause passive verbs. Circle examples of introductory *it*. Bracket [ ] the complement introducer *that* or *to*. State whether you think each complex passive expresses an opinion or a fact. The first one, in sentence (6), is done as an example. It expresses a fact.

THE GUINNESS BOOK OF WORLD RECORDS: TREASURE OR TRIVIA?

(1)Have you ever wondered what the name of the rarest spider in the world is? (2)Or who holds the record for performing the most somersaults? (3)Or the width of the largest pizza ever made? (4)Probably not. (5)Nevertheless, the answers to questions such as these, as well as numerous other facts about the natural and man-made world, have made the *Guinness Book of World Records* a continual best-seller since it was first published in 1956. (6)In fact, (it) is claimed [to be the top-selling copyright book in publishing history].

(7)The *Guinness Book of World Records* presents hundreds of fascinating, if not immediately useful, facts and figures for those who are curious about the superlatives of the world (and even of the known universe), whether they concern the biggest, the longest, the oldest, or the smallest. (8)Here are just a few examples:

(9)The longest-living fish is thought to be the lake sturgeon. (10)It was reported that one specimen lived for 82 years.

(11)It is believed that Sirius A, the Dog Star, is the brightest of the 5,776 stars we are able to see.

(12)The Library of Congress on Capitol Hill in Washington, D.C., is known to be the largest library in the world.

(13)It must be admitted that many of the "facts" in this compendium are concerned with trivia or with rather bizarre feats. (14)For example, consider the following:

(15)The most overdue library book in the United States is reported to have been checked out in 1823 and returned by the borrower's great-grandson in 1968. (16)The fine, which was waived, is said to have been $2,264.

(17)A British woman is alleged to have eaten 2,780 cold baked beans, one by one with a cocktail stick, in 30 minutes.

(18)It is believed that the ultimate writing under handicap involved the ability to write backward, upside down, and laterally inverted (mirror-image) with both hands simultaneously while blindfolded. (19)Three people are known to have performed this feat.

(20)As useless as some of this information may seem, it could be conjectured that the lists of oddities, rather than the "hard facts" of science, are what accounts for the tremendous popularity of the *Guinness Book of World Records*.

Focus 2

Discourse Function of Introductory *It*

USE

- The two complex passive forms given in Focus 1, with and without introductory *it*, often have much the same meaning:

    (a) It is said that the number 13 is bad luck.

    (b) The number 13 **is said** to be bad luck.

    The discourse context will, however, influence the selection of one over the other.

- To introduce a topic, the introductory *it* form may be preferred because it puts the new information at the end of the sentence. For example, if you were listening to a news report, there would be less chance that you would miss hearing part of the information if all of it came after an introductory phrase:

    (c) It was reported today that a power failure in Montreal has caused a blackout.

- We might use the form with *to*-infinitive after a topic has been introduced. In other words, the subject is then known through previous mention:

    (d) The power failure is believed to have affected the entire city.

    The information in the subject—*the power failure*—helps to create a link to the previous example by repeating part of the predicate.

Exercise 4

For each of the following numbered sentence groups, choose and circle the sentence that best fits the context, using the principles of presenting old and new information discussed in Focus 2. Consider each numbered group to be the beginning of a written article or spoken announcement.

1. It is believed by some that to open an umbrella in the house will bring bad luck. In parts of Asia, as early as the eleventh century,
    (a) it was thought to be an insult to open an umbrella inside a building.
    (b) opening an umbrella inside a building was thought to be an insult.

2. **(a)** It has been alleged that an employee of the museum is responsible for the theft of dozens of paintings.
    (b) An employee of the museum is alleged to be responsible for the theft of dozens of paintings.

    Police are currently investigating the claim.

3. **(a)** It was reported this morning that a Pacific blacktip shark gave birth to three healthy pups at Sea World.
   (b) A Pacific blacktip shark was reported to have given birth to three healthy pups at Sea World this morning.
   Officials commented that this marks the first documented birth of the species in captivity.

4. Of the comets that have been recorded, the least frequently returning one is Delavan's Comet, which appeared in 1914.
   (a) This comet is not expected to return for 24 million years.
   (b) It is not expected that this comet will return for 24 million years.

Focus 3

Contexts for Use of Complex Passives

USE

- We often use complex passives in journalism, in business, and in academic writing to achieve an impersonal tone or to report information that is not known to be a fact. We don't commonly use complex passives in informal spoken English; they are, however, frequent in formal spoken English (e.g., news reports, speeches) and in a variety of written contexts.

- Some of the most common uses of complex passive are

  - to achieve an impersonal tone; the writer/speaker wants to avoid using first person *I* or *we*.

in explanations/ observations:	**(a)** It **should be noted** that these results cannot be generalized. **(b)** This product **is known** to be inferior.
in statements of desired or expected behavior:	**(c)** It **is assumed** that all employees have completed the necessary hiring papers. **(d)** All homework **is expected** to be turned in on time.
in evaluations or judgments:	**(e)** It **has been ruled** that the prisoner was unfairly convicted. **(f)** The house **was considered** to be overpriced.

  - to express information about the past or present that has not been verified as factual or true, even though it may be widely believed to be true.

    (g) It **is believed** that baseball was being played in England in the early eighteenth century.
    (h) The highest price paid for a bottle of wine **is thought** to be $157,500.
    (i) Mr. Blau **is alleged** to have stolen several car stereos.

- to describe past beliefs that are no longer regarded as true, especially ones that were once considered truths but are now regarded as myths:

> **(j)** In the nineteenth century, it **was thought** that personality traits and mental abilities could be detected by bumps on the head.
>
> **(k)** In ancient Greece, lightning bolts **were believed** to be weapons used by Zeus, the king of the gods.

- to express a general expectation about some future event:

> **(l)** It **is assumed** that more and more species will become extinct if we continue to destroy the world's rain forests.
>
> **(m)** The weather **is expected** to be warm and sunny all weekend.

Exercise 5

Imagine that you are a television news commentator. The following are questions you have been asked about past and current events. Give a response to each question by making a complex passive statement from the information in brackets: [ ]. Include an agent only if you think it is needed. Try to use a variety of verbs.

EXAMPLE: Q: Why didn't Mr. Smith get elected mayor? [people thought he was corrupt]

A: *He was alleged to be corrupt.*

OR *It was alleged that he was corrupt.*

1. Q: Why didn't Congress pass the defense bill? [The legislators said it was a waste of taxpayers' money.]
2. Q: Why were people surprised that the Minnesota Twins won the World Series in 1987? [They didn't think the Twins were the best team.]
3. Q: Why were scientists surprised when the *Voyager* satellite discovered that Neptune has a ring around it? [They had thought Neptune had only arcs around it, not a complete ring.]
4. Q: Can acid rain really prevent global warming? [Some scientists think that by-products of acid rain may cause solar energy to be mirrored back into space. This would cool the atmosphere.]
5. Q: Why were the local beaches closed for swimming last weekend? [City officials believed they were polluted.]
6. Q: Why did the chief of police resign? [Some citizens provided evidence that he was accepting bribes.]

Focus 4

Verbs Occurring with Complex Passives

USE

- We commonly use the following verbs with complex passives.
  - to express information considered or demonstrated to be a fact:

    know understand prove show

  - to present information or report events that the speaker/writer does not want to claim is a fact:

    allege consider presume say
    assume feel report suppose
    believe imagine rumor think

  - to present observations/discoveries:

    find discover note mention observe reveal show

  - to express speculation:

    conjecture hypothesize speculate suggest

  - to express expectations/recommendations/decisions:

    agree assume decide expect presume suggest

  - to express evaluations:

    consider deem judge rule

Exercise 6

Here are some more facts and trivia from the *Guinness Book of World Records*. Information considered to be a fact is indicated by (F); information thought to be possibly true is indicated by (?). Make up a complex passive sentence for each, using introductory *it* + "that" clause. Then make a sentence for each, using a "*to*-infinitive" clause. Do any of your sentences sound awkward? Discuss your responses.

EXAMPLE: (?) Greatest number of letters received by any private citizen in a year: 900,000 (by baseball star Henry Aaron in 1974).

It is believed that the greatest number of letters received by any private citizen in a year is 900,000.

The greatest number of letters received by any private citizen in a year *is believed to be* 900,000.

(With the verb *believe*, either form is OK)

1. (F) Tallest living animal: giraffe
2. (?) Longest time that anyone has gone without sleep: 453 hours, 41 minutes

3. (?) Total number of active volcanoes: 850
4. (F) Widest street: the Monumental Axis in Brasilia, Brazil
5. (?) The smelliest animal in the world: the African zorilla
6. (?) The earliest false teeth: 700 B.C. in what is now Tuscany, Italy
7. (?) The most chronic sneezing fit: 978 days
8. (?) The fastest flying insect: the American deer bot-fly
9. (F) The longest United Nations speech: 4 hours and 29 minutes (by Cuban President Fidel Castro, on September 26, 1960).
10. (?) The longest prison sentence: 10,000 years, imposed on a convicted murderer in Alabama, 1981.

Focus 5

FORM

That Clause Subjects Raised to Main Clause Subjects

FORM

- Introductory *it* with active verbs also introduces *that* clauses:

  ***That* Clause**
  (a) It appears that some superstitions are shared around the world.
  (b) It seems   that many superstitions have religious origins.

- As with the second type of complex passive structure, when you want to put more focus on the subject of the *that* clause, you may "raise" it to the subject position of the main clause. The *that* clause, now missing its subject, changes to an infinitive (*to* + verb) clause:

  It appears that **some superstitions** —> **Some superstitions** appear

- The *that* clause, now missing its subject, changes to an infinitive (*to* + verb) clause:

Raised Subject	Clause Verb	Main Infinitive Clause
(c) Some superstitions	appear	to be shared around the world.
(d) Many superstitions	seem	to have religious origins.

- The infinitive of the dependent clause should be perfective if the main clause verb is present tense and the event of the clause occurs at a definite time in the past.

Present	Past
(e) It **appears** that Dr. Samuel Johnson, who lived in the eighteenth century,	**was** very superstitious. —>
(f) Samuel Johnson, who lived in the eighteenth century, **appears**	**to have been** very superstitious.

- Sometimes a *that* clause modal verb needs to be changed to make an infinitive clause:

(g) It seemed that the magician **could make** himself disappear. —>

(h) The magician seemed $\left\{\begin{array}{l}\text{to be able to}\\\text{to have been able to}\end{array}\right\}$ make himself disappear.

Past **Present or Past**

As **(h)** shows, either a present or perfective infinitive is acceptable; the main clause verb **seemed** is past tense.

- We can use these verbs with either introductory *it* or subjects raised from a *that* clause:

   appear   chance   happen   seem   turn out

Exercise 7

Restate each of the (b) sentences below. Put focus on the subject of the *that* clause by raising it to the main clause and by changing the *that* clause to an infinitive clause. Use an appropriate infinitive form.

> **EXAMPLE:** (a) There are numerous superstitions regarding animals and weather. (b) For example, to many people, it appears that animals can predict earthquakes.
>
> Restated: (b) For example, to many people, *animals appear to be able to* predict earthquakes.

1. (a) It was once believed that the earth was the center of the solar system. (b) Of course, it turned out that this belief was wrong, as the Polish astronomer Copernicus discovered.

2. (a) Not too long ago, those who believed in extraterrestrial beings were thought to be a bit crazy. (b) Now it appears that even the United States government is interested in exploring the possibility of life on other planets.

3. (a) The men who sailed with Christopher Columbus to the new world were said to be superstitious. (b) To them, it seemed that the sharks that pursued their ship were a bad omen.

4. (a) A pair of identical twins were separated at birth and adopted by two different families. (b) Amazingly, it happened that they met each other 19 years later when they enrolled at the same university.

5. (a) In Cheshire, England, legend has it that an old beech tree is cursed and that anyone who tries to lop its limbs will suffer. (b) It happened that two men lost their own limbs just days after cutting branches off the tree.

6. (a) In Europe, it was believed that donkeys could predict wet weather. To some, it seemed that donkeys twitched their ears and brayed whenever a storm was on its way.

7. (a) William Henry Harrison was elected President of the United States in 1840 and died in office. (b) A century later, it happened that President Franklin D. Roosevelt also died in office.

8. (a) It was once believed that a sudden coughing fit was caused by the devil entering someone who was telling lies. (b) It appears that this idea has died out in most places.

Exercise 8

The following drawings illustrate geometrical illusions. The sentences underneath them express the reality. State the illusion achieved by each, using *appears to be* or *seems to be*. The first has been done as an example.

EXAMPLE:

UPSIDE-DOWN T

1. The vertical and horizontal lines are of equal length.

   Illusion: *The vertical line appears to be longer.*

   OR *The horizontal line seems to be shorter.*

PONZO

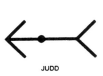

JUDD

POGGENDORFF

2. The horizontal lines are equal in length.

3. The dot is at the midpoint of the horizontal line.

4. The oblique lines can be connected by a straight line.

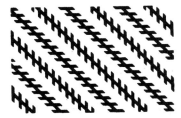

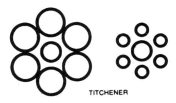

TITCHENER

5. The oblique lines are parallel.

6. The two inner circles are the same size.

Look at the pictures below. Describe what you think each of them shows, using *appears to be* or *seems to be*. Compare your descriptions with others in your class to see if they differ.

7.

8.

Focus 6

FORM

Verbs That Require Subject Raising

FORM

- We cannot use a larger set of verbs with introductory *it* + *that* clause; that is, they require a raised subject:

Raised Subject	Main Clause Verb	Infinitive Clause
(a) Religious beliefs	tend	to influence superstitions.
(b) Superstitions	continue	to be observed even though we no longer believe them.

(c) NOT: It tends that religious beliefs influence superstitions.

(d) NOT: It continues that superstitions are observed even though we no longer believe them.

- The following verbs require subjects of the dependent clause to be raised. A few can be followed by a gerund rather than an infinitive:
  - + Infinitive:

    come*   fail   grow*   proceed   prove   tend

  - + Infinitive or Gerund:

    begin   commence   cease   continue   commence

  - **(e)** I began $\begin{Bmatrix} \textbf{to climb} \\ \textbf{climbing} \end{Bmatrix}$ the hill.

*with the meaning of "to develop gradually": He finally *came to* appreciate his family. After many years, she *grew to* enjoy the quiet country life.

Exercise 9

Twelve people participated in a year-long medical study intended to change their eating habits and help them to become healthier. The following chart gives facts about each of them before and after the study. Make up a sentence for each fact in the "After the Study" column. Use a verb from the list below. Rephrase the information as necessary.

begin	proceed	grow	continue	fail
commence	come	tend	cease	

EXAMPLE: Esther grew to like eggplant.
Hal failed to reduce his cholesterol level.

Participant	Before the Study	After the Study
1. Esther	disliked eggplant	liked eggplant
2. Hal	had a high cholesterol level	had a high cholesterol level
3. Perrin	never ate breakfast	usually ate breakfast
4. Anthony	thought oat bran was for horses	recommended oat bran to all his friends
5. Rose	weighed 200 pounds	weighed 200 pounds
6. Sylvia	ate fried chicken	ate broiled chicken
7. George	had ice cream for dessert after dinner	had ice cream for dessert after dinner
8. Ellen	ate meat	became a vegetarian
9. Dominic	hated seaweed	liked seaweed a little bit
10. Warren	had pizza once a week	had pizza once a month
11. Gail	seldom ate fruit	ate fruit almost daily
12. Steve	had eggs for breakfast every morning	had eggs for breakfast every morning

Exercise 10

Get responses from a classmate to each of the following questions. Then tell him/her your responses. Use *tend* + infinitives in your responses:

EXAMPLE: When do you usually get sleepy during the day?
A: *I tend to get* the sleepiest late in the afternoon.
B: *I tend not to get* sleepy at all during the day; I guess I have a lot of energy.

1. What academic subjects do you usually have the most trouble with?
2. Which aspects of using English do you typically have difficulty with?
3. What do you usually do on Saturday nights?
4. What kinds of magazines do you usually like to read?
5. If you have a problem, do you typically tell someone about it or keep it to yourself?
6. What do you and your friends usually talk about?

7. Do you usually dress conservatively or follow the fashion trends?

8. Do you get angry easily or are you "slow to burn"? What kinds of things generally make you angry?

9. How do you handle a very stressful situation? How do you usually react?

10. If you disagree with a friend about something, do you usually say something or keep quiet?

Focus 7

FORM

To Be Deletion with Raised Subjects

FORM

- A few of the verbs listed in Focus 5 and Focus 6 permit deletion of *to be* in the infinitive clause: *seem, appear, turn out,* and *prove.*

   (a) That superstition **seems to be universal.** —>

   (b) That superstition **seems universal.**

   (c) Your prediction **turned out to be wrong.** —>

   (d) Your prediction **turned out wrong.**

   (e) NOT: Your prediction happened wrong.

- *To be* deletion tends to be more common before an adjective phrase than before a noun phrase. In some contexts, you may need *to be* for clarity with noun complements:

   Adjective

   (f) That belief appears <u>false</u>.

   Noun

   (g) Questionable usage: That belief appears a <u>myth</u>.

   If you are in doubt whether you can omit *to be* in a sentence, you should probably keep it there.

- We cannot delete *to be* if *be* is part of a progressive verb in the infinitive clause:

   (h) The birds seemed to be listening to us.

   (i) NOT: The birds seemed listening to us.

Exercise 11

The following passage summarizes Guy De Maupassant's most famous short story, "The Necklace." First, put [ ] around (a) introductory *it* + *that* clauses and (b) raised subjects + infinitive clauses. Then restate each introductory *it* sentence with a raised subject and infinitive clause.

> **EXAMPLES:** (1) [who happened to be born into a poor family during the 19th century]
>
> (2) [Since it appeared that she had no chance to marry a rich man] —>
> Since she appeared to have no chance to marry a rich man

(1)Mathilde Loisel was a pretty and charming French girl who happened to be born into a poor family during the 19th century. (2)Since it appeared that she had no chance to marry a rich man, she accepted the proposal of a junior clerk in the Ministry of Education. (3)As time went by, it seemed that Mathilde grew more and more discontent. (4)She tended to spend her days longing for the beautiful furnishings, the elegant clothes, and the extravagant entertainment that the wealthy enjoyed. (5)Her husband, though a kind man, failed to please her.

(6)One day, Monsieur Loisel came home with an invitation to a grand reception at the Ministry of Education. (7)He expected her to be delighted, but it turned out that Mathilde was quite upset by the invitation because she had no lovely dress to wear. (8)Finally, her husband agreed to let her spend what was to him an exorbitant sum on a new dress. (9)Mathilde continued to be distressed, however, because she had no fine jewelry. (10)Monsieur Loisel suggested she borrow something from her rich friend, Madame Forestier. (11)At Madame Forestier's, Mathilde's friend told her to pick out whatever she liked. (12)Mathilde proceeded to try on all of Madame Forestier's jewelry and finally selected a magnificent diamond necklace.

(13)The reception proved to be a dream come true for Mathilde. (14)It seemed that every man wanted to dance with her. (15)Even the Minister of Education appeared to be watching her. (16)On the way home, however, disaster struck when Mathilde lost Madame Forestier's necklace. (17)She and her husband went into tremendous debt to replace the necklace without letting Madame Forestier know of its loss. (18)As Mathilde spent her days doing heavy domestic work to repay the debt, she began to look coarse and unattractive. (19)She ceased to be the lovely young woman she had once been. (20)One day, ten years later, it chanced that her path crossed with Madame Forestier for the first time since the loss of the necklace. (21)She finally confessed to her friend what had happened many years ago. (22)Imagine poor Mathilde's shock when it turned out that the original necklace had been only an inexpensive imitation, not a real diamond necklace.

Exercise 12

The picture below illustrates several geometrical illusions. How many can you identify? State the illusions with *appears* or *seems*, deleting the *to be* infinitive.

> **EXAMPLE:** The front edge of the carpet seems shorter than the width of the back wall.

Focus 8

Adjectives with Subject Raising

- Adjectives following **be** verbs also allow subjects of *that* clauses to be raised to main clause subjects:

Raised Subject	*Be* Verb	Adjective	Infinitive Clause
(a) The party	is	certain	to be a success.
(b) My parents	were	bound	to discover the vase was missing.
(c) They	are	liable	to disagree with us.

- As with verbs, some adjectives allow the introductory *it* + *that* clause as well as the raised subject + infinitive clause.

  (d) It is certain that the party will be a success.

- Other adjectives require the subject to be raised:

  (e) NOT: It was **bound** that my parents would discover the vase was missing.

  (f) NOT: It is **liable** that they will disagree.

- Adjectives allowing either introductory *it* or raised subject

  certain   likely   sure   unlikely

- Adjectives requiring raised subject + *to* + verb

  apt   bound   liable

Exercise 13

Below is another set of superstitions. Each condition is separated from the result by a slash (/). A result considered certain (according to the superstition) is indicated by a plus sign (+). A result considered probable is indicated by a question mark (?). Make a sentence for each, using a raised subject. For results that are certain, use one of the following adjectives: *certain, sure, bound*. For results that are probable, use one of the following: *likely, apt,* or *liable.*

> **EXAMPLE:** A person with a prominent nose is apt to be intelligent.

1. (?) Person with prominent nose/intelligent.
2. (+) Person who laughs before breakfast/cry before supper.
3. (+) Any food stirred counterclockwise/not taste right.
4. (?) Redheads/hot tempered.
5. (+) Wearing earrings/ keep evil spirits out of your ears.
6. (+) Woman who gets a haircut when the moon is on the wane/lose her hair.
7. (+) Putting shoes on the table/bring you bad luck.
8. (?) Person with a crooked little finger/become wealthy.
9. (?) Kissing someone on the nose/lead to a quarrel.
10. (?) Washing your car/bring rain.

Exercise 14

Ask the first four questions of one of your classmates and get responses. Then have him/her ask you the last three.

1. On what occasions are you likely to use your native language instead of English?
2. In what aspects of your life do you think you are bound to be successful?
3. If you were giving advice to someone just starting to learn English, what would you be certain to tell him/her?
4. What is one possession you own that you would be unlikely to share with someone else?
5. What topics are you most liable to discuss at a party with people you don't know too well?
6. On what days of the week are you likely to be in a good mood? Why?
7. Where, if at all, are you apt to sing to yourself?

Now write two questions to ask your teacher, using adjectives in Focus 9 + infinitive clauses. Your teacher, of course, may reserve the right to be silent in response to some questions!

Focus 9

Infinitive Clause Objects Raised to Main Clause Subjects

FORM

- Another structure in English raises the **object** of an infinitive clause after introductory *it* + adjective + *be* into the subject position of a main clause:

Introductory *it*	*Be* Verb	Adjective	Infinitive Clause
(a) It	is	easy	(for me) to do **this exercise.**
(b) It	was	unsafe	(for us) to drive **that car.**

Raised Object	*Be* Verb	Adjective	Infinitive Clause
(c) This exercise	is	easy	to do.
(d) That car	was	unsafe	to drive.

- We can infer the performer of the action (e.g., *I, we*) from the context. Sometimes the performer is not specific; it may be **anyone**.
- The raised object can also be the **object of a preposition** in the infinitive clause:

Introductory *It*	*Be* Verb	Adjective	Infinitive Clause
(e) It	is	dangerous	to skate **on thin ice.**

Raised Object	*Be* Verb	Adjective	Infinitive Clause
(f) Thin ice	is	dangerous	to skate on.

- Some adjectives that allow object raising:

amusing	*dangerous*	*hard*	*nice*
annoying	*difficult*	*harmful*	*pleasant*
appropriate	*easy*	*horrible*	*safe*
bad	*entertaining*	*illegal*	*simple*
beneficial	*evil*	*instructive*	*stupid*
boring	*fun*	*interesting*	*tough*
convenient	*good*	*marvelous*	*useful*

Exercise 15

Complete the following sentences by inserting nouns, adjectives, and verbs from the lists below that fit the contexts. The first one is done as an example.

Nouns	Adjectives	Verbs
a river with swift currents	annoying	complete
a thank-you letter	appropriate	develop
crossword puzzles	bad	eat
one habit	beneficial	fill out
insulting greeting cards	dangerous	get
many United States citizens	evil	pronounce
telemarketing phone calls	hard	read
shrimp	harmful	send
television	humorous	swim
words	simple	watch

1. *Telemarketing phone calls* are *annoying* to *get* just as you sit down for dinner.

2. _____ in the newspaper are often _____ to _____

   unless you have a good vocabulary.

3. _____ can be _____ to _____ if you are allergic

   to seafood.

4. _____ is _____ to _____ if you've been a week-

   end guest at someone's house.

5. _____ is _____ to _____ in; you should be sure

   that someone is nearby if you need help getting out.

6. Some superstitions involve _____ that are considered _____

   to _____ , such as ones used to cast spells on people.

7. Smoking is _____ that is _____ to _____ de-

   velop, especially when you're young.

8. _____ think that the federal tax forms are not _____ to

   _____ .

354

9. _____ can be _____ to _____ if you need to improve English listening comprehension skills.

10. Do you think that _____ are _____ to _____ or do you find them in bad taste most of the time?

Exercise 16

Discuss with classmates answers to the following questions, giving your opinions or information about where you live. Use a "raised object" structure in your responses. An example is given for the first one.

1. What kinds of television programs do you think are the most boring to watch?

   EXAMPLE: To me, *game shows* are the most boring to watch.

2. What is one of the most entertaining things to do where you live?
3. What music do you think is most pleasant to listen to?
4. What's hard to remember about English?
5. Do you think drugs such as marijuana or heroin should be illegal to use, to sell, or both to use and sell?
6. In your opinion, what's horrible to eat?

Activities

Activity 1

Imagine that you work as a local news reporter on television. One of the stories to which you have been assigned involves a rather strange case of stolen houseplants. The information below describes the suspected thief, who was seen briefly by one houseplant owner. Since the thief has not yet been proven guilty and the person who saw her isn't absolutely sure of her description, only the information about the number and kinds of plants stolen can be considered factual. Write a news report of the case, using complex passive constructions where you think they would be appropriate.

The events:

   Plants were stolen from 30 houses on the east side of the city.
   Most plants missing are begonias and ivies.
   Most victims think the plants were stolen in the morning.

The suspect:
Information based on a report by one witness:

   female   was wearing a green jumpsuit
   between 50 and 60 years old   geranium tatooed on left forearm
   about 5' tall   drives a blue Chevy van
   red hair

Activity 2

Interview a classmate about family history or hometown history. Ask him/her to tell you about some events that are thought to be true but are not documented. The events might concern some long ago period (e.g., "Juan's great-grandfather was believed to have been born in Guatemala. The family is thought to have moved to Mexico in the early 1900s."). They could also be information about your classmate's youth as reported by his/her parents (e.g., "Sonia is said to have been very good-natured as a baby."). Take notes during the interview. Then write up a report from your notes, using complex passives where appropriate to express some of the information. You will probably want to use both active and passive sentences in your report. If time permits, present your report orally to the class.

Activity 3

Select an article or a passage that contains speculative information. Rewrite the passage, rephrasing some of the information as *that* clauses and infinitive clauses in complex passive constructions or with raised structures reviewed in this unit.

Activity 4

Discuss with your classmates eating habits that have changed since you were young. What types of food have you grown to like that you used to dislike? What foods did you begin to eat when you were older that you had never tried as a child, such as food from other countries?

Activity 5

Many cultures have superstitions about numbers. For example, in many places, 13 is an unlucky number and in some, three is a magical or lucky number. Conduct library research and/or interview people you know from different cultures about superstitions involving numbers. Write a report of your findings, using complex passive or raised structures. (As an alternative, you could research topics suggested at the end of the Task.)

Task

When someone mentions the film industry, people usually think first of actors and directors, who are often featured in the entertainment news. When film awards are handed out, however, we are reminded that behind every good movie stands a creative scriptwriter (or scriptwriters).

Form groups with members of your class. Each group will be a team of scriptwriters. Imagine that you are being considered for a film company contract based on your imaginative ideas. For each of the scenarios below, think of a completion for the last line of dialogue or description. When you are finished, read your completions and, as a class, vote on the ones you think are the most creative for each scenario.

FILM 1: SCIENCE FICTION

Scenario: For weeks, the townspeople of Spooner, a small lake resort town, have observed signs that something horrible has invaded their community. Trees, shrubs, and even the flowers have begun to die. Dogs howl at night and cats are afraid to leave their houses. One summer Saturday night, many of the townsfolk are, as usual, celebrating the end of the week at the local dance hall, when they become aware of an eerie green glow outside. They rush out to see what it is. Moving slowly toward them across a field is . . .

FILM 2: HORROR STORY

Scenario: Ten people have agreed to spend a week in a large and decrepit old mansion on the edge of town. Strange events have occurred in this house over the past few years, and the people assembled on this evening want to find out if there is truth to rumors that the house has been cursed. They are all seated at the dining room table, with their leader, Madame Montague, at the head.

Madame Montague:
My friends, you all know why we are here. Before we spend another hour in this house, there is one thing that I must demand of all of you. Under no circumstances should. . . .

FILM 3: ROMANCE

Scenario: Max and Ramona are a young couple in their 20s who have been dating for a year. Max is passionately in love with Ramona and wants to marry her, but he's not sure if she's as much in love with him as he is with her. Max is trying to find out how Ramona feels about him.

Max: Ramona, you know how much I love you. (Long pause. No response from Ramona.) Tell me, what do you think of me?

Ramona: Max, never have...

FILM 4: MYSTERY

Scenario: Detective Hendershot has been called to the scene of a crime—a murder, to be exact. He is now in the master bedroom, where the unfortunate victim was discovered. Hendershot opens and searches the dresser drawers one by one, hoping to find the murder weapon or some other clue to the crime. He opens the last drawer, the bottom one, and sifts through its contents. There, buried under a pile of silk scarves, is...

FILM 5: ADVENTURE STORY

Scenario: After three days of wandering aimlessly in the heart of a Brazilian jungle, a group of scientists are forced to acknowledge that they are hopelessly lost. The head of the expedition, Professor Winbigler, feels it is time to warn the others of a great danger to them that she has encountered while trying to find the trail back to civilization.

Professor Winbigler:

I didn't want to tell you this, but now that we may not get out of here for a while, I believe you should be alerted. Far more threatening to our survival than the poisonous snakes and spiders are...

Focus 1

FORM

Fronted Adverbials

FORM

- In English, you can signal special emphasis or contrast by moving words or phrases from their typical order in a sentence to the front of a sentence or clause. We call this process **fronting** and the result **fronted** structures.
  - **(a)** The townspeople went outside **because they were curious.**
  - **(b)** Fronting: **Because they were curious,** the townspeople went outside.
  - **(c)** I would **not** leave this town **for anything**.
  - **(d)** Fronting: **Not for anything** would I leave this town.

358

- When you front some constituents, you must also change the subject/auxiliary order or, in some cases, subject/main verb order. As the second example above shows, you move negative adverbs to the front of the sentence or clause:

Subject	Auxiliary	Negative	Verb
(e) I	would	not	leave this town for anything. —>

Negative	Auxiliary	Subject	Verb
(f) Not for anything	**would**	I	leave this town.

- The following types of adverbials do not affect the subject/auxiliary/main verb order when we front them.
  - Adverbials of time:

    (g) She works on her novel **during the evenings. —>**

    (h) During the evenings, she works on her novel.
  - Adverbials of manner:

    (i) Detective Dubrow sorted the evidence **with great care. —>**

    (j) With great care, Detective Dubrow sorted the evidence.
  - Adverbials of condition:

    (k) Something strange must be happening **if the dogs are howling. —>**

    (l) If the dogs are howling, something strange must be happening.
  - Adverbials of purpose:

    (m) Max showered Ramona with gifts **in order to win her heart. —>**

    (n) In order to win her heart, Max showered Ramona with gifts.
  - Adverbials of reason:

    (o) The townspeople left **because they were afraid. —>**

    (p) Because they were afraid, the townspeople left.
  - Adverbials of frequency that follow verbs:

    (q) The group would meet **every night** in the living room of the old mansion. —>

    (r) Every night the group would meet in the living room of the old mansion.
- We may front two other types of adverbials without subject/main verb inversion, although they may optionally have inverted subjects and main verbs:
  - Adverbials of direction:

    No Inversion

    (s) From the bushes, **a leopard** suddenly **appeared.**

    Optional Inversion

    (t) From the bushes suddenly **appeared a leopard.**
  - Adverbials of position:

    No Inversion

    (u) In the far corner of the library, **a small boy sits.**

    Optional Inversion

    (v) In the far corner of the library **sits a small boy.**

The difference in use between the uninverted and inverted forms will be discussed in Focus 6.

Exercise 1

Use the cues in parentheses to add a phrase or clause to each sentence. To emphasize the description you added, move it to the front of the sentence. If you wish, you can add other descriptive words or phrases.

EXAMPLE: The odd creatures were standing in front of them. (manner)

The odd creatures were standing in front of them *with hungry looks on their angular faces.*

Fronted: *With hungry looks on their angular faces,* the odd creatures were standing boldly in front of them.

1. The townspeople were absolutely terrified.

    a. (time)_____.

    b. (reason)_____.

    c. (frequency)_____.

2. Detective Hendershot will find the murderer.

    a. (condition)_____.

    b. (purpose)_____.

    c. (manner)_____.

3. The group explored every nook and cranny of the old house.

    a. (time)_____.

    b. (manner)_____.

    c. (reason)_____.

4. The scientists wandered.

    a. (direction)_____.

    b. (manner)_____.

    c. (frequency)_____.

5. Professor Winbigler faithfully writes in her journal.

    a. (purpose)_____.

    b. (position)_____.

    c. (condition)_____.

Focus 2

Fronted Structures Requiring Subject-Auxiliary Inversion or Subject-Verb Inversion

FORM

- Some fronted adverbials and other fronted constituents require the subject/auxiliary or subject/verb order to be reversed, or **inverted.** The auxiliary or verb comes before the subject instead of after it.
- Fronted structures requiring subject/auxiliary or subject/verb inversion include:
  - Adverbials of extent or degree:
    - **(a)** The townspeople were **so afraid** that they hardly ventured out of their neighborhoods. —>
    - **(b) So afraid** were the townspeople that they hardly ventured out of their neighborhoods.
  - Adverbials of position when the main verb is *be*:
    - **(c)** A small boy is **in the far corner of the library.** —>
    - **(d) In the far corner of the library is** a small boy.
    - **(e)** NOT: In the far corner of the library a small boy is.
  - Negative adverbials of frequency that come before the main verb:
    - **(f)** We have **rarely** seen such generosity.
    - **(g) Rarely** have we seen such generosity.
  - Other negated constituents:
    - **(h)** Max would **not** leave Ramona **for anything.** —>
    - **(i) Not for anything** would Max leave Ramona.
  - Present participles + modifiers:
    - **(j)** A beam of light was **moving toward them.** —>
    - **(k) Moving toward them** was a beam of light.
  - Past participles + modifiers:
    - **(l)** A note was **stuck in a branch of the willow tree.** —>
    - **(m) Stuck in a branch of the willow tree** was a note.
  - Comparative fronting:
    - **(n)** The cinematography was **more interesting than the plot.** —>
    - **(o) More interesting than the plot** was the cinematography.
  - Implied negation:
    - **(p) Little** did the soldiers know that the enemy was just over the hill.

    Because the negation is implied rather than explicit, there is no corresponding non-fronted form with *little.* A nonfronted version would be something like: *The soldiers did not know the enemy was just over the hill. Little + do + (someone) + know* is an idiom in English. It is often followed by a *that* clause.

Exercise 2

Use an appropriate word or phrase from the list below to complete the blanks with fronted structures.

little did I know	peeking out from under a snowdrift
not for anything	stuffed into the toe
never	so embarrassed
sitting at the bottom of the hill	worse than the beginning of my
coming toward me from the right	excursion

I'm not sure if I ever want to go skiing again. (a) _____ have I felt so frustrated

trying to have fun! First, I had trouble just getting on the boots and skis I had rented. One

of the boots wouldn't fit; then I discovered that (b) _____ was an old sock. I

was so nervous that I hadn't realized what it was. Next I discovered that getting to the top

of the hill on the chair lift was no small feat. (c) _____ that one could fall nu-

merous times before even getting started. Once I made it to the top, I couldn't believe how

small everything looked down below. (d) _____ was a tiny building that I rec-

ognized as the chalet. My first thought was "(e) _____ am I going to go down this slope." As it turned out, my first thought was probably better than my second, which was to give it a try. (f) _____ was the end of it. As I raced uncontrollably down the slope terrified, I suddenly saw that (g) _____ was another skier. We collided just seconds later. (h) _____ , I muttered an apology. That was it for me for that day. (i) _____ did I feel that I spent the rest of the afternoon finding out how to enroll in a beginning ski class.

Focus 3

Patterns of Subject/ Auxiliary/Verb Inversion

FORM

- With negatives and frequency adverbs that follow verbs, there are several patterns of inversion, depending on the verb:
  - Complex verb: we invert the first auxiliary and the subject:

	Negative + Word	First + Auxiliary	Subject +	(Other + Auxiliary)	Main Verb +	Modifiers
(a)	Never	**could**	**Max**	have	left	Ramona.
(b)	Not for anything	**would**	**they**		stay	in that house.
(c)	Seldom	**have**	**we**		witnessed	such a spectacle.

- Simple verb (no auxiliary): we add a form of *do* before the subject
  - **(d)** I never **said** such a thing! —>
  - **(e)** Never **did I say** such a thing!
- Main verb *be*: *be* and the subject are inverted
  - **(f) The director is** rarely here on time. —>
  - **(g)** Rarely **is the director** here on time.
- *Not* + a noun beginning a sentence: subject-verb inversion occurs only if the noun is a fronted sentence object, not a grammatical subject:

Inversion: Negated Object	No Inversion: Negated Subject
Object Aux Sub Verb **(h)** Not **a word did we say.**	**Subject Aux Verb** **(i)** Not **a word was said.**

363

- For other fronted constituents, usually the verb is a form of *be*, which is moved before the subject. If the form of the main verb *be* includes an auxiliary, it too is inverted.
  - Adverbials of extent or degree:

        ***Be* Subject**
    (j) So boring **was the speaker** that many in the audience fell asleep.
  - Participles:

        ***Be* Subject**
    (k) Placed on the shelf **was an elegant silver letter opener.**

        Be   **Subject**
    (l) Waiting for her at the restaurant **had been all of her friends.**
  - Comparatives:

        ***Be* Subject**
    (m) More beautiful than the stars **were her eyes.**

Exercise 3

Add a main clause after each of the following phrases, expressing your opinions or providing information. If the fronted constituent is a position adverb, use a *be* verb to follow it.

> **EXAMPLE:** Near the school *is a small coffee shop.*

1. Seldom during the past few years
2. More fascinating than my English class
3. Rarely during my lifetime
4. In my bedroom
5. More important to me than anything
6. Seldom in the history of the world
7. More of a world problem than air pollution
8. So interesting . . . that
9. Stored in the recesses of my brain, never to be forgotten,
10. Waiting for me in the future
11. In the front of my English textbook
12. Better than ice cream for dessert
13. Loved and respected by many admirers
14. So terrible . . . that

Exercise 4

Make up a sentence in response to each of the following. Use a fronted structure for emphasis.

> **EXAMPLE: In the back of our classroom** are posters of many countries of the world.

1. Describe what is in some area of your classroom.
2. State how exciting something is to you by comparing it in degree to something else. (Start with "More exciting . . . ")
3. Tell how infrequently you have done something.
4. Describe how angry you were in a certain circumstance. (Start with "So angry . . . ")
5. Describe how happy you were in another circumstance.

Focus 4

Fronted Negatives
with Explicit Negation

- Some negatives that we may front have an explicit negative word such as *no, not,* or *neither.* Most of them have meanings of "never," "none," or "no one" in context.
- **Adverbs and adverb phrases**
  - For some negative adverbs, fronting simply involves moving the negative and inverting the subject and auxiliary or main verb *be.*

never	**(a) Never** have I laughed so hard!
not once	**(b) Not once** have I missed my Portuguese class this year.
not + for + (noun)	**(c) Not for all the money in the world** would I commute four hours a day!
not + until + (noun)	**(d) Not until the morning** did she realize the ring was missing.
not since + (noun)	**(e) Not since April** have we had so much rain.

- Another group of negative adverbs includes *not + any* (or *anywhere, anything*) in non-fronted forms:

  (f) We can **not** allow you to enter under **any** circumstances.

  When we front these forms, the negative shifts to the fronted constituent: *not any* changes to *no,* either as a modifier or as part of an adverb.

  not under **any** circumstances —> under **no** circumstance

  not anywhere —> **no**where

  These adverbs include:

in no case	**(g) In no case** can we make an exception.
under no circumstances	**(h) Under no circumstances** will the prisoner be allowed to leave.
in no way	**(i) In no way** will this affect your grade.
no way (informal)	**(j) No way** am I gonna miss that concert!
nowhere	**(k) Nowhere** have I been that is this peaceful.

- **Adverb time clauses:**

not + until + (clause)	**(l) Not until I see it** will I believe it!
not since + (clause)	**(m) Not since I started school** have I had so much spare time.

- **Noun phrase objects**

  *not + noun (singular)**

  (n) The sky was brilliant; **not one** cloud could he see in any direction.

  * a plural form is possible with *no* (no clouds could he see), but the emphasis would not be as strong as with the singular form.

- **Conjunctions**
  - With negative conjunctions, fronting changes the form of negation:

      not + either —> **neither, nor**
      no one + either —> **neither + anyone**

(o) I have no idea why the mail didn't come.
(p) My mother does **not either.** —>   **(q) Neither** does my mother.
                                                 (r) Nor does my mother.

(s) No one else does **either.** —>   **(t) Neither** does **anyone** else.

Negative Conjunctions	Example
neither + sentence	**(u)** Peter couldn't read the signature. **Neither** could his friends.
nor + sentence	**(v)** Rhoda has never had her ears pierced. **Nor** does she ever intend to do so. When fronted, *neither* and *nor* usually follow negative sentences to which they are semantically joined.
not only . . . but also	**(w) Not only** does frozen yogurt taste good, **but** it's **also** good for you.
no sooner . . . than	**(x) No sooner** had the exam started **than** we had a fire drill.

Exercise 5

Add the negative fronted structure in parentheses to the following sentences for emphasis. Make any other changes that are necessary.

    EXAMPLE: I hadn't ever been so upset. (never)
               Never had I been so upset.

1. We can't let you retake the examination. (under no circumstances)
2. I haven't missed a class. (not once)
3. Homer won't miss graduation. (not for anything)
4. This didn't change my attitude about you. (in no way)
5. I haven't finished the homework assignment. No one else has. (neither)
6. She hasn't allowed any misbehavior. (in no case)
7. You may not have access to the files. (under no conditions)
8. I wouldn't trade places with him. (not for a million dollars)

Exercise 6

Complete the following statements with information about yourself.

1. Not since I was a child . . .
2. Not until I am old and gray . . .
3. Not until years from now. . . .
4. Not since I started. . . .
5. Nowhere . . .
6. Not for anything . . .

Focus 5

Near Negation and Implied Negation

MEANING

- Words and phrases of near negation express the meanings "almost never," "almost not," and "not very much." They can also trigger subject–auxiliary inversion.
- Expressions of near negation include:
  - **Adverbs:**

seldom *rarely*	**(a) Seldom** **(b) Rarely** } will honeybees sting unless provoked.
scarcely ever *hardly ever* *almost never*	**(c) Scarcely ever** **(d) Hardly ever** } does he travel anymore. **(e) Almost never**
only + once, *twice, etc.*	**(f) Only once** has she gotten a speeding ticket.
barely *scarcely + when/* *hardly before*	**(g) Barely** **(h) Scarcely** } had Nan left **when** the tornado struck. **(i) Hardly** (= almost not)
little	**(j) Little** do they care what we think! (= not much)

- Phrases of implied negation include:
  - Time adverbials:

    Only + Time Phrase/Clause

    (k) Only { **later**
after I finished } did I realize my error. (= not until then)

  - Reason adverbials:

    Only + Reason Phrase/Clause

    (l) Only because { **of your plea**
you are my friend } will I do this.

  - Conditional clauses:

only + if clause *only + when* clause	**(m) Only if you stay** will I stay. (Otherwise I won't stay.) **(n) Only when I laugh** does it hurt. (Otherwise it doesn't hurt.)
had + subject + verb (= *If* + subject + *had* + verb)	**(o) Had Ken known** the traffic would be so bad, he would have stayed home. (= he didn't know)

Exercise 7

In the dialogue below, a group of friends who have just been backpacking in the mountains are telling some other friends about their trip. Emphasize the negatives or implied negatives in each underlined statement by rephrasing the statement with a fronted negative. Make other changes as necessary.

> **EXAMPLE:** We didn't see a wild animal even once.
>
> *Not even once did we see a wild animal.*

Karen: Well, to begin with, we had to hike straight uphill for six miles. I couldn't believe how steep it was! (1) I had never been so tired in my whole life!

Toshi: Really! (2) My feet stopped hurting only when we reached the campsite. Listen, next time all the food will be freeze-dried. (3) I wouldn't carry a 20-pound pack uphill again for anything!

Phan: Anyway, when we finally got up to our campsite, it was gorgeous! (4) We were on the shores of a pristine mountain lake, surrounded by pine trees, and we couldn't see another person anywhere.

Kent: (5) However, we had no sooner dumped all our stuff on the ground when the storm clouds rolled in and it started to pour.

Mario: (6) Yeah, and I didn't discover until then that I hadn't packed my rain poncho.

Karen: (7) The rest of us hadn't either.

Toshi: We tried to pitch the tents as fast as we could, but it wasn't fast enough. (8) We got soaked, and some of our food got wet too. [change to *not only . . .*]

Phan: But fortunately the storm ended almost as quickly as it had started. (9) We had scarcely finished pitching our tents when a rainbow appeared on the other side of the lake.

Kent: It was not just a rainbow, it was a double rainbow. (10) I've seen one of those only once before.

Mario: All in all, even though it was a hard climb getting there, it was worth it. (11) You know, you seldom realize how peaceful life can be until you get away from civilization!

Karen: That's true. (12) And I began to appreciate the beauty of the mountains only after I got back to the city.

Exercise 8

The statements below are film reviewers' comments about two movies. The comments in Part A are about a beach movie for teenagers; those in Part B are about a suspense thriller. To make the comments more emphatic, rewrite them with preposed negatives. Feel free to paraphrase, adding and deleting words as you think appropriate, but try to keep the general meaning the same.

> **EXAMPLE:** I wouldn't recommend this movie to any of my friends—or to any of my enemies, for that matter.
>
> I wouldn't recommend this movie to any of my friends. *Nor would I recommend it* to my enemies, for that matter.

A. *BORN TO SURF*

1. Moviegoers haven't been exposed to anything so silly since *Beach Bingos*.
2. I yawned more in this movie than in any other I've seen.
3. *Born to Surf* is supposed to be a comedy, but the corners of my mouth didn't turn up once.
4. I wouldn't tell anyone to waste their money on this movie under any circumstances.

B. *THE EDGE OF THE EDGE*

1. You shouldn't miss this thriller. [hint: use "no way"]
2. *The Edge of the Edge* has just started when you become aware that **you** are on the edge—of your seat. [hint: use "not until"]
3. You won't have any idea who the killer is until the very last moment.
4. Every actor in this film gives a good performance. [hint: change *good* to *bad.*]

Focus 6

USE

Uses of Fronted Structures: Emphasis, Contrast, and Focus on Unexpected Information

USE

- In this unit, you have learned the role of fronted structures for emphasis. There are a few other uses for these structures. The main reasons you would move constituents from their normal order to the front of the sentence or clause are
  - To emphasize the fronted constituent.
  - To contrast the meaning of the fronted constituent with that of another constituent (or more than one other).
  - To move new or unexpected information expressed by the subject to the end of the sentence or clause.

- For adverb phrases such as those expressing time, place, and frequency, the context determines whether **emphasis** or **contrast** is intended.

Emphasis	Contrast
(a) In the evenings, she writes. It is a time when the house is quiet and peaceful and she can concentrate.	**(b) In the evenings** she writes. **The mornings** are devoted to gardening and **the afternoons** to her job at the publishing company.
(c) On the first floor are men's clothes. This floor also has luggage.	**(d) On the first floor** are men's clothes. **On the second floor** are women's clothes and linens.

As the contrast examples illustrate, the repetition of modifiers also creates parallelism, a stylistic device we use for emphasis and rhythm. Fronting the modifiers makes the parallelism more obvious.

- We can also front adverb clauses either for emphasis or contrast.

Emphasis	Contrast
(e) When it's very hot, I try to stay inside. The heat makes me lethargic.	**(f) When it's very hot,** I try to stay inside. **When the weather is cool,** I spend a lot of time outdoors.

- We may front adverbials of direction or position either to emphasize the adverbial or to put focus on a subject with new or unexpected information. Because these adverbials have optional subject-verb inversion, when inversion occurs, it puts greater focus on the subject.

Emphasis on Adverbial	Focus on Subject
(g) The raccoon who visited our cabin regularly was scurrying back and forth on the front deck. Then we heard the door open and **into the kitchen the raccoon came**.	**(h)** We called for our dog to come in the cabin since it was getting late. Then we heard the door open and **into the kitchen came a raccoon**.

- We typically front **participles** with their modifiers and comparatives to delay a subject that presents new or unexpected information and thus to put focus on the subject.

Focus on Subject

Participle	Comparative
(i) Who could be at her door at this late hour? Sara squinted through the peephole to see who the mystery caller was. Staring back at her was **her long-lost brother**.	**(j)** What do I value most? More important to me than anything else is **my family**.

- We may front negative structures to emphasize:
  - Unusual or unexpected events or actions:

    (k) Never have I seen such a display of virtuosity!
  - Particular aspects of events or actions:

    (l) Not until the last votes were counted would the mayor admit defeat.
  - Prohibited actions expressed by strong commands:

    (m) Under no circumstances may you leave this building.
  - The "negativeness" of things, events, or actions:

    (n) Not a single word did she utter that was true.

    These uses often overlap; a fronted negative may emphasize in several different ways at the same time.

Exercise 9

State what you think is the main reason for fronting each of the underlined structures. Do you think it is primarily for (1) emphasis of the fronted structure, (2) contrast of the structure, or (3) focus on the delayed subject?

1. Only when Marta drives does she get nervous. At other times, she's quite calm.
2. The phone rang. Howard was sure it was his best friend Miguel calling. Picking up the phone, he shouted, "Yo!" Responding to his greeting was his biology professor.
3. Not since I was in elementary school have I been to the circus. Believe me, that was a long time ago!
4. This is your room. I hope you'll enjoy your stay here. To your right is a cooler with ice and the soft drink machines. To your left and around the corner is the swimming pool.
5. To start this lawnmower, you need to pull the cord very hard and quickly. To keep it going, you should set the lever in the middle.
6. Minh heard a noise coming from underneath his parked car. Getting down on his knees, he looked under the front of it. There, crouched on the right front tire was a tiny kitten.
7. Not until I hear from you will I leave. I promise I'll stay here until then.
8. During the long winters, Bonnie does a lot of reading. She loves to lounge by the fire with a good book.
9. The crowd was waiting excitedly to see who would win this year's Boston marathon. A few minutes later, across the finish line came a runner from Argentina.
10. Had I known the movie was so long, I doubt I would have gone to see it. I had no idea that it would last for five hours!

Exercise 10

In each of the students' responses to the teacher's questions below, there is something wrong either with the *form* of the statement or the *use* in context. Identify the problem. Correct errors in form and explain problems with usage.

1. **Teacher:** Meeyung, is it true that you got to see the fireworks during the Statue of Liberty's anniversary celebration?

   Meeyung: Oh, yes! Never I have seen such a beautiful display of fireworks!

2. **Teacher:** Alex, the bell rang five minutes ago. Please turn in your exam.

   Alex: No way am I gonna finish this test.

3. **Teacher:** Wilai, I don't seem to have your homework. Did you turn it in to me?

   Wilai: No, I'm sorry, never have I turned it in.

4. **Teacher:** Javier, did you find that chapter explaining verb tenses helpful?

   Javier: Yes, not only it helped me with present perfect, but it also explained conditional tenses well.

5. **Teacher:** Patrice, I'm really sorry to hear you've been so ill. I hope you're better now.

   Patrice: Thank you. I *was* really sick all month. No sooner I got rid of the flu when I got pneumonia.

6. **Teacher:** Kazuhiko, I could help you after class if you can stay for a while.

   Kazuhiko: I'm sorry. Not for an hour could I stay because I have another class at 4:30.

Activities

Activity 1

Write a paragraph in which you describe one of the following:

1. the contents of a room as someone might see the room upon entering it
2. a machine or appliance with a number of parts

Use some fronted adverbials of position for contrast or emphasis in your description.

EXAMPLES: As you come into the living room, there is a large chintz sofa. In front of the sofa is a maple coffee table. To the left of it is an end table that matches the coffee table, and to the right stands a bookcase. On top of the bookcase sits my favorite vase. It's a deep turquoise blue.

The parts of my computer include the monitor, the printer, the computer itself, and the control panel. On the control panel are four switches. To the far left is the switch for the computer. Next to it is the switch for the monitor. To the right of the monitor switch is the one for the printer.

Activity 2

Imagine that someone has spread some rumors about you, each of which, of course, is untrue. They are stated in 1–6 below. Set the record straight by doing the following:

a. Deny the statement using a fronted negative phrase (Some common informal "protest phrases" you might also want to use: "Wait a minute!" "Oh, come on!" "Are you kidding?" "Are you serious?")

b. Justify or further explain your denial.

> **EXAMPLE:** So, I hear you are always late for school.
> Response: **a.** Wait a minute! Only once have I been late this year!
> **b.** And then it wasn't even my fault; the bus was late.

1. Someone said that you often sleep until noon.
2. Rumor has it that you spend most of your free time (when you're not sleeping) watching soap operas.
3. Is it true that you eat ice cream for breakfast?
4. I heard that you drive like a maniac.
5. Is it a fact that your favorite pastime is shopping?
6. Did you really fail all of your courses?

Activity 3

What are some things you would have done (or not done) in the past had you been better informed about a situation or as wise as you are now? Make a list of statements, using past conditionals without *if* to express them. Take turns sharing statements with members of the class. Here are a few examples:

> Had I known the English exam was going to be so hard, I would have started studying for it weeks ago.
> Had I heard about the storm predictions on Friday, I never would have tried to go sailing on Saturday.

After each statement, someone in the class should respond with an appropriate comment or question; e.g, "Well, I hope you did O.K. on your exam even if you didn't study enough;" "Why? What happened to you when you went sailing?"

Activity 4

Make a list of some things you believe you would *never* do under any circumstances. For emphasis, start your statements with a negative word or phrase. Then share your list with one or more classmates to see if they also would never do the things on your list. Have them discuss their lists with you. Finally, write a summary of your discussion, pointing out your similarities and differences on this topic.

> A few examples:
> Under no circumstances would I take an advanced course in physics.
> No way would I ever eat squid.
> (informal usage)

Activity 5

Write a paragraph in which you describe an event that affected you strongly; for example, a time when you were especially happy, excited, angry, frightened, surprised, etc. Use a fronted structure, such as a comparative, somewhere in the paragraph to emphasize the way you felt.

Activity 6

Advertisements and commercials often use strong claims to sell products. Imagine that you are a copywriter for an ad agency. Choose a product (one that already exists or make one up) to sell; write an advertisement for either print media (magazine, newspaper), radio, or television. In your ad, use at least two fronted structures to emphasize something about your product. Present your ad/commercial to the class and give them a chance to discuss your claims.

Activity 7

Write a review or synopsis of a book, television show, or movie that you especially liked or disliked. Use some fronted structures for emphasis, contrast, or focus.

25

It as a Focusing Device

Cleft Sentences

Task

If you have brothers or sisters, you may have at times judged a sibling's behavior in terms of his or her position in the family as the oldest, youngest, or middle child. For example, you might have considered a brother's or sister's "take charge" attitude as characteristic of an oldest child, or another's "spoiled" behavior as a result of being the youngest. If you are an only child, you may have heard generalizations about only children being very confident or expecting a lot of attention.

In *First Child, Second Child . . .* , clinical psychologists Bradford Wilson and George Edington present research findings and their observations about personality traits often associated with particular birth orders. Some of these traits are listed below. Based on your knowledge of your family members' personalities (including yours) and the personalities of friends whose birth order you know, try to guess which order each trait characterizes: the only child, the oldest child, the middle child, or the youngest child. Here are answers to the first two:

It's the oldest child who's often the most self-critical and perfectionist.

It's the middle child who tends to be secretive.

1. tends to be self-critical and perfectionist
2. is often the most secretive
3. is usually very comfortable with older people
4. tends to be skilled at defending himself or herself
5. may sometimes try to be all things to all people
6. as a child, may find others of the same age immature

7. often feels most obligated to follow the family rules and routines
8. may be confused about self-image as a result of being simultaneously welcomed, adored, bossed around, and disliked by siblings
9. tends to be the most conservative
10. is typically self-sufficient
11. often subject to self-doubt due to not being taken seriously by family members
12. may often feel like a "fifth wheel" (a feeling of not belonging or being an "extra")

Discuss your choices in small groups; try to reach a consensus. Then report the groups' guesses to the rest of the class. Tally the results for each trait to see which ones you agree on. If there is disagreement, explain some of your reasons for assigning a trait or attitude to a particular birth order.

Focus 1

FORM ● USE

Structure and Discourse Function of Cleft Sentences

- Cleft sentences put special emphasis on one part of a message. As its name suggests, the cleft sentence divides a sentence into two parts: (1) a focus element and (2) a clause beginning with *that, who, which, when,* or *where:*

Focus Element	Clause
(a) It is the youngest child	who is often both a rebel and a charmer.

(Unstressed version: The youngest child is often both a rebel and a charmer.)

- We introduce the focus element of a cleft sentence with *it* plus a singular form of *be.* The verb is singular even when the focus element is plural:

Focus Element	Clause
(b) It **is** oldest children and only children	who tend to be the most assertive.

- The *be* verb is often present tense *is*; however, we use other tenses in cleft sentences:

Focus Element	Clause
(c) It **was** the last street sign	that said Ocean Avenue.
(d) It **used to be** my mother	who did all the cooking, but now we all help.
(e) It **will be** on a Saturday	that we leave, not a Sunday.

- The tense of the focus element and the clause do not need to be the same:

Focus Element: Present	Clause: Past
(f) It **is** the man near the phone booth	who **lent** me a dollar.

- We can also use modal verbs with cleft constructions to express logical probability:

Focus Element	Clause
(g) It **must** be red wine	that stained this carpet.
(h) It **can't** be the youngest child	who is the most conservative.

- There are a number of grammatical structures that can be the focus of a cleft. These will be presented in Focus 3.

Exercise 1

Complete each blank below with a word or phrase that fits the context.

1. It couldn't be _____ who are confused about self-image because they don't have any siblings.

2. I think it must be _____ who often has the self-image problem because the older ones might have mixed feelings about the baby of the family.

3. It might be _____ who is generally self-sufficient because as a child he/she might have had to do a lot of things alone.

4. Wilson and Edington claim that, of all birth order positions, _____ the middle child who is apt to be the most popular among other people.

5. The two psychologists say it is because _____ often feels protected by older siblings that he or she may be fearless and have a strong sense of exploration.

6. They have also observed that _____ who tend to have difficulty dealing with interruptions from others because they did not have brothers or sisters who interrupted them.

Focus 2

MEANING

Distinguishing One or More of a Group

MEANING

- The cleft sentences in both the Task and Exercise 1 distinguish one member of a group as having certain traits or qualities:
  (a) It is **the middle child** who is most secretive.
  (The middle child here is distinguished from the eldest and youngest children.)
- We can also use plural focus elements to distinguish more than one member of a group:
  (b) It is **my oldest brother and my middle brother** who most resemble my father. My two younger brothers look more like my mother.
- In some cases, the implied **group** may include all other things; that is, the cleft sentence implies that the focus element is the only thing that fits the clause description. This meaning may be made explicit with the word *only*:

Focus Element	**Clause**
  (c) It is only love   that can bring world peace
  (Love is the only thing that can bring world peace.)

Exercise 2

Which person in your family or circle of friends best matches the following descriptions? Use a cleft sentence beginning with "it is" (or "it's") in your response.

> **EXAMPLE:** would be most likely to complain about young people's behavior
> *It's my grandmother who* would be most likely to complain about young people's behavior.

Note: If you yourself are the one who best matches the description, there are two ways to use the first person singular in cleft sentences.

It is I.... (Formal usage)

It is me... (Informal usage; the form many native speakers of English use in spoken English)

1. tends to watch the most TV (family member)
2. has the best sense of humor (family member or friend)
3. would be most likely to park a car and forget where it was (family member or friend)
4. has the most trouble getting up in the morning (family member)

5. is the most artistic (friend or family member)

6. would be most likely to stop and help if he/she saw someone in trouble (friend or family member)

7. most often tries to get out of doing housework (family member)

8. most enjoys gossiping (friend or family member)

Exercise 3

Choose a word from the list for a focus element and complete each blank so that the sentence is a cleft construction. The first has been done for you as an example.

anger	music
curiosity	pride
faith	a sense of humor

1. *It was anger* that made God banish Adam and Eve from the Garden of Eden, according

   to the Bible.

2. _____ that often keeps us from admitting our mistakes.

3. _____ that caused Pandora's downfall in the Greek myth; she had to find

   out what was in the box.

4. _____ that has been called the language of the soul.

5. _____ that keeps most of us from taking ourselves too seriously.

6. _____ that has helped many people to withstand religious persecution.

Focus 3

FORM

Structures Used as Focus Elements

FORM

- So far, most of the words or phrases following the *It + be* have been nouns or noun phrases in subject position. Although these are common focus elements, we can use a number of structures as focus elements.
  - Subject
    (a) It is **the President** who appoints the Cabinet.
  - Direct Object
    (b) It is **the Cabinet** that the President appoints.

379

- Object of a Preposition

  (c) It is **the Senate** that the President often disagrees with.

- Complement (noun)

  (d) It was **an awful shade of yellow** that they painted the Oval Office.

- Complement (adjective)

  (e) It was **greenish yellow** that they painted it.

- Prepositional phrase

  (f) It was **due to illness** that the Vice-President resigned.

- Adverb

  (g) It was **only begrudgingly** that the two senators admitted they had erred.

- Dependent clause

  (h) It was **after World War II ended** that the baby boom began in the United States.

- Infinitive Clause

  (i) It was **to ensure the right of women to vote** that the Twelfth Amendment to the United States Constitution was passed.

Exercise 4

Restate the following sentences about the U.S. civil rights movement of the 1960s to emphasize the information indicated in parentheses. Change any other wording as necessary. The first one has been done as an example.

1. Black students staged the first sit-in at a lunch counter in Greensboro, North Carolina, in 1960. (Emphasize the date.)

   It was in 1960 that black students staged the first sit-in at a lunch counter in Greensboro, North Carolina.

2. White and black civil rights workers sat together in "white only" sections of restaurants and other public places to protest segregation. (Emphasize the purpose.)

3. In 1962, President Kennedy sent U.S. Marshalls to protect James H. Meredith, the first black student at the University of Mississippi. (Emphasize the place.)

4. The civil rights movement reached a climax in 1963 with the march on Washington. (Emphasize the event.)

5. Martin Luther King delivered his famous "I Have a Dream" speech during the march on Washington. (Emphasize the speech.)

6. Three young civil rights workers were tragically murdered on June 22, 1964. (Emphasize the date.)

7. Martin Luther King led massive civil rights marches in Selma, Alabama, and Montgomery, Mississippi, in 1965. (Emphasize the places.)

8. King was assassinated by James Earl Ray in Memphis, Tennessee. (Emphasize the assassin.)

9. We now celebrate the achievements of this great civil rights leader in January. (Emphasize the month.)

Exercise 5

The following sentences explain either causes or effects of an action. Use a cleft construction with an appropriate tense and either *out of* (reason) or *for* (purpose) plus a word from the list to complete them. The first has been done as an example.

adventure   greed
envy   ignorance
fame and glory   love

1. *It was out of envy* that Cinderella's wicked stepsisters made her stay home and work.

2. _____ that some people have stereotyped ideas about different

   cultures.

3. _____ that some people seek careers as professional athletes

   or actors.

4. _____ that the evangelist solicited more and more money

   from his followers.

5. _____ for each other that Romeo and Juliet ended their lives.

6. _____ that they signed up for the African safari trip.

Exercise 6

Imagine that each of the situations is true. Provide an explanation, either serious or humorous, emphasizing the reason. The first one has been done as an example.

1. You were late to class yesterday.
   It was because the bus didn't come that I was late to class.
2. You didn't have an assignment done that was due.
3. You missed a medical appointment.
4. You forgot a relative's birthday. (You choose the relative.)
5. You didn't eat anything for two days.
6. You stumbled and fell crossing the street.

381

Focus 4

Contrasting Focus

USE

- We sometimes use cleft sentences to point out a contrast to something said or done, or commonly believed but not true:

  (a) I think the youngest child is the one who tends to be secretive.

  (b) No, **it's the middle child** who is often secretive.

  In spoken English, *middle* in sentence (b) would receive extra stress because it is the word that contrasts with what the other speaker has said. This type of cleft, with added stress on a word or phrase, implies a negative statement more strongly than clefts of the type in Focus 2: It is *X*, **not** *Y*.

- As with other types of clefts, we may use a variety of focus elements:

  (c) No, it was **with his teeth** that he took off the bottle cap, not a can opener. (prepositional phrase)

  (d) What color paint is this? It was **blue** that I ordered, not green! (adjective)

  (e) You fixed my what? It was **to get my brakes repaired that I brought my car in,** not to get the transmission replaced! (nonfinite clause)

Exercise 7

You have been asked to edit a reference book manuscript for errors. Unfortunately, much of the book turns out to be a veritable treasury of misinformation. As you read each fact, identify the part that is incorrect. Make up a statement indicating to the author what needs to be corrected, using a cleft sentence to highlight that element.

> **EXAMPLE:** Mark Twain wrote the classic novel *Huckleberry Flan* in 1884.
> **Correction:** It is *Huckleberry **Finn*** that Mark Twain wrote.

1. The U.S. Congress first began meeting in Washington State in 1800.
2. New York City has two baseball teams: the Mets and the Blue Jays.
3. One of the most famous tragedies of all times, "Romeo and Juliet" was written by Moliere in 1595.
4. Christopher Columbus discovered Portugal in 1492.
5. U.S. astronauts first landed on Mars in 1969.
6. In 1260, Kublai Khan founded the Yuan dynasty in Japan.
7. Leonardo da Vinci painted the famous *Moaning Lisa* around 1500.
8. The brain, the spinal cord, and the nerves are parts of the body's digestive system.
9. Nefertiti ruled India along with her husband King Akhenaton during the fourteenth century B.C.

Focus 5

Gradable Contrast

MEANING

- The contrast expressed by a cleft sentence may also be a gradable one; that is, it may refer to something that exceeds others on a certain scale:

  My older brother is a good pianist. My older sister plays the cello quite well. However, **it is my younger brother** who has exceptional musical talent in our family.

Exercise 8

First, complete each list below with four examples:

FAVORITE FOODS

1.

2.

3.

4.

FAVORITE MOVIES [OR TV PROGRAMS]

1.

2.

3.

4.

FAVORITE SCHOOL SUBJECTS

1.

2.

3.

4.

FAVORITE [YOUR CHOICE]

1.

2.

3.

4.

Now, to indicate which items rank highest from each of the first three lists, fill in the blanks of the sentences below. Share one of your responses with classmates.

1. I love to eat _____ , _____ , and _____ . But it is _____ that I would choose if I had to eat only one food for a week.

2. I could watch _____ , _____ , and _____ quite a few times, but it is _____ that _____ .

3. I enjoy _____ , I like to study _____ , and I also like _____ . However, if _____ , it is _____ that I would choose.

4. With the fourth list of your favorites, make up a sentence using the pattern above.

Focus 6

Establishing Time, Place, and Characters in Narrative

USE

- In narratives, such as stories and historical accounts, we may use cleft sentences to establish the time, the place, or the characters (or actual people) of the narrative.
  - **Time**
    - **(a)** It was **in the early spring** that Jane finally felt well enough to make the trip to Waterbury.
    - **(b)** It was **on a cold day in February 1860** that Abraham Lincoln delivered his eloquent "Cooper Union" speech against slavery.
  - **Place**
    - **(c)** It was **in Barbizon** that Rousseau founded the modern school of French landscape painting.
  - **Person**
    - **(d)** It was **Shakespeare** who inspired Beethoven's creation of his String Quartet opus 18, number 1.
- We may also use cleft sentences to describe things as they are happening. This is often done:
  - in journalism:
    - **(e)** **It is shortly after dusk when** a tired Vin Ho steps off the plane.
  - in a summary or review of books, films, etc.:
    - **(f)** **It is to Italy that Mark escapes** when his troubles begin.
    - **(g)** **It is the parish priest** who rescues our hero from a life of crime.

Exercise 9

Choose one feature to highlight in the following historical facts and write an introductory sentence for a historical narrative about each person.

EXAMPLE: It was around 2700 B.C. that Cheops began building the pyramids of Egypt.

Person	Date	Place	Event
Cheops (king)	around 2700 B.C.	Egypt	started building the pyramids
Machiavelli (statesman)	1513	Florence, Italy	accused of conspiracy
John James Audubon (artist)	April 26, 1785	Cayes, Santo Domingo	born
Emily Dickinson (poet)	1862	Amherst, Massachusetts	began correspondence with Thomas Wentworth Higgins
Joaquium Machado de Assis (writer)	1869	Rio de Janeiro, Brazil	married Portuguese aristocrat, Carolina de Novaes
Jean Sibelius (composer)	1892	Helsinki, Finland	wrote the symphonic poem, "Kullervo"
Rin-Tin-Tin (dog)	1950s	Hollywood, California	became a star on his own TV show

Focus 7

FORM ● USE

Other Forms of Cleft Constructions

FORM
USE

- *It* + *be* does not always start sentences in cleft constructions.
  - In questions, we invert *it* + *be* (*be* + *it*) after a question word:
    - **(a) Who was it** that gave you that information?
    - **(b) Why was it** (that) they decided to move?
  - In yes-no questions, the inverted form *be* + *it* also occurs:
    - **(c) Was it out of pity** that he let the old man move into his house?
  - *it* + *be* may follow a *What a* + noun phrase in a cleft construction that expresses wonder, delight, surprise, etc.
    - **(d) What a nice essay it was** that you wrote about your father.
      (It was a nice essay that you wrote about your father.)

385

- As you have already seen in some of the exercises in this unit, a cleft construction may also be part of a *that* clause (with or without *that*) in reported speech:

(e) I told you before (that) **it was Marsha who called you, not Marianne.**

(f) The President announced (that) **it was because he was ill that he would not be seeking reelection.**

In the last sentence above, it would probably sound better to delete the first *that* so that the sentence doesn't have two consecutive *that* clauses. However, either form is grammatical.

Exercise 10

Make up a cleft sentence for each situation that follows. The first has been done as an example.

1. You told a friend that *E. T.* was going to be on TV on Monday night. He thought you said Sunday. Tell him what you said.

   I told you (that) it was on Monday night that it was going to be on, not Sunday!

2. You're not sure why a customer service representative at a bank wanted to know your place of birth for a checking account application you were filling out. Ask him.

3. You want to compliment a classmate on a great speech that she gave in class the day before.

4. You've been listening to a history lecture about China and missed hearing the date when the Chinese revolution ended the Manchu Dynasty. Politely ask your instructor to tell you the date again.

5. You and your family are watching the news. The newscaster has just announced the cause of a major plane crash to have been an engine failure. A member of your family was distracted and didn't hear this information. Tell him/her what the newscaster said.

6. You tried to call a close friend for three hours, but the line was busy. You wondered whom she could be on the line with. When you finally get through, you ask her.

Activities

Activity 1

Make up five descriptions that could be used for members of your class. Write your descriptions as verb phrases, similar to Exercise 2. (Be careful not to write any descriptions that would offend anyone or hurt someone's feelings!) Write down who you think best fits the description. Take turns reading your descriptions and have classmates say who they think matches each, using a cleft sentence. Then tell them whether you agree or disagree. Here are a few examples to get you started:

A: Tells the funniest stories
B: I think it's Josef who does that.
A: I agree.
B: Always has the right answers
C: I'd guess that it's Greta who's always right.
B: Hmm . . . well, frankly, I thought it was me!

Activity 2

In teams, write questions for a trivia quiz, using cleft constructions. Consider history, sports, the arts, geography, science, and entertainment as possible categories. (Don't make your questions too hard!) Take turns asking your classmates the questions. Score one point for each correct answer.

> **EXAMPLE:** Where was it that the first Olympics were held? (Greece)
>
> Who was it who became President of the United States after Jimmy Carter? (Ronald Reagan)
>
> What is it that you need to make salt besides chloride? (sodium)
>
> What decade was it that World War II ended? (the 1940s)

Activity 3

People who are against the government controlling the sales of guns often say "It's not guns that kill; it's people who kill." Do you agree with this logic? Write a paragraph giving your opinion about this statement.

Activity 4

Consider some films you have seen or books, poetry, or short stories that you have read. For each, what was one of the main things you admired or that you felt made it good? Write your responses in a list. Then elaborate on one of them by writing a paragraph about it. Here are a few examples of the types of comments that might be made:

It is the beautiful cinematography and interesting story that make *Out of Africa* such an enjoyable movie.

It is Rebecca West's careful observations about people and places in Yugoslavia that make *Black Lamb and Grey Falcon* such an interesting book.

Activity 5

Write a narrative paragraph describing the place, time, and other significant information about one of the following:

The circumstances of your birth or someone else's you know.

A historical event

A current event

To begin your narrative, choose one of the features to highlight in a cleft construction, as was discussed in Focus 5.

Activity 6

Which of the personality traits listed in the Task seem to fit you or members of your family? Write a paragraph describing who it is that they fit.

Activity 7

If you live in an area that has "tabloid news" shows on TV—the ones that tend to focus on crimes and various celebrity scandals—listen to a few of them. See if they use cleft sentences in their narration to highlight times, dates, places, or people for a dramatic effect.

26

Preposition Clusters

Task

Look at the following pictures and captions describing immigrants and refugees from around the world.

Italian immigrants arriving in Australia

Vietnamese refugees being accepted by the Federal Republic of Germany

Jewish immigrants pouring into Israel

Now consider one group of refugees or immigrants that have recently settled in your native country or in a country you are familiar with. Think about the circumstances surrounding their departure from their homeland and their present living conditions in the new country. Jot down notes about these circumstances in the chart below.

Immigrant or Refugee Group = _____	
1. Why they departed from their country	
2. What they hope for in their new country	
3. What group (if any) they are at odds with in the new country	
4. What aspects of life they are unaccustomed to in the new country	
5. Who they associate with in the new country	
6. What jobs they are good at in the new country	
7. How their contributions result in a richer cultural heritage for the new country	

Now discuss with your classmates the results of your brainstorming.

Focus 1

Overview of Preposition Clusters; Verb + Preposition

FORM

- This unit will provide extensive practice with preposition clusters of three types:
  verb + preposition
  adjective + preposition
  preposition + noun phrase + preposition

- Some verb + preposition clusters are *consist of, count on, differ from, hope for, plan on,* etc.
- Verb + preposition clusters must be followed by noun phrases or gerunds.

> Refugees differ from **immigrants** in that they have not chosen to leave their homeland. They have usually fled from **their homeland** to escape war, famine, or persecution. Refugees often plan on **returning** to their homeland as soon as the problems are over. They hope for **a better future** when they return.

Exercise 1

There are four verb + preposition clusters in the chart prompts in the Task. Can you identify them? Now, use your notes from the chart and write four sentences about the immigrant or refugee group you described, using verb + preposition clusters.

> **EXAMPLE:** The Vietnamese *departed from* Vietnam in order to find better economic and political conditions.

Exercise 2

The following sentences contain verb + preposition clusters. Complete them in two ways, with a noun phrase and with a gerund.

> **EXAMPLE:** The new parents marveled at *seeing their son for the first time.*
> *the beauty of their child.*

1. Staying healthy consists of _____.

2. The plan called for _____.

3. Does anyone object to _____?

4. Ever since I was a child, I have counted on _____.

5. Since it is very late, you can dispense with _____.

6. After the accident, Jaime withdrew from _____.

7. Will the president succeed in _____?

8. The protesters were demonstrating furiously against _____.

9. Why can't she distinguish between _____?

10. I don't agree with the senator who voted for _____.

Focus 2

MEANING

Verb + At

MEANING

- Several verb + *at* clusters relate to facial expressions.
  - **(a)** She **looked at** the spectacle and then **smiled at** the person who was sitting next to her.
- Some verb + *at* clusters relate to sight.
  - **(b)** She **stared at** the broken windshield.
    stare at = see with steady, wide-eyed appearance
  - **(c)** They **glared at** the intrusive visitor.
    glare at = stare angrily
  - **(d)** We **gazed at** the beautiful painting.
    gaze at = see intently, with fixed attention
  - **(e)** He **glanced at** his watch.
    glance at = look at briefly
  - **(f)** He **winked at** the cab driver.
    wink at = close and open one eye deliberately
- Other verb + *at* clusters relate to other facial expressions that express an emotion.
  - **(g)** The model **grinned at** the camera.
    grin at = smile broadly, showing the teeth
  - **(h)** She **frowned at** the children's mischief.
    frown at = to wrinkle the brow with displeasure
  - **(i)** We **scowled at** the convicts as they left the courtroom.
    scowl at = to wrinkle the brow with anger or disapproval
  - **(j)** They **sneered at** the opposing team.
    sneer at = raise one corner of the lip to show contempt

Exercise 3

Fill in the following blanks using verb + *at*. In some cases, more than one answer is possible.

EXAMPLE: The flight attendant <u>*smiled at*</u> me as he asked if I wanted coffee, tea, milk, or soda.

1. "Open your mouth wide," said Peter's mother. Peter _____ the spoonful of medicine and then reluctantly swallowed it.

2. It was wonderful to finally reach the mountain summit. The hiking party sat down and _____ the scenery around them.

3. "Doctor, would you mind _____ my throat? It feels rather sore."

4. The man acknowledged the child by _____ her from across the room.

5. I haven't seen my ex-husband since he _____ me from across the court-room.

6. The politician quickly _____ his notes before delivering his speech.

Focus 3

MEANING
Verb + *With*

MEANING

- Verb + preposition clusters with *with* (such as *associate with, cooperate with, consult with, deal with, join with, side with, unite with*) imply association between or among different parties.

   The laborers **consulted with** their union. They decided not to **cooperate with** management.

Exercise 4

Select one word or phrase from the following three columns to create a question using verb + *with*.

EXAMPLE: Do *homeowners deal with realtors to sell their homes?*

Column #1	Column #2	Column #3
a. homeowners	their children	under most circumstances
b. criminals	the poor	to gain social approval
c. the rich	opthamologists	to reduce jail terms
d. parents	the police	to sell their homes
e. patients	realtors	in the fight against AIDS
f. young people	gangs	about their eyes

Focus 4

MEANING

Verb + *From*

MEANING

- Verb + preposition clusters with *from* imply separation.

   You must not **deviate from** the rules. If you **dissent from** authority, you will be punished.

Exercise 5

Fill in one of the following verbs + *from* in each blank.

abstain   differ   flee   separate

desist   dissent   recede   shrink

detach   emerge   recoil   withdraw

deviate   escape   retire

1. Certain groups follow restrictive dietary laws. For example, Orthodox Jews

   (a) _____ pork and shellfish. Sometimes these and other groups who

   (b) _____ the status quo or (c) _____ the norm are considered

   strange by outsiders but extremely religious by those from within the same community.

2. Immigrants come to a foreign country to live for many different reasons. They want to (a) _____ persecution, war, disaster, or epidemics. Certain Indochinese have (b) _____ impoverished conditions in their native lands but have become successful in their new homes around the world.

3. Some newcomers to a country go through culture shock. This phenomenon makes some people (a) _____ social relationships. Because of depression, they also sometimes (b) _____ responsibilities. They may even (c) _____ psychological help because they are not used to dealing with doctors for psychological problems.

4. Mr. Johnson is getting older. His hair (a) _____ his forehead. Next year he plans (b) _____ his job.

Focus 5

MEANING

Verb + *For*

MEANING

- Several verb + *for* clusters relate to desire or need:

ask for	pray for
crave for	thirst for
hope for	wish for
long for	yearn for

I **crave for** a cigarette nearly every hour. I **pray for** the strength to stop smoking.

Exercise 6

A. Study the following chart about immigration movements to the United States. Use different verbs + *for* to describe why the different groups came to the United States.

Major Immigration Movements To The United States

Who	When	Number	Why
Irish	1840s and 1850s	About $1\frac{1}{2}$ million	Famine resulting from potato crop failure
Germans	1840s to 1880s	About 4 million	Severe economic depression and unemployment, political unrest and failure of liberal revolutionary movement
Danes, Norwegians, Swedes	1870s to 1900s	About $1\frac{1}{2}$ million	Poverty; shortage of farmland
Poles	1880s to 1920s	About 1 million	Poverty; political repression; cholera epidemics
Jews from Eastern Europe	1880s to 1920s	About $2\frac{1}{2}$ million	Religious persecution
Australians, Czechs, Hungarians, Slovaks	1880s to 1920s	About 4 million	Poverty; overpopulation
Italians	1880s to 1920s	About $4\frac{1}{2}$ million	Poverty; overpopulation
Mexicans	1910 to 1920s	About 700,000	Mexican Revolution of 1910; low wages and unemployment
	1950s to 1990s	About 2 million	Poverty; unemployment
Cubans	1960s to 1990s	About 700,000	Communist take over in 1959
Dominicans, Haitians, Jamaicans	1970s and 1990s	About 900,000	Poverty; unemployment
Vietnamese	1970s and 1990s	About 500,000	Vietnam War 1957 to 1975; communist take over

Source: U.S. Immigration and Naturalization Service

EXAMPLE: Cubans   The Cubans *craved for* freedom in a non-Communist country.

1. Irish
2. Germans
3. Norwegians
4. Poles
5. Jews
6. Austrians
7. Italians
8. Mexicans
9. Haitians
10. Vietnamese

B. What other immigrant groups are coming to the United States today? Why?

395

Exercise 7

Create short paragraphs with the verb + preposition clusters provided below.

EXAMPLE: rebel at, shudder at, jeer at

The refugees were *rebelling at* leaving their homeland. They *shuddered at* the sight of the guns that the soldiers were carrying. But they held up their fists while the crowds *jeered at* them and shouted, "We shall return!"

1. talk of, think of, disapprove of
2. listen to, object to, reply to
3. plan on, embark on, live on
4. believe in, persist in, result in
5. look at, laugh at, point at

Focus 6

FORM

Adjective + Preposition

FORM

- Some adjectives can precede prepositional phrases.
  (a) The hut stands **adjacent to the river.**
  (b) The people are **dependent on fishing.**
  (c) They are **burdened with high taxes.**
- Some adjective + preposition clusters are:

free *immune* *safe* } *from*	*eager* *homesick* *sorry* } *for*	*compatible* *unfamiliar* *content* } *with*
expert *good* *swift* } *at*	*proficient* *rich* *successful* } *in*	*careless* *happy* *enthusiastic* } *about*
ignorant *afraid* *proud* } *of*		

- Adjective (*-ed*) + Preposition
  (d) Miwa is **accustomed to** living on only two meals a day.
  (e) Ho is **tired of** no meat in his diet.
  (f) They are **concerned about** surviving the drought.
  (g) The old men are **addicted to** opium.

Exercise 8

Create your own questions for the following answers, using two different adjective + preposition phrases from Focus 6.

EXAMPLES: A healthy mathematician
Who is *free from* disease and *good at* math?
A sloppy executive
Who is *careless about* his appearance and *successful in* his job?

1. A calm athlete
2. A claustrophobic politician
3. An anxious addict
4. A clean mechanic

5. A weary worrier
6. A joyful seamstress
7. A repentant runner

Exercise 9

Discuss what the following organizations are *interested in, concerned about, accustomed to, committed to, dedicated to,* and/or *preoccupied with.*

EXAMPLE: The World Bank is interested in aiding the world's poor.

1. Greenpeace
2. European Community
3. The Peace Corps
4. The United Nations

5. The Red Cross
6. UNICEF
7. The Fulbright Program
8. Amnesty International

Focus 7

FORM

Multiword Preposition Clusters

FORM

- Multiword preposition clusters follow the following pattern: preposition + (+ article) noun + preposition. Many clusters use *in* or *on* as the first preposition and *of* as the second preposition.

in + **noun** + *of*	*on* + **noun** + *of*	*in* + *the* + **noun** + *of*	*on* + *the* + **noun** + *of*
in case of in charge of in place of in lieu of in favor of	on account of on behalf of on top of on grounds of	in the course of in the event of in the habit of in the name of in the process of	on the advice of on the basis of on the part of on the strength of on the face of

- There are less regular combinations as well:

by means of	in return for	at odds with	with the exception of
with respect to	in addition to	for the sake of	

Exercise 10

Write *in (the)* or *on (the)* in the following blanks.

EXAMPLE: <u>*On the*</u> basis of no evidence, the case is dismissed.

1. _____ case of an emergency, duck under your desks and cover your heads.

2. _____ account of his great skill, he completed the task.

3. _____ advice of my physician, I must take these pills and get plenty of rest.

4. I have decided to buy the warehouse _____ strength of expert opinion.

5. _____ event of an earthquake, do not panic.

6. She wants a divorce _____ grounds of mental cruelty.

7. He will pay the bail _____ lieu of staying in jail.

8. She is _____ habit of joking when she should be serious.

9. _____ behalf of the committee, I would like to thank you for all of your work.

Exercise 11

Working with a partner, fill in the following blanks with the expressions below. Compare your answers with those of your classmates.

in the habit of   with reference to
as a consequence of   with the purpose of
for lack of   with an eye to
on account of   in addition to
for the sake of   in lieu of

EXAMPLE: <u>*With reference to*</u> Afghans, many are living in Pakistan and Iran.

1. The United States is _____ turning back many Mexicans from its southern border.

2. Bulgarians of Turkish descent are emigrating from Bulgaria _____ reuniting with their families in Turkey.

3. Europeans Jews and North American Jews have inhabited Israel _____ recreating a Jewish homeland.

398

4. _____ experiencing persecution, many Tamils have left Sri Lanka and gone to England.

5. One reason some Vietnamese have been turned back to Vietnam from Hong Kong _____ space.

6. Nicaraguans have fled to the United States _____ escaping war.

7. Many Cambodians have escaped into Thailand _____ humane treatment.

8. _____ Moroccans, Tunisians, and Senegalese have immigrated to Italy to find work.

9. _____ starvation, Nigerians, Ugandans, Sudanese, and Chadeans have fled to other African countries.

10. _____ staying in Romania, many Romanians of Hungarian descent are moving to Hungary.

Focus 8

USE

Introducing a Topic/ Identifying a Source

USE

- We use some preposition clusters to introduce a topic.
  - **(a) Pertaining to** immigrant quotas, the United States has tightened its restrictions in recent years.
  - **(b) Speaking about/of** persecution, certain immigrant groups have endured more than others.
  - **(c) With respect to** culture shock, most immigrant groups experience it in one form or another.
- We use other preposition clusters to identify a source.
  - **(d) Based on/upon** immigration statistics, more men than women emigrate from their native countries.
  - **(e) According to** Professor Herbert, many immigrants decide to return to their native countries after a few years.

Exercise 12

Complete the following sentences.

     EXAMPLE: Based on the weather report, *it will rain tomorrow.*

1. According to scientists, _____.

2. With respect to our solar system, _____.

3. With reference to recent political events, _____.

4. Speaking about discrimination, _____.

5. Relating to my last conversation with my family, _____.

6. Based upon my own observations, _____.

7. According to the dictionary, _____.

8. Pertaining to the death penalty, _____.

9. With respect to the students in this class, _____.

10. Speaking of good movies, _____.

Exercise 13

Supply the appropriate prepositions for the blanks in the following passage adapted from John Crewdson's *The Tarnished Door* (New York: Times Books, Inc., 1983, pp. 96–97).

The reforms of the McCarran Act limited annual immigration to the U.S. to 290,000, with 120,000 of the immigrants coming (1) _____ Western Hemisphere countries and the other 170,000 coming (2) _____ Eastern Hemisphere countries. Preference was given (3) _____ the reunification of families by reserving three-quarters of each year's visas for relatives of resident aliens and citizens of the U.S. Thus, most immigrants over the 290,000 were family members who were exempted (4) _____ the numerical limits of the preference system. Because one-fifth of the visas were reserved (5) _____ persons with needed talents or skills, many of those who did get visas were unsuited (6) _____ all but the most menial work. The year the law was passed, the U.S. admitted 113,000 immigrants from Europe and only 71,300 from Asia, Mexico, Africa, and Latin America. By 1977 the number of European immigrants had fallen (7) _____ 70,000, while the number of Asian, African, Mexicans, and Latin Americans had risen (8) _____ 231,000.

In 1976, in an effort to increase the equitability of visa distribution still further, the 20,000 annual ceiling on immigrants from each Eastern Hemisphere nation was also imposed (9) _____ all Western Hemisphere countries, including Mexico, which until then had by itself accounted (10) _____ about half the Western Hemisphere's quota of 120,000 visas a year.

Activities

Activity 1

The suffix -*ism* refers to a doctrine, practice, system, quality, or theory. For example, "terrorism" is a practice of using terror to accomplish a particular end. Below you will find various sentences about terrorism that utilize adjective + preposition phrases. Create more sentences about other "isms," using the same adjective + preposition phrases or others of your choice.

> **EXAMPLE:** Terrorism is often *associated with* hijacking. It is usually *accompanied by* violence. It is *based on/upon* perceived injustices among groups. It is *dependent on* people willing to risk their own lives. It is *harmful to* innocent bystanders.

How about. . . .

commercialism?
internationalism?
capitalism?
Communism?

racism?
socialism?
feminism?
nationalism?

Activity 2

In small groups, brainstorm answers to the following questions. When you are finished, see which group has the most answers to each of the questions.

1. Which groups abstain from certain types of food or drink?

   EXAMPLE: Muslims,

2. What are some terms for people who deviate from the law?

   EXAMPLE: robbers,

3. Which immigrants have had to flee from their native lands?

   EXAMPLE: Vietnamese,

4. Why do some people shirk their responsibility?

   EXAMPLE: lazy,

5. What American or British customs differ from the customs of your native country?

   EXAMPLE: kissing in public,

6. What foods do some people recoil from?

   EXAMPLE: snails,

7. What do people do once they have retired from their jobs?

   EXAMPLE: travel to India,

8. What types of household tasks do people like to escape from?

   EXAMPLE: scrubbing the floor,

Activity 3

The following terms relate to intercultural contact or movement from, to, or within a country. Try to find definitions of the following terms from dictionaries, encyclopedias, classmates, your teacher, etc. Give definitions of these terms while citing your sources, using the expression *according to*.

   EXAMPLE: *According to* the encyclopedia, a refugee is any uprooted person who has a well-founded fear of persecution for reasons of race, religion, nationality, membership in a particular social group or political opinion.

1. refugee
2. emigrant
3. guest workers
4. brain drain
5. multiculturalism
6. political correctness
7. melting pot
8. Zionism

Activity 4

The Statue of Liberty in New York Harbor has a plaque at its base that states the following:

> Give me your tired, your poor,
> Your huddled masses yearning to breathe free,
> The wretched refuse of your teeming shore.
> Send them, the homeless, tempest-tossed to me,
> I lift my lamp beside the golden door!

Do you believe it is possible for countries such as the United States to have an open–door policy? Should all people who desire it be allowed to freely immigrate and settle in the United States? What, if any, limits should be put on immigration? Should there be quotas? What obligation would the new country have to support the immigrants? Write a short composition on this topic, incorporating at least five preposition clusters you have learned in this unit.

Activity 5

Form two teams. Have each team create a set of eight cards which contain various types of preposition clusters with one or more prepositions missing. For example:

hint _____	dream _____
eligible _____	happy _____
astonished _____	shocked _____
_____ reference _____	_____ favor _____

Exchange cards with another team. See which team is most accurate at producing sentences with *because* clauses and the preposition cluster on the card.

1. I like to *hint at* what I want for my birthday because my family never knows what to buy.
2. I was *shocked at* hearing the news because I did not expect it.
3. *In reference to* his request, I do not feel that we should grant it because he is very irresponsible.

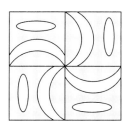

Index